Wanted To Buy

2nd Edition

A listing of serious buyers paying CASH
for everything collectible!

COLLECTOR BOOKS
A Division of Schroeder Publishing Co., Inc.

The current values in this book should be used only as a guide. They are not intended to set prices, which vary from one section of the country to another. Auction prices as well as dealer prices vary greatly and are affected by condition as well as demand. Neither the Author nor the Publisher assumes responsibility for any losses that might be incurred as a result of consulting this guide.

Drawings by Beth Summers with the exception of those on pages: 11, 18, 19, 39, 43, 48, 79, 134, 172, 195, 197, 213, 223, 234, 260, 276, 279, 303, 311, 313, 326, 336, 350, 364, 368, 385, 386, 392, 397, 399, 413, 421, 426, 429, 433, 442.

Introduction

This book was compiled to help put serious buyers in contact with the non-collecting sellers all over the country. Most of us have accumulated things that are not particularly valuable to us, but could very well be of interest to one of the buyers in this book. Not only does this book list the prices that collectors are willing to pay on 1,000's of items, but also lists 100's of interested buyers along with the type of material each is buying. *Wanted To Buy* is very easy to use. The listings are alphabetically arranged by subject, with the interested buyer's name and address preceding each group of listings. In the back of the book, we have included a special section which lists the names and addresses of over 250 buyers along with the categories that they are interested in. When you correspond with these buyers, be sure to enclose a self-addressed, stamped envelope if you want a reply. If you wish to sell your material, quote the price that you want or send a list and ask if there are any items on the list that they might be interested in and the price that they would be willing to pay. If you want the list back, be sure to send a S.A.S.E. large enough for the listing to be returned.

Packing and Shipping Instructions

Special care must be exercised in shipping fragile items in the mail or U.P.S. Double-boxing is a must when shipping glass and china pieces. It is extremely importat that each item be wrapped in several layers of newspaper. First, put a 4-inch layer of wadded newspaper in the bottom of the box. Secondly, start placing the well-wrapped items on top of the crushed newspaper, making certain that each piece of glass or china is separated from the others. Make sure that there is at least 4 inches of cushioning newspaper or foam between each item. When the box is nearly full, place more cushioning material on top of the contents and then seal the box.

Finally, place this box and contents in a larger box cushioned again with at least 4 inches of newspaper on all 4 sides, top and bottom. This double-boxing is very important. Our Postal Service and United Parcel Service are efficient, however, we must pack well just in case there is undue bumping in handling.

When shipping coins and precious metals be sure and register your shipment and request a return slip so that you will know that the buyer received the goods and the date that it was delivered. All material should be insured for the full value and remember, always use strong boxes, lots of packing and good shipping tape.

ABINGDON POTTERY

Abingdon pottery was produced from 1936 to 1951 in Abingdon, Illinois. It was made of vitreous china. Abingdon pottery was marked in several ways: ink stamp, incised emblem with model number, and paper labels. I am looking primarily for brown, black, or red pieces. Also being sought are figurals such as nudes or animals, bookends (no horse heads), large garden vases, and cookie jars. When contacting me, state size, model number from bottom, color, condition, and price. Thank you.

Mary Weldi-Skinner
1656 Farragut Ave.
Chicago, IL 60640-2010

ADVERTISING

In an effort to present a product to the customer, every imaginable gimmick was put into play. Colorful and artfully-decorated signs and posters, thermometers, hand mirrors, neon clocks and signs, and attractive tin containers—all with catchy slogans, familiar logos, and often bogus claims—are only a few of the many examples of early advertising that are of interest to collectors today.

Porcelain signs were made as early as 1890 and are highly prized for their portrayal of life as it was then. I will buy various advertising items in good, clean condition. The following list is an example of prices I will pay.

Richard T. Rautwein
437 Dawson St.
Sault Ste. Marie, MI 49783

We Pay

Blatz Beer Old Heidlberg Girl Sign.............................300.00
Coca-Cola Clock, Gilbert...350.00
Coca-Cola Neon Clock...125.00
Edison Mazda Sign, lighted......................................400.00
Green River Whiskey Sign, tin..................................310.00
Lion Gas Sign, porcelain..200.00
Lucky Strike Clock...300.00
Moxie Ice Cooler..300.00
Pepsi Cola Radio, bottle..150.00
RCA Dog, tin w/glass eyes......................................500.00
RCA Nipper, plaster, 36″...525.00
R&G Corsets Clockwork Sign, woman w/corset moves, 24x36″.........550.00
Red Raven Tray (Ask the Man)...................................115.00
Republic Tires Sign, paperboard................................150.00
Rye-Ola Syrup Dispenser..250.00
Senaca Camera Sign, tin..225.00
Standard Gas Sign, tin, w/Mickey Mouse, 30″ round..............200.00
Weatherbird Shoe Sign, porcelain & neon........................375.00
Western Union Sign, porcelain...................................50.00

Antique advertising consists primarily of giveaways from before 1920 that could be found in most stores, ice cream parlors, and tobacco shops. It also consists of the containers or packages that the product came in or was served on. A representation would be spoons, plates, trays, tins, store clocks, foam scrapers, dispensers, jars, signs, calendars, etc. The average collector is concerned mainly with the condition of the article, the product represented, and the graphics. Obviously, a person or building shown on the advertisement is more desirable than just writing. Age is another important factor. We can date the first advertisement printed in English to the year 1480. It advertised a religious book by William Caxton. The offset lithography came into being in approximately 1875; we seek out anything from the 1800's. When purchasing, we use a scale of 1-10, with 10 being mint condition, and rarely will purchase anything below a grade 7. When writing to us, always mention your asking price—we won't make offers. Be accurate on your grading. Photos would of course be helpful and would be returned to you. The following list is just

Advertising

a few of the things we purchase. The prices shown in no way reflect a minimum or a maximum. Let us know what you have.

House of Stuart
Box 387
Huntington, NY 11743

We Pay

Tins	50.00	Dye Cabinets	250.00
Signs	500.00	Glasses	10.00
Dispensers	300.00	Syrup Bottles	25.00
Gum Packages	10.00	Soda Fountain	700.00
Displays	200.00	Cigar Lamps	150.00
String Holders	300.00	Cigar Cutters	110.00
Tobacco Cabinets	550.00	Show Cases	150.00
World's Fair Items	15.00	Coffee Grinders	200.00
Clocks	400.00	Gum Machines	250.00
Jars	50.00	Catalogs	10.00
Straw Holders	75.00	Cracker Jack Items	10.00
Lamps	65.00		

———

I am interested in buying insurance advertising plaster plaque medallions for St. Paul Fire & Marine Insurance Co., St. Paul Mercury, St. Paul Mercury Indemnity, etc. I pay $50.00.

Donald A. Shaurette
#21 1240 Bryant Ave.
St. Paul, MN 55075

———

Collector is interested in purchasing for his own collection any pre-1935 calendars, paper posters, trade signs, window-display cardboard signs from these companies:

Austin Cartridge Co.
Austin Powder Co.
The Black Shells
DuPont Gunpowders
Harrington & Richardson Arms Co.

Hopkins & Allen Arms Co.
Hazard Powder Co.
Hunter Arms Co.
Infallible Gunpowders
Ithaca Guns

6

King Powder Co.	Robin Hood Ammunition Co.
Laflin & Rand Powder Co.	Robin Hood Powder Co.
Marble Arms & Mfg. Co.	J. Stevens Arms & Tool Co.
E.C. Meacham Arms Co.	Smith Guns (L.C. Smith)
Miami Powder Co.	Savage Arms Company
Marlin Firearms Co.	Selby Shells
Oriental Powder Co.	Selby Smelting & Lead Co.
Parker Brothers-Gunmakers	San Francisco U.M.C.
Meriden, Conn.	Union Metallic Cartridge Co.
Peters Cartridge Co.	U.S. Cartridge Co.
Remington-U.M.C.	Walsrode Gunpowder
Remington Arms Co.	Winchester Repeating Arms Co.

Bill Bramlett
P.O. Box 1105
Florence, SC 29503-1105
(803) 393-7390 (home)
(803) 665-3165 (work)

Advertising graphics from the 1800's and early 1900's have become popular collectibles over the past twenty years. Signs, calendars, and trays with colorful images are the most desirable; but small novelty items are popular as well. We will buy any advertising items in excellent condition if you contact us.

Roger Baker
P.O. Box 620417
Woodside, CA 94062

Firearms & Ammunition   **We Pay**

Calendar 20.00-400.00
Sign 40.00-500.00
Envelope 5.00-20.00
Watch Fob 5.00-25.00

General Store   **We Pay**

Food 20.00-200.00
Druggist 25.00-300.00
Dry Good 15.00-300.00

Beer,Whiskey,Tobacco   **We Pay**

Calendar 25.00-300.00
Sign 40.00-1,000.00
Tray 25.00-200.00

Advertising

Old advertising signs are one of the most sought-after items in collecting today. They were made of wood, tin, glass, and paper. Depending upon the subject matter, some of these early lithographs bring high prices.

Terrell W. Allen
1705 2nd Ave.
Manchester, TN 37355

We Pay		**We Pay**	
Coffee	25.00 +	Thermometers	25.00 +
Tobacco	25.00 +	Gasoline	50.00 +
Flour	25.00 +	Tires	50.00 +
Wagon	100.00 +	Oil	25.00 +
Carriage	100.00 +	Plows	100.00 +
Whiskey	100.00 +	Medicine	25.00 +
Beer	100.00 +	Thread	100.00 +
Bread	25.00 +	Candy	25.00 +
Overalls	50.00 +	Trays	25.00 +
Soft Drinks	25.00 +		

AFRICAN AND TRIBAL ART

Tribal art plays an essential role in the lives of many so-called 'primitive' peoples. It functions, within a given culture, in three basic areas. First and foremost, it is a means by which the adult society transmits its laws, moral codes, and history to the younger generations. Secondly, it allows man to transcend everyday life and communicate with man and the supernatural. In its final stage, it is an indication of wealth and status for its tribal owner.

We are interested in preserving this art, history, and culture. To this end, we would like to purchase tribal artifacts from the American Indian and African nations. We ask that the items offered us be made and used by the tribal members (no tourist items, please).

African items must pre-date 1945, and missionary artifacts and collections especially are sought. American Indian items must pre-date 1920. We would also like pre-1940 Mexican and South American Santos, Retablos, Ex Votos, crucifixes, religous carvings, and religious items. Please describe and price in first letter. Photos are a big help.

African

Masks	Drums
Fettishes	Household Objects
Figural Carvings	Musical Instruments
Weapons	Textiles
Shields	Clothing

American Indian

Pipe Bags	Bows & Arrows
Quillwork	Quivers
Parfleche Cases	Toys
Beaded Items	Eskimo Items
Clothing	Baskets
Moccasins	Pottery
Leatherwork	Old Pawn Jewelry

Museum of Classical Antiques & Primitive Arts
P.O. Box 2162
Medford Lakes, NJ 08055

I am looking to buy African and South American artifacts. Some of the tribal items sought are spears, masks, shields, arrows, weapons, wildlife products, skins, mounts, ivory, clothing, art, tools, body adornments, etc. Please reply with a picture, price, and description.

Richard McCoy
1119 Michigan Ave.
St. Joseph, MI 49085

AKRO AGATE

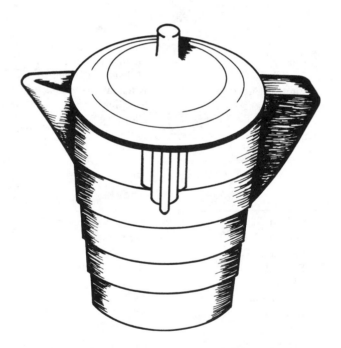

The Akro Agate Company of Clarksburg, West Virginia, produced a general line of household wares in addition to its well-known marbles and children's dishes. From the early 1930's to the late 1940's, ash trays, flowerpots, vases, powder jars, and other items were produced for the dime-store trade.

The colors of Akro products range from the familiar orange, green, blue, and red marbleized pieces to the solid opaques such as milk glass, black amethyst, pumpkin, yellow, and a wide variety of blues and greens. They also produced a limited amount of transparent clear, amber, green, and red pieces. Listed below are some of the specific pieces I want to buy and the prices I will pay for mint-condition pieces. I will also buy pieces not listed here, as well as pieces with minor damage. Contact me with your list of items for sale.

Albert Morin
668 Robbins Ave. #23
Dracut, MA 01826

We Pay

Ash Tray, Hotel Lincoln or Edison.............................15.00
Ash Tray, Advertising..20.00
Bell...25.00
Creamer, large, 3"...35.00
Sugar, large, 3"...35.00
Candlesticks, pair, 3¼"......................................35.00
Flowerpot, Graduated Darts, #308, 7".........................25.00
Flowerpot, #1307, #1308, or #1309............................20.00
Flowerpot, #1310 or #1311....................................20.00
Powder Jar, Ivy, #323..25.00
Powder Jar, Apple..75.00
Vase, Graduated Darts, #316..................................15.00
Vase, Ribs & Flutes, #311, 8"................................20.00
Apothecary Jar, pink or blue.................................20.00
Treasure Trunks..15.00
Company Brochures or Literature..............................25.00

AMERICAN ILLUSTRATOR'S ART

American Illustrator's Art

Harrison Fisher (1875-1934), the late, great American illustrator, was the creator of 'The Fisher Girl.' Born in Brooklyn, he moved to San Francisco at an early age; his career began in his teens. He was hired by the Hearst papers to do artwork for their publications. Later in New York, his illustrations of beautiful women attracted much attention and graced the covers and contents of the most popular magazines of the day, *Puck*, *Ladies' Home Journal*, *Saturday Evening Post*, and *Cosmopolitan*. He also illustrated books and painted portraits of his favorite subject, 'The American Beauty.'

The Harrison Fisher Society preserves, promotes, and publishes the works of Harrison Fisher. Collectors and dealers are invited to send a SASE regarding the society.

The Harrison Fisher Society
P.O. Box 81868
San Diego, CA 92138
(619) 488-8170

Books Illustrated by Harrison Fisher: **We Pay**

Hiawatha	75.00 +
Bachelor Belles	75.00 +
A Dream of Fair Women	75.00 +
The Harrison Fisher Book	100.00 +
American Belles	100.00 +
Maidens Fair	100.00 +
Fair Americans	100.00 +
Harrison Fisher's American Beauties	100.00 +
Harrison Fisher's American Girls in Miniature	100.00 +
A Garden of Girls	100.00 +
The Little Gift Book	100.00 +
The American Girl	100.00 +
Beauties	100.00 +
Harrison Fisher Girls	100.00 +
Pictures in Color	175.00 +
A Girl's Life and Other Pictures	175.00 +
30 Favorite Paints: and The Social Comedy	100.00 +
A Book of Sweethearts (includes other illustrators)	50.00 +
Lovely Women (includes other illustrators)	50.00 +

Other Collectibles   **We Pay**

Candy Tins	15.00 +
Old Prints	Write
Originals	Write
Pocket Mirrors, Calendars	Write

We buy original art prints by major American artists. The term original print refers to those works of art achieved through the specific processes known in print-making as relief intaglio, lithography, and other surface-printing methods. These include woodcut, engraving, etching, drypoint, and lithography. Many of these prints were signed in pencil and are not often numbered, especially those from before the 1950's.

Listed below are a few of the major American artists and the prices we are willing to pay for their works. Prices will vary by individual artist based upon subject matter, technique, and rarity.

Patrick Albano
Aaron Galleries
209 Main St.
Festus, MO 63028

We Pay

G. Bingham	1,000.00-3,000.00
George Bellows	500.00-20,000.00
Thomas Hart Benton	300.00-5,000.00
Grant Wood	750.00-3,000.00
Mary Cassatt	1,000.00-5,000.00
John James Audubon	500.00-5,000.00
Nathaniel Currier	250.00-7,000.00
Currier & Ives	500.00-3,000.00
J. Curry	300.00-2,000.00
Winslow Homer	50.00-15,000.00
Martin Lewis	500.00-3,000.00
Reginald Marsh	250.00-2,500.00
James A. Whistler	200.00-5,000.00
John Sloan	300.00-2,500.00
Childe Hassam	400.00-3,000.00

The turn of the century brought many changes in the book-publishing trade. One of the most important was a carry over from the Art Nouveau poster era when the various illustrators painted beautiful color plates to illustrate the many stories, fairy tales, and classics popular at that time.

Illustrators such as Philip Boileau, Harrison Fisher, Clarence Underwood, Charles Dana Gibson, Henry Hutt, Coles Phillips, and others painted beautiful pictures of the women of the period. Many of these were published and placed in fine gift books. These books range in size from 8" x 10" to 15" x 22" and are not to be confused with the small fiction novels in the 5" x 8" size.

We pay these prices for books with color plates by the following illustrators if the books are in fine condition. We pay lesser prices for examples in less-than-fine condition. Ship books for immediate payment. I you have any questions, please call or write.

Mashburn Books & Cards
P.O. Box 609
Enka, NC 28728
(704) 667-1427

Books Illustrated by Harrison Fisher   We Pay

Dream of Fair Women..**35.00**
American Girls in Miniature................................**25.00**
The American Girl..**50.00**
A Garden of Girls..**60.00**
The Harrison Fisher Book...................................**60.00**
American Beauties..**50.00**
Bachelor Belles..**60.00**
Fair Americans...**60.00**
American Belles..**50.00**
Harrison Fisher Girls......................................**75.00**
Others..**Write or Call**

Books Illustrated by Coles Phillips   We Pay

A Young Man's Fancy.......................................**60.00**
A Gallery of Girls...**60.00**
Others..**Write or Call**

Books Illustrated by Clarence Underwood   We Pay

American Types...**40.00**
Love's Young Dream...**20.00**
Others..**Write or Call**

Books Illustrated by Henry Hutt   We Pay

The Henry Hutt Picture Book................................**35.00**
Others..**Write or Call**

Books Illustrated by Howard C. Christy   We Pay

The Christy Girl...**25.00**
The American Girl..**35.00**

We Pay

The Princess...**20.00**
The Lady of the Lake.......................................**20.00**
Others..**Write or Call**

Other Illustrators

We Pay

Charles D. Gibson...Write
Philip Boileau..Write
Others ....Write

AMISH ITEMS

I am interested in Amish items, pre-1930's only. This category includes rag dolls, quilts, toys, rugs, furniture, or any small Amish-made items. In every category, I need a full description and price. A photo is most helpful. As an example, I am paying $50.00 and up for pre-1930's Amish rag dolls and $100.00 and up for pre-1930's Amish quilts.

Linda Grunewald
P.O. Box 311-X
Utica, MI 48087
(313) 739-4053

AMUSEMENT PARK

At one time there were nearly two thousand roller coasters operating in the United States. Amusement parks were situated everywhere. Most popular were the early trolley parks. I collect virtually anything relating to amusement parks, even items remotely related. I have visited nearly every amusement park in the United States and even have a nine hundred pound restored antique roller coaster car in my home. Listed here are some of the items I am looking for: signs, tickets, carousel horses, tokens, photos, movies, letterheads, ride manufacturer's catalogs, ride blueprints, posters, paintings, advertising items, post cards, and buttons.

Amusement Park Man
Tom Keefe
P.O. Box 464
Tinley Park, IL 60477

AQUARIUMS

Antique aquariums are wanted by collector. Also I am buying all related tropical fish items such as Art Deco fishbowl stands and bowls, old aquarium heaters, filters, ornaments, and air pumps. I am especially interested in finding Eagle-type aquariums from the 1800's, Jewel aquariums (made in Chicago in the 1930's), and the Fiske Fountain aquarium. Please send a description and a photo of each item if possible, along with your asking price.

Gary Bagnall
c/o Zoo Med Laboratories, Inc.
1406 S. Ritchey St. Unit D
Santa Ana, CA 92705

(714) 835-7418
(714) 642-7064

ART GLASS

I want to buy any 1950's art glass, but I am especially looking for pieces signed Venini, Sarpaneva, Tapio Wirkkala, Kosta, Orrefors, Kaj Franck, Nuutajarvi-Notsjo, Flysfors, Seguso, Flavio Poli, Holmgaard, Leerdam, Barovier and Toso, etc. If you are unsure of what you have, send a photo. I am interested in buying all mint pieces, small or large.

Also, I buy 1950's ceramics. I especially need pieces marked Gustavsburg (sometimes AG and a hand), signed Stig L, Kage 'Farsta,' and Friberg. I also buy Rorstrand and other Swedish and Finnish pieces. I also need ceramics signed by Hans Coper and Lucie Rie.

Let me know what you have. Photos are helpful. Thanks.

Dennis Boyd
211 S. Mulberry St.
Richmond, VA 23220

I want to buy art glass or colored pattern-glass sugar shakers, cruets, syrup pitchers, and castor sets. All four of these items were used on the late Victorian dinner table. All except the cruet had metal lids. The cruet, of course, had a glass stopper most often of matching design.

I particularly want decorated items, cranberry opalescent items, pigeon blood items, cased glass items, ornate patterns, or ornately trimmed items. I will pay from $50.00 to $350.00 for each item. If you can't identify an item, please send a photo.

Juanita Wilkins
P.O. Box 1884
Lima, OH 45802

ART NOUVEAU

We are interested in Art Nouveau items from the 1880's to 1915. This includes paper goods, vintage clothing, glass, or anything else from this period. I pay $5.00 and up for all categories.

Bird-in-the-Cage
201 King St.
Alexandria, VA 22314

ATLANTIC & PACIFIC TEA CO.

A&P (or The Great Atlantic & Pacific Tea Company) was established in 1859. Over the years, hundreds of items have produced as give-aways, promotions, etc. Prior to 1964, such items included spice tins, trading cards, brochures, and publications.

We pay according to condition. Please send photo or complete description for instant quote from private collector.

C.T. Peters, Inc.
P.O. Box 2120
Red Bank, NJ 07701

AUTOGRAPHS

Autographs

For the collector with a strong historical interest, the collecting of autographs in the form of letters, notes, documents, and manuscripts is especially rewarding. When collected by theme or time period, the resulting focus enables the collector to become more of an expert in a specific area. Also he is more apt to be approached by those with unique and original items for sale.

There certainly is some delight in collecting autographs of the famous. Far greater delight and pleasure, though, come from collecting those written pieces that make an important statement. In other words, it is indeed nice to have an autograph of Ulysses S. Grant framed with a vintage steel engraving, but it is a veritable height of excitement to have a hand-written telegram of Grant informing the President that Lee's army cannot escape far from City Point! This year I have bought and sold both, as well as numerous similar items.

The following values are what I will pay for the few items listed below. There are, of course, many more that could be listed, as well as other categories such as signed photographs. For a firm quote, it is best to send me a photocopy of your item. You are also welcome to call; leave a message in the daytime, or personally speak with me almost any evening.

Will Paulsen, Autographs
969 Rock Creek Rd.
Charlottesville, VA 22903
(804) 971-6864

Civil War Period	Signature	Autographed Signed Letter
P.G.T.Beauregard	50.00	200.00
Ambrose E. Burnside	20.00	100.00
George A. Custer	300.00	1000.00
Jefferson Davis	150.00	500.00
Jubal A. Early	35.00	150.00
David G. Farragut	25.00	100.00
Ulysses S. Grant	100.00	400.00
A.P. Hill	200.00	800.00
T.J. "Stonewall" Jackson	500.00	2000.00
Albert S. Johnston	150.00	600.00
Robert E. Lee	400.00	1500.00
James Longstreet	35.00	175.00
John S. Mosby	75.00	250.00
Philip H. Sheridan	25.00	100.00
J.E.B. Stuart	100.00	600.00

Early American Patriots	Signature	Autographed Signed Letter
George Rogers Clark	300.00	1500.00
Benjamin Franklin	650.00	1800.00
John Hancock	500.00	1000.00

Early American Patriots	Signature	Autographed Signed Letter
Patrick Henry	200.00	500.00
Sam Houston	100.00	350.00
Light Horse Harry Lee	100.00	250.00
Meriwether Lewis	300.00	700.00
Paul Revere	300.00	1500.00
John Marshall	200.00	600.00
Dolley Madison	250.00	600.00
Martha Washington	500.00	
George Wythe	100.00	300.00

American Presidents	Signature	Autographed Signed Letter
George Washington	1500.00	4000.00
John Adams	300.00	1000.00
Thomas Jefferson	750.00	3000.00
James Madison	200.00	600.00
James Monroe	200.00	400.00
John Quincy Adams	100.00	300.00
Andrew Jackson	150.00	400.00
Martin Van Buren	75.00	150.00
William Henry Harrison	100.00	350.00
John Tyler	75.00	200.00
James K. Polk	100.00	300.00
Zachery Taylor	200.00	600.00
Millard Fillmore	75.00	150.00
Franklin Pierce	75.00	150.00
James Buchanan	75.00	150.00
Abraham Lincoln	800.00	2000.00

The field of autograph collecting extends far beyond the teenager who screams for a signature at a stage door. Autographs are collected from the earliest known writings of man to the explorers of the universe today.

The value of an autograph depends on who signed the piece, what was signed (a slip of paper, a letter, a document, a photo, etc.), condition, and so on. Therefore it is impossible to quote buying prices. In general I am always interested in purchasing letters, documents, signed photos, checks, etc., from people in the following categories:

Scientists	First Ladies
Aviators	Authors
Presidents	Inventors

Autographs

Artists
Statesmen
Actors

Actresses
Supreme Court
Signers of the Declaration of Independence

Paul Hartunian
47 Portland Place
Montclair, NJ 07042

I buy autographs! I have several areas of special interest: the Civil War, Hollywood, signed photos of famous people, space and early aviation, old diaries, and old letters having news and/or happenings of the period. Being an avid and constantly active collector, I am interested in many related artifacts and paintings circa 1830 through 1930. Please let me hear from you!

Michael Reese II
715-9 One Appian Way
South San Francisco, CA 94080
(415) 588-7608

We Pay

Civil War Letters, Union	5.00 +
Civil War Letters, Confederate	10.00 +
General Custer Signed Photo	1,000.00 +
General Robert E. Lee CDV	500.00
Hollywood Letters	20.00 +
Hollywood Signed Photos	20.00 +
Early Aviation Letters or Signed Photos	75.00 +
Artists Letters or Autographs	20.00 +
Revolutionary War Items	10.00 +

Wanted: collections and accumulations of family and business letters, manuscripts, documents, diaries, ledgers, photographs, newspapers, ephemera, and trade catalogs. We are seeking material from all states and countries of any period. All quotes will be acknowledged. Prices paid will depend upon quantity, quality, and condition. Please send a full description and (if possible) a Xerox copy. Immediate payment made upon acceptance of offer. We don't deal in sports or entertainment material. This is a full-time business. Our shop is open by appointment; wants are cheerfully solicited, and your catalogues are always appreciated. We buy and sell. We are a member of the Manuscript Society and have been established since 1978. Authenticity is guaranteed on all material.

Mr. Carmen D. Valentino
Rare Books & Manuscripts
2956 Richmond St.
Philadelphia, PA 19134
(215) 739-6056

AUTOMOBILIA

Buick promotional items wanted. Looking for any factory-issued items such as paperweights, desk sets, ash trays, banks, key chain tags, promotional models, matchbooks, advertising literature, showroom items, awards, etc. Also looking for toy Buicks, dealer-issued items, and Buick accessory items.

Alvin Heckard
R.D. 1, Box 88
Lewistown, PA 17044

Automobilia

I collect automobile literature and accessories such as owner manuals, shop manuals, and sales brochures. I am also interested in buying accessories which were offered as extras by the dealer or after-market manufacturers. These would include compasses, license plate attachments, flag holders, radios, temperature or oil pressure meters, mirrors for sun visors, car vases, clocks, fog lights, etc. The value depends very much on the item, its condition, and its circa.

Besides these items, I buy miniature key chain license plates (or tags). These were made by D.A.V. (Disabled American Veterans) as a fund raiser from 1942 to 1976. B.F. Goodrich (as well as several other companies) made them from 1939 until 1942. Of the D.A.V. tags, the hardest to find are the early ones, those from the smaller or less-inhabited states (WY, MT, SD, NC, SC, OR, WA, AK, DE, and HI), and those from 1943 (due to WWII). Tags from 1968 and after are hard to find with a date because many states began utilizing window stickers or tabs. The easy-to-find tags are those from NY, PA, IA, KS, and WI; and those made from the 1950's up to 1968. Common D.A.V. tags are worth 50¢ to $8.00; harder-to-find examples range from $2.00 to $15.00. The B.F. Goodrich tags are worth $10.00 to $30.00--again depending upon state and date. Of course, condition is also a factor, and some collectors consider matched pairs especially valuable. Contact me for more information, offers, and names of collectors.

Donald L. Fehr
P.O. Box 872
Northfield, NJ 08225

I want automobile literature dating from 1900 through 1975. I buy sales brochures, repair manuals, parts catalogs, owner's manuals, showroom items or any other literature pertaining to automobiles. I travel to purchase literature.

Walter Miller
6710 Brooklawn Pkwy.
Syracuse, NY 13211
(315) 432-8282

AVIATION

I am buying commercial aviation items. I prefer items from the 1920's through the 1970's whether a single piece or a collection. Listed below are some of the things I am seeking. I also want anything old and unusual.

John R. Joiner
245 Ashland Trail
Tyrone, GA 30290

	We Pay
Pilot Wings	25.00 +
Pilot Hat Emblems	25.00 +
Flight Attendant Wings	25.00 +
Flight Attendant Hat Emblems	25.00 +
Timetables	3.00 +
Playing Cards	1.00 +
Post Cards	.50 +
Anniversary Pins	5.00 +
Pilot Manuals	25.00 +
Maintenance Manuals	25.00 +
Display Models	50.00 +
Early Signs	20.00 +
Dining Service Items	1.00 +
Posters	5.00 +

Commercial airline memorabilia is a growing hobby and collectible field. I will buy or trade any item—quantities are always of interest. Specific interests include playing cards, schedules, posters, kiddie wings, wings, and all logo-marked items.

Bill Rosenbloom
1893 Worcester
St. Paul, MN 55116

I need for my personal library World War I 1914 through 1918 squadron memorial volumes and squadron histories. I need the two-volume set *Lafayette Flying Corps* by Nordhoff and Hall, published by Houghton and Mifflin. I also need the two-volume set *New England Aviators of 1914-1918*. I collect aviation-related photos and negatives from the 1920's through the 1940's and various other relics, as well. I will buy an entire collection to get what I want.

Charles Donald
P.O. Box 822
Union City, NJ 07087

BADGES

I am actively seeking operator's badges from Pennsylvania only. There are three different types that were issued; they are very similar—all were oval pin-backs with a keystone center.

The most common type is the 'Pennsylvania Licensed Driver,' issued from 1910 through 1919. The 1910 badge is keystone shaped; after 1911, they were oval. The second type is identical, only the wording has been changed to 'Pennsylvania Licensed Operator.' These were issued to paid employees from 1915 through 1929. The 1929 badge was round, rather than oval—about the size of a silver dollar. The third type is 'Special Licensed Driver,' issued from 1911 through 1916. Though we aren't really sure why these were issued, we suspect they were for non-residents who lived in Pennsylvania temporarily. They are also oval in shape.

Prices paid for badges are as follows. These are only guidelines; much depends on condition.

Edward Foley
227 Union Ave.
Pittsburgh, PA 15202

PA Licensed Driver	We Pay		We Pay
1910	50.00	1921	45.00
1911	35.00	1922	45.00
1912	30.00	1923	40.00
1913	25.00	1924	40.00
1914	25.00	1925	40.00
1915	25.00	1926	40.00
1916	25.00	1927	35.00
1917	20.00	1928	35.00
1918	20.00	1929	40.00
1919	20.00		

PA Licensed Operator	We Pay	PA Special Licensed Driver	We Pay
1915	50.00	1911	45.00
1916	50.00	1912	45.00
1917	50.00	1913	40.00
1918	50.00	1914	40.00
1919	45.00	1915	35.00
1920	45.00	1916	35.00

BANKS

Banks

I am collecting old banks of any material composition—cast iron, tin, glass, and wood. I am especially interested in cast iron and mechanical banks, but am willing to pay good prices for any old banks. I will pay retail prices for banks listed in Don Cramer's *The Collector's Encyclopedia of Toys and Banks*, or I will negotiate with anyone. I am a collector, not a dealer.

Don Eigenberg
1595 Beverly
Gering, NE 69341

Collecting glass banks has been a popular hobby for many years. This is probably due to the fact that nearly all children had a bank when they were young. Glass banks remain very easy to find and are relatively inexpensive. A certain class of glass banks has become more collectible in recent years, and that is the figural glass bottle bank. This is a glass bottle which originally held some product such as mustard, flavored syrup, olives, shaving cream, etc., and when empty could be used as a coin bank due to its slotted lid. We buy any of the following bottle banks if they have their original lid and are not damaged. A label may increase its value; contact me for these prices.

Bonnie Hare
311 Fairview St.
Carlisle, PA 17013
(717) 243-5378

We Pay

Bear Snowcrest Baby 4¾"	20.00
Bear Snowcrest Papa 8½"	20.00
Bee Hive Honey Jar	35.00
Burma Shave	20.00
Cat Grapette	18.00
Clown Snowcrest	60.00
Donald Duck	25.00
Elephant Vandor 'Made in Taiwan'	20.00
Lion Vandor 'Made in Taiwan'	20.00
Jocko the Monkey	40.00
Lucky Joe w/Clown Lid	14.00
Lucky Joe w/Deerwood Lid	16.00
Lucky Joe w/Royal Blue Lid	16.00
Lucky Joe w/All Paper Face	20.00
Mickey Mouse Jam Jar	50.00
Owl Gattuso	35.00
Penguin Snowcrest	60.00

We Pay

Pig Forbes Tea..20.00
Pig Gattuso..25.00
Pig 'Brother can you spare a dime'....................................25.00
Seal Snowcrest...60.00
Spacemen...12.00
Tankcar..18.00
Uncle Sam Bond Bank..60.00

Toy penny banks are collected by all those who have an interest in 'saving' a part of American History. Before 1930 they were usually made of cast iron. The companies that produced these toys made thrift a very important part of American society. Coin banks were made in themes depicting people, animals, safes, and architectural buildings. They convey a realistic image of life styles, sometimes portraying sports figures or occupations.

There were over three hundred mechanical types produced between 1870 to 1930. Still banks and registering types were manufactured around the same period. It is very difficult to catalog all of these because 'new' finds keep being discovered. We buy all toy banks in good condition; photographs are helpful. No reproductions are bought. We pay according to original condition.

Mark & Lynda Suozzi
Antiques & Americana
P.O. Box 102
Ashfield, MA 10330
(413) 628-3241

We Pay

Dentist..2,000.00 +
Oriental Camel...300.00 +
Girl Jumping Rope..7,500.00 +
U.S. & Spain...1,500.00 +
Independence Hall..300.00 +
Baby Elephant at 10 O'clock..5,000.00 +
Army-Navy Safe...200.00 +
Eagle & Eaglets..300.00 +
10¢ Registering Bank...500.00 +
Paddy & Pig..600.00 +
Owl (head turns)...200.00 +
Statue of Liberty (large)..200.00 +
Basset Hound...400.00 +
Apple Bank...300.00 +
Darktown Baseball..600.00 +
Jonah & Whale..600.00 +

We Pay

Columbian Bank Building...200.00 +
Giant Bank...4,000.00 +
Lion Hunter...1,000.00 +
Mikado Bank...10,000.00 +
Reclining Chinaman...2,000.00 +
Roller Skating...7,000.00 +
Camera (Kodak) Bank...200.00 +
Boy Scout..1,000.00 +
Bad Accident...600.00 +
Board of Trade...3,000.00 +
Tugboat..4,000.00 +
Breadwinners...8,000.00 +
Teddy & Bear...500.00 +
Many Others..10.00-10,000.00

The first patented cast iron mechanical bank was invented by John Hall on December 21, 1869. Since that time, literally thousands of banks have been manufactured in almost every country in the world. The United States historically has remained in the forefront of mechanical bank production, with early subjects spanning everything from biblical themes to the circus. Racial and nationality prejudice served as a popular theme during the 1800's, represented by such mechanicals as 'Reclining Chinaman,' 'Jolly Nigger,' 'Darkey Watermelon,' 'Paddy and the Pig,' and 'The Dentist Bank.'

I am interested in purchasing any mechanical bank manufactured in the United States, England, or D.R.G.M. Germany between the years 1869 and 1939. They may be made from iron, tin, lead, wood, or cardboard, as long as they are old.

Regarding the prices I will pay for the rare banks on the following list: name your price—$5,000.00, $10,000.00, $25,000.00—depending upon condition.

Name of Bank:
Baby Elephant, bank opens at X o'clock, lead with wood base
Springing Cat, cat jumps mouse, lead with wood base
Chinaman in Boat, food tray flips over, lead
Darkey Fisherman, 'Dis Pond Am Boss Place,' lead
Clown on Bar, clown spins around, tin clown on iron base
Presto, mirrors inside, iron & glass
Mama Katzenjammer, eyes move, iron
Turtle, head moves, iron
Bowling Alley, man tosses ball, iron
Mikado, Magic Bank; covers coin with cups, iron
Merry-Go-Round, turn crank, revolves, iron
Roller Skating, figures skate around, iron
Girl in Chair with Dog, dog moves, iron

Little Red Riding Hood, Grandma reveals Wolf's face, iron
Old Woman in Shoe, holds stick in hand, iron
Panorama Building, wood roller with pictures, iron & paper
Bank Teller, man stands behind iron desk, iron
National Building Bank, cardboard figure inside, iron & paper
Rival Bank, monkey jumps into dormer window, iron
Clown, Harlequin, Ballet Dancer; figures spin, iron
Germania Exchange, goat on beer barrel, lead
Darkey Kicks Football into Watermelon, arms & foot move, iron
Jonah and Whale, Jonah emerges from whale's mouth, iron
Seek Him Frisk, dog chases cat up tree, tin & iron
Zig Zag Bank, coin causes jack-in-box to open, tin & iron
Tin Characters, coin is placed on extended tongue, tin
Spring Jaw Characters, coin makes jaw wiggle, lead

Sy Schreckinger
P.O. Box 104
East Rockaway, NY 11518

Old cast iron mechanical banks were made between 1860 and 1930. These banks display some form of action while utilizing a coin (as opposed to a still bank which has no moving parts.) The majority of mechanical banks were made by the J.E. Stevens Co. of Cromwell, CT.

Reproduction and fakes exist in many banks, and some forgeries were made as early as 1935. One must be aware that condition is very important to the value of banks; there are often broken parts on the old mechanical banks. We buy all old banks, both in good condition and poor. I will buy other banks not listed; contact me for prices. We will pay up to the price indicated for banks in good condition.

Kittelberger Galleries
82½ E. Main St.
Webster, NY 14580
(716) 265-1230

We Pay

Bowling Alley Bank..**10,000.00**
Darktown Battery...**1,200.00**
Butting Buffalo..**2,000.00**
Boy Scout..**3,000.00**
Boy Steals Watermelon...**1,500.00**
Bread Winner's Bank..**10,000.00**
Bulldog..**700.00**
Bad Accident...**1,500.00**
Circus Bank..**5,000.00**

We Pay

Dentist	2,000.00
Freedman's Bank	40,000.00
Girl Skipping Rope	10,000.00
Indian & Bear	1,000.00
Leap Frog	3,000.00
Lion & Monkeys	1,000.00
Chinaman in Boat	10,000.00
Darkey Fisherman	10,000.00
Confectionery	5,000.00
Merry-Go-Round	10,000.00
Roller Skating Bank	10,000.00
Old Woman in Shoe	50,000.00
Jonah & Whale on Pedestal	10,000.00

_____

Mechanical banks (often originally the rich kid's toy) have remained popular since they were first introduced in the late 1800's. Mechanical banks made saving money fun, since the way the bank 'swallowed' the coin was entertaining for children to watch. Some banks had very simple movement, such as the movement of just one hand or arm. Others had lots of action—these tend to be the most desirable and the easiest to break. Beware! Reproductions (some of which themselves were made forty years ago) are more common than originals.

Jeff Bradfield
745 Hillview Dr.
Dayton, VA 22821

We Pay

Creedmore, good paint	250.00
William Tell, good paint	400.00
Darktown Battery	850.00
Two Frogs	500.00
Gem Bank	150.00
Dentist	2,200.00 +
Lion & Monkeys	550.00
Eagle & Eaglets	400.00
Trick Dog	250.00

_____

I buy broken, incomplete, or partial mechanical banks. I pay a good, fair price. Look up the value in a current antique price guide, and let us set a mutually acceptable price. I always give a fair market value. Of course, I'll buy complete banks, too, but so will a lot of folks. Lets make a deal—call or write. I also want wooden bank shipping boxes, colored trade cards, and catalogues of banks. Prices I'll pay are listed below.

Greg Zeminick
1350 Kirts #160
Troy, MI 48084
(313) 244-9426

We Pay

Darktown Battery (broken)	**500.00-700.00**
Calamity (broken)	**1,000.00-1,500.00**
Mammy (broken)	**1,800.00**
Picture Gallery (broken)	**1,600.00**
Weeden's Tin Windup	**550.00**

These tin (or tin with paper label) miniature oil-can banks are usually four ounces in size and represent a specialty within the collectible bank category. Beginning in the early 1940's, these banks were produced as a promotional tool for gasoline and motor oil dealers. In addition to motor oil, many specialty oils and fluids were promoted with these banks including antifreeze, top oil, and lubricants. There are well over one hundred to one hundred fifty different versions known to date. Many oil companies offered five or six different banks representing most, if not all, of their oil products. Most common is Cities Service with Koolmotor tin banks for various grades of oil (HD, 5D, Premium, etc.). Another is Wolf's Head Motor Oil with a number of versions, the most desirable being Wolf's Head Light Duty and Heavy Duty Motor Oils. (The Super Duty version is the most common.)

Listed below are some of the brands I seek to expand my collection of eighty-six different oil-can tin banks. Please drop me a card with your find and the price desired (range is from $5.00 to $20.00, based on condition and rarity). I'll respond immediately.

Peter Capell
1838 W. Grace St.
Chicago, IL 60613

Banks from These Companies   **We Pay**

Bardahl Top Oil	**5.00-20.00**
Cross Country Motor Oil (Sears)	**5.00-20.00**

	We Pay
Conoco 'Nth' Motor Oil	5.00-20.00
Co-op Diesel Oil	5.00-20.00
Esso Motor Oil	5.00-20.00
Lion Motor Oil	5.00-20.00
Kendall 2,000 Mile Motor Oil	5.00-20.00
Mobil Upper Lube	5.00-20.00
Marathon Motor Oil	5.00-20.00
Pure/Purol Motor Oil	5.00-20.00
SOHIO-The Standard Lubricant	5.00-20.00
Shell X-100 Motor Oil	5.00-20.00
Tenneco Motor Oil	5.00-20.00
Tiolene (Pure) Motor Oil	5.00-20.00
Triton Motor Oil	5.00-20.00
Wolf's Head LIGHT Duty Motor Oil	5.00-20.00
Wolf's Head HEAVY Duty Motor Oil	5.00-20.00
Worthmore Solvent Refined Oil	5.00-20.00
Skelly Motor Oil, etc.	5.00-20.00

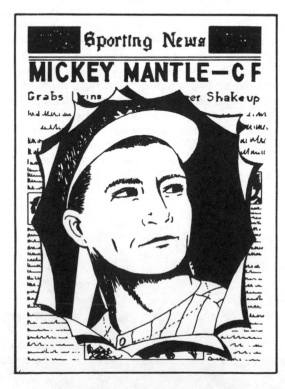

BASEBALL CARDS

Baseball card collecting has become very popular in the past eight years. Once thought of as a hobby for children, it has grown to attract people of all ages. The hobby has watched cards such as the 1933 Goudy Babe Ruth climb from $35.00 in 1979 to over $2,300.00 in 1988. This hobby is definitely based on supply and demand. A ball player in your part of the country will bring a premium price, as opposed to one who's not in your area. Condition is a big factor in determining price. A card will bring top dollar if it is in mint condition and the photo is well centered on the card.

We are constantly buying cards—any kind, year, or amount. Please send a list with a description of your cards, condition, and price. Below you will find a list of cards we are currently buying with the price. The price reflects mint-condition cards.

The Shortt Stop
Michael Shortt
557 Richmond Ave.
Syracuse, NY 13204

We Pay   **We Pay**

	We Pay		We Pay
1984 Mattingly	15.00	1985 Eric Davis	8.00
1978 Murray	12.00	1985 Mark McGwire	10.00
1980 Henderson	12.00	1983 Wade Boggs	10.00
1956 Mantle	250.00	1973 Mike Schmidt	50.00
1956 Mays	50.00	1974 Dave Winfield	6.00
1956 Aaron	50.00	1972 Rod Carew	10.00
1960 Yastrzemski	65.00	1972 Steve Garvey	10.00
1960 Mantle	75.00	1953 Mickey Mantle	300.00

We are always looking for baseball cards, statues, pins, or anything pertaining to baseball. We are especially seeking older, high-quality, unique items to purchase. Just write us and turn those old pieces of cardboard into cash.

The following list represents only a small number of cards that we are looking for. If you have any cards not on the list, please write us with the description, condition, quality, and quantity. We will respond immediately with a purchase offer.

Peace Antiques
Rt. 1, Box 176
Remer, MN 56672

Pre-1940 Undamaged Cards   **We Pay**

Pre-1940 Undamaged Cards	We Pay
Babe Ruth	250.00 +
Lou Gehrig	250.00 +

Baseball Cards _____

	We Pay
Ty Cobb	100.00 +
Honus Wagner	150.00 +
Hundreds of Others	50¢-1.00

1940-1970 Undamaged Cards	We Pay
Mickey Mantle	75.00 +
Joe DiMaggio	100.00 +
Ted Williams	50.00 +
Roger Maris	15.00 +
Jackie Robinson	40.00 +
Hundreds of Others	1.00-50.00

Baseball cards have been with us for one hundred years now. Although there have been collectors all this time, in the last decade the hobby has really come of age. It's no longer just a 'kid's pastime.' Still it covers all age groups and interests. The fun thing is that there are thousands of cards available for pennies. Then there are the cards that are worth hundreds and even thousands of dollars to advanced collectors and investors. As with most collectibles, condition is of prime importance. For example, a card valued at $100.00 in mint condition may be worth less than $5.00 in fair condition. Regardless of the age of cards, strict grading is always required.

The following list includes some cards I'm currently buying. Prices are for cards in mint condition. I will pay approximately 70% for excellent and 30% for very good cards. Refer to *Beckett Price Guide* for grading standards. All St. Louis Cardinal cards wanted! Many other cards 1933 through 1985 wanted!

B.A. Murry
709 Taylor Dr.
Carbondale, IL 62901
(618) 529-4391

	We Pay
Stan Musial	75.00-175.00
Ted Williams	75.00-175.00
Mickey Mantle	75.00-3,500.00
Yogi Berra	20.00-175.00
Jackie Robinson	50.00-175.00
Duke Snider	20.00-175.00
Roy Campanella	20.00-175.00
Willie Mays	30.00-400.00

We Pay

Commons 1948...4.00-8.00
Commons 1949...3.00-15.00
Commons 1950...4.00-8.00
Commons 1951...3.00-10.00
Commons 1952...3.00-8.00
Commons 1953...4.00-10.00
Commons 1954...2.00
Commons 1955...1.00-3.00
Topps 1952 Mantle.......................................4,500.00
Topps 1953 Mantle...650.00
Topps 1956 Mantle...275.00
Topps 1957 Mantle...225.00
Topps 1958 Mantle...175.00
Topps 1959 Mantle...125.00
Topps 1959 Musial...30.00
Topps 1960-63 Musial..20.00
Topps 1954 Williams.......................................100.00
Topps 1954-67 Williams......................................50.00
Topps 1953 Robinson.......................................100.00
Topps 1954 Aaron..250.00
Topps 1955 Clemente.......................................150.00
Topps 1955 Koufax...125.00
Topps 1955 Snider...125.00
Topps 1958 Maris...80.00
Topps 1959 Gibson...100.00
Topps 1973 Schmidt...80.00
Topps 1977 Murphy..30.00
Topps 1979 Ozzie Smith......................................8.00
Topps 1980 Henderson.......................................12.00
Topps 1983 Boggs...15.00
Topps 1984 Mattingly.......................................15.00
Fleer 1984 Mattingly.......................................15.00
Donruss 1985 E. Davis......................................15.00

BATHING BEAUTIES AND OTHER NAUGHTIES

As the Victorian era passed into the Edwardian and roaring twenties, a market developed for bisque and china figurines of women in revealing outfits and bawdy novelties. Bathing beauties, women dressed in molded swimsuits or bits of lace,

37

were produced from 1910 through the 1930's. Sometimes the ladies were left nude or were clad only in molded underwear or long stockings; these are 'naughties.' Hollow figurines with suggestive themes, such as a little boy on a chamber pot or a woman cupping her breasts, were meant to be filled with water. When a rubber bulb was squeezed, water would squirt out of an appropriate orifice. Other naughties appeared to be innocent figurines but, when turned over or around, displayed a risque character. For example, turning over a figurine of a fully-dressed woman revealed her to be nude beneath. Germany first produced these pieces; but as Japan flooded the market with often crude copies, the novelties fell out of favor.

I will buy quality German pieces. The prices are only estimates, depending on size, subject, position, molding, and decoration. I will pay less for poorer pieces or more for excellent ones.

S. Weintraub
2924 Helena
Houston, TX 77006

We Pay

Tinted (not pre-colored) Bisque Bathing Beauty, molded suit:
Less than 5"..**50.00-150.00**
5" or more..**150.00-250.00**
Bathing Beauty, net suit, mohair wig:
Less than 5"..**100.00-175.00**
5" or more..**150.00-350.00**
Nude Figurine:
Less than 5"..**50.00-150.00**
5" or more..**125.00-300.00**
Molded Underwear or Stockings:
Less than 5"..**75.00-175.00**
5" or more..**150.00-350.00**
Hollow Naughty (meant to squirt water):
Boy or child..**25.00-100.00**
Woman..**75.00-165.00**
Naughty (reveals 'surprise' when turned over or around):
Child..**50.00-100.00**
Woman..**75.00-250.00**
Black Woman..**100.00-300.00**

BB GUNS

I am especially interested in older pre-1915 guns, preferably cast iron-framed guns. There are many different models and variations to these early guns. Some are very fancy and ornate; others are very plain and simple—a factor that does not decrease or increase the value.

To list a few names that may appear on the gun or the stock of the gun (some stocks are made of iron or steel) would be as follows: Daisy, Atlas, New Dandy, King, Columbian, Adams Westlake, Heilprin, Cycloid, New Rapid, Dewey, Crescent, Oziehs, Globe, Dunbar, Special, Warrior, Magic Bijou, and Matchless. There are a few others. Bear in mind there may be fifteen models or variations per trade name.

Prices vary according to the condition, completeness, and rarity of the gun. The values of most guns if complete and undamaged start at $100.00 and go upwards rapidly depending on the above variables.

A picture of the gun would help a great deal. I will pay top dollar for any guns I can use in my collection. I also collect cast iron cap guns and single-shot rifles.

Terry Burger
2323 Lincoln
Beatrice, NE 68310
(402) 228-2797

BEATLES

Items relating to the Beatles, who revolutionized pop music in the 1960's, have become very collectible over the past ten years. The original memorabilia generated from this era is vast and almost countless. Almost any item which could be branded with the Beatles' pictures or logos were manufactured. There are three categories into which these items can be placed. The first and the most common group is the mass-produced items and toys that were available in most department stores. The second category includes promotional items of limited production which were given out to radio stations and a selected few. Last is the category which contains personal items that actually were owned by the Fab Four. These are extremely rare pieces and usually surface only in major auctions. Unfortunately, many of the smaller mass-produced items have been counterfeited and have in turn made their original counterparts practically worthless.

I have collected Beatles items for over ten years and am looking for 1960's original memorabilia only. I will buy only items in near-perfect condition unless the item is rare. Contact me for other prices for less-than-perfect examples. Near-perfect condition includes original packaging.

Joseph Hilton
6 Wheelwright Dr.
Lee, NH 03824

We Pay

Balloon in package	20.00
Banjo, plastic, by Mastro	200.00
Bongos, plastic, by Mastro	200.00
Bedspread, English	150.00
Binders, plastic, 3-ring	25.00
Blanket, English	150.00
Bubble Bath, Paul & Ringo	35.00
Case, Air Flite Bag	75.00
Colorforms, 1966, NEMS	100.00
Coloring Book, 1964	20.00
Curtains, English, 1964	150.00
Disk-Go-Case, plastic, 1966	35.00
Dolls, 1964, by Remco (4)	100.00
Dresses, English, 1964	150.00
Flip Your Wig Game, Milton Bradley	50.00
Guitar, plastic, various sizes	100.00 +
Hairspray Can, 1964, NEMS	100.00
Halloween Costumes, boxed	75.00
Lampshade, English, 1964	100.00
Lunch Box & Thermos	50.00
Pen, faces on clip, 1964	25.00
Pillow, 3 variations, 1964	50.00
Purse, vinyl, rope handle, 1964	50.00
Record Carrying Cases, 45 or LP sizes	50.00 +
Record Player, 1964 (working)	250.00

We Pay

Tennis Shoes, boxed, 1964	75.00
Talcum Powder, tin, English, 1964	100.00
Wallet, w/all inserts, 1964	30.00
Yellow Sub Ceramic Bank	75.00
Yellow Sub Colorforms, 1968	100.00
Yellow Sub Corgi Toy, 1968	100.00
Yellow Sub Coat Hangers, 1968	25.00
Yellow Sub Puzzles, by Jaymar	30.00 +
Autographs, 1964-1969, genuine	300.00 +

Beatles memorabilia is becoming increasingly collectible to Yuppies who grew up in the '60s. From 1964 after the Beatles appeared on the 'Ed Sullivan Show' until their break-up in 1970, the Beatles totally dominated the music industry. As they changed and progressed, so did the entire generation, from long hair, folk-rock, moustaches, granny glasses, acid-rock, stereo, mysticism, revolution, and self-awareness.

Most Beatles memorabilia has the initials NEMS printed on it. Wigs were the first big item (so everyone could look like them). Then came bubble gum cards, lunch boxes, and the rest.

I buy all types of Beatles and rock memorabilia––those in mint condition and damaged, individual pieces and box lots––if you contact me for prices.

Cindy Oakes
34025 W. 6 Mile
Livonia, MI 48152
(313) 591-3252

We Pay

Buttons	50¢-1.00
Magazines	1.00-5.00
Bubble Gum Cards	25¢-50¢
Dolls, vinyl, 4", ea	25.00-50.00
Drums	10.00
Lunch Pail	25.00
Thermos	10.00
Yellow Submarine	5.00
Plastic Models	10.00
Wig	15.00
Flip Your Wig Game	5.00
Necklace	5.00
Books	1.00-5.00
Nodder Dolls, ea	10.00

Beatles

We Pay

Original Beatle Concert Programs or Ticket Stubs.................**1.00-5.00**
Beatles Blow-up Dolls, set of 4....................................**40.00**
Beatles Clothing w/Original Labels...............................**10.00 +**

The Beatles were the first rock and roll group to be marketed in a massive way. Hundreds of Beatles items were produced, but because many were cheap and poorly made, they have become hard to find. Unfortunately, as Beatle collecting has become more popular, the incidence of counterfeiting has also increased. Some items (for example Beatles Soap Bubbles and a coloring set) are newly made. Autographs need proof of authenticity. We buy Beatle items in good to mint condition. For paper items, this means no marks or tears. No common LPs, please. Bootleg or unusual albums and singles—especially with jacket covers—are welcome. Listed below is only a sampling of our wants; please contact us with any items you might have.

Dziadosz
327 Washington S.E.
Grand Rapids, MI 49503

We Pay

Bubble Gum Card..**25¢**
Beatle Magazine...**5.00**
3-Ring Binder (red, white, or blue).............................**25.00**
Charm Bracelet...**12.00**
Flip Your Wig Game...**30.00**
Blue Meanie Halloween Costume, boxed...........................**25.00**
Drinking Glass, yellow...**30.00**
Drinking Glass, clear..**15.00**
Phonograph, blue..**100.00**
Hair Spray..**50.00**
Air Flite Carrying Case, round, vinyl..........................**30.00**
Remco Doll, w/instrument, NEMS, 4½"............................**25.00**
Disk-Go-Case..**20.00**
Sweatshirt, white...**10.00**
Talc Powder...**40.00**
Magazine w/Beatles Cover (Time, Life, Post, Newsweek, Rolling Stone)...**2.00**
Tennis Shoes, Wing Ding, boxed................................**40.00**
Tennis Shoes, high back, boxed................................**50.00**

BEER CANS

I am buying beer cans—complete collections or single cans. They must be mint condition and bottom opened. Beer cans from all countries are wanted, both U.S. and foreign, in sizes from 8¾-ounces to gallons. I also want these complete sets: Piper Sets, Tennants Girls Sets, German Train Sets, German Balloon Sets, etc. Price varies from set to set, depending on the number of cans in each, and will fluctuate as supply and demand changes. I will be glad to have your offers or lists and will quote a fair price. I am a collector, so I can pay a fair price. Listed below are some sample sets wanted and the prices I will pay.

AAACRC
P.O. Box 8061
Saddle Brook, NJ 07662

We Pay

28-Can Simba Set	**30.00**
24-Can Lion Set	**30.00**
New Olympic Set, Lababatt, Canada, 15-Can Set	**18.00**

BILLIARDS

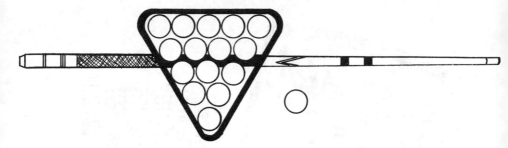

The game of billiards has a rather obscure origin. It is believed that the game developed as an outgrowth of lawn bowling and was originally played with clay balls and large wooden sticks (having no special tips) on a large rectangular table.

During the 16th century, the game was brought to this part of the world by the Spaniards and was avidly played in Europe even prior to its introduction in North America. Over the years, variants of the game have developed, the most noted of these being pocket billiards or pool. Various refinements of the early equipment used include the addition of live rubber cushions on the table and the introduction of pockets; the cue stick was tapered, and a leather tip was added at its end so that English or spin could be imparted to the cue ball.

Most strikingly (no pun intended), billiards and its variants have attracted devotees and casual players of both sexes, all ages, and of all socio-economic strata. Numbered among its players are George Washington, Thomas Jefferson, Alexander Hamilton, the Marquis de Lafayette, and Abraham Lincoln to name but a few.

The game has also been used by some for its therapeutic value and was recommended to Louis XIV of France by his physician as a 'tonic exercise.'

My own interest in the game spans more than thirty years. I seek to purchase the following: photos, advertisements, catalogues, books, two-piece pool cues, and other related items. Due to the wide variety of items which fall under these headings, buy prices will necessarily have to be determined on an individual basis depending upon the nature and condition of the item(s) offered. Please write giving a complete description and enclosing photo(s) if at all possible.

Marc L. Ames
539 Lyme Rock Rd.
Bridgewater, NJ 08807

We Pay

Zambodie & Balabushka 2-Piece Cue . . . . **100.00 +**
Old Pool & Billiards Lithographs . . . . **5.00 +**
Old Instructive Material (books, etc.) . . . . **5.00 +**
Tobacco Cards Featuring Billiard Players . . . . **1.00 +**

BLACK MEMORABILIA

Black memorabilia is probably one of the most unique and unusual forms of collecting. Due to the subject matter, the Black collector stands alone. Offering a mixture of elegant to derogatory items, Black collections are either revered or criticized by the viewer.

Due to the fact that there are such a wide variety of items, it is impossible to list each one and its price. I will purchase nearly all Black items. All items must depict Black people (no native items). You must call or write to the provided address. Some of the items in which I am most interested are listed below.

Tim Schnitzer
P.O. Box 5512
Yuma, AZ 85364
(602) 783-4816

45

Black Memorabilia

We Pay

Aunt Jemima Items (spices, cookie jars, sugar & creamer, etc.)..........**10.00+**
Tobacco Humidors Depicting Black People..........................**25.00+**
Black Bisque Figurines..**15.00+**
Terra Cotta Items...**20.00+**
Majolica Figurines, Vases, Etc....................................**25.00+**
Chalkware, Wall Plaques, Etc.......................................**5.00+**
Cast Iron Figures (no reproductions)..............................**10.00+**
Linens (tablecloths, towels, aprons, etc.)........................**10.00+**
Cruets (ceramic salt & pepper sets, etc.).........................**10.00+**

During the past eighteen years I have enjoyed searching for many types of Black items. Since thousands were commercially produced and hundreds more were one-of-a-kind folk art, the search is endless. Several of my favorite categories are: rag dolls, carved walking sticks, Weller Mammy kitchen set, jigsaw puzzles, valentines, paper dolls, playing cards, skill games, sewing items, children's books, souvenir spoons, watercolors, prints, jewelry, and advertising items. These can reflect Black images from both realistic and stereotype viewpoints. I am interested in items that represent both aspects as long as they are not common (such as Mammy/chef salt and pepper sets, Mammy shopping reminder lists, outhouse figures, and linen post cards).

Fortunately, many unusual items are available in every part of this country. I can usually buy from a photo or Xerox copy as long as condition is clearly described. The following are some of the items I am buying and the prices I will pay for them in fine condition. I am interested in other items and will consider higher prices than those listed.

Jan & Bruce Thalberg
23 Mountain View Dr.
Weston, CT 06883

We Pay

Cloth Doll, Beloved Belindy......................................**150.00**
Print, My Honey, by Guttman......................................**150.00**
Print, Mammy's Angel Child, by Gimball...........................**150.00**
Print, Four Seasons, by Maud Humphrey............................**50.00**
Cookie Jar, Mammy, by Pearl China................................**200.00**
Cookie Jar, Mammy, by Weller.....................................**300.00**
Bottle, Mammy, by Robj...**150.00**
Cup & Saucer, Coon Chicken Inn...................................**50.00**
Flatware, Coon Chicken Inn, ea...................................**10.00**
Lamp, Mammy, full-figure, glass..................................**250.00**

We Pay

Wall Lamp, Mammy head, ceramic	125.00
Wall Clock, Mammy, full-figure, metal	200.00
Playing Cards, pre-1930	25.00
Mechanical Valentines, pre-1920	20.00
Mechanical Valentines, 1920-1940	10.00
Greeting Cards, pre-1950	5.00
Sheet Music, by E.T. Paull	10.00
Pincushion & Emery, Mammy face	25.00
Paper Mask, Aunt Jemima	25.00
Pencil Sharpener, Our Gang	15.00
Papier-mache Candy Container	75.00
Papier-mache Christmas Figural Ornament	150.00
Cotton Batting Christmas Figural Ornament	100.00
Glass Christmas Figural Ornament	150.00
Appliqued or Embroidered Dishtowel	20.00
Recipe Box, Mammy, green plastic	45.00
Ronson Bartender Lighter	250.00

I am interested in buying Black memorabilia of every sort and description—ceramic figurines, banks, ash trays, soap holders and dispensers, post cards, old sheet music, salt and pepper shakers, bells, posters, and other forms of graphic arts. I am particularly interested in rare (i.e., 19th century) items described in the preceding sentence. One example is a bottle opener fashioned like protrusive lips. I must have a detailed description of any and all items.

William E. Perkins
4937 Catharine St.
Philadelphia, PA 19143

BOOKS

The price a dealer suggests for a book can only be used as a guide; value depends on the edition, the publisher, the condition, the demand, the rarity, and more. Signed and inscribed volumes have value if the author or the person to whom the book is inscribed is important. There are simply some books that have no value in the marketplace, for the subject matter or the author may not be of interest at the moment. Eventually there may be renewed interest in the author or the subject.

Listed below are some of the authors, titles, and subjects that interest me. Besides these I am interested in out-of-print books on antiques and decorative arts––rugs, silver, lamps, quilting, furniture, pottery, porcelain, and many others. Also wanted are color-plate books printed before 1860, many juveniles, and books with leather bindings in very good condition.

Robert L. Merriam
Newhall Rd.
Conway, MA 01341

Authors   We Pay

Mary P. Wells Smith, The Old Deerfield Series...................**up to 6.50**
Mary P. Wells Smith, The Young Puritan Series..................**up to 6.50**
Mary P. Wells Smith, Jolly Good Times Series....................**up to 6.50**
Joel Chandler Harris, 1st editions..............................**up to 20.00**
Thornton Burgess, 1st editions.................................**up to 10.00**
Mark Twain, 1st editions......................................**up to 200.00**

Illustrators, Derrydale Press   We Pay

Frederic Remington..**up to 75.00**
N.C. Wyeth...**up to 75.00**
Howard Pyle...**up to 75.00**
Willy Pogany..**up to 75.00**
Maxfield Parrish...**up to 75.00**
Edmund Dulac...**up to 75.00**
Frank Schoonover..**up to 75.00**
Arthur Rackham...**up to 75.00**

Western Massachusetts History   **We Pay**

Everts, The Connecticut River Valley...............................**45.00**
Holland, History of Western Massachusetts, 2 vols....................**45.00**
Sheldon, George; History of Deerfield, original edition, 2 vols...........**50.00**
Kellogg & Thompson, History of Greenfield, 4 vols...................**65.00**
Many Others Wanted

Wanted: collections and accumulations of family and business letters, manuscripts, documents, diaries, ledgers, photographs, newspapers, ephemera, and trade catalogues. We are seeking material from all states and countries of any period. All quotes will be acknowledged. Prices paid will depend upon quantity, quality, and condition. Please send a full description and (if possible) a Xerox copy. Immediate payment made upon acceptance of offer. We do not deal in sports or entertainment material. This is a full-time business. Our shop is open by appointment. Your wants are cheerfully solicited. Your catalogues are always appreciated; we buy and sell. We are a member of the Manuscript Society and were established in 1978. Authenticity is guaranteed on all material.

Mr. Carmen D. Valentino
Rare Books & Manuscripts
2956 Richmond St.
Philadelphia, PA 19134
(215) 739-6056

Antique books are always in demand in my shop. Some collectors are more interested in their covers than in their contents. Georgetown, Colorado, is a Victorian village, and my shop sells many books from that era. Earlier books are always welcome, but books with publishing dates newer than 1915 are not purchased. Books of the West and mining are in great demand. Antique children's books find favor with collectors. As a result of having been an English teacher for many years, there will always be old school books and classics on the shelves. Prices paid depend on age, condition, edition, book jacket, and publisher.

Betty Schoon
The Betty Lamp
Box 1038
Georgetown, CO 80444

Books

The late 1950's and early 1960's witnessed the emergence of the fascinating hobby of barbed-wire collecting. As interest in the hobby heightened, collectors realized that a source of information regarding barbed wire was not readily available. Early books and publications on the subject arose from the collector's need to identify his wire, establish value guides for trade purposes, and to promote the hobby.

Wire-related books can be separated into three basic groups. Excellent books pertaining to patents have been published. Books designed to identify wire usually consist of sketches of the wire and pertinent information. The bulk of the publications are in this group. Lastly, several outstanding books addressing the subject of barbed-wire history and the prominent position it occupied in the 'winning of the west' have been written.

Collector associations were formed to promote the hobby. Each group published periodical newsletters containing information such as membership rosters, group activities, and articles about barbed wire. Today they serve as historical records of the associations and the hobby they loved.

I am interested in buying books, periodicals, and articles relating to barbed wire. Below is a list of titles, authors, and estimated values for items in mint or near-mint condition.

Ken Norris
P.O. Box 476
Grandfalls, TX 79742

We Pay

The Barbed Wires, Allison	6.00
Barbed Wire and Related Fencing Items, Allison	10.00
Patents, Pictures, and Pertinent Points, Allison	10.00
The Fence Tie, Allison	12.50
The American Barbed Wire Journal (periodical, per copy)	60¢
Antique Wire Illustrated, Chandler	10.00
The Barbed Wire Time (periodical, per copy)	50¢
A Guide to Prices of Antique Barbed Wire, Boyd	4.00
Barbed Wire, CWCA (periodical, per copy)	50¢
Antique Barbed Wire-Identification Index, Campbell	12.00
Barbs, Prongs, Points, Prickers, and Stickers, Clifton	35.00
Lone Rider, CWCA (periodical, per copy)	50¢
Early Barbed Wire Specimens, R.E. Productions	15.00
Unusual Fence Wires, Edwards	5.00
Barbed Wire Manual with Pricing Guide, Fountain	10.00
'Bobbed' Wire, Glover	27.50
More 'Bobbed' Wire, Glover	25.00
The 'Bobbed' Wire Bible, Glover	22.50
The 'Bobbed' Wire Bible II, Glover	22.50
The 'Bobbed' Wire Bible III, Glover	20.00
The 'Bobbed' Wire Bible IV, Glover	15.00
The 'Bobbed' Wire Bible V, Glover	12.00
Barbed Wire Identification, Grant	7.50
Happiness Is Being a Barbed-Wire Collector, Grauberger	8.00
Barbed Wire, Harris and Hill	5.00
Simplified Handbook for Wire Collectors, Hauff	7.00
Planter Wire, Hauff	5.00
The International Barbed Wire Gazette, Glover (periodical, per copy)	75¢
Early United States Barbed-Wire Patents, James	37.50
Old West Barbed Wire and Patent Dates, Jenkins	10.00
Little Joe's Antique Barbed-Wire Manual, Little	9.00
The Wire That Fenced the West, McCallum	10.00
Panhandle-Plains Historical Review, McClure	20.00
Fences, Gates, and Bridges, Martin	8.00
The Fencing Tool Bible, Marquis	8.00
The National Barbed Wire Trader, Allison (periodical, per copy)	50¢
Wire Bard, NRMBWCA (periodical, per copy)	25¢
Northern Wire, NRMBWCA (periodical, per copy)	25¢
'Bob' Wire, Prickette	5.00
Texas Barbed Wire, TBWA (periodical, per copy)	25¢
The Complete Encyclopedia of Barbed Wire, Thurgood	3.00
You As a Barbed-Wire Collector, Trocin	6.00
Barbed Wire Handbook, Turner	8.50
Barbed Wire Handbook and Pricing Guide, Turner	8.50
'Ole Timey Stuff', Turner	8.50
Relic Collectors Book for Treasure Hunters and Collectors, Turner	8.50

Books

Barbs and Snags, WBWCA (periodical, per copy)......................25¢
Antique Barbed-Wire Collecting, Wolf..............................3.50
Barbed-Wire Collectors Handbook, Kreigh...........................5.00
Barbed-Wire Buyers Guide, Koltra..................................5.00

The fairy tales and folklore which we first read as children have remained etched in our memories. Through the mid-eighteenth century, nearly all books produced for children were either grammar, history, morality, or mathematics. However, in the latter part of the century, books were written primarily for the amusement of children. Illustrated books were a luxury that most adult readers could not afford. Because rapid improvements in the photoengraving process in the late 1890's, children's picture books became available to everyone. The sale of children's books illustrated by such noted artists as Kate Greenaway, L. Frank Baum, and Beatrix Potter flourished in the early 1900's.

Please write me with the following information on the children's books which you have to sell: the date of publication, publisher, author, and condition of book. Very good shows some small signs of wear; good describes the average used book that has all pages present; fair is a worn book that has all pages with worn binding. Higher prices will be paid for books in fine condition.

Ruppert Books
5909 Darnell
Houston, TX 77074

We Pay

Baum, L. Frank; Oz title, pre-1940.................................14.00
Burroughs, Edgar Rice; Tarzan titles..............................3.00
Dick & Jane Readers...3.00
Disney, Walt; pre-1940's
    Mickey Mouse...4.00
    Donald Duck..4.00
    Minnie Mouse...4.00
    Pinocchio 4.00
    Snow White...4.00
    Dumbo..4.00
    Uncle Remus..4.00
    Bambi..4.00
    Fantasia...4.00
    Three Little Pigs..4.00
Dixon, Franklin; Hardy Boys w/dust jackets........................2.00

We Pay

Keene, Carolyn; Nancy Drew w/dust jackets..........................6.00
Mother Goose, pre-1930 editions......................................6.00
Newbery & Caldecott Award Winners..............................3.00
Parrish, Maxfield; any illustrated including:
    Bolanyo, by Opie Read..15.00
    Golden Treasury of Song & Lyric..............................15.00
    Poems of Childhood, by Eugene Field..........................15.00
    The Golden Age, by Kenneth Grahame.........................15.00
    Dream Days, by Kenneth Grahame.............................15.00
    Wonder Book & Tangleood Tales, by Nathaniel Hawthorne.........15.00
    Italian Villas, by Edith Wharton...............................15.00
    Knave of Hearts, by Louise Saunders...........................15.00
Scribners Illustrated Classics.......................................10.00
Seuss, Dr. (No Weekly Reader editions)..............................2.00
Wiggin, Kate Douglas; A Bird's Christmas Carol.....................4.00
Wiggin, Kate Douglas; Mother Carey's Chickens.....................4.00
Books illustrated by:
    N.C. Wyeth..8.00
    Jesse Wilcox Smith...8.00
    Harrison Fisher (American Girls)..............................8.00
    Beatrix Potter..8.00
    Bessie Pease Gutmann.......................................8.00
    Tasha Tudor...8.00
    Kate Greenaway..8.00
    Randolph Caldecott...8.00
    Edmund Dulac..8.00
    Walter Crane..8.00
    Howard Pyle...8.00
    Arthur Rackham..8.00
    W.W. Denslow...8.00
    Maud Petersham...8.00
    Lois Lenski...8.00
    Wm. Pene DuBois..8.00
    Maurice Sendak..8.00

Patten Beard apparently wrote or compiled several books of humorous children's stories in the late 1800's and early 1900's to about 1928. Some of the titles include *What-Happened-After Stories*, *Twilight Tales*, and others. I first learned of his stories and books in *Book Trails*, a multi-volume set that carried one of his stories (The Little White Bed That Ran Away) in Volume I. I will pay $6.50 per book including postage. Books must be in good condition––no mold and no missing pages. Please write first, we want only one copy of each of his titles. No crafts books please––he wrote some of these, too. Many thanks!

Mrs. Vicki Jones
19225 Center Ave.
Homewood, IL 60430

I am collecting 'Oz' books by L. Frank Baum, Ruth Plumly Thompson, John Neill, Jack Snow, Rachel Cosgrove, Eloise McGraw, Lauren Wagner, and W.W. Denslow. Especially wanted are *Who's Who in Oz*, by Jack Snow; *Snuggle Tales*, by Laura Bancroft; *Boy Fortune Hunter Series*, by Floyd Akers; *Sam Steele Adventure Series*, by Hugh Fitzgerald; and other books by Schuyler Stanton and Edith Van Dyne. I am also interested in all children's books illustrated by John Neill and W.W. Denslow. Please send description, condition, publisher, and price when writing.

Edwin Wilder
P.O. Box 175
Northland, WA 98358

I want to buy pre-'50s fashion pattern books such as Simplicity, Vogue, etc. I pay $15.00 to $30.00 for Simplicity fashion pattern books, $20.00 to $35.00 for Vogue fashion pattern books, and $15.00 to $30.00 for other fashion pattern books. I also want to buy the pre-'50s patterns shown in these books. Please note that I only need the pattern envelope; the pattern is not necessary. For pattern envelopes with color photos, I pay 25¢ to 50¢ each. For pattern envelopes with black and white photos, I pay 15¢ to 25¢ each.

Beatrix Brockerman
730 W. Gaines St.
Tallahassee, FL 32324

I want to buy German language books. This includes Bibles, children's books, and other books in German. Describe and price, or mail and I will return pre-paid if rejected.

R.L. Rice
612 E. Front St.
Bloomington, IL 61701

The Kurdish Program, Cultural Survival, Inc., is a private non-profit organization which operates a Kurdish Library seeking books and memorabilia relating to the culture, archaeology, geography, and history of the Kurdish people of the Middle or Near East. Publications related to the following would be of interest: Ottoman Empire, Babylonia, Median Empire, Turkey, Iraq, Iran, Syria, as is material on Saladin and the Crusades. We also collect books on the geo-political or regional interests of European countries, the United States, and the Soviet Union as they relate to the Middle East. The geographical area of our interest falls into such places as Southeastern Turkey (Anatolia), Northern Iraq, Northern Syria, and Western Iran. Please send description and price list, or we will be happy to make you an offer.

The Kurdish Program
Cultural Survival, Inc.
1133 Ave. of the Americas
New York, NY 10036
(212) 764-1133

I have a wide variety of interest in paperback books. I am looking for any and all books dealing with TV-related shows from the 1950's and 1970's. Examples would be shows like 'The Untouchables,' 'Maverick,' 'Bonanza,' 'The Saint,' 'The Man from U.N.C.L.E.,' 'The Avengers,' 'Batman,' 'The Monkees,' 'The Invaders,' 'Dark Shadows,' and many, many others too numerous to mention. Books must be in at least very good condition with no major defects such as water damage, broken spines, heavy creases, or stains. I will pay up to $1.00 each if in fine condition. Please write with description of items.

Rick Nosker
8519 E. Sheridan
Scottsdale, AZ 85257

Books

I'm looking for books and magazines on tropical fish. I will buy any quantity of older issues (pre-1960's) and any quantity of current (the last 20 years) titles. I also purchase old Aquarium Society publications and broadsides dealing with P.T. Barnum's American Museum. As for books, I am looking for pre-1950's titles only except for books by the authors Sterba or Hoedeman. Please send information on what you have and your asking price.

Gary Bagnall
c/o Zoo Med Laboratories
1406 S. Ritchey St. Unit D
Santa Ana, CA 92705
(714) 835-7418
(714) 642-7064

As a collector of sports memorabilia, I am interested in any 19th-century non-fiction books about baseball, football, or boxing. Listed are some of the books wanted. This being an incomplete listing, please contact me if you have any other books in this category. I am paying $50.00 and up for 19th-century non-fiction baseball books, and $20.00 and up for 19th-century non-fiction boxing books. Let me hear from you!

John Buonaguidi
2830 Rockridge Dr.
Pleasant Hill, CA 94523

Books Wanted:

Baseball Players Book of Reference, by Henry Chadwick, 1866-1872
The Game of Baseball, by Henry Chadwick, Munro, 1868
Chadwick's Baseball Manual, Henry Chadwick, Holland, 1888-89
Book of American Pastimes, Charles Peverelly, 1866
Baseball, 1845-1871, Seymour Church, 1902
Baseball, John Ward, Athletic Publishing Co., 1888-89
The National Game, Alfred Spink, National Game Publishing Co., 1910
Poe's Football, Street & Smith, 1891
American Football, Walter Camp, Harper, 1892-96

BOTTLES

Bottles have long been collected for their beauty and legend. They come in a wide variety of shapes, sizes, and colors. Bottles date back as far as the first century B.C. to the late 1800's. Many bottles were embossed with raised lettering of company names, advertising slogans, ingredients, etc. One way to date old bottles that were hand blown in a mold is to look for the mold seams running up each side of the bottle. On bottles dating before 1905, mold seams ended one-half inch below the top of the bottle. By 1906 the Owens automatic bottle-making machine was perfected, and all seams ran to the top of bottles. We are buying all bottles that are free of cracks, chips, or any heavy discolorations. Below is a partial listing of prices we are paying for various bottles:

Loring T. Sollender
528 E. Cloud Ridge St.
Sierra Vista, AZ 85635

Bitters   We Pay

Acorn Bitters, amber, 9"...15.00
Aimar's Fly Trap Bitters, aqua, 7"..................................35.00
American Life Bitters, cabin shape, light amber.....................45.00
Dr. Ball's Vegetable Stomach Bitters, pontil, aqua, 7"..............15.00
Bender's Bitters, aqua, 10"...15.00

Bottles

Big Bill Best Bitters, cabin shape, amber, 10"........................20.00
Boston Malt Bitters..10.00
Clark's Vegetable Bitters, pontil, aqua, 8"...........................35.00
Favorite Bitters, barrel shape, amber, 9"............................15.00
Globe Bitters, amber, 9" or 10"....................................25.00
Hall's Bitters, 1852 on back, amber, 9"............................25.00
Plow's Sherry Bitters, large leaf on back, amber, 8".................75.00
St. Gotthards Bitters, amber, 8"...................................20.00
Suffolk Bitters, pig shape, amber, 9x3"...........................100.00
Universal Bitters, pontil, aqua....................................25.00
Zingari Bitters, lady's leg type, amber, 11".......................40.00

Medicine   We Pay

Abbott Bros., Chicago; rheumatic remedy, amber, 6"..................3.00
Dr. H. Anders & Co., pontil, pictures sun, aqua.....................9.00
Brant's Indian Pulmonary, aqua, 7"................................10.00
E.A. Burkhouts Dutch Liniment, N.Y.; pontil, aqua, 5"...............20.00
Dalby's Carminative, pontil, aqua, 3"..............................5.00
G.W. House Indian Tonic, ring top, aqua, 5".......................15.00
Kidney Bottle Pills, kidney shape, clear, 5".......................5.00
Geo. L. Laird & Co., cathedral type, blue, 7"......................9.00
McCombies Restorative, pontil.....................................7.00
Pine Tree Tar Cordial, blob top, patent 1859, green..................9.00
Roshton & Aspinwall, N.Y.; pontil, Compound Chlorine Tooth Wash on
    back, golden olive...35.00
Saver, 3-sided, amber, 3½"...5.00
Smith Green Mt. Renovator, Stoddard glass, olive amber..............30.00
Swaim's Panacea, Philadelphia; pontil, olive, 8"....................9.00
Tippecanoe, amber, clear, or aqua, 9", ea...........................8.00
Dr. Townsend Sarsaparilla, pontil, amber, 9".......................10.00
Turner Bros., N.Y.; graphite pontil, amber.........................10.00
U.S.A. Hospital Dept., oval, cornflower blue, 2"....................7.00
J.B. Wheatley's Syrup, graphite pontil, aqua, 6"....................8.00
Dr. Wynkcop's Catharismic Honduras, N.Y.; 10".......................7.00

Poisons   We Pay

Carbolic Acid (on each side), crosses, cobalt, 5"...................4.00
Hobnail Poison, clear, 6"..10.00
J.T.M. & Co. (under bottom), 3-cornered, amber, 3".................8.00
Lin Bellad, label, cobalt, 7".....................................7.00
Not To Be Taken, 12 on bottom, cobalt, 8".........................7.00
Poison Flask (very rough), sheared top, aqua, ½-pint...............15.00

We Pay

Syr:Fer:Iodid, cobalt, 7″ **8.00**
Tinct., opil-poison on base, cobalt, 7″ **5.00**

Sodas

We Pay

Barclay St. (in center), applied lip, green, 7″ **3.00**
Bessemer Coca Cola, aqua, 6½″ **10.00**
Christian Schlepegrell & Co., ground pontil, 8-panel, blue, 8″ **7.00**
W.M. Eagle, NY; graphite pontil, blob top, cobalt, 7″ **12.00**
Guyette & Co., MI; G under bottom, cobalt, 7″ **7.00**
Heatly Bros. Mangnum, aqua, 7″ **7.00**
Hulshizer & Co. Premium, graphite pontil, green, 8½″ **8.00**
T.&R. Morton, Newark, NJ; graphite pontil, squat type, green, 7″ **6.00**
Olsen & Co., Memphis, TN; blob top, cobalt, 7½″ **9.00**
John Ryan, 1859, GA, cobalt, 7½″ **8.00**
E. Sheehan, 1880, GA, R.J.B. on back, cobalt, 7½″ **10.00**
Tear Drop Shape, crude top, dark olive, 8″ **7.00**

Ale & Gin

We Pay

A.I., anchor in seal, honey amber, 9″ **7.00**
B.C.W., pontil, dark olive, 9″ **7.00**
Flora Temple Harness Trot, horse on front, amber, 8½″ **12.00**
L.&T. Gin, anchor on front, olive, 9″ **8.00**
Woodman's, pontil, 3-part mold, black **20.00**

Spirits

We Pay

Andresen & Son, MN; amber, 5x5x3″ **30.00**
Belfast Malt Whiskey, aqua, 11″ **9.00**
Henry Chapman & Co., pumpkin-seed type, amber, 5½″ **8.00**
Neal's, cobalt, 9″ **7.00**
Roth & Co., San Francisco, amber, quart **10.00**

Food

We Pay

Cannon Bottle, amber or olive, 9½″ **5.00**
E.H.V.B., 6-panels, graphite pontil, light blue, 9″ **8.00**
Horton-Cato & Co., Detroit; celery salt, gold, 8″ **5.00**
My Wife's Salad Dressing, blue-green, 8″ **3.00**
Pepper Sauce, fifteen rings, cathedral type, aqua, 1875, 8″ **4.00**
Olive Oil, pontil, free blown, aqua, 13½″ **4.00**

Bottles

Pickle Label, sheared top, aqua.......................................5.00
Planter's, peanut figures, glass top, peanut knob, clear................10.00
Tobasco (or dry food), pontil, wide mouth, dark green, 2½" opening......5.00
M.T. Wallace & Co., Brooklyn, NY, Purifying Extract 1850; pontil, aqua,
9½"..7.00

Inks
We Pay

Alonzo French, patent 1870, aqua, 2".................................9.00
Brickett J. Taylor Ink, flared lip, cylindrical, 4½"....................12.00
Carter's House Ink Turtle, double, 2 windows & Carter on roof........12.00
Coventry Geometric Ink, open pontil, amber, 1½"....................8.00
Farley's Ink, pontil, 8-sided, aqua, 2x2"............................8.00
Octagon Ink, pontil, mushroom shape, aqua.........................5.00
Pitkin Inkwell, 36-rib mold, flared lip, lime green...................25.00
Tea Kettle Ink Label, 8-panel, sheared top, cobalt, 2x4"...............18.00
Waters Ink Troy, NY (on panels); pontil, ring shoulder & top, aqua,
2½x2"...12.00

We are especially interested in American-made bottles from before 1900 which feature embossed product names or full labels. Americans bottled countless products during the 1800's. We are interested in any type of bottle, from food to medicine to alcoholic beverages. These might be clear, amber, aqua, blue, green or milk glass. No machine-made bottles, please. The prices below are starting prices for the pieces we need; your bottle could easily be worth more to us. Please contact us for prices paid for specific items.

Steve Ketcham
Box 24114
Edina, MN 55424
(612) 920-4205

We Pay		We Pay	
Historical Flasks	50.00 +	Whiskeys	10.00 +
Bitters	25.00 +	Bar Decanters	25.00 +
Barber Bottles	50.00 +	Sodas	10.00 +
Patent Medicines	10.00 +	Fruit Jars	25.00 +
Inks	10.00 +	Poisons	10.00 +
Figurals	25.00 +	Miniatures	15.00 +
Beers	5.00 +		

Miniature beer and soda bottles were produced from about 1900 until around 1963. The earliest were made by breweries and usually contained beer, but primarily it was novelty companies who made and distributed them. Some were also distributed by breweries and liquor stores. Two of the largest manufactuers were Edward A. Muth & Son, Inc., and Bill's Novelty & Premium Manufacturing Co.

Below is a list of prices I will pay for bottles that are in very good condition, showing the full label design. I will buy bottles not listed here as well, and you can contact me for prices. If you have doubt of its identity, feel free to send a description or picture, and I will make an offer.

John Carver
4668 Evelyn St.
Milton, FL 32570
(904) 994-9419

We Pay | | **We Pay**

White Cup	10.00	Primo Beer	15.00
Gold Bond Beer	10.00	Ambrosia Beer	15.00
Milan Springs	8.00	Nectar Beer	15.00
Tiptop Beer	12.00	Fredericks 4 Crown	12.00
Crystal Rock	15.00	Manhattan Beer	15.00
Iron City	15.00	Topper Beer	18.00
Old Dutch	12.00	Citizens' Beer	20.00
Harry Mitchell	10.00	Fehr's Beer	10.00
Pennsy Beer	12.00	Old Craft Beer	20.00
Magnolia Beer	10.00	Manru Lager	25.00
WV Special Export Beer	10.00	Doershuck Beer	20.00
Golden Drops	10.00	Good Host Beer	15.00
All Pre-Prohibition	25.00	Red Ribbon	8.00
Walter Beer	10.00	Jung Old Country	15.00
Tivoli Beer	8.00	Apache Beer	20.00
Stoeckle Beer	20.00	Old Glory	15.00
Spearman Beer	20.00	Senate Beer	15.00
Black River Ale	12.00	Wagner Beer	20.00
Congress, short	8.00	Atlantic Beer	15.00
Congress, tall	18.00	All Soda Bottles	10.00

We are wanting to buy beer or pop bottles in cobalt blue or milk glass. We pay from $10.00 to $50.00, depending on the bottle. We prefer Michigan bottles but will buy any.

Mr. & Mrs. Robert McLachlan
5191 S. Moore Rd.
Cass City, MI 48726

Bottles

I want to buy Erie, Pennsylvania, bottles. Embossed bottles of all kinds which say 'Erie' on them are of the most interest to me, especially medicines, beers, sodas, and mineral waters. I will also buy other Pennsylvania bottles.

Jim Finn
P.O. Box 7306
Erie, PA 16510

We Pay

Mizpah Cure for Weak Lungs	**60.00**
Bentle & Andrews Drugs	**10.00**
H.V. Claus, beer	**10.00**
Carter's Extract of Smart Weed	**3.00**
John J. Graney, beer	**10.00**
P. Minnig & Co., medicine	**10.00**
Ackerman	**25.00**
Wayne Brewery, green	**40.00**
J. Kretz, beer	**10.00**
Doc. P. Hall's, iron pontil	**30.00**
Steven's & Co., blue	**75.00**
F. Nick's Pharmacy	**4.00**
Lancaster, Erie Co., NY; flask	**80.00**
Cunningham & Co., Pittsburgh, fruit jar, iron pontil	**100.00**
A. Stone & Co., Philadelphia, fruit jar, iron pontil	**100.00**
For Pike's Peak, Pittsburgh, PA; flask	**100.00**
Jas. Shaughnessy, Erie, PA	**20.00**
J.H. Welsh, Erie, PA	**20.00**

Wanted to buy: Daisy and Button castor bottles to fit Victorian silverplate frames. We will pay up to $40.00 a bottle depending on the color. Also wanted are Bell Flower castor bottles for the same type frame. Price is negotiable.

S. Cohen
7457 LeClaire
Skokie, IL 60077
(312) 677-5650

Wanted: Hutchinson sodas and whiskeys from western mining towns—especially Black Hawk, Breckenridge, Buena Vista, Central City, Cripple Creek, Georgetown, Idaho Springs, Leadville, Ouray, Silverton, Telluride, and Victor, Colorado.

Wanted from all states! Embossed round milk quarts, druggists, Hutchinsons, amber whiskeys, and bitters.

Ed Krol
Star Rt. #2, Box 15A
Derning, NM 88030

Bottles shaped like violins were made from 1930 through 1950. These bottles often came with snap-on metal brackets for hanging on a wall as a flower vase. They came in assorted colors.

We are looking for the 6″ bottle with 1¼″ width, the 8″ bottle with 1½″ base, and the 10″ bottle with 1¾″ base. We no not want the 11″ brown one with 2¾″ base or the 9″ blue one with 2½″ base, as these were recent and designed as wine bottles.

Lawrence Hartnell
Box 352
Collingwood, Ontario
Canada L9Y 3Z7

BOY SCOUT MEMORABILIA

In 1910 the Boy Scouts of America was organized. With such notable people as James E. West, Earnest T. Seton, Daniel C. Beard, and Collen Livenston, this program got under way. Its true founder, Lord Baden-Powell, was the moving force to get the organization started. His leadership and guidance made scouting a success in the U.S. Scouting collectibles include books, patches, pins, novelty items (banks, games, etc.), uniforms, magazines, equipment, flags, National and World Jamboree items, statues, belts, etc. Over the past seventy-three years, millions of boys and men have gone through the scouting program. Although collectibles are vast and varied, few are really worth much money due to the fact that the National Council of BSA issued millions of most items to fill the required needs of the boys. Listed below are items that we are seeking and prices we will currently pay—help!

R.J. Sayers
P.O. Box 246
Andrews, TX 79714
(915) 523-2902

We Pay

1910 BSA Handbook	50.00
1912 Parker Games	15.00
1920 Scout Iron Bank	25.00
1924 World Jamboree Patch	800.00
1929 World Jamboree Patch	75.00
1933 World Jamboree Patch	110.00
1937 World Jamboree Patch	200.00
1947 World Jamboree Patch	75.00
1920 BSA Eagle Medal (BSA)	35.00
1930 BSA Eagle Medal	25.00
1935 US Scout Jamboree Patch	30.00
1937 US Scout Jamboree Patch	25.00
1911 BS Handbook (proof copy)	75.00
1911 BSA Handbook	45.00
1910 BSA Handbook (special presentation copy), in case	1,000.00
1920-30 Scout Contest Medals	15.00
1910-20 Lifesaving Medal	200.00
1910-20 Medal of Merit	150.00
1950 Scout-Explorer Silver Medal	100.00
1950-60 Explorer Ranger Medal	100.00
1920 Eagle Scout Patch	10.00
1913-30 Boys Life Magazine	5.00
1950 Scout Eagle Ring	20.00
1950 Scout Eagle Pin	15.00
1930-50 OA Patches	2.00-25.00
1916-19 WWI Posters	40.00
1916-19 Liberty Medals	20.00
1912-30 Pins (leaders or boys)	10.00
1925-50 Rockwell Calendars	7.00

We Pay

1920 Remington Knives	30.00
1930 Ulster Knives	12.00
1930-60 Sheath Knives	7.00-20.00
1930 Cub Scout Uniforms	15.00
1910-20 Scout Uniforms	35.00
1910-30 Leader Uniforms	45.00
1910-30 Achievement Medals	30.00
1910-30 Leader Collar Pin (brass)	12.00
1910 Baden-Powell Plates	25.00
1920 Dresden Scout Plates	15.00
1920-40 Scout Lead Figure	7.50
1910-30 Merit Badge Sash	30.00

Below is a partial listing of scout items I am looking for. I am interested in buying one piece or large collections of scout and scout-related items. The variety of items issued by or about the scouts is too large to list in entirety. I have an interest in nearly everything. When writing, please describe your item, its condition, and what you want for it. I am willing to go through your collections and estimate what I would be willing to pay for them. I am home most evenings if you want to call.

Doug Bearce
P.O. Box 4742
Salem, OR 97302
(503) 399-9872

We Pay

Books: Boy Scout Handbook 1910-1940, merit badge books pre-1945, Handbook for Scoutmasters pre-1945, Patrol Leaders Handbook pre-1945, official publications (senior scout, sea scout, Order of the Arrow, professional scout), pre-1940 cubbing publications, annual reports to Congress, etc. ... 2.00-150.00

Books (fiction): Every Boy's Library, unusual titles, w/dust jackets ... 1.00+

Boy's Life: pre-1950 ... 50¢-12.50

World Scouting Magazine: all issues ... 50¢-2.00

Baden-Powell: books by or about, china, prints, letters, etc. ... 3.00+

Lone Scout: degree books, pins, etc. ... 5.00+

Post Cards: most older cards ... 25¢+

Jamboree: patches, neckerchiefs, coins, pins, posters, decals, pillows, & other items issued at National & World Jamborees ... 50¢-125.00

Philmont Scout Ranch: patches, post cards, other items issued by or about the ranch & its operation ... 50¢-100.00

Uniforms: adult pre-1940, cub pre-1945, air scout all parts & patches, scout pre-1940 (if it has patches & most parts), explorer pre-1957 (if it has patches) ... 2.50-200.00

We Pay

Patches: merit badges on square cloth, merit badges pre-1950, badges of
    office or rank, patches pertaining to national events, patches of local
    councils (only if very old), or patches for council uniform . . . . . . **50¢-20.00**
Order of the Arrow: all patches, handbooks pre-1960, any written
    material about the order, felt sashes **4.00-100.00**
World's Fair: anything having to do w/scout activities at the fairs . . . **2.50-50.00**
Dan Beard: books, letters, pictures, & anything pertaining to Dan Beard
    & outdoor work w/boys **1.00-50.00**
Pins: all pins pre-1960 (many current pins are dated 1911) **2.00-25.00**
Medals: all medals are of interest if they are scout-related **2.00-150.00**
Posters: all posters w/scouting as the subject **2.00-100.00**
China: plates, items w/Rockwell scout designs, scout personality
    items, etc. (no interest in scout coffee mugs) **5.00-50.00**
Seton: letters, books, artwork, Woodcraft Rangers items, & anything
    by or about Seton **2.50-150.00**
Coins: anything w/Boy Scouts as the subject . . . . **25¢-10.00**
All of the following are in my area of interest: pictures (Jamboree or
    older pictures that carry information about the activity photo-
    graphed or names of people), scout toys, scout banks, scout sheet
    music, stamps (covers only), recordings of scout programs, movies
    w/scouts as subjects, etc. . . . . **25¢-150.00**

BREWERIANA

At one time, thousands of breweries existed in the United States. There were over five hundred breweries in the five boroughs of New York City alone! American breweries were mostly owned and operated by German immigrants. The beer industry thrived until 1919 when prohibition started. Millions lost their jobs and the era known for its great advertising art came to an end. Prohibition forced most breweries out, others either merged or were bought out by the larger, stronger breweries that were able to cling to survival by the manufacture of near-beer (non-alcoholic). Then came 1933 and prohibition was repealed. Out once again rolled barrels of legal 'Real Beer.' But the damage was done; most breweries were never to open again, and no more of their great, signed trays, steins, and other giveaways were to be made.

We are looking to purchase all pre-prohibition and repeal-movement campaign items. Items must be in good condition. We will consider unususual brewery items from the 1930's and 1940's. We are also interested in other miscellaneous, old American beer-advertising items such as: match safes, corkscrews, unusual bottle openers, paperweights, smoking pipes, etched glassware, etc. Please describe items and send a photo whenever possible.

Bob Miller
386 Pennsylvania Ave.
Mineola, NY 11501

We Pay

Serving Trays	**15.00-450.00**	Post Cards	**50¢+**
Tip Trays	**15.00-300.00**	Photographs	**5.00-25.00**
Foam Scrapers	**2.00-15.00**	Pin-Back Buttons	**1.00+**
Tin Signs	**15.00-500.00**	Shaving Mugs	**100.00+**
Reverse Glass Signs	**20.00-700.00+**	Salesmen Pins	**2.00-20.00**
Paper Coasters	**50¢+**	Driver Pins	**2.00-20.00**
Mugs	**15.00+**	Pre-'59 Beer Cans	**5.00+**
Steins	**40.00+**		

We are interested in buying all types of pre-prohibition brewery memorabilia. These items were generally given away by breweries to advertise their products during the latter half of the 1800's and the early 1900's. The prices below are only starting prices; your item could easily be worth much more to us. Please contact us for the price we would pay for your specific item.

Steve Ketcham
Box 24114
Edina, MN 55424
(612) 920-4205

	We Pay		We Pay
Bottles	5.00 +	Steins w/Brand Name	35.00 +
Calendars	20.00 +	Openers	10.00 +
Corkscrews	10.00 +	Photos	10.00 +
Etched Glasses	35.00 +	Pin-Backs	10.00 +
Enameled Glasses	75.00 +	Playing Cards	20.00 +
Foam Scrapers	10.00 +	Post Cards	10.00 +
Industrial Publications	10.00 +	Signs	75.00 +
Knives	35.00 +	Trays	75.00 +
Match Safes	10.00 +	Tip Trays	25.00 +
Mirrors, large	35.00 +	Tokens	10.00 +
Pocket Mirrors	35.00 +	Watch Fobs	25.00 +
Mugs w/Brand Name	35.00 +		

BREYER HORSES

My love for horses is exemplified by the marvelous Breyer plastic horses. I will purchase whole collections or one piece. Please describe and price. All letters will be answered.

Edythe Shepard
German Shepherd Memorabilia
1334 E. Suncrest Dr.
Tuscon, AZ 85706

BRIDE'S BASKETS

I would like to buy bride's dishes to go in frames that I already have. I would also like to buy frames. I need all sizes of both. I pay from $25.00 to $125.00.

Jean Ryan
P.O. Box 1381
Springfield, IL 62705
(217) 787-0598

BUCKLES

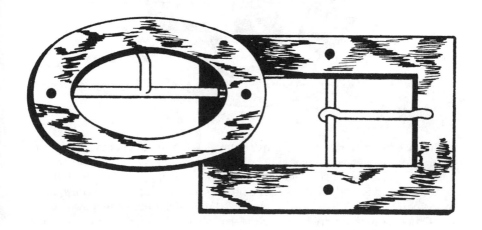

Mother-of-pearl is the inner shell layer of shelled mollusks from salt water or fresh water. It has a natural pearly sheen and can be polished as well. It has been used for centuries for decorative clasps and ornaments including buckles, buttons, brooches, etc.

We buy dress buckles of mother-of-pearl, preferring the fancy, ornamented, highly-carved ones, or those of unusual shape and size––very small as well as very large. Brass posts and tongues will add to the price. More common ones will range from $2.00 to $4.00 each.

Pictures of buckles can be made by using a copying machine at your local library or post office. Descriptions and sketches or photos should be addressed to:

D.M. Diabo
19953 Great Oaks Circle S.
Mt. Clemens, MI 48043

BUTTONS

Buttons, an art form in miniature, date back to the 13th century. It is an interesting and monetarily-reasonable hobby. Early buttons were primarily for ornamentation and clothing fasteners. Most buttons surviving are from the 18th, 19th, and 20th centuries; and the most desirable ones are the elegant types designed for the aristocratic class. There are innumerable kinds of buttons sought by collectors, more than over four hundred categories—by subject, topic, size, and material, etc. Buttons were made all over the world, but the most desired and collected today are French, English, and American made.

The most popular varieties are porcelain, metal, gilt, and Satsumas with pictures, fables, buildings, and heads of famous people. Modern buttons produced after 1900 were made of plastic, leather, wood, glass, or metal. Another interesting type is the china buttons made around 1850. They were printed with calico-like designs transferred from paper.

We buy some specialized buttons in good condition. Add twenty-five cents if buttons are on an original card. The price list below is reflective of prices now being paid by me according to kind, material, and condition.

Georgia Fox
Foxes' Den Antiques
P.O. Box 846
Sutter Creek, CA 95685

We Pay

Animal	25¢-10.00
Bimini Glass	25¢-1.50
Celluloid	10¢-2.00
China, Calico & Stencil	10¢-25¢
Copper	50¢-1.00
Cut & Pressed Glass	10¢-25¢
Drums Type	10¢-25¢
Enamel/Porcelain Figure	2.00-20.00
Fables	50¢-6.00
Fabric/Embroidered	10¢-25¢
FOX Buttons, any	10¢-5.00
Gay Nineties (Jewel)	50¢-2.00
Gilt Brass	50¢-3.00
Indian Silver	50¢-3.00
Inlaid, small	10¢-1.50
Japanese Brass Painted & Tole	25¢-10.00
Jasperware/Steel	1.00-15.00
Jewel/Gemstone	50¢-15.00
Lithograph-People	50¢-3.00
Modern Glass	15¢-50¢
Mother-of-Pearl or Cameo, 18th Century	3.00-20.00
Nut, Palm, Tagua	5¢-50¢
Paperweights	50¢-5.00
Pearl	5¢-50¢
Pearl & Shell, 1900-1910	50¢-6.00
Railroad	10¢-50¢
Realistics	5¢-2.00
Satsumas	1.00-10.00
Silver	1.00-5.00
Steamship	5¢-25¢
Religious	50¢-6.00
Steel, 18th-19th Century	10¢-6.00
Steel Cups	25¢-5.00
Tombac, 1760-1800's	25¢-5.00
Vegetable Ivory	5¢-50¢
Waistcoat	25¢-4.00
Wood & Bone, 18th Century	25¢-3.00
Wood/Metal Trim	10¢-3.00
Work Clothes	10¢-35¢
Uniform	10¢-50¢
Pewter	10¢-5.00
Victorian Glass	10¢-50¢

I want to buy antique buttons—no 'pearlies' or common ones. I am looking for enamels, old metal picture buttons, porcelain, unusual materials, 'pretty' ladies, children, animals, and flowers. I will buy the above by the piece, a full collection, or stock from a retiring dealer.

Betty J. Rundell
Rt. 1, Box 444
Leander, TX 78641
(512) 267-2286

I am a serious collector and author seeking to purchase fine antique American military buttons for my private collection. I am very interested in acquiring fine to mint, non-excavated specimens dating from 1812 to 1865. Although I collect all pre-1865 U.S. Military buttons, I am especially interested in obtaining Confederate States buttons, pre-1865 southern state seals, and pre-1865 southern military school buttons. I am also very eager to purchase any pre-1865 U.S. Military buttons including artillery, cavalry, dragoons, engineers, ordnance, infantry, naval, marines, riflemen, topographical engineers, voltiguers, corps of artificers, regimentals, and state militias. I am also seeking any 1812-1865 military buttons with unusual, rare, or unlisted backmarks.

I pay top prices for buttons I need for my collection. I am willing to pay up to $2,000.00 per button. Prices vary greatly depending on rarity, desirability, and condition.

Daniel J. Binder
927 20th St.
Rockford, IL 61104

Peace, anti-war, anti-nuke, etc., buttons (pins) were popular during the late '50s and turbulent '60s. To date they have not surfaced as a collectible; but, to those of us brought up during those times, they do have nostalgic appeal. I will purchase peace and anti-war buttons of the '50s and '60s only for 25¢ to $2.00 each. If a really unusual one is offered, a higher payment would be considered.

W.A. Schroeder
1354 93rd Ave.
Kenosha, WI 53142

CALENDAR PLATES

Calendar plates were introduced in the early 1900's as advertising items. They were usually china, but some were tin. They had pictures such as Gibson girls, country scenes, flowers, animals, Christmas, New Year, patriotic, or advertising themes in the center along with the name and address of the merchant who was giving the plate away to customers. The calendar of the specific year was usually around the border of the plate.

We buy all years of calendar plates. Remember that plates in mint condition are worth more than damaged or worn specimens. Plates with more interesting themes are also worth more. Please contact us regarding calendar plates that you have for sale. Please state year, size of plate, theme, colors, etc., as well as the maker's name (usually found on the reverse) and the name and address of the merchant. Note: not all have a maker's name or a merchant's name.

Jane Cummings
37943 Wright St.
Willoughby, OH 44094
(216) 949-2174

	We Pay		**We Pay**
Pre-1906	**50.00-150.00**	1916-1917	**15.00-35.00**
1907	**25.00-50.00**	1918-1919	**15.00-40.00**
1908-1915	**15.00-40.00**	1920-1921	**15.00-35.00**

We Pay

1922-1924	20.00-50.00
1925-1927	25.00-50.00
1928-1930	25.00-60.00
1931-1940	35.00-75.00

We Pay

1941-1949	40.00-80.00
1950-1960	5.00-15.00
1960-1970	5.00-10.00

CALIFORNIA PERFUME COMPANY

In New York City, New York, in 1886, Mr. D.H. McConnell, Sr., founded the California Perfume Company (C.P.C.). These toiletries continued to be manufactured with the C.P.C. label until 1929 when 'Avon Products Inc.' was added. Both names appeared on the label until about 1939 when 'C.P.C.' was removed, and the labeling continued as 'Avon Products.' The name 'Perfection' was used on the household products issued by these companies.

I am interested in buying certain C.P.C. items from the circa 1900 period. I am particularly interested in the Natoma Rose fragrance and will pay good prices for such items. I do not want anything bearing the Avon name. When writing please send a complete description, including condition, and any note of importance. A self-addressed stamped envelope is required if you are seeking information only. Please, no collect calls.

Mr. Richard G. Pardini
3107 N. El Dorado St.
Stockton, CA 95204
(209) 446-5550 (7 am to 11 pm Pacific)

CAMERAS

Very tiny cameras have been produced since the late 1800's; the major countries of origin are the United States, Japan, Germany, and England. Often novelty items, a large number of varieties were sold and produced in Japan from the 1940's through the 1950's. Seldom functional because of the nonavailability of film, small cameras have a wide range of value depending upon variety and degree of sophistication.

I am interested in acquiring subminiature cameras, including those built into other items such as binoculars, lighters, rings, pencils, etc. I will provide a listing of over three hundred miniature cameras with estimated values from $5.00 to $500.00.

Bob Johnson
P.O. Box 71687
Marietta, GA 30007-1687

CANDY CONTAINERS

Candy Containers

Glass candy containers, once a mere gimmick to help sell candy, have rapidly become collectible. Candy containers were first used in the late 19th century and saw continued use until the mid-20th century. They often would depict a famous person, comic character, animal, event, or a common household item. Though made of glass, many of the earlier containers often had tin parts such as movable wheels, windmill blades, horns, or closures to keep the product sealed. Perfect condition is extremely important in commanding top dollar as many people will repair the rare ones and repaint them to hide any damage. Original paint also enhances their values.

We buy all types of candy containers from common to rare. Original paint and candy add greatly to prices below. Prices are for candy containers in mint condition. We especially desire to purchase collections.

Jeff Bradfield
745 Hillview Dr.
Dayton, VA 22821

We Pay

Spirit of St. Louis, original metal	**150.00**
Amos & Andy, heads painted	**225.00**
Limousine, red tin wheels	**45.00**
Baseball Player	**250.00**
Submarine, all original metal	**250.00**
Felix by Barrel	**225.00**
Flossie Fisher Furniture, yellow & black paint, depends on piece	**Please Call**
Tin Dollhouse Furniture	**Please Call**
Jack-O'-Lantern, good orange paint	**50.00**
Soldier by Tent	**Please Call**
Rabbit w/Hat	**500.00 +**
Swan Boat	**275.00**
Rabbit Family	**400.00**
Windmill, metal blades	**250.00**
Dolly's Bathtub	**Please Call**
Cannon, tin carriage	**150.00**
Santa by Chimney	**115.00**
Pocket Watch w/Fob	**100.00**
Mantel Clock w/Face	**55.00**

Shortly after the turn of the century candies (primarily hard candies) were packaged in figural glass containers which could be played with, displayed, or used as toys, knick-knacks, salt and pepper shakers, etc. These became very popular. They were produced mainly in the glass factories of Western Pennsylvania, but some were made in the east as well.

By the mid-1950's, plastic had replaced glass in their manufacture. Among the most popular plastic 'toy'-type candy containers is the PEZ dispenser—a hollow box that holds candy pellets which are dispensed by tipping back the 'head' at the top, thereby releasing a PEZ candy. You have to load them yourself! The following list is what I will generally pay for glass and plastic candy containers in good shape. Glass containers should have most of their original paint and closure; a few small chips may be acceptable. Plastic examples must be complete with little fading.

Ross Hartsough
98 Bryn Mawr Rd.
Winnipeg, Manitoba
Canada R3T 3P5

We Pay

Glass Halloween Theme Container	**200.00 +**
Glass & Tin Furniture Type	**100.00 +**
Glass & Paper Lamp Type	**100.00 +**
Glass Dirigible	**90.00 +**
Glass Airplanes, some w/tin	**25.00-150.00**
PEZ Container, full body (no 'box')	**25.00 +**
PEZ Yo-Yo, tin	**35.00 +**
PEZ Container, early 1950's	**10.00 +**
PEZ Movie Promo, w/containers, for 'Stand by Me' cardboard display	**45.00**
Plastic Candy Container, common	**2.00-10.00**

We will pay high wholesale prices for uncommon glass, tin, and papier-mache candy containers. Please let us hear from you!

Childhood Memories
P.O. Box 96
Ashford, CT 06278
(203) 429-8876

Papier-mache candy containers made for the dime-store market at the turn of the century were used by many families as holiday decorations. Santas, boots, candles, snowmen, stars, and fruits were some of the designs for Christmas. Halloween saw an array of hunch-backed black cats, jack-o'-lanterns, witches, goblins, and other weird creatures. The Fourth of July was a time for flags, Uncle Sam, the presidents, firecrackers, and other patriotic motifs. I collect these molded paper candy containers and use them as decorations for the holidays to bring back those carefree days of long ago. Actually, I am interested in any old decorations no matter what the holiday. I cannot list any prices paid because it all depends on the rarity of the piece, its condition, and how badly I want it. A good written description or Polaroid photo helps me make up my mind. Put a price range on what you have to sell and I'll make an offer. Thanks!

Bill Boyd
4922 State Line
Westwood Hills, KS 66205
(913) 831-0912 (7 pm to 10 pm)

CANTON

    Canton ware is a Chinese export porcelain that is easily recognized by its familiar blue and white 'hills and streams landscape' pattern. At the extreme outer edge is a narrow white rim with a wider blue band that is diapered. Inside this band is a border of short diagonal lines contained by a continuous, scalloped line called the rain-and-cloud pattern. The central decoration consists of a stream with a bridge (that typically has three arches) flanked on each side by a pagoda (tea house), a willow and a pine tree, rocks, one or more boats, and hills in the background with pagodas.

    Canton was a very popular Chinese export porcelain manufactured primarily for the American marketplace during the nineteenth century. There was so much shipped from the port of Canton that it took on the Canton name. In colonial days, Canton was so common and inexpensive that it was not considered an important porcelain. The quality of Canton varies widely. Some of it is very fine, but much of it is coarse, pitted, carelessly decorated, and marred by many different kinds of imperfections. The color of Canton varies from faded light blue or gray-blue to an almost navy blue. Dating Canton with high certainty is very difficult. Age and value are determined by texture and form, rather than by color or quality, and is best left to the experienced.

Mellin's Antiques
P.O. Box 134
Redding, CT 06875

CARNIVAL GLASS

We buy all good, old pieces in any color including dark marigold, green, blue, amethyst (purple), lavender, white, red, aqua opalescent, peach opalescent, etc. Pieces need not be marked but must be in excellent condition.

We pay good prices for good pieces. Although carnival glass is difficult to photograph due to its iridescence, it can be done by focusing the camera at an angle rather than straight onto the subject. Please send us your photos, descriptions, condition, etc. We will reply with prices we pay for each item. Please also remember to include the phone number where you can be reached during the day, should we have a question. Thank You!

The Antique Place
1524 S. Glenstone
Springfield, MO 65804

Carnival glass cannot yet be classified as antique, but it is surely one of our fastest-growing collectibles with about eight thousand organized collectors actively seeking it out. The shimmering, ever-changing iridescence that overlays the basic color of each piece is what makes it so fascinating. Even with over twelve hundred named patterns and thirty-plus shapes to choose from, one thing——color——is surely what carnival glass is all about. Inordinate amounts were produced in the basic glass colors of marigold, green, blue, and purple/amethyst; however, the makers also made limited amounts in colors of pastel blue and green and in many off-color shades of blues, greens, reds, aqua, lavender, smoky, and vaseline. Most of these colors were also opalized in small amounts. We are interested in acquiring these color oddities in certain shapes and patterns. We will pay up to the following amounts for certain specific colors, patterns, and shapes, or combinations thereof.

Wesley or Betty Strain
(314) 524-5608

Item Color	We Pay
White, Ice Blue, or Green	up to 1,000.00
Ice Green or Red	up to 1,500.00
Vaseline	up to 2,000.00
Opalized Colors	up to 2,500.00
Plates, Bowls, or Tumblers	up to 1,000.00
Vases	up to 2,000.00
Water Pitchers	up to 3,500.00
Punch Sets	up to 7,500.00

CASH REGISTERS

Cash registers are becoming increasingly popular as collectibles, particularly within the past five years——especially the earlier wood and brass cabinet models.

From the late 1800's until the outbreak of World War I, cash-register companies, primarily in the United States, made hundreds of different fancy machines in an effort to please business owners all over the world and to more accurately and securely manage and control 'cash flow.' The beginning and primary company, National Cash Register Company of Dayton, Ohio, continues to this date to strive to meet the changing needs of businesses throughout the world.

We buy most nice wood or ornate brass cash registers that are in good condition, that can easily be restored, and are not missing major functional and/or cosmetic parts. We also buy other machines; however, prices paid for those machines tend to be lower. The following price list is reflective of prices we have paid or are now paying for such noted 'National' cash registers—unrestored, in good working order, and with no major parts missing. We urge you to contact us for prices paid on any of the hundreds of models not listed.

Kathryn D. Danielson
1612 Queen City Ave.
Tuscaloosa, AL 35401

Unrestored   **We Pay**

National #1, brass	**800.00**
National #2, brass	**400.00**
National #3, brass	**400.00**
National #4, brass	**700.00**
National #4, wood	**1,350.00**
National #5, fleur-de-lis	**650.00**

Cash Registers

National #6, extended base.....................................**1,000.00**
National #7, brass..**550.00**
National #7, brass w/clock.....................................**650.00**
National #8, brass w/clock.....................................**550.00**
National #92, bronze..**650.00**
National #12, brass...**650.00**
National #130, brass..**700.00**
National #202, brass..**300.00**
National #211, brass..**500.00**
National #216, brass..**600.00**
National #215, fleur-de-lis.....................................**650.00**
National #226, brass..**450.00**
National #232, brass..**250.00**
National #247, brass..**350.00**
National #250, barber shop.....................................**550.00**
National #27478, scrolls & devil-head pull.......................**1,200.00**
National #310, brass..**350.00**
National #313, brass..**450.00**
National #323, brass..**450.00**
National #324, brass..**400.00**
National #347, 2-2, 2-drawer...................................**450.00**
National #35, brass...**450.00**
National #356G, brass...**200.00**
National #47¼, wood..**900.00**
National #442, brass..**350.00**
National #50, brass...**400.00**
National #542, brass..**350.00**
National #452C, brass...**1,500.00**
National #47½, inlaid wood.....................................**950.00**
National #50¼, brass..**400.00**
National #747..**100.00**
National #333, brass..**250.00**
Premier #1, ornate...**300.00**
World...**400.00**
American, oak, dtd 1887.......................................**100.00**
McCaskey, oak, pat 1906.......................................**100.00**
Michigan, wood base..**100.00**
Simplex, oak...**550.00**
Ideal...**50.00-150.00**

CAST IRON

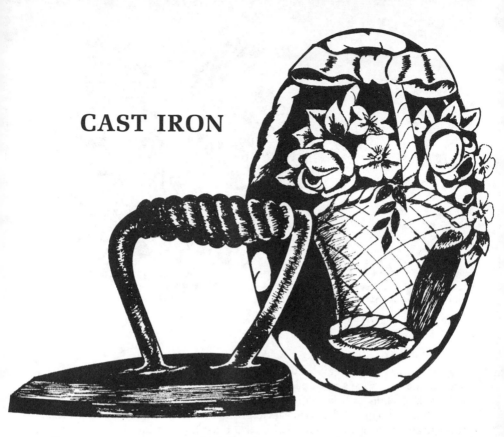

I buy various iron items in the following categories that are free from rust and defects, cracks, or other damage. In the case of painted cast iron, paint must be old and at least 70%. No reproductions or repaints are acceptable. I need pictures, full descriptions, and price desired when writing. I am interested in buying the following items.

Cast or Wrought Trivets
Match Holders
Unusual irons
Children's Irons
Still or Mechanical Banks
Children's Stoves
Advertising Skillet Ash Trays
Other Advertising Items

Cigar Cutters
Corkscrews
Cap Exploders
Figural Cap Pistols
Cap Canes
Griswold & Wagner Items
Miners' Candle Holders
Unusual Items

J.M. Ellwood
8220 E. San Miguel
Scottsdale, AZ 85253
(602) 947-6220

CAT COLLECTIBLES

If you are a cat lover you probably are or soon will be a collector of cat memorabilia. America's most popular cat is probably Chessie, the mascot of the Chesapeake & Ohio Railroad. Other famous cats include Felix and Morris. Carter's Ink and Clarke's Thread also used cats to promote their products. The most famous cat illustrator is probably Louis Wain, who illustrated children's books and post cards. Cat statues are also in abundance. I buy and sell collectible and cute cat items. Listed below are some of the prices I pay for items in good condition.

Jackie Durham
P.O. Box 2426
Rockville, MD 20852

We Pay

Chessie Calendar, 1936-1937	**30.00**
Chessie Calendar, 1942-1946	**35.00**
Chessie Calendar, 1950's	**20.00**
Chessie Color Advertisements	**1.00**
Chessie Candy Dish	**20.00**
Children's Book, illustrated by Louis Wain	**25.00**
Puzzle, illustrated by Louis Wain	**35.00**
Louis Wain Post Card	**5.00**
Trade Card	**1.00**
Carter Ink Advertisement	**1.00**
Morris Water Glass	**1.00**
Cat Statue, Staffordshire	**45.00**

We Pay

Cat Statue, Royal Doulton..**20.00**
Cast Iron Doorstop...**25.00**

I buy small or large cat collections. Special interests are quality figurines in perfect condition, Currier & Ives prints (framed), oil paintings, jewelry, needlework, books illustrated by Louis Wain (plus anything pertaining to Wain), etc. I buy post card collections but no individual cards except 'squeak' cards, for which I pay $2.00 to $5.00. Special items I'm looking for: majolica cats, Royal Bayreuth cats, cats on spoons (sterling or plate), bronze cats by The Animaliers, and cat-shaped inkwells. Signs of wear on chalkware and other fragile items are OK; but do not contact me with chipped, cracked or repaired pieces. I will consider folk-art items of various levels of quality––price will depend on the quality of the artwork. I could go on and on, as I buy just about anything with cats!

Marilyn Dipboye
31311 Blair Dr.
Warren, MI 48092

We Pay

Figurine, Royal Doulton 'Lucky'.................................**45.00**
Figurine, Rosenthal, small.....................................**35.00-45.00**
Figurine, Rosenthal, large.....................................**50.00-75.00**
Print, Currier & Ives, framed..................................**45.00**
Oil Painting...**50.00 +**
Individual Playing Card..**15¢**
Pin (costume jewelry)..**3.00-20.00**
Needlework, framed or unframed.................................**5.00-50.00**
Old Calendars, complete & unused...............................**1.00-10.00**
Books, illustrated by Louis Wain...............................**20.00-75.00**
Sheet Music, illustrated w/cats................................**5.00-15.00**

CATALOGS

As secretary of The Antique Stove Association, I'm in touch with serious stovers nationwide. It's a thin market, but I do find considerable demand for pre-1935 stove manufacturers' catalogs—the older, the better. Missing pages are a serious short-coming, but decrepit condition is tolerable. I find no demand for furnace items, commercial-institutional (hotel range) items, foreign items (except Canadian), in-ventors' prospectuses or patents, items from suppliers to the stove industry, stove-polish items, trade cards that don't illustrate a stove, and ads clipped from periodicals. Gasoline and kerosene (oil) stoves have no present following, and in-terest in electric stoves is only beginning. There's a striking lack of interest in the South, so southern manufacturers have hardly any following. I do not make a market in posters and signs, since they're non-informational, and demand is spotty and unpredictable at prevailing price levels. I have never charged my customers more than $45.00 for even the finest, large-format stove catalog from the 1880's.

The Antique Stove Information Clearinghouse
417 N. Main St.
Monticello, IN 47960

We Pay

Stove Catalog, 80 + pages, 1885, 6x9″ **20.00**
Stove Catalog, 80 + pages, 1900, 6x9″ **17.00**
Stove Catalog, 80 + pages, 1920, 6x9″ **13.00**
Stove Catalog, 80 + pages, 1935, 6x9″ **10.00**
Stove Catalog, 80 + pages, 1940, 6x9″ ....**too modern, I don't buy**
Repair Parts Catalog, w/model names & part numbers.................**20.00**
Repair Parts Catalog, w/model names & no part numbers..............**10.00**
Repair Parts, universal parts only.....................................**3.00**
Brochure, one stove model or partial line, 1910......................**3.00**
Stove Manufacturer's Official Cookbook.............................**10.00**

I am interested in obtaining catalogs featuring American decorative arts for a research library. Of particular interest are those which include pictures and/or information on manufacturing techniques. Catalogs featuring china, glass, silver, and/or furniture are needed. Sears & Roebuck catalogs prior to 1910 would be con-sidered.

The following list is a sample of possibilities and prices paid. Please send descrip-tion, date, number of pages, photocopy of sample pages (if possible), and price of items you have for sale.

H. Gold
2173 Fenway Dr.
Beachwood, OH 44122

We Pay

Associated Tile Manufacturing Home Suggestions, 1920...............**4.00**
Complete Book of Interior Decorating, 1948........................**3.00**

We Pay

Kirsch Book, 1929	5.00
Larkin Club Magazine, 1927	5.00
Luce Furniture Co., Grand Rapids, Michigan, 1922	25.00
Marshall Fields, 75th Anniversary, 1927	20.00
My Better Homes & Gardens Home Guide, 1933	5.50
Old China, 1902	7.00
Spiegel Furniture, 1941 (catalog extraction)	6.50
Studio Yearbook of Decorative Art, 1925	5.00
Tomlinson Chair Co., High Point, North Carolina, 1906	35.00
Zangerle & Peterson Co., Chicago, Illinois, 1923	20.00

CEREAL
BOXES

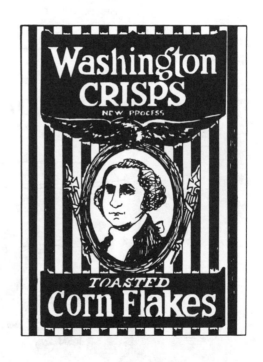

I will purchase all complete or near-complete cereal boxes and cereal-advertising displays. Boxes that feature the Lone Ranger, cartoon characters, sports, movie stars, and radio show premiums are especially wanted. I also purchase the premiums that are shown on the packages. I have illustrated want lists of the items I regularly buy and will send them to all who request a list. I will pay top dollar for the cereal boxes listed below.

Kix, Atom Bomb Ring, 1947   Cheerios, Lone Ranger
Nabisco, Straight Arrow   Cheerios, Disney Comic Books, 1946

Ralston, Tom Mix
Quaker, Sgt. Preston
Kellogg's Pep, Superman
Quaker, Bugs Bunny Comics
Post Toasties, Disney Cutouts
Wheaties, Sports Cards
Quaker, Gabby Hayes
Kellogg's, Pep Pins
Post, Roy Rogers
Quaker, Gene Autry Comics

Wheaties, Lone Ranger
Wheaties, Jack Armstrong
General Mills, 10 Pack-City
Ovaltine, Capt. Midnight
Kellogg's, Superman Display Figure
Quaker, Roy Rogers Display Figure
Nabisco, Straight Arrow Display Figure
Wheaties, Disney Comic Books Boxes
Others

John Fawcett
R.R. 2
720 Middle Tpk.
Storrs, CT 06268

CHILDREN'S DISHES

Children's dishes, larger than doll dishes but smaller than regular adult-sized china, have been popular for several hundred years. These play sets have often been made by famous makers of china such as Ridgway, Noritake, R.S. Prussia, Royal Bayreuth, etc. Sets were made by well-known U.S. china firms as well: Salem, KT&K, Warwick, etc. Children's dishes over one hundred years old are difficult to find. We concentrate on children's china of more recent issue but will buy complete or partial sets, whether new or old. We are particularly interested in buying teapots from children's sets, whether or not accompanied by sugar bowls, creamers, cups, saucers, and/or plates. We also buy odds and ends of lids from small china. Children's sets with original boxes are more valuable.

Prices will be quoted on receipt of letter with details as to the number of pieces, the labeling or marking, and the condition. Letters should preferably be accompanied by a photograph of pieces offered. We do not buy metal or plastic dishes.

D.M. Diabo
19953 Great Oaks Circle S.
Mt. Clemens, MI 48043

CHINA

We purchase all major brands of fine china and some of the lesser ones. We also buy earthenware and stoneware. Some of the ones we purchase are: Aynsley, Castleton, Franciscan, Haviland, Lenox, Oxford, Adams, Minton, Noritake, Royal Doulton, Spode, Syracuse, and Wedgwood. Others we like are Adderly, Ancestral, Baronet, Block, Booths, Ceralene Raynaud, Coalport, Dansk, Denby, Easterling, Edelstein, Fine Arts, Flintridge/Gorham, Richard Ginori, Grace, Hammersley, Hutschenreuther/Pasc, Pickard, Princess, Radcliff, Rosenthal/Continental, Royal Albert, Royal Caulon, Royal Copenhagen, Shelley, Tirschenreuth, and many, many more.

All china must be in like-new condition—no cracks, chips, crazing, or worn patterns. We always need good china. We will pay the following prices for five-piece place settings which consist of: dinnerplate, salad plate, bread and butter plate, cup and saucer. Hope to hear from you, and thanks to all.

Windmill Antiques
600 W. Burt
Lincoln, NE 68521

We Pay

Famille Rose, Aynsley	25.00
Sunnyvale, Castleton	25.00
Mariposa, Franciscan	35.00
Cambridge Blue, Haviland	45.00
Westport D518, Lenox	50.00
Maldon, Oxford	50.00
Georgian 2609, Adams	25.00
Cheviot S503 Green, Minton	50.00
Embrace 2755, Noritake	15.00
Wincanton Blue, Woods	15.00
Chateau Rose H4940, Royal Doulton	50.00
Lancaster Blue, Spode	50.00
Royal Court Cobalt Blue, Syracuse	45.00
Prairie Flowers, Wedgwood	50.00
Dynasty, Minton	50.00
Laurentian S659 Pink, Minton	50.00
Flora Danica, Royal Copenhagen	75.00
Blue Sprays Z2817 Rib., Royal Worcester	50.00
Geisha (any), Spode	50.00
Kensington Y8051, Spode	50.00
Irene Y6470, Spode	50.00
Old Colony Rose Y6447, Spode	50.00
Shima, Spode	50.00
Blueberry, Stangl	15.00
Grace, Syracuse	30.00
Susanne, Vogue	20.00
Caernarvon Black, Wedgwood	45.00
Columbia Ruby, Wedgwood	50.00
Della Robia Multicolor, Adams	25.00
Embassy Cobalt Blue, Aynsley	25.00
Beatrice, Castleton	30.00
Lyric, Castleton	35.00
Ma Lin, Castleton	30.00
Royal, Castleton	30.00
Admiral Cobalt Blue, Coalport	30.00
Athlone (any), Coalport	30.00
Hunting Scene 12748, Staffordshire	30.00

We Pay

English Garden, Denby..25.00
Baronial, Gorham...30.00

I am trying to complete an inherited set of Minton Hazelmere-B1220. My prices are negotiable for pieces in good condition. Having been unable to find much available, I can only guess at the correct market price range. Please write concerning availability and asking price.

H. McKinney
16 California #205
San Francisco, CA 94111

We Pay

Place Settings...250.00
Dinner Plates..75.00
Salad Plates...50.00
Bread & Butter Plates..50.00
Cup & Saucer Sets..75.00
Serving Pieces...Write

CHRISTMAS

Skinny, old artificial trees; faded, ugly old Santas; and glass ornaments wrapped in tarnished tinsel are among our prized possessions. We collect anything old having to do with Christmas, such as the old trees, ornaments, decorations, lights, books, animals, candy containers, fences, and Santas. Most of these items were made in Germany in the late 1800's and early 1900's.

The old trees were actually made of goose feathers. The sheep have wooden legs and cloth bodies. Tree decorations were made of delicate blown glass, cotton, wood, metal, paper, wax, spun glass, and tinsel. Many of the ornaments and decorations come apart and originally held candy. Cardboard, metal, or wooden fences are placed beneath the tree to create a scene with houses, animals, or the nativity.

We'll pay $100.00 for almost any old original feather tree. Six- to eight-foot trees can go as high as $500.00. Round bases are more desirable than square. Good green color is sought, as well as blue and other colors. Most have berries or candle holders.

The following is a sample of some of the items we are seeking and the approximate price we will pay. Much depends on the condition and age of the item and whether or not it is complete. So check out the attic and contact us about any old Christmas items you have for sale. We purchase one item or whole collections. We do not buy reproductions.

Bill & Treva Courter
Rt. 1
Simpson, IL 62985
(618) 949-3884

We Pay

Tree Stands, musical & revolving	200.00-300.00
Sheep or Goats (depending on size, color)	15.00-45.00
Wooden Fences (metal ones are less)	20.00-75.00
Father Christmas (Santa), red cloth suit, fur beard	200.00-400.00
Father Christmas (Santa), other color suits, fur beard	300.00-500.00
Ornaments, wax angel w/wings, 6"	20.00-75.00
Ornaments, cotton, human figures w/paper faces	25.00-100.00
Ornaments, cotton, human figures w/bisque faces	50.00-125.00
Ornaments, cotton, animals	20.00-75.00
Ornaments, cotton or glass, vegetables or fruits	15.00-25.00
Ornaments, glass, peas in a pod	75.00-100.00
Ornaments, glass, kerosene lamps	15.00-45.00
Ornaments, glass, lamps w/removable shades	45.00-95.00
Ornaments, glass, Aladdin Genie	50.00-60.00

Buying pre-'30s Chistmas items such as feather trees, unusual ornaments, cotton ornaments, Santas, paper or cardboard ornaments, and candy containers. No bulbs please.

John & Jenny Tarrant
67 May Valley
Fenton, MO 63026

We Pay

Feather Trees, small...**40.00-60.00**
German Santas...**40.00 +**
Japan Santas...**15.00-30.00**
Cotton Batten Fruit..**5.00-10.00**
Cotton Batten Animals..**15.00-30.00**
Cotton Batten People or Santas...............................**30.00-60.00**

Sterling and silverplated Christmas ornaments were made by many silver companies from 1970 until the present; a different design was produced every year. Collectors try to complete each series. Gorham made 'Snowflakes' of sterling silver starting in 1970. Towle made 'The Twelve Days of Christmas' in 1971. Metropolitan Museum made 'Snowflakes' starting in 1971. Wallace's most collectible series, the silverplated 'Sleigh Bell' (ball shaped), started in 1971. International made 'Santas' of silverplate in 1972. Oneida made 'Joy to the World,' 'The Nativity,' and 'The Magi' of sterling starting in 1973—also 'Reindeer's Cupid' in 1974 and 'Vixen' in 1975. Cazenovia made 'Raggedy Ann and Andy' of sterling. Hallmark made 'Halls of Kansas,' composed of several charming sterling ornaments. All are collectible. Original boxes, flannels, etc. add to the value. Tell us what you have in silver ornaments, and we will make offers. We pay according to condition and desirability.

Overtons
200 Ave. Santa Margarita
San Clemente, CA 92672
(714) 498-5330

We Pay

Gorham, Snowflakes, sterling, 1971-1988......................**15.00-75.00**
Towle, Twelve Days of Christmas, sterling, 1971..............**100.00**
Metropolitan Museum, Snowflakes, sterling, 1971-1988.........**20.00-40.00**
Wallace, Bell, silverplate, 1971-1980........................**10.00-25.00**

We Pay

International, Santas, silverplate.............................**10.00-30.00**
Oneida, Religious Series.....................................**20.00-40.00**
Oneida, Reindeer..**20.00-40.00**
Cazenovia, Animals & Others.................................**20.00-40.00**
Hallmark, sterling...**50.00-65.00**
Gorham, Icicle, sterling...**35.00**

CIGAR STORE ITEMS

I collect cigar store items: cigar store figures of wood, zinc, or iron (Indians, Blacks, sultans, sultanas, pretty girls, Punches, etc.); cigar counter-top lighters and cutters; and old photos of cigar stores (wooden Indians at the storefront). Also wanted are trade cards, catalogues, etc. No cigar boxes or bands collected. I'll pay a good, fair price. Write or call. Thanks.

Greg Zemenick
1350 Kirts #160
Troy, MI 48084
(313) 244-9426

CIGARETTE HOLDERS

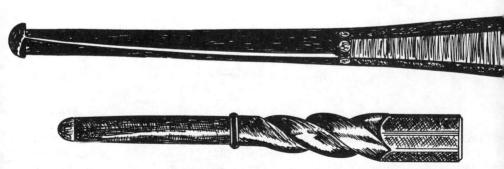

Glass cigarette holders, sometimes with matching match holders, were produced for a short time in the 1930's. These often looked like a stemmed wine glass with the foot rim turned up at the edges. A second shape had a rectangular top that looked as though it would hold calling cards or playing cards.

Lawrence Hartnell
Box 352
Collingwood, Ontario
Canada L9Y 3Z7

We Pay

Clear Glass..**15.00-20.00**
Colored Glass...**20.00-25.00**
Engraved Colored Glass..................................**25.00-30.00**
   In metal holders....................................**30.00-35.00**
Stretch Glass...**40.00-45.00**

CIVILIAN CONSERVATION CORPS

The 'Tree Army,' as it was affectionately called by some of its former members, was established April 5, 1933, by President Franklin Roosevelt. The C.C.C. was to provide useful work and vocational training for unemployed young men between the ages of 18 and 25. At that time, there were a quarter of a million men out of work. The first 'camp' was established at Luray, VA. There would be at its height over fifteen hundred spread across the country. Because of Congress' unwillingness to appropriate the funds necessary to continue the program, the C.C.C. closed its doors in 1942. During the brief existence of the Civilian Conservation Corps, many items were produced with the C.C.C. initials or emblem. Below is a brief list of the items I am looking for. Should you have anything not listed below, please send a photo or sketch along with your asking price. Please, no 'make offers.'

Thomas W. Pooler
21948 McCourtney Rd.
Grass Valley, CA 95945

We Pay

Tokens, brass or aluminum...............................**15.00**
Camp Script...**1.00-5.00**
Triangular Pennants, felt...............................**15.00**

Civilian Conservation Corps _____

We Pay

Unit Patches (insignia w/camp no.).............................25.00
Specialty Patches, w/rank stripe............................5.00-10.00
Square Company or Camp Flags.................................50.00
Honor Award Medal, w/blue ribbon...........................100.00
Collar Insignia..5.00-10.00
Tie Clips..5.00-10.00
Belt Buckles...5.00-20.00
Lapel Buttons...10.00-15.00
Rings 15.00-35.00

_____

The Civilian Conservation Corps was authorized by the passage of 'The Emergency Work Act' in March, 1933. It was a program to put thousands of young men in a peacetime army to work in the national forests, state parks, and other public lands. The U.S. Army operated the camps while the Departments of Agriculture and Interior supervised the work projects in cooperation with the State Department of Forests and Parks. The program ended with the start of World War II which drained the supply of young men and also improved the economy.

I am interested in purchasing any items which are associated with the C.C.C. era. The range of collectibles is unlimited, so if you have anything marked with the following, please contact me: C.C.C., E.C.W., W.P.A., U.S.D.A., U.S.F.S., U.S.D.I., S.C.S., F.S.R., F.S.F., F.S.N., or L.E.M.

Larry Jarvinen
313 Condon Rd.
Manistee, MI 49660

We Pay

Axes 6.00
Belt Buckles...8.00
Belts 12.00
Brass Collar Tabs..4.00
Camp Newspapers..2.00
Canteens 5.00
Cooking Utensils..3.00-8.00
Crosscut Saws..12.00
Photographs 1.00-5.00
Pins...5.00
Planting Bars..8.00
Plates 3.00
Pruning Saws...3.00
Pruning Shears...12.00
Rings 15.00-50.00

We Pay

Shovels..6.00
Cups..3.00
Firehose Nozzles...5.00
Flags..20.00
Furniture...10.00-30.00
Hammers...4.00
Hand Saws...4.00
Hats..6.00
Knapsacks...8.00
Knives..4.00
License Plates...10.00
Medals..5.00-20.00
Patches...3.00
Paper Items...2.00
Signs..3.00-20.00
Silverware..2.00
Tie Clasp...3.00
Uniforms..5.00-25.00
Watch Fobs..4.00
Wood Boxes..6.00
Wood Branding Irons..50.00
Wrenches..2.00

CLARICE CLIFF POTTERY

Clarice Cliff 'Bizarre Ware' was made in England from the late 1920's through the early 1950's. It is all hand-painted and is characterized by bright, colorful, whimsical designs based on flowers, fantasy scenes, or simple geometric patterns. Almost all pieces carry the 'Clarice Cliff' signature. Most will also be marked 'Bizarre.' Other markings which appear include: Crocus, Fantasque, Lotus, Caprice, Latone, Inspiration, Delicia, and many others.

I am interested in buying only the hand-painted Bizarre Ware line (especially the Fantasque pattern), not the later pictorial Tonquin and other similar frilly patterns. Prices listed below are general examples and depend on the particular pattern and condition.

Darryl Rehr
3615 Watseka Ave. #101
Los Angeles, CA 90034
(213) 559-2368

We Pay

Conical Sugar Shaker..**50.00**
Teapot or Coffeepot..**100.00**
Dish or Bowl, 6″..**50.00**
Demitasse Cup & Saucer...**25.00**
Vase, small..**75.00**
Vase, large...**135.00**
Conical Bowl..**125.00**
Complete Coffee Set...**200.00**
Dinner Service for 8..**400.00**

Clarice Cliff designed and produced hand-painted pottery in England from 1928 to 1938. She worked in the factories of Newport and Wilkinson. The designs were decidedly Deco and brilliant in color and form. Our book on Cliff is widely available. We will buy work which relates to the items illustrated therein and will pay as below.

Louis K. Meisel Gallery
141 Prince St.
New York City, NY 10012
(212) 677-1340

We Pay

12″ Jugs & Vases......................................**400.00-1,500.00**
18″ Chargers..**500.00-1,500.00**
Tea Sets..**500.00-1,000.00**
Small Items...**100.00-400.00**
Bowls (conical).......................................**300.00-900.00**
Bowls (other)...**100.00-600.00**

CLOCKS

I collect various types of Regulator schoolhouse clocks. I am looking for more in good-to-mint condition. Most clocks will be of oak wood and have brass pendulums. Sizes vary from 24″ through 36″ and up.

School clocks were manufactured by many companies such as Waterbury, Seth Thomas, New Haven, Gilbert, Ansonia, etc. The prices below are for clocks with cases in excellent condition, in good running order and with all original parts including the face and pendulum. Clocks should be well packed with the pendulum wrapped separately. A key should be included.

Dennis F. Kickhofel
20863 Lancaster Rd.
Harper Woods, MI 48225

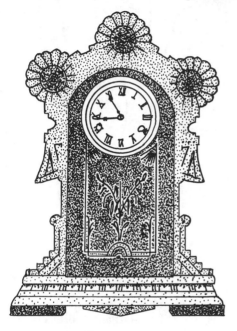 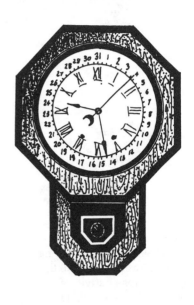

We Pay

Oak Schoolhouse Regulators.......................................**125.00**
Small Regulators...**100.00**
Large Square Regulators..**145.00**

We are seeking European clocks. Clocks of the 16th, 17th, 18th, and early 19th centuries are preferred. Lantern, bracket, grandfather, automation, chinoiserie, fusee chain, inlaid, and ormolu are examples of our wants. Please send photo, information, condition, price, and SASE.

Barbara N. Cohen Galleries
115 E. Main St.
Waterloo, NY 13165

CLOTHING

Clothing makes the man! What I want are the clothes that made the women and children from 1850 through 1950. I am interested in only the fashions that are good representatives of the period. For example: crinolines (Gone-with-the-Wind period), bustles, hobble skirts, flapper dresses, and Gibson-girl and World War II styles.

We are especially looking for bustle-style dresses and Gay 90's bicycling costumes. Children's and women's clothing must be in good condition. Pastel colors are preferred.

Linda Hood
5828 Brentwood Trace
Brentwood, TN 37027

We Pay

Crinoline Dresses	25.00-125.00
Bustle Dresses	15.00-100.00
Edwardian Dresses	15.00-100.00
Flapper Dresses	15.00-75.00
Dresses, ca 1930-1950	10.00-50.00
Lace Wedding Dresses	25.00-250.00

I am a serious buyer of vintage clothing from about 1880 to the 1950's. I prefer good quality, pretty things with great style. Of course, this is subjective. I'll be happy to look at any older clothing you have. Exact prices depend upon condition, material, quality of workmanship, size, and style. Damaged items are assessed individually. All inquiries enclosing a SASE are answered. I also buy nice accessories.

Pahaka September
19 Fox Hill
Saddle River, NJ 07458

We Pay

Daytime Outfits, 1880's-1919	**5.00-7.00**
Daytime Outfits, 1920's (flapper)	**5.00-45.00**
Daytime Outfits, 1930's	**5.00-35.00**
Daytime Outfits, 1940's	**3.00-25.00**
Daytime Outfits, 1950's	**3.00-20.00**
Fancy Evening Wear, 1880's-1919	**15.00-100.00**
Fancy Evening Wear, 1920's (beaded/fancy)	**25.00-150.00**
Fancy Evening Wear, 1930's	**15.00-75.00**
Fancy Evening Wear, 1940's	**10.00-65.00**
Fancy Evening Wear, 1950's	**5.00-35.00**
White Cotton Victorian & Edwardian Outfits	**20.00-125.00**
Wedding Dresses, 1880-1930's	**20.00-125.00**
Designer Label Clothing (Poiret, Worth, Boue Soeurs, Fortuny, Adrian, Schiaparelli, etc.)	**25.00-1,000.00**
Children's Fancy Dresses	**10.00-45.00**
Older Lace Bridal Veils & Headpieces	**10.00-50.00**
Embroidered Robes, Shawls	**10.00-100.00**
Parasols	**5.00-50.00**
Men's Suits, 1920's (button fly, no vents)	**10.00-35.00**
Men's Clothing, 1880-1940	**5.00-50.00**
Shoes, 1880-1940's	**3.00-50.00**
Fashion Magazines & Patterns, 1880-1930's	**1.00-7.00**
Jewelry, Victorian	**5.00-150.00**
Jewelry, 1920's-1930's	**5.00-30.00**
Costume Jewelry, 1930's-1950's	**1.00-50.00**
Purses (beaded or mesh)	**7.00-50.00**
Dresser Accessories	**3.00-50.00**
Hats, 1880-1920 (fancy, wide-brim, feathers, fruit, etc.)	**12.00-60.00**
Hats, 1920's (cloche)	**8.00-50.00**
Hats, 1930's	**4.00-25.00**
Hats, 1940's	**3.00-20.00**

Dresses, suits, and accessories from the 1940's are my thing. The following is an example of prices I will pay for items; but if you have something of interest for me that is not listed, or if you want a higher price, contact me for negotiation. What I purchase must be in very good-to-excellent condition.

Lynda Long
8517 Crestview Dr.
Fairfax, VA 22031

We Pay

Shoes, size 7½ B..10.00-18.00
Dresses, size 9 to 11..20.00-30.00
Business Suits, size 9 to 11...................................25.00-40.00
Bakelite Pins...5.00-12.00
Purses 5.00-15.00
Jewelry, large or chunky.......................................5.00-30.00
Hats 5.00-15.00
Hat Boxes...4.00-10.00
Compacts..5.00-25.00

COAL-MINING EQUIPMENT

The coal-mining industry as we know it dates to about 1840. Related items are as diverse as their origins and the persons responsible for them. Mining gear and equipment were usually commercially manufactured. By 1890 such items could be ordered from mail-order catalogs. Miners had to buy their own equipment including tools, black powder, and blasting caps. Many bought them at the local company store. This constituted a major investment for the miner, and he kept his equipment in good repair.

I am interested in all actual objects used in connection with mining, such as tools, helmets, lanterns, and dynamite detonators—also in sales brochures and catalogs. I will buy other mining items not listed. Contact me. Let me know what you have.

Frank Fazzini
227 Castner Ave.
Donora, PA 15033

We Pay

Sticking Tommy...20.00 +
Sunshine Lights..10.00 +

Leather Caps..5.00 +
Cloth Caps...2.00 +
Lunch Bucket......................................2.00 +
Powder Flasks.....................................5.00 +
Carbide Containers................................3.00 +
Powder Boxes......................................5.00 +
Squib Boxes.......................................5.00 +
Carbide Lights....................................3.00 +
Carbide Guns......................................5.00 +
Bird Cages.......................................10.00 +
Surveyor's Lights................................10.00 +
Carbide Light Repair Kits........................10.00 +
Safety Lamps.....................................10.00 +
Hanging Oil Lamps................................15.00 +
Powder Jugs.......................................5.00 +
Catalogs ....5.00 +

American carbide miners' lamps were manufactured from about 1900 until 1985. Although the exact number of manufacturers is unknown, there were at least forty with thousands of varieties produced. I am generally not interested in the common brands such as Justrite, Auto-Lite, Guysdropper, DeWar, Premier, and Butterfly; but I will buy some varieties of these makes. Please describe all markings on the lamp, the material it is made of, and the overall condition. Prices quoted below are for complete lamps in excellent condition and represent a small sample of the types I will buy. Incomplete or damaged lamps may be of interest, but quoted prices will be less. I am also interested in related items such as lamp parts, catalogs, and carbide flasks.

Ken Gaska
1688 E. Corson St.
Pasadena, CA 91106

We Pay		**We Pay**	
American	350.00	Little Giant	100.00
Anton	400.00	Maple City	300.00
Bright-Lite	300.00	Maumee	500.00
Copper Queen	300.00	Ni Ba	200.00
Dry-Lite	400.00	Norleigh Diamond	400.00
Ever Ready	300.00	Pocahontas	200.00
Fulton	350.00	Red Star	350.00
Gem	250.00	Scronto	250.00
Imperial	350.00	Snell	350.00

	We Pay		We Pay
Squarelite	300.00	What Cheer	400.00
Standard	300.00	Zar	250.00

COAT
OF ARMS

Since the middle ages, noble European families have proudly displayed on their armour and other possessions pictorial symbols representing the character traits and personal interests they wanted to be known by. Family crests can be found on every type of material, either painted, embroidered, engraved, or otherwise affixed. I buy all examples of all age categories. Condition and color must be excellent. Information or history about your crest makes it even more desirable. Hand-painted crests as well as embroidered ones are highly prized.

Steve Whysel
103 NE 99th St.
Miami Shores, FL 33138
(305) 754-3070 (evenings & weekends)

	We Pay
Crests on Tile	15.00-100.00
Crests on Paper	10.00-100.00

Crests on Fabric (Tapestry)................................**25.00-250.00**
Crests on Wood...**15.00-150.00**
Crests on Cups...**15.00-50.00**
Crests on Plates...**20.00-75.00**
Books on Heraldry..**5.00-50.00**

COCA-COLA

The Coca-Cola Company has spent more money advertising a single product than any other company in the world. This is evidenced by the numerous types of items which bear the Coca-Cola trademark. The earliest advertising dates back to the 1880's, even before Coca-Cola was sold in bottles. The bottling of Coca-Cola began in the 1890's, but fountain sales were far greater until the 1920's.

I am interested in all items pertaining to or advertising Coca-Cola, many of which space would not permit me to list. I prefer the older items, but will consider all. I also prefer the items to be in extremely good condition, but I make an exception if I don't have the item in my collection. The following list reflects the current prices being paid by me for items in extremely good condition. I also buy items advertising other brands of soft drinks.

Mr. & Mrs. Marion Lathan
Rt. 1, Box 430
Chester, SC 29706
(803) 377-8225

We Pay

Calendars, 1890's..**2,000.00**
Calendars, 1900-1910..**900.00**
Calendars, 1911-1919..**400.00**
Calendars, 1920-1925..**200.00**
Calendars, 1926-1937..**100.00**
Calendars, 1938-1940...**50.00**
Calendars, 1941-1950...**25.00**
Calendars, 1951-1969...**14.00**
Serving Trays, 1890's...**1,900.00**
Serving Trays, 1900-1909..**700.00**
Serving Trays, 1910-1928..**175.00**
Serving Trays, 1929-1936...**75.00**
Serving Trays, 1937-1942...**40.00**
Serving Trays, 1948-1958...**18.00**
Chewing Gum Jars..**250.00**
Metal Signs, 12″ round...**29.00**
Metal Signs, 16″ round...**33.00**
Metal Signs, 18″ round...**33.00**
Metal Signs, 24″ round...**37.00**
Metal Signs, 36″ round...**37.00**
Cardboard Signs, 1900-1920..**200.00**
Cardboard Signs, 1921-1930..**100.00**
Cardboard Signs, 1931-1940...**50.00**
Cardboard Signs, 1949-1950...**35.00**
Cardboard Signs, 1951-1969...**18.00**
Menu Boards, 1930's..**50.00**
Menu Boards, 1940's..**25.00**
Menu Boards, 1950's..**13.00**
Light-up Signs, 1950's..**115.00**
Light-up Signs, 1960's...**65.00**
Thermometers, through 1915..**110.00**
Thermometers, 1920's-1930's..**40.00**
Thermometers, 1940's-1960's..**16.00**
Clocks, 1880's-1900..**1,200.00**
Clocks, 1900-1940...**450.00**
Clocks, 1940-1950...**110.00**
Clocks, 1950-1969..**45.00**
Cooler Radios, 1950's...**100.00**
Toy Trucks w/Bottles, 1930's......................................**100.00**
Salesman Sample Coolers, 1920's...................................**900.00**
Salesman Sample Coolers, 1930's...................................**250.00**
Bottles, stopper top..**150.00**
Bottles, paper labels..**30.00**
Bottles, straight sided..**10.00**
Display Bottles, usually 20″ tall & up.............................**65.00**
Syrup & Seltzer Bottles..**25.00**

We Pay

Wood Syrup Kegs	**30.00**
Wood 6-Packs	**15.00**
Display Racks, 1930's	**40.00**
Display Racks, 1940's-1950's	**20.00**
Watch Fobs, w/celluloid facing	**100.00**
Bookmarks, early 1900's	**75.00**
Post Cards, early 1900's	**50.00**
Coupons, early 1900's	**45.00**
Blotters, early 1900's	**35.00**
Playing Cards, early 1900's	**75.00**
Sheet Music, early 1900's	**100.00**
Records, 1950's	**5.00**
Fans, early 1900's	**60.00**
Photos (originals only), 1900-1930's	**15.00**
Letterhead & Invoices, early 1900's	**10.00**
Cigar Bands	**40.00**
Advertising Manuals, 1930-1950's	**10.00**
Decals, 1930's-1950's	**8.00**
Magazine Ads, 1900-1906, color	**20.00**
Magazine Ads, 1900-1906, black & white	**5.00**

We buy Coca-Cola items in mint or near-mint condition. Lady calendars and signs are of special interest. We also buy Pepsi Cola, Hires, Moxie, Nu Grape, Orange Crush, Dr. Pepper, Cherry Smash, etc. We are interested in purchasing pre-1940 calendars with guns, ammunition, soda fountain, automobiles, pretty girls, etc., as well as advertising calendars and those illustrated by Maxfield Parrish or any other recognized artist.

Buck Fever Studio
Box 230
961 Country Club Rd.
Marion, VA 24354

We Pay

Calendars, 1891-1900	**1,200.00-5,000.00**
Calendars, 1901-1913	**800.00-1,800.00**
Calendars, 1914-1940	**75.00-500.00**
Calendars, 1941-1954	**25.00-200.00**
Serving Trays, 1897-1909	**300.00-3,000.00**
Serving Trays, 1910-1934	**75.00-350.00**
Serving Trays, 1936-1957	**25.00-100.00**

	We Pay
Topless Trays, 1908	300.00-1,500.00
Framed Vienna Art Plates, 1908-1912	100.00-500.00
Small Change Trays, 1899-1920	75.00-1,200.00
Leaded Glass Shades	1,500.00
Ceramic Syrup Dispenser, 1896	1,500.00
Cameo Paper Signs, 1895-1900	100.00-2,000.00
Cardboard Cutouts, 1895-1930	100.00-2,000.00
Cardboard Cutouts, 1930-1955	25.00-100.00
Early Cardboard Signs, w/sports figures or movie stars	25.00-250.00
Self-Framed Tin Signs, pre-1920	500.00-2,000.00
Signs, pre-1942, celluloid, tin, glass, porcelain, arrow type	25.00-500.00
Baird Clocks	1,500.00-3,500.00
Clocks, pre-1920	350.00-1,500.00
Clocks, up to 1950	10.00-200.00
Radio, 1933, 30" Bottle	600.00
Radio, 1950, Cooler	225.00
Metalcraft Trucks	150.00-650.00
Salesman Sample Coolers, 1929-1939	250.00-2,000.00
Leaded Glass Display Bottle, 1920	3,000.00
Syrup & Seltzer Bottles	25.00-200.00
Pocket Mirrors, 1905-1922	125.00-500.00
Post Cards, pre-1920	2.00-200.00
Blotters, pre-1940	2.00-200.00
Magazine Ads, pre-1940	1.00-100.00
Photos, Catalogues, Checks, & Related Ephemera	2.00-200.00
Coupons, Menus, Bookmarks, Stamp Holders, Note Pads, or Folding Cards, pre-1920	25.00-250.00

COFFEE GRINDERS

I collect American and German coffee grinders. This includes the wood kind that sit on counters and the hanging ones that are attached to a wall. They must be in good-to-excellent condition with no missing parts. The wooden grinders should have the original drawer. The wall-type grinder should have the original glass (usually marked 'Arcade'). I buy any of the above. Please pack in a sturdy box and wrap carefully.

Dennis F. Kickhofel
20863 Lancaster Rd.
Harper Woods, MI 48225

We Pay

American Grinders, wood...**25.00**
American Grinders, tin...**20.00**
German Grinders...**30.00**
Wall Grinders, glass..**35.00**
Wall Grinders, all tin..**25.00**
Toy Grinders..**20.00**

COIN-OPERATED MACHINES

Gumball machines, penny arcade machines, pinball machines, vending machines, and jukeboxes are all coin-operated machines. The use of coin-operated machines began in the 1880's—now they are everywhere. Coin-operated machines are one of the few antiques that you can play with and admire at the same time. Prices are still reasonable, starting at $50.00. I buy, sell, and play with all kinds of coin-operated machines. Listed below are some of the prices I pay for machines that are in good working condition.

Ken Durham
P.O.Box 2426
Rockville, MD 20852

We Pay

Victor Gumball	25.00
Masters Gumball	75.00
Columbus Gumball	75.00
Snoopy Gumball	250.00
Pikes Peak	100.00
Smiley	100.00
Poison This Rat	200.00
Strength Machines	75.00
Kicker-Catcher	95.00
Love Meter	85.00
Shooting Gallery	95.00
Pinballs, 1930's	150.00
Card Machines	35.00
Diggers/Cranes	300.00
Penny Drops	75.00

We are interested in procuring antique coin-operated vending machines made prior to 1930. We prefer working models, but will purchase machines with parts missing if you send us photos and descriptions so we may ascertain a very fair and equitable price.

Harold Adler
Mantiques
14572 Deervale
Sherman Oaks, CA 91403

As slot machines are not patentable by law, being considered an item not in the public interest, very little reference material exists. So paper items such as trade catalogs, manuals, and photographs having anything to do with coin-operated rarities are of interest to me––as long as they are pre-'60s!

Gambling machines of every kind come under the heading 'Slot Machines.' Some shook dice; others were roulette wheels under glass that took coins from several players and paid different odds. The jukebox, the gumball machine, and the arcade device had a coin slot; and they are of interest to us also. I am interested in devices, regardless of condition, and any amount of parts from a handle to a truckload. All letters will be answered.

RYAN
7217 N. Jersey
Portland, OR 97203
(503) 286-3597

We Pay

Manuals & Catalogs, w/amusement devices..........................**20.00 +**
Magazines: Billboards, Coin Machine Journal, Cashbox, etc..........**2.00-5.00**
Trade Stimulators, small counter gambling or gum machine......**40.00-600.00**
Photographs, old business interiors w/unusual items in view......**10.00-40.00**
Slot Machines, every type & purpose, from 'One Arm Bandit' to
    exotic floor machine (send a photo for evaluation)........**300.00-3,000.00**
Arcade Machines & Scales...................................**up to 300.00**

COMIC BOOKS

_____

Comic books have become one of today's top collectibles. All those comic books that you threw out when you were a kid have become very valuable indeed. With an ever-increasing number of comic book collectors throughout the United States, the supply cannot meet the demand. Since comic books that were published in the 1930's and 1940's were printed on such poor-quality paper, books in the higher grades such as near-mint or mint are quite rare.

We are buying all comic books that were published between 1930 and 1950 and most books that were published between 1951 and 1964. All books must be complete with no covers or pages missing. The following list reflects the minimum price we will pay for comic books in fine condition. We will buy other comic books not listed here as well as comic and pulp original art.

Metropolis Comics
7920 19th Ave.
Brooklyn, NY 11214
(718) 837-2538

We Pay

Marvel Comics #1	5,000.00
Marvel Mystery #2	600.00
Human Torch #1	500.00
Sub-Mariner #1	450.00
Red Raven #1	300.00
All-Winners #1	250.00
Capt. America #1	1,000.00
Classic Comics #1	250.00
Mystic Comics #1	300.00
More Fun Comics #55	300.00
Amazing Man #1	200.00
Police Comics #1	200.00
Plastic Man #1	100.00
Ace Comics #1	150.00
X-Men #1	70.00
Planet Comics #1	250.00
Jumbo Comics #1	400.00
Wings #1	75.00
Gene Autry #1	100.00
Reform School Girl	200.00
Mickey Mouse #16	200.00
Blue Beetle #1	150.00
New Comics #1	300.00
New Fun Comics #1	700.00
The Arrow #1	250.00
The Flame #1	100.00
Superman Comics #1	5,000.00
Superman #2, #3, #4, or #5	30.00-300.00
Batman #1	1,500.00

We Pay

Batman #2, #3, #4, or #5	**25.00-300.00**
Flash Comics #1	**900.00**
Action Comics #1	**6,500.00**
Action Comics #2 through #100 ea	**20.00-700.00**
Green Lantern #1	**500.00**
Wonder Woman #1	**400.00**
Detective Comics #1	**1,500.00**
Detective Comics #27	**5,000.00**
All-Star Comics #1	**600.00**
All-American Comics #1	**250.00**
Capt. Marvel #1	**1,200.00**
Whiz Comics #1	**2,000.00**
Wow Comics #1	**1,000.00**
Master Comics #1	**300.00**
Archie Comics #1	**400.00**
Pep Comics #1	**200.00**
Daredevil Comics #1	**300.00**
Silver Streak #1	**300.00**
Donald Duck #9	**400.00**
Walt Disney #1	**500.00**
The Yellow Kid #1	**7,000.00**
Fantastic Four #1	**300.00**
Spiderman #1	**200.00**

COOKBOOKS

Cookbooks

When the Civil War was over, thousands of widows and orphans were left without homes or providers, and it became necessary to come up with a way of raising money to care for the destitute. Recipe collections were gathered into charity cookbooks which were sold to benefit the poor. While today these cookbooks are generally called 'fund raisers,' they are still used to support good causes.

We buy pre-1970 cookbooks in good condition with working bindings and no lost pages. Minor use marks or marginal notes are fine, but stained pages will reduce the book's value. We will also consider books that were published by community organizations for other than fund-raising purposes; i.e., to commemorate a special anniversary or other occasion. The following is a general guide. I am also interested in buying books in poor condition if the text is complete.

Mary Barile
P.O. Box 642
Margaretville, NY 12455

We Pay

1950-1970 Cookbook	**4.00**
1930-1949 Cookbook	**5.00-6.00**
1920-1929 Cookbook	**6.00**
Pre-1920 Cookbook	**7.00-20.00**
Pre-1900 Cookbook	**15.00-30.00**

Wanted: cookbooks—especially the old Rumford Baking Powder pamphlet-type with little girls in full-color lithographs on the cover. Some of these little girls wore large bonnets and long curls; one has wheat in her mouth. Some cookbooks were made in the shape of loaves of bread. Others had unique covers made from wood or metal. Also highly collectible are the 18th- and 19th-century cookbooks which depict old stoves and kitchen utensils peculiar to that era.

Of special interest are wartime recipes and booklets explaining how to prepare meals with scarce commodities. I appreciate the single sheet of paper folded so that every inch of space was utilized and imprinted with excellent recipes. Rumford Baking Powder published the following:

HELP FOR YOUR WAR-TIME FOOD PROBLEMS

1. Your Meat Problem: *Rumford Meat-Extenders*
2. Your Bread-Delivery Problem: *Rumford Quick Breads*
3. Your Time-Shortage Problem: *Rumford Time-Saver Plan* (Bake All At Once)
4. Your Lunch-Box Problem: *Rumford Lunch Box Ideas*
5. Your Sugar Problem: *Rumford Sugarless Recipes*
6. Your Ration-Point Problem: *Rumford Point Savers*

Any of the above are worth $25.00 each. Cookbooks by famous chefs (first editions only) and pamphlets featuring radio and TV stars are highly desirable.

Bernice Stafford
332 Vineyard Rd.
Warwick, RI 02889

As secretary of The Antique Stove Association, I'm in touch with serious stovers nationwide. It's a thin market, but I do find considerable demand for stove manufacturers' official cookbooks dating from before 1935 (other types not wanted). I'm prepared to pay $10.00 for any such cookbook, unless I'm overstocked in that brand. Missing pages are a serious defect, reducing price by half.

The Antique Stove Information Clearinghouse
417 N. Main St.
Monticello, IN 47960

COOKIE
CUTTERS

Cookie Cutters

Cookie cutters are not a common collectible at this time. I started my own collection recently and am hoping to add many more soon. The type I am most interested in are Hallmark and Ambassador cutters, both of which have been made for seventeen years. Most are plastic with details or impressions on them. Some are painted on top. Shaper or outline cutters were also made. I am interested in acquiring all made by Hallmark and Ambassador. The first cutters made by Hallmark were three small, thin, plastic ones that appeared on the front of greeting cards. They are a bunny, a heart, and a gingerbread boy. I am interested in boxed sets and cutters with logos, painted details, advertising, and copper coloring. I particularly like the detailed metal cutters and the toy or miniature-type sets made for children. I have also found that plastic cutters from craft sets such as those found in Play Dough are just as collectible as actual cookie cutters. Below is a list of specific cutters I would like to have.

Mrs. Gari McCallum
918 Rosewood
Wasco, CA 93280

Hallmark and Ambassador   We Pay

Cupid, Heart, Bunny, or Gingerbread Boy, translucent, (sold in greeting cards in 1960's)	5.00
Peanuts, painted, set of 4	5.00
Raggedy Ann & Andy	5.00
Snoopy on Pumpkin	5.00
Pink Panther	2.00
Winnie the Pooh	2.00
Snoopy, set of 4	8.00
Miss Piggy	1.00
Snoopy, What's Cooking	1.00
Snoopy, Hi Sweetie	1.00
Count, Sesame Street	1.00
Dove	50¢
Cornucopia	50¢
Reindeer, painted	1.00
Snoopy Astronaut	5.00
Dumbo	50¢
Any Peanuts Characters	1.00
Any Disney Characters	1.00
Koala Bear w/Heart	50¢
Candy Box	50¢
Leprechaun	50¢
Easter Designs	50¢
Valentines	50¢
St. Patrick's	50¢
Autumn	50¢
Halloween	50¢
Thanksgiving	50¢

We Pay

Christmas	50¢
Gingerbread People	50¢
Turtle	50¢
Wedding Bell	50¢
Baby Bootie	50¢
Baby Rattle	50¢
Butterfly	50¢
Ice Cream Cone	50¢
Smiling Star	50¢
Strawberry	50¢
Smiling Sun	50¢
Train Engine	1.00
Fire Chief Badge	2.00
Fozzie Bear	1.00
Panda Bear	1.00
Scooby Doo	50¢
Crisco 3-D, set	5.00
Avon	1.00
Mr. Peanut Hat or Cane	2.00
Robin Hood, set of 8	5.00
Robin Hood, 1 of set of 8	50¢
Seagrams 7 Crown (metal)	3.00
Kenmore K (Sears)	2.00
Betsy McCall (metal)	10.00
Borden's Beulah	4.00
Wrigley & Mirro Troll	4.00
Mirro Windmill	2.00
Pillsbury Dough Boy	2.00
Pillsbury Dough Girl	2.00
Allstar-Master Set	5.00
Allstar-Disney Set	5.00
Allstar-Fairy Set	5.00
Hershey Bar, painted	1.00
Twelve Days of Christmas Set	5.00
Chilton Sets	3.00
Any San Diego Zoo	50¢
Any Sea World	50¢
Any Disneyland	50¢
Any Disney World	50¢
Any Alice in Wonderland	50¢
Stanley Home Products	50¢
Premium	50¢
Advertising	50¢
Any Novelty (toy, puzzle, 3-D)	50¢
Any Metal or Plastic Miniature Sets	1.00
Single of Metal or Plastic Miniature Set	25¢
Lone Toy Tree (on card)	50¢

	We Pay
Mennegasco Indian Maid.............................	2.00
Holly Hobbie Set..................................	4.00
Sesame Street Alphabet.............................	5.00
Plastic or Painted Backs...........................	50¢
A.F. Perry Goldilocks w/3 Bears Set (boxed).........	10.00
Pillsbury Comicooky...............................	50¢

COOKIE JARS

I am extremely interested in collecting cookie jars. Those that interest me most are the ones made in the U.S.A. of ceramic or china composition. Any manufacturer is fine. The figurals are my favorite, but I really love them all. I would like them to be in good condition. The older jars are acceptable if they have just a tiny stress crack or defect. I love the old jars as well as the new. The only glass jars that I collect are advertising jars. Some jars I have are also made of plastic, wood, or celluloid. Some of the older manufacturers would be McCoy, Brush, Shawnee, and Red Wing. Let me know what jars you have to sell and I will consider all offers. The following are just a few examples of the jars wanted.

Mrs. Gari McCallum
918 Rosewood
Wasco, CA 93280

Abingdon   We Pay

Granny **30.00**
Black Lady **50.00**
Humpty Dumpty **40.00**
Jack-in-the-Box **30.00**
Little Miss Muffet **40.00**
Mother Goose **40.00**
Little Bo-Peep **40.00**

Brayton   We Pay

Large Mammy **75.00**

Brush   We Pay

Little Boy Blue **50.00**
Humpty Dumpty **30.00**
Davy Crockett **50.00**
Peter Pumpkin Eater **40.00**
Red Riding Hood **50.00**
Little Girl **30.00**
Puppy Police **30.00**
Formal Pig **30.00**
Circus Horse **25.00**
Clown **25.00**
Elephant w/Ice Cream **30.00**

Hanna Barbara Productions   We Pay

Yogi Bear **40.00**

Harvey Productions   We Pay

Casper the Ghost **70.00**

F.&F. Mold   We Pay

Aunt Jemima **50.00**

Hall China   We Pay

Jewel Tea Jar **50.00**

Cookie Jars

Maddux of California   **We Pay**

Humpty Dumpty...25.00

Pearl China   **We Pay**

Chef 75.00
Mammy 75.00

Poppytrail   **We Pay**

Rose 25.00
Raggedy Ann...30.00
Raggedy Andy..30.00

Walt Disney   **We Pay**

Mickey Mouse Clock..30.00
Donald Duck...45.00
Donald Duck w/Pumpkin.....................................40.00
Mickey Mouse w/Drum.......................................40.00
Mickey Mouse on Cake......................................40.00
Snow White..35.00

Pottery Guild   **We Pay**

Elsie the Cow...35.00

NAPCO   **We Pay**

Little Bo-Peep..25.00

Doranne of California   **We Pay**

Fire Plug...20.00

DeForest of California   **We Pay**

Cookie King...20.00

National Silver   We Pay

Mammy **50.00**
Chef **50.00**

McCoy   We Pay

Indian **70.00**
Tepee **60.00**
Davy Crockett Head **150.00**
Coke Can **20.00**
Barnums Animals **30.00**
Mammy w/Cauliflower **150.00**
Black Train Engine **35.00**
Caboose **35.00**
W.C. Fields **50.00**
Friendship 7 Spaceship **30.00**
World Globe **40.00**
Astronauts **35.00**
Apollo **60.00**
Snoopy in Doghouse **35.00**
Rocking Chair w/Dalmations **45.00**
Woodsy Owl **30.00**
Mr. & Mrs. Owl **25.00**
Football Player **20.00**
Baseball Player **20.00**
Koala Bear **20.00**

Regal China   We Pay

Churn Boy **40.00**
Baby Pig **30.00**
Quaker Oats **25.00**
Davy Crockett **50.00**
Goldilocks **50.00**

Red Wing   We Pay

Dutch Girl, blue **30.00**
Pineapple, blue **20.00**

Robinson Ransbottom   We Pay

World War II Soldier **30.00**
Sheriff Pig **20.00**

	We Pay
Peter Pumpkin Eater	30.00
Cow Jumped Over Moon	20.00

American Bisque

	We Pay
Sandman	20.00
Umbrella Kids	30.00
Blackboard Bum	30.00
Blackboard School Boy	25.00
Blackboard School Girl	25.00
Cheerleaders	25.00
Yarn Doll	20.00
Boots	25.00
Wooden Soldier	20.00
Pig w/Painted Dots	20.00
Farmer Pig	20.00
Seal on Igloo	20.00
Spaceship	30.00

COUNTRY STORE STRING HOLDERS

From the 1840's up until the 1950's, string was used to tie up packages. In the early 1950's, tape came into use and the use of string began to decline. For some time advertising country store string holders have been sought by collectors. I am interested in advertising and non-advertising types of string holders or twine boxes made of metal, glass, or wood. This type of string holder can hold a ball, cone, or cylinder of string. Basically there are models that hang from the ceiling, attach to the wall, or sit on the counter.

I am also interested in any advertising for wrapping-type string or twine, including wholesale hardware catalogs and twine-cutting knives and devices.

Little is known about the non-advertising types of string holders, so I am putting together a book on identifying all types. A drawing or photo is necessary to determine if I already have the one you want to sell. I have at this time over 250 different string holders in my collection. I am not interested in chalk or china types that hang in the kitchen.

Charlie Reynolds
Reynolds Toys
2836 Monroe St.
Falls Church, VA 22042

	We Pay
Cast iron, w/paper cutter, Egyptian motif	500.00
Cast iron, ball string type	35.00 +
Cast iron, figural, horizontal string in back	250.00
Cast iron, counter type, cone string	20.00
Glass, clear, open bottom, counter type	45.00
Glass, red, tin bottom	75.00
Advertising	Negotiable
Any I do not have	Write

COW CREAMERS

Little cream pitchers that were molded in the form of a cow are becoming very popular items among the country-minded collector. Cow creamers produced in the 18th and early 19th centuries are the most desirable to the serious collectors. Many of these creamers were made in Holland, Germany, and France, as well as other countries such as Czechoslovakia, Japan, Occupied Japan, and the Staffordshire district of England.

Traditional-style cow creamers made in the late 19th and 20th centuries are also very collectible; they are found in standing or sitting positions, in plain colors, or with designs. Some even have a matching sugar bowl or salt and pepper shakers!

I buy only cow creamers that are free from chips or cracks. Send a picture or information concerning creamers not listed. Prices listed below are for examples either with or without designs.

LuAnn Riggs
1818 Beacon
Mexico, MO 65265

We Pay		**We Pay**	
White	5.00	Pearlized	7.50
Cobalt Blue	10.00	Signed	10.00
Pink	2.50	Sponged	15.00
Brown	6.00	Silver	5.00
Black & White	7.50	Gold	5.00
Yellow	3.00	Advertising	12.50
Orange	4.00	Rare	15.00

COWBOY AND TACK ITEMS

I am very interested in buying items related to the American cowboy from the 1860's through 1940's. I want older guns, especially Colts and Winchesters, gun leather such as saddle scabbards, pistol holsters, and cartridge belts. I also want chaps, the cowboy leggings of either leather or 'hair' hides, wrist cuffs, old or fancy gauntlet gloves, early cowboy boots, hats, neckerchiefs, and clothing. Nice old spurs and bits, law badges, saddle catalogs before 1940, brand books, early hunting or Bowie knives, braided horsehair or other fancy bridles, quirts, and braided rawhide ropes are also needed.

I am an eager buyer of older spurs in particular—especially the big Western or cowboy styles. Of particular interest are spurs with a maker's name (usually stamped inside the bands or near the strap buttons) and those with inlaid or overlaid silver mountings. Silver-mounted bits are also wanted, as well as old or fancy spur straps and other nice cowboy tack.

I am a private collector and will pay the very highest prices for outstanding items. I will consider buying entire collections.

Bill Mackin
P.O. Box 555
Meeker, CO 81641
(303) 878-4525

CRACKER JACK PRIZES

Cracker Jack prizes were first inserted in the popcorn and molasses confection in 1912. These tiny prizes have mirrored the interests of this century's children. Both World War I and World War II brought an assortment of Cracker Jack prizes reflecting the times.

The 1920's and 1930's were the 'Golden Era' of Cracker Jack prizes with many colorful prizes being made of tin. Many were marked Cracker Jack, but just as many were unmarked.

Another similar popcorn confection was called Checkers and was manufactured by the Shotwell Manufacturing Co. of Chicago. Checkers also had a prize in every box, and many of their prizes had corny little four-line poems on them. The Cracker Jack Co. bought Checkers and distributed both products for many years.

In 1948 plastic prizes were introduced. While interesting, these are not nearly as valuable as the earlier prizes. Prizes should be free of rust if tin and have all parts with good color and no tears if paper. I would be interested in hearing about any unusual items you might have to sell.

Harriet Joyce
16144 Woodhaven Ct.
Granger, IN 46530
(219) 272-3283

We Pay

Story Book, 1920's & 1930's, small, marked..........................**30.00**
Drawing Book, small, marked..**35.00**
Paper Doll, foldouts, small, marked................................**65.00**
School Tablet, marked..**55.00**

We Pay

Paper Jigsaw Puzzle, marked	35.00
Stickpin on card, marked	35.00
Felt Anniversary Pennant, 1972, marked	75.00
Cracker Jack Match Safe, marked	125.00
Tin Pea Shooter, marked	85.00
Painter's Hat, marked	65.00
Ink Blotter, marked	40.00
Matchbook, marked	45.00
Golf Tee, in matchbook, marked	75.00
Goat, Elephant, Leopard, or Rhino; tin w/movable head, unmarked	45.00
Piano, red-painted tin, unmarked	35.00
Mantel Clock, lithographed tin	10.00

CREDIT CARDS

Credit card collecting increased in popularity when collectors realized most cards were destroyed upon expiration as the issuers recommended.

The first credit cards were issued in the early 1900's. They were generally made from paperboard. Plastic credit cards were first issued in the late 1950's. Collectors eagerly seek paperboard and pre-1970 plastic credit cards issued by nationally-known companies.

There is a market for all problem-free credit cards issued before 1980. The condition, variety, and age are just some of the factors involved in determining a card's value. A credit card's value can only be arrived at by examination on an individual basis.

I will make an offer for all the credit cards you wish to sell, not just the better ones. Send any quantity. Within 24 hours of receiving your credit cards, an offer will be made by return mail in the form of a check. If you don't accept the offer, simply return the check and your credit cards will promptly be sent back. All prices are for problem-free cards in average condition.

Greg Tunks
150 Hohldale
Houston, TX 77022
(713) 691-1387

Plastic Cards

We Pay

American Express, violet	10.00
ARCO	50¢

We Pay

BankAmericard...5.00
Chevron, 1967...4.00
Choice...50¢
Cupid Candies, 1964.......................................2.00
Diners C, red top..12.00
Esso (U.S.)..3.50
Frederick's..4.00
W.T. Grant...50¢
Gulf, 1960...4.00
Husky, 1973..2.00
Lit Bro, stripes..1.00
Macy's, red star...1.00
MasterCard...1.00
Master Charge..4.00
Phillips 66, executive......................................3.00
Standard Oil, map..4.00
Sunoco, 1975...2.00
Texaco, 1960...3.00
TWA, 1968..6.00
Visa..1.00
Wards, data card...4.00

Paper Cards   We Pay

Aetna Oil...5.00
American Express...50.00
Diners Club...35.00
Hilton Hotels...2.50
Mobil...8.00
Mohawk Gasoline...6.00
Saks Fifth Ave..5.00
Shannon Furniture...2.00
Sheraton Hotels..3.00
Texaco..8.00

Miscellaneous   We Pay

Celluloid Card..15.00
Charge Coin...4.00
Laminated Paper..5.00
Metal Plate..2.50
Plate Cover..1.00
Playboy, metal..5.00

CROCHET HOOKS

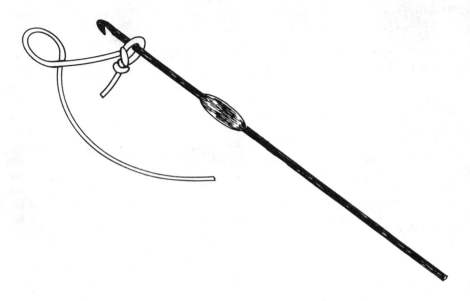

Crocheting has once again become popular. Thus the collecting of crochet hooks is on the rise. A crochet hook is a single eyeless needle having a hook at one end. There are many different stitches that can be made with one hook and unlimited items to be made (doilies, collars, bedspreads, etc.). The finished product depends on the learned ability of a crocheter.

Most hooks are nickel-plated steel (sizes 00-14). Those from the 1940's are usually priced right on the hook (10¢, 15¢). Hooks from earlier times are made of various materials such as ivory, wood, or other metals.

Very few companies still make hooks today; we particularly like examples that were made by companies that no longer exist. We are interested in buying older hooks——elegant, unusual, ivory, one-of-a-kind, homemade, etc. Hooks other than those listed below, tatting shuttles, crochet books, and other crochet-related items would also possibly be purchased. Get in touch with us for prices.

Hicker' Nut Hill Antiques
c/o Genie Prather
Rt. 2, Box 532-Y
Tyler, TX 75704

We Pay

Hero (name brand)..**50¢**
Boye (w/price)..**50¢**
De Lux (name brand)..**50¢**
Milward (England)..**50¢**

We Pay

Susan Bates (plain)	50¢
Susan Bates (plastic holder on end)	50¢
Plastic	25¢
Wood	50¢
Ivory (plain)	2.00
Ivory (carved)	5.00
Unusual	up to 5.00
Elegant	up to 8.00
Susan Bates (brightly-colored tip, metal)	1.00

CURRENCY AND COIN-RELATED COLLECTIBLES

I am seeking a variety of items relating to currency, coins, and counterfeiting. Counterfeit currency detectors, scales, scanners, grids, books, reporters, recorders, magnifiers, Detectorgraphs, Laban Heath detectors, or anything to do with the detection of counterfeit currency or stocks is sought. Coin detectors may be marked with names such as Herpers, Seymour, Smith, Thompson, Maranville, Lueders, Fairbanks, McNalley, MBT, Rice, Bathcelder, Statler, Street, Ewing, or Myers.

Scales may have slots or recesses for the weighing of coins—either gold or silver, or a combination of both. Scales may be marked with denominational markings such as $20.00, $10.00, $5.00, etc. They may also be marked with a name (but not necessarily). The main feature of these scales is that they all have some way of weighing a coin and then checking its thickness or diameter. They do not have pans or weights like a gold scale. Besides coin scales, I would also be interested in coin balances and counterfeit coin scales.

Another related area of interest is macerated currency—any item made of ground-up money pulp, usually souvenir items such as statues, plaques, plates, post cards, animals, shoes, hats, etc. These often have a small tag affixed stating 'This item made of U.S. greenbacks redeemed and macerated by the U.S. Government.'

Donald Gorlick
P.O. Box 24541
Seattle, WA 98124

CUSTARD GLASS

Custard glass was first developed in England in the early 1880's. The first American custard glass was made in 1898 by Harry Northwood. It was made in patterned tableware pieces as well as in souvenir items and novelties.

We buy custard glass in good condition, no reproductions please. The following list reflects the prices we will pay; we will also buy pieces not listed.

Delores Saar
45 5th Ave. NW
Hutchinson, MN 55350

Northwood Grape   We Pay

Tumbler	25.00
Pitcher	175.00
Cologne Bottle	250.00
Cracker Jar	250.00

Northwood Inverted Fan & Feather   We Pay

Tumbler	25.00
Pitcher	175.00
Butter Dish	150.00
Sugar	75.00
Spooner	50.00
Creamer	60.00
Cruet	250.00

Northwood Maple Leaf   We Pay

Tumbler	40.00
Pitcher	175.00
Salt & Pepper	200.00
Jelly	175.00

CYLINDER PHONOGRAPHS AND RECORDS

Cylinder phonographs were made from about 1890 to 1929. Early unusual models and later wooden-horn machines are the most sought after today. Phonographs which are complete and in good condition of course bring the most money, but incomplete or damaged machines are desirable as sources for parts.

Cylinder records were primarily made by Edison and Columbia, but minor makers such as U.S. Everlasting and Lambert had brief but extensive outputs. Condition is all important for cylinder records—mildewed, cracked, or very dirty cylinders have little or no value.

The following list is a sample of prices paid by me for various cylinder phonographs and cylinder records in good condition. Extra would be offered for phonographs with optional accessories such as repeat mechanisms or for cylinders with unusual cases.

Paul E. Newth
26 Gail Dr.
Ellington, CT 06029

131

Cylinder Phonographs

	We Pay
Maroon Gem	500.00
Columbia BO	600.00
Columbia BGT	450.00
Columbia BET	400.00
Columbia AA	325.00
Triumph Model F	500.00
Triumph Model C	375.00
Edison Opera	1,200.00
Edison Idela (Ideal)	1,400.00

Cylinder Records

	We Pay
Presidential (Taft, Roosevelt, Bryan)	15.00
Let Us Not Forget	35.00
Uncle Josh on Statue of Liberty	25.00
Uncle Josh on Weather Bureau	25.00
Uncle Sam to George	15.00
Sophie Tucker	15.00
Pink Lambert	12.00
Columbia, 6"	12.00
Dream House	25.00
Cylinder Cabinet, rounded front	325.00
Cylinder Cabinet, 6-drawer	200.00 +
'5000' Series Cylinders	6.00

CZECHOSLOVAKIAN COLLECTIBLES

At the close of World War I, Czechoslovakia was declared an independent republic and immediately developed a large export industry. The factories produced a wide variety of glassware as well as pottery and porcelains until 1939 when the country was occupied by Germany.

The following list reflects prices we will pay. We will consider buying other items not listed. The pieces must be marked 'Made in Czechoslovakia.'

Delores Saar
45 5th Ave. NW
Hutchinson, MN 55350

We Pay

Art Glass Vases	**15.00**
Art Glass Candy Baskets	**25.00**
Pottery, Porcelain, or Semi-Porcelain:	
Wall Pocket, bird/birdhouse, 5½″	**9.00**
Bird Flower Holder, 5⅜″	**8.00**
Creamer, parrot, 4½″	**10.00**
Teapot, girl finial, 8″	**40.00**
Creamer, swan, 5⅛″	**9.00**
Creamer, moose, 4⅞″	**15.00**
Basket, 7⅝″	**30.00**
Art Deco Figure, 9¾″	**30.00**
Wall Candlestick, 9⅛″	**30.00**
Box, 3″	**20.00**
Salt, 8″	**30.00**
Vinegar, 9¼″	**18.00**
Clock, 7¼″	**40.00**

DEPRESSION GLASS

Depression glass is one of America's most popular and universal collectibles. Many companies produced glass dinnerware in clear, transparent, and opaque colors as well. The term 'depression glass' refers principally to mass-produced patterns that were sold inexpensively or given away as premiums. The term 'elegant glassware' refers to hand-made or hand-finished glassware made with a touch of class by such companies as Cambridge, Fostoria, and Heisey. It was often promoted for wedding presents, giftware, and special occasions. The most widely-used pattern identification and price guides are those by Gene Florence and Hazel Weatherman.

Not listed below but also of interest to us are the many types of colored kitchenware produced during the 30's and 40's: mixing and batter bowls, butter and cheese dishes, cruets, funnels, glass knives, ladles, measuring cups, range sets, reamers, refrigerator dishes, rolling pins, shakers, spice sets, straw holders, sugar dispensers, syrup pitchers, toilet accessories, water bottles, etc. Contact us for prices.

We will buy any and all dinnerware and stemware items in 'depression,' 'elegant,' and 'kitchenware' patterns in perfect, like-new condition (free from mold roughness, nicks, cracks, bruises, scratches or other signs of wear). Listed below are prices that we are currently paying. Other pieces, colors, and patterns are priced accordingly.

Fenner's Antiques
Osna & Jim Fenner
2611 Ave. S
Brooklyn, NY 11229

134

AMERICAN SWEETHEART
Pink

Berry Bowl.................**15.00**	Bread & Butter Plate..........**75¢**
Oval Vegetable.............**18.00**	Dinner Plate...............**9.00**
Cup & Saucer Set............**7.00**	Platter **12.00**

BUBBLE
Blue

Berry Bowl.................**4.50**	Bread & Butter Plate..........**75¢**
Oval Vegetable.............**4.50**	Dinner Plate...............**2.50**
Cup & Saucer Set............**1.50**	Platter **5.00**

CAMEO
Green

Oval Vegetable..............**8.00**	Dinner Plate................**7.00**
Cup & Saucer Set............**6.00**	Platter **8.00**
Bread & Butter Plate..........**75¢**	Salt & Pepper Set...........**30.00**
Lunch Plate.................**3.75**	

CIRCLE
Pink

Berry Bowl.................**1.50**	Bread & Butter Plate..........**75¢**
Oval Vegetable..............**3.75**	Lunch Plate.................**1.75**
Cup & Saucer Set............**2.00**	Dinner Plate...............**3.00**

COLONIAL
Pink

Berry Bowl.................**3.50**	Lunch Plate.................**3.00**
Oval Vegetable.............**12.00**	Dinner Plate...............**16.00**
Cup & Saucer Set............**6.00**	Platter **12.00**
Bread & Butter Plate.........**1.50**	Salt & Pepper Set...........**60.00**

DOGWOOD
Pink

Berry Bowl.................**7.50**	Lunch Plate.................**2.00**
Oval Vegetable.............**22.00**	Dinner Plate...............**8.75**
Cup & Saucer Set............**7.00**	Platter **150.00**
Bread & Butter Plate.........**2.00**	

FLORAL
Pink

Berry Bowl	5.50	Dinner Plate	5.50
Oval Vegetable	5.00	Platter	5.50
Cup & Saucer Set	6.75	Salt & Pepper Set	21.00
Bread & Butter Plate	1.50		

FLORENTINE 2
Green

Berry Bowl	4.50	Dinner Plate	5.00
Cup & Saucer Set	4.00	Platter	5.00
Bread & Butter Plate	1.00	Salt & Pepper Set	21.00

HOLIDAY
Pink

Berry Bowl	3.50	Bread & Butter Plate	1.00
Oval Vegetable	6.00	Dinner Plate	4.75
Cup & Saucer Set	4.00	Platter	4.50

IRIS
Clear

Berry Bowl	2.00	Lunch Plate	21.00
Cup & Saucer Set	6.75	Dinner Plate	18.00
Bread & Butter Plate	3.75		

MADRID
Green

Berry Bowl	2.00	Lunch Plate	2.75
Oval Vegetable	6.25	Dinner Plate	15.00
Cup & Saucer Set	3.75	Platter	5.00
Bread & Butter Plate	1.00	Salt & pepper Set	23.00

MANHATTAN
Clear

Cup & Saucer Set	7.50	Dinner Plate	5.00
Bread & Butter Plate	1.50	Salt & Pepper Set	8.75

MAYFAIR
Blue

Oval Vegetable	21.00	Dinner Plate	27.00
Lunch Plate	15.00	Platter	21.00

MISS AMERICA
Pink

Berry Bowl	6.25	Dinner Plate	8.50
Oval Vegetable	8.25	Platter	8.00
Bread & Butter Plate	9.25	Salt & Pepper Set	25.00

MODERNTONE
Blue

Berry Bowl	6.75	Dinner Plate	4.75
Cup & Saucer Set	4.75	Platter	12.00
Bread & Butter Plate	1.50	Salt & Pepper Set	16.00
Lunch Plate	3.00		

PATRICIAN
Green

Berry Bowl	4.25	Lunch Plate	3.50
Oval Vegetable	9.00	Dinner Plate	16.00
Cup & Saucer Set	6.50	Platter	7.50
Bread & Butter Plate	2.50	Salt & Pepper Set	27.00

PRINCESS
Pink

Berry Bowl	6.00	Dinner Plate	6.00
Oval Vegetable	7.50	Platter	22.00
Cup & Saucer Set	5.25	Salt & Pepper Set	27.00
Bread & Butter Plate	1.25		

ROSEMARY
Amber

Berry Bowl	1.50	Dinner Plate	2.75
Oval Vegetable	4.50	Platter	4.75
Cup & Saucer Set	3.00		

ROYAL LACE
Green

Berry Bowl	12.00	Lunch Plate	5.00
Oval Vegetable	13.00	Dinner Plate	9.00
Cup & Saucer Set	9.50	Platter	15.00
Bread & Butter Plate	3.00	Salt & Pepper Set	60.00

ROYAL RUBY
Red

Berry Bowl	1.50	Bread & Butter Plate	75¢
Oval Vegetable	16.00	Lunch Plate	1.50
Cup & Saucer Set	2.50		

SHARON
Green

Berry Bowl	4.25	Dinner Plate	6.00
Oval Vegetable	8.75	Platter	8.00
Cup & Saucer Set	8.75	Salt & Pepper Set	33.00
Bread & Butter Plate	2.00		

TEA ROOM
Pink

Oval Vegetable	24.00	Lunch Plate	12.00
Cup & Saucer Set	24.00	Salt & Pepper Set	22.50
Bread & Butter Plate	9.00		

WINDSOR
Green

Berry Bowl	3.50	Dinner Plate	4.75
Oval Vegetable	7.50	Platter	5.50
Cup & Saucer Set	5.00	Salt & Pepper Set	22.50
Bread & Butter Plate	1.50		

Depression glass is the colored glass made primarily during the years of 1920 through 1930. It came in pink, green, blue, amber, yellow, white, and crystal. It was given away in cereal and soap powder, at movies and gas stations, and even for selling greeting cards. We buy all patterns and colors. Condition must be mint or near-mint. Prices should be reasonable enough to allow for resale. We also buy 'elegant glass' of the depression era such as Fostoria, Cambridge, Heisey, Paden

City, etc. Also of interest to us is kitchen glassware (butter dishes, cruets, mixing bowls, reamers, canister sets, refrigerator dishes, etc.).

Please list the pattern name, color, article, and price. If you have a large number of items, please quote a price you would take for the entire lot.

The Monkey House Antiques
Attention: Juanita B. McGuire
31887 O'Neal Dr.
Springfield, LA 70462

I am wanting to complete sets of Cherry Blossom (pink) depression glass and Mt. Pleasant Double Shield (black) depression glass. I do not want reproductions but am willing to pay retail prices listed in *The Collector's Encyclopedia of Depression Glass* by Gene Florence. I particularly need tumblers, berry bowls, cereal bowls, serving bowls, and coasters in Cherry Blossom; cups in the black glassware are wanted. I am a collector, not a dealer.

Joan Eigenberg
1595 Beverly
Gering, NE 69341

These are items I am looking for: pink Royal Lace salt and peppers, pink Holiday butter dish top, pink Sierra butter dish top, pink Strawberry butter dish top, pink Floral & Diamond butter dish top, crystal Iris butter dish top, pink American Sweetheart saucer, pink Holiday cup, green Dogwood saucer, green Princess cookie jar top, and green Royal Lace cookie jar bottom.

Ray Richardson
P.O. Box 292
St. Paul, VA 24283-0290

Wanted: depression glass cake plates in all colors. I will pay $8.00 to $35.00 depending on pattern and color.

Mr. & Mrs. Robert McLachlan
5191 S. Moore Rd.
Cass City, MI 48726

DIONNE QUINTUPLETS

I am a fairly new collector, so there are many items I don't have. Name your price, and if it is something I want I will consider it. I am looking for anything pertaining to the Dionne Quints, Dr. Dafoe, Nurse Yvonne Leroux, or any of their other nurses, family, mid-wives, Madame Legros and Lebel, Quintland items, etc. Some are marked Corbeil or Callander, Ontario, Canada.

I am especially looking for any paper items, also china, metal, cloth, plaster, including little china and celluloid dolls. (I am not interested in Alexander dolls.)

I want scrapbooks, anything inscribed 'Good Luck Babies,' green china bowls with heads of the Quints, and blue glassware depicting the Quints, as well.

Mrs. Donald Hulit
R.F.D. 1, Rt. 35-A, Box 547
West Buxton, ME 04093

DISNEY COLLECTIBLES

Just about anything in the Disney line from the late 1920's on up to the present time is collectible, with usually the earlier pieces being the most desirable. I am primarily interested in items from the late 1920's through the 1940's. The items listed below are from the 1920's and 1930's (unless noted otherwise). Prices indicated are the minimum amount that I'll pay for items in excellent condition. Please contact me if you have any of these or any other examples of the Disney line from the 1940's. I also want Disney figurines that were produced through the 1950's. I am a serious buyer, and I'm always interested in nice items. If you have any questions, please feel free to write or call. Thanks!

Bob Havey
P.O. Box 3
W. Sullivan, ME 04689
(207) 442-3083

_____

We Pay

Mickey Mouse Radio	300.00
Snow White Radio	250.00
Mickey Lamp in Chair	350.00
Donald Lamp by Post	350.00
Mickey Pocket Watch	150.00
3 Pigs & Wolf Pocket Watch	150.00
3 Pigs & Wolf Wrist Watch	150.00
Mickey Mouse Pin-Back	20.00
Pop-Up Book	100.00
Tin Pails, Sprinklers, Etc.	25.00
Donald Bisque Figure, 4″ or larger	75.00
Mickey Bisque Figure, 5″ or larger	100.00
Complete Tea Set	75.00
Movie Poster	200.00
Store Advertising Piece	75.00
Paperdoll Book	75.00
Punch-Out or Cut-Out Book	50.00
1st Mickey Book, 1930	200.00
Mickey Waddle Book w/Waddles	250.00
Milk Bottle	50.00
Merchandise Catalogue	100.00
Christmas Promotion Book	100.00
Studio Fan Card	50.00
Reverse Painting, large	75.00
Reverse Painting, small	40.00
Mickey Mouse Phonograph	200.00
Picture Disk Records	100.00
Wind-Up Celluloid or Tin Toy	200.00
Minnie's Yoo Hoo, store music	100.00
Bavarian China Pieces	35.00
Mickey Mouse Magazine	15.00
Mickey Post Card, 1930's	10.00
Vernon Kilns Pieces, 1940's	50.00
Laguna Pottery Pieces, 1940's	50.00
American Pottery Pieces, 1940's	25.00
Evan K. Shaw Pieces, 1940's	25.00
Goebel Pieces, 1940's	50.00
Mickey Mouse Clock	75.00
1st Mickey Mouse Club Items, 1930	25.00
Mickey Boxed Games, large	50.00

I will purchase all 1930's Disney items—everything featuring Mickey Mouse and friends (Mickey Mouse bisque figurines, dolls, toys, games, paper, radios, lamps, rubber stamp sets, advertising, Disney autographs, movie posters, greeting cards, tin and celluloid wind-up toys, banks, original art, studio Christmas cards, trains, artwork pull toys, etc.) Everthing with the pie cut-eyed Mickey or the long-billed Donald Duck is wanted. I have picture want lists of the items I seek and will send them to all who request a copy. I will pay top dollar for any of these listed items:

Fantasia Cut-Out Books, mint
Mickey Mouse Bisque Figures, w/movable arms, 9″
Mickey & Donald Figural Lamps & Lamp Shades
Kay Kamen Disney Merchandise Catalogs
Mickey Mouse Movie Stories Book 2
Mickey Mouse Tin Oval Lunch Boxes
Mickey Mouse Steiff Dolls
Mickey Mouse Post Toasties Cereal Boxes
Mickey Mouse Radios
Mickey Mouse Movie Posters
Mickey Mouse Lionel Circus Train
Mickey Mouse Lionel Santa Handcar
Disney Cheerios Cereal Boxes
Disney European Toys & Figures

John Fawcett
R.R. 2
720 Middle Turnpike
Storrs, CT 06268

DOG
COLLECTIBLES

Through the centuries man's best friends have been his dog and his horse. My passion centers on the noblest of the canines, the German Shepherd. As an advanced collector, my interest lies mainly in the older items, but I still seek Rin-Tin-Tin, Strongheart, and Flame novelties.

Edythe Shepard
German Shepherd Memorabilia
1334 E. Suncrest Dr.
Tuscon, AZ 85706

I collect dog-related items on any breed. I buy whole collections or one piece. Examples of items sought are pictures, post cards, statues, and books.

Mary Devlin
9726 Philadelphia Rd.
Baltimore, MD 21237
(301) 686-9212

DOG LICENSE

I want to buy old dog license tags. Buying prices are listed below. Certain common tags from some New York towns were purchased at lower prices, such as Rush or Wheatland, 1913; Scio, 1912; and Woodbury, 1916. These would be valued at $2.00 to 3.00 each. I will also buy other types of license tags (line tags, minnow net tags, fyke net tags, eel pot tags, and sidepath or bike tags).

James C. Case
Box 1076
Corning, NY 14830
(607) 962-2504

Date	NYS	Figural
Pre-1865	50.00-150.00	50.00-150.00
1865-1876	35.00-100.00	40.00-100.00
1877-1889	20.00-75.00	25.00-75.00
1890-1899	15.00-35.00	15.00-50.00
1900-1906	6.00-15.00	10.00-20.00
1907-1916	5.00-12.00	9.00-15.00

Date	Other State	Figural
Before 1865	50.00-150.00	
1865-1876	30.00-50.00	30.00-75.00
1877-1889	10.00-50.00	15.00-50.00
1890-1899	10.00-30.00	15.00-40.00
1900-1906	5.00-15.00	5.00-20.00
1907-1916	3.00-15.00	2.00-15.00

State Issue

1917-1930	50¢-2.00
1931-date	5¢-50¢

Conservation Department Issue

1917 NYS	25.00-50.00
1918-1935	5.00-25.00

DOLLS

Automatons are mechanical figures or dolls made to look like a person or an animal that can apparently move by themselves. They have fascinated collectors since the 18th century when they reached the height of their popularity. Queen Marie-Antoinette was so taken by them that in 1780 she commissioned two Germans, Roentgen and Kintzing, to make her a doll capable of movement that would contain a music box with a dulcimer player. Gluck composed the music especially for the automaton they created.

Mechanical dolls have been produced by French and German firms; even Thomas Edison was fascinated by automatons. His phonograph dolls are especially collectible. Modern-day reproductions of antique musical dolls are still being produced by Dynasty Dolls.

We buy all types of dolls, especially musical dolls in working and non-working condition. Original clothing and condition of mechanism determine price. Pictures are helpful when evaluating dolls, and I will travel to see an interesting collection. If the mechanical doll works, it is worth more than an ordinary doll; if it does not work, it's not worth much more than a non-mechanical doll. Contact me for further details. Sample prices below are for dolls in working condition.

Cindy Oakes
34025 W. 6 Mile
Livonia, MI 48152
(313) 591-3252

We Pay

Modern Dynasty Mechanical Doll	30.00-50.00
Unmarked Bisque Movable Doll	200.00+
Ballerina, pivots on wheeled base	500.00+
German Mechanical Bank Player, carries a drum & cymbals	750.00+
German Steiff Display, w/tagged animals	500.00+
Jumeau Lady, reclines on chaise lounge, holds fan & lace hanky	1,500.00+
Simon & Halbig Lady, sits at boudoir table w/toiletry	2,000.00+
French School Teacher, inside a classroom; moves to teach pupils	1,000.00+
Bru Fashion Guitar Player	3,000.00+
Jumeau Lady Magician, taps 3 boxes to reveal monkey, dog & baby	1,000.00+

I am looking for a **Bonnie Braids** doll. She is Dick Tracey's daughter. She is all rubber, buck-toothed, and her yellow hair is in two braids that are inserted through holes in her head. She must be in good condition—no cracks, no toes or fingers missing, and with original clothes. I will pay $20.00. I also will buy other dolls, doll furniture, doll clothes, dishes, or toys. Doll clothes must be clean, with no tears or holes. Doll furniture must be original, not re-done. Doll dishes are preferred in sets. Accessory pieces are also wanted. Add $1.00 if sets are in original boxes. The toys I prefer are old tin, wood, or metal ones. If painted, paint must be in good shape.

L.A. Smith
1504 W. Iowa
Norman, OK 73069

We Pay

Bonny Braids..20.00
Plastic Dolls..50¢-5.00
Rubber Dolls...50¢-5.00
Doll Clothes...50¢-1.00
Furniture...1.00-10.00
Dishes 1.00-5.00
Toys 1.00-5.00

We buy all types of dolls; listed below are specific examples. Prices are given for dolls in good-to-fair condition. If a doll is mint with original clothes and box, we would pay more. Please send us your list of dolls for sale (with prices)—we want many other dolls that are not listed here as well.

MaryAnn Polidoro
41 Vermont Ave.
N. Babylon, NY 11703
(516) 587-4959

We Pay

Ideal Toni..40.00
American Character Sweet Sue.............................40.00
F&B Honey...40.00
R&B Nanettes..40.00
F&B Patsy Family..60.00
Terri Lee...60.00
Valentine, hard plastic....................................20.00
NASB 10.00
NASB Muffies...25.00
Mary Hoyer...50.00
Ayers, human hair...25.00
Ginnys, hard plastic.......................................15.00
Ideal Compos...25.00
Madame Alexander, hard plastic.........................25.00
Madame Alexander Compo................................25.00
Ideal, hard plastic...20.00
Barbie & Family..10.00
Shirley, composition......................................75.00
Shirley, 1957, vinyl..35.00
Shirley, 1982, 12"...20.00
Shirley, 1982, 8"..10.00
Personality Dolls...35.00

We Pay

Unmarked, hard plastic..**15.00**
Unmarked, composition...**25.00**
Old Doll Clothes...**5.00**
Old Doll Shoes...**2.00**
Doll Boxes..**5.00**
Doll Books..**5.00**

I would like to buy **bisque doll heads**. I will buy damaged heads with pieces missing, as well as old bodies or body parts. I will pay up to $100.00 on a damaged item if I like it.

Jean Ryan
P.O. Box 1381
Springfield, IL 62705
(217) 787-0598

I'm interested in buying antique **bisque dolls, heads, parts** from 1800 to the 1930's. I'm especially interested in closed-mouth dolls without any chips or cracks. I prefer the composition, ball-jointed bodies. The prices on the dolls vary because of rarity, style, etc. Heads start at $50.00 and go up. Complete dolls start at $300.00 and go to $2,000.00 or even more.

Dorothy Grinewitlki
3428 Napier Rd.
Benton Harbor, MI 49022

Barbie has become dolldom's most popular representative. Introduced in 1959, she did not excite dealers but charmed her little girl owners and soon gathered an adult collector following. An 11″ dimensional 'paper doll.' Barbie's success was insured by the many and varied clothing outfits that were sold with her.

Barbie catapulted the Mattel Toy Company into the world's number-one position as producer of women's wear. Her tiny garments reflected the western world's fashion evolution through hem lengths, accessories, sewing methods, and textile development. Mattel offered little girl Barbie owners greater play opportunities and attracted new adult fans each year as Barbie and her expanding family reflected new cultural and racial attitudes through changes in hairstyle, makeup, friends, and relatives.

Prices fluctuate widely on collectible Barbie and her possessions. They are based on age, desirability, and condition. Deduct 50% from the listed price if the item has been removed from its box or package; deduct another 25% if the item shows use or wear. We are also interested in G.I. Joe and other personality celebrity dolls.

Gretchen & Wildrose
Playdolls
5816 Steeplewood Dr.
North Richland Hills, TX 76180
(817) 485-7189

We Pay

#1 Barbie	1,200.00 +
#2 Barbie	1,200.00 +
#3 Barbie	350.00 +
#4 Barbie	250.00 +
Barbie w/Bendable Limbs	200.00 +
Bubble Cut Barbie	90.00
#1 Ken	125.00
#2 Ken	75.00
#1 Alan	65.00
First Ken w/Bendable Limbs	250.00
#1 Midge	65.00
Midge w/Bendable Limbs	200.00
Other Barbie & Family Dolls	10.00-500.00
3 Rare 900-Series Outfits	250.00
Other 900 Series	10.00-200.00
1600 Series Outfits	10.00-250.00
Pan American, Other Rare 1600's, Pucci, & Other Specials	400.00 +
Structures & Accessories	5.00-350.00

Doll collecting is one of the most popular hobbies in the country today, and **Barbie** dolls represent one of its most rapidly-growing facets. These dolls were produced in large quantities and are still available at a relatively low cost when compared to antique dolls.

The first Barbie was produced in 1959. Since then other dolls of the Barbie type have been introduced. Some of these are Midge, Ken, Allen, Ricky, Skipper, Scooter, Tutti, and Todd. All have outfits and other accessories that may be purchased separately.

Prices I pay will vary according to condition and my needs at the time of purchase. I will buy in quanity and purchase all items related to Barbie in less-than-new condition for lesser prices. I am also interested in all antique dolls and related items, as well as miniatures.

Donna Purkey
2430 W. Random Dr.
Anaheim, CA 92804

We Pay

Barbie . . . . **15.00 +**
Midge . . . . **10.00 +**
Ken . . . . **10.00 +**
Ricky . . . . **10.00 +**
Skipper . . . . **5.00 +**

I will buy almost any kind of doll––I will pay about one-half book price. I am interested mostly in small **jointed bisque dolls**, also **celluloid dolls**, or **Indian dolls**––new or old. I seek **rag dolls** also.

Betty Clark
Clark's Antiques
Rt. 2, Box 106
Houston, MS 38851

I want a doll-size camel-back trunk in good condition. I am also interested in **Dionne and Shirley Temple doll items**. Does anyone have a wicker doll buggy?

Sandi Waddell
2791 C.R. 302
Durango, CO 81301
(303) 247-1568

I am interested in buying **dolls and dollhouses**. This category reflects my interest in a broader framework. These lovely houses and old dolls represent history in costume and interior design and man's ingenuity at creating very small replicas of real life. I am specifically looking for interesting and well-formed **half dolls**–– sometimes called dresser dolls or bathing dolls. They decorated a lady's dresser in the 20's and 30's. I need a book called *Sewing for Twentieth Century Dolls*, by Johanna Anderton, which is out of print. I am willing to pay up to $25.00 for a copy in good condition. I am also looking for a two-story dollhouse built or made in the early 1940's. (My brother threw mine in the garbage while I was away at college, and I would like to replace it.) The price would depend on the house and its condition.

Sharon Wilkins
1105 Burnham St.
Cocoa, FL 32922

I am interested in old **Lenci (cloth and painted) dolls**, and **bed (composition) dolls** with lashes and high wigs. These dolls were popular in the late 30's. Most had long legs, high heads, and wore full, silky, flowing dresses which were very ornate. I will pay $25.00 to $35.00 if condition is extra nice (no cracks -- light hairlines OK). Does anyone have an old **Cosmopolitan bed doll** named 'Marie Antoinette'? I am interested in ornate, fancy types and **pincushion dolls** too. I'll give $15.00 to $20.00 for pincushion dolls that are extra pretty (nice wigs and fancy dress). Call me collect; leave your number and I'll call you back. I also want dolls to sell and trade.

Doris J. Reissig
(305) 724-2375 (after 6 pm)

Hello! I really want a marked, hard plastic **Mary Hoyer doll**. I hope you have one for me! I am also looking for the *Wee Friends Book*, by Eleanor Watson. I collect **Madame Alexander dolls** and need some of the 1949 14" Little Women, a 21" Madame Alexander in a pink formal, 11" Cissettes from the 50's and 60's, and various other hard plastic dolls from the 50's. Please write about dolls you have for sale. I will pay a fair price and will answer all mail. Thank you!

Elaine DeVylder
2 Weed Circle
Stamford, CT 06902

Raggedy Ann and Andy are truly American dolls. These dolls, originated by Johnny Gruelle, have been loved by children and adults alike who are charmed by their saucy, pert expressions. They were made by the Gruelle family prior to 1918. Voland Manufacturing acquired the manufacturing rights from 1918-1934, and in

1935, Exposition Doll & Toy produced Raggedys. Mollye Goldman also made them in 1935, but because she did not obtain the manufacturing rights, she had to discontinue making the dolls. Her dolls have multi-striped legs and the words 'Manufactured by Mollye Doll Outfitters' across their chests. In 1938 Georgene Novelties began making the dolls; they continued production until 1963.

I buy good condition Raggedys made prior to 1950 including early hand-made Raggedys, Raggedy books, and books about other characters. I also buy **teddy bears, Lulu and Tubby, Nancy and Sluggo, and Howdy Doody**.

Gwen Daniel
18 Belleau Lake Ct.
O'Fallon, MO 63366
(314) 281-3190

We Pay

Early Raggedy Ann, dated	**150.00-350.00**
Early Raggedy Ann, undated	**150.00-300.00**
Early Raggedy Andy	**150.00-300.00**
Beloved Belindy, by Voland	**100.00-250.00**
Pirate Chieftan, by Voland	**100.00-250.00**
Percy Policeman, by Voland	**100.00-250.00**
Uncle Clem, by Voland	**100.00-250.00**
Eddie Elephant, by Voland	**100.00-250.00**
Beloved Belindy, by Georgene	**100.00-250.00**
Exposition Raggedy	**100.00-250.00**
Black Outline Nose Raggedy, by Georgene	**50.00-150.00**
Raggedy Ann, Andy, or Baby, by Mollye	**100.00-250.00**
Raggedy Ann or Andy, by Georgene	**5.00-75.00**
Books by Voland, Donahue, Gruelle	**5.00-25.00**

Among the more elusive of the modern collector's dolls is this series of character dolls by American Doll and Toy Company of New York. Though these 21″ to 23″ vinyl dolls were made as recently as 1960-1961, they apparently didn't sell well at the time, judging from their scarcity today.

There are sixteen known dolls in the **Whimsey Series**. Two of these were marketed in 1961 with different names. Most came with small accessories which were easily lost and a cardboard tag on a string which was usually thrown away. Two similar dolls made by the company have been accepted as part of the series by most collectors. They are the relatively popular Hedda Get Bedda––a three-faced doll exhibiting various states of discomfort and contentment––and the wide-eyed Astro Nut. There is also one sandy-haired Whimsey not mentioned in any ads. This was possibly marketed through Montgomery Ward or a similar mail-order chain. Following are the items I'm missing and what I'm willing to pay.

Jeanne Demers
100 Main St., Apt. 211
Suncook, NH 03275

We Pay

Samson the Strong	110.00
Betty the Beauty	100.00
Astro Nut	100.00
Tillie the Talker's Tag & Telephone	30.00
Zack the Sack's Tag	15.00
Dixie the Pixie (Polly the Lolly) Tag & Lollipop	25.00
Bessie the Bashful Bride's Tag & Veil	25.00
Fannie the Flapper's Tag & Cigarette Holder	25.00
Freddie the Friar's Tag	15.00
Hilda the Hillbilly's (Raggie) Corncob Pipe	15.00
Lena the Cleaner's Tag, Fork, Knife, & Spoon	25.00
Susie the Snoozie's Tag	15.00
Trixie the Pixie's Tag, Horns, & Trident	30.00
Zero the Hero's Tag, Pennant, & Football	30.00
Hedda Get Bedda's Adjustable Hospital Bed	35.00

DR. PEPPER COLLECTIBLES

Dr. Pepper was introduced in 1885 at Waco, Texas, by the Artesian Mfg. & Bottling Co. They produced many advertising products that were given to their customers. They distributed nearly as many different items as Coca-Cola, Pepsi Cola, Moxie, etc. If you have an unusual item, please send a description (a photo, if it is difficult to describe); be sure to mention condition, and I will try to give you a fair offer for it. Pre-1950 items are preferred, but I would consider any good piece. Please include SASE.

Bob Thiele
620 Tinker
Pawhuska, OK 74056

ENGLISH POTTERY & PORCELAIN

I am interested in buying any piece of porcelain, pottery, or stoneware of English origin. Items do not necessarily have to be marked. I prefer pieces made before 1870. Prices noted are for examples in perfect condition. A color photo along with a detailed description and a sketch of any mark should accompany correspondence to assure a quick reply.

Heritage Antiques
516 S. Holland Ave.
Bellville, TX 77418

We Pay

ABC Plates & Mugs	10.00 +
Art Deco	5.00 +
Art Nouveau	5.00 +
Banks, ceramic	10.00 +
Bisque	10.00 +
Blue Willow	10.00 +
Butter Pats	3.00 +
Children's Plates	5.00 +
Children's Mugs	10.00 +
Creamware	30.00 +
Cup Plates	5.00 +
Fairings	15.00 +
Flow Blue	15.00 +
Gibson Girl Plates	30.00 +
Historical	20.00 +
Ironstone, white	5.00 +

We Pay

Jasper	10.00 +
Lustre Wares	10.00 +
Majolica	10.00 +
Match Strikers	15.00 +
Mocha Ware	30.00 +
Miscellaneous Items	Write
Pitchers	15.00 +
Pot Lids	15.00 +
Pratt Wares	30.00 +
Royal Doulton	30.00 +
Royal Worcester	30.00 +
Salt-Glazed Wares	10.00 +
Spatterware	10.00 +
Spongeware	10.00 +
Staffordshire Figures	20.00 +
Stoneware	10.00 +
Tea Leaf Ironstone	10.00 +
Wedgwood	15.00 +

FAIRBANK

I collect most any item marked 'Fairbank.' A photograph or photocopy would be helpful in describing an item. I pay 15% finders fee if the information leads to a purchase. Please, no magazine ads for Fairy Soap or Gold Dust. Also no expensive tin signs are wanted. Reproductions will not be considered; originality must be guaranteed. Listed are items I am interested in buying—it is in no way complete. Items must be in good-or-better condition.

Soap: Fairy, Santa Claus, Sunny Monday, Pumo, Clarette, Mascot, White Star, Golden West, Gold Dust, Dandy, & Silver Dust. (Especially wanted are mint bars.)
Cottolene Cooking Oil: Tins & dated items, especially Gold Label.
Fairbank Scales: Small counter-top size, any related item, or any dated advertisements.
Fairbank Lard Co.: Any dated item.
Fairbank Meat Co.: Any dated item.
Fairy Calendars: Must be in excellent-to-mint condition.

There were a lot of items offered either as gifts, premiums, or by mail order. A few that I know of are: Gold Dust jewelry, watch fobs, children's fairy tale books or kitchen toys, gift plates, and a Fairy Soap doll made in 1912. I will pay book price if there is one or a 'value to me' negotiated price. Contact Jim or Ellen at the address or phone number given below.

Fairbank House of Antiques & Upholstery
113 E. 5th
Kennewick, WA 99336
(509) 586-6836

FARM COLLECTIBLES

I want to buy horse-drawn wagons, fifth-wheel farm wagons, light delivery wagons, or stagecoaches (Yellowstone or Yosemite)—restored or parts. Send photo with description and best time to be reached by phone. Reward is offered for a successful lead.

Fifth Wheel
P.O. Box 1392
Santa Rosa, CA 95402-1392

FAST-FOOD COLLECTIBLES

Collector glasses from fast-food restaurants and food products are a new type of collectible that is growing in respect. Over the past twenty years restaurants have been offering promotions of glasses decorated with cartoon characters, sports figures, and more.

I buy all different types of glasses that have a restaurant or food product indicated on them. Glasses must be in mint condition with no fading, chips, or scratches. I will buy any of the following types of glasses listed and more. I will pay between 50¢ and $3.00 (plus postage) per glass, depending on type and quantity. Let me know what you have to offer.

McDonald's	7-UP	Currier & Ives
Arby's	Walt Disney	Howdy Doody
Burger King	Walter Lantz	Archies
Wendy's	MGM	Flintstones
Taco Bell	PAT Ward	Norman Rockwell
Pizza Hut	Looney Tunes	Cinderella
Dr. Pepper	Sports Related	Wizard of Oz
H Salt	Hanna Barbara	Holly Hobbie
7-11	Sunday Funnies	Al Kapp
Pepsi	Christmas	More
Coca-Cola		

Mark E. Chase
RD #3, Box 360
New Wilmington, PA 16142

FINE AND DECORATIVE ARTS

Paintings, pastels, drawings, prints, sculpture, photographs, pottery, iron work, and fabrics done by established and recognized artists of Wisconsin (pre-1945), including American Indian, Euro-American, and native Wisconsins are wanted. We will purchase works in any condition that suit our collection.

West Bend Gallery of Fine Arts
300 S. 6th Ave.
West Bend, WI 53095

FIRE DEPARTMENT

Items dealing with firemen are a part of our history as fire companies have been serving America since the early 1700's. Many of our founding fathers, including George Washington and Benjamin Franklin, were firemen. There are many items relating to firemen. These should be in good condition without major defects. Helmets, badges, belts, certificates, shaving mugs, and lanterns are just a few of the many fire-department items collected.

I buy fire items from the 1700's to the 1920's. This includes hand and steam engines, buckets, trumpets, helmets, toys, badges, etc. The following price list indicates prices paid by me. I will pay top dollar for quality items. Many people list prices and then try to buy for a lower figure––I don't. The only stipulation is condition; damage of any kind will affect price. I will buy one item or an entire collection.

M. Grimley
P.O.Box 244
Oakland, NJ 07436

We Pay

Presentation Badges......................................100.00
New York City Fire Badges.................................75.00
Bells from Fire Engines..................................200.00
Book, History of New Orleans FD..........................100.00
Book, History of Pittsburgh FD............................75.00
Buckets w/Fire Scenes....................................400.00
Buckets w/Fine Paintings.................................400.00
Steam Fire Engine Catalogs................................50.00
Hand Steam Fire Engine Catalogs...........................50.00
Certificates, pre-1850....................................75.00
Engine Lights..2,000.00
Gongs w/Wooden Cases.....................................750.00
Indicators w/18" Bells & Oak Cases.....................1,500.00
Fire Marks..100.00 +
Grenades..50.00 +
Fire Helmets w/Presentation Plates.......................600.00
Fire Helmets w/Sea Horses................................300.00
Fire Helmets w/Greyhounds................................275.00
Fire Helmets w/Painted Fronts............................375.00
Fire Helmets w/Beavers...................................300.00
Fire Helmets, unusual styles.............................450.00
Stovepipe Parade Hat...................................2,000.00
Lanterns, engraved.....................................350.00 +
Fireman Magazines, pre-1900...............................5.00
Shaving Mugs...200.00
Ambrotypes of Firemen....................................150.00
Ambrotypes of Fire Engines...............................300.00
Tintypes, full plate.....................................100.00
Daguerreotypes...300.00 +
Commemorative Plates, pre-1915............................50.00
Presentation Shields, 24" & up.........................1,200.00
Prints, pre-1900...200.00
Statues of Firemen.....................................150.00 +
Nameplates from Steam & Hand Fire Engines..............200.00 +
Torches Engraved w/Fire Department.......................500.00
Trumpets, extra fancy..................................1,500.00
Presentation Trumpets....................................600.00

We Pay

Work Trumpets, engraved...400.00
Steam Fire Engines...1,0000.00 +
Hand Fire Engines..5,000.00 +
Ahrens Fox Piston Pumpers....................................7,500.00

FIREWORKS MEMORABILIA

I am one of the few fireworks memorabilia collectors in the United States. I mainly collect old firecracker packs; there are thousands of these stashed or forgotten packs in barns, attics, basements, etc. Some of the really rare ones are worth $50.00 or more. Dig out your old packs and send me a Xerox, so we can talk a deal. I also collect old labels, catalogs, etc. I pay top dollar for this type of memorabilia. This means money in your pockets. Start digging! Thank you.

Ricks
740 Southampton
Auburn Hills, MI 48057

Not many people are interested in this field, which includes old firecracker packs, labels, and old fireworks catalogues; but it seems to be slowly gaining in popularity. Fireworks have always been an integral part of our nation's heritage and despite efforts to minimize celebration of the Fourth of July, there is a definite increase in the use of fireworks to honor the birthday of our country. Firecrackers and other fireworks items began to be imported from China during the 1800's, and the old firecracker packs and labels from that date until the 1960's are popular collectibles—although they are extremely difficult to find.

Especially wanted are packs of Picnic, Golliwog, Lone Eagle, Oh Boy, Typewriter, Evergreen, Atlas, Tank, Minute Man, and Spirit of '76—$25.00 to $50.00 is paid for each of these. Also in the $25.00 to $50.00 range are old fireworks catalogues from National, Spencer, Baltimore Fireworks Co., Butler Bros., Masten & Wells, Hitt's, UNXLD, Havre de Gras Co., and many others.

I pay cash—very generously—for any old packs, labels, and catalogues I can use. The more desirable the item, the more money I'll pay. Please contact me for cash offers for your material.

William Scales
130 Fordham Circle
Pueblo, CO 81005
(719) 561-0603 (evenings best)

Fireworks catalogs and related artifacts are wanted by an historian! We are paying cash for old fireworks catalogs, boxed items, salesmen's display boards and samples, sparkler and cap boxes, Chinese cracker packs, posters, banners, photos of old fireworks plants, and anything related to the old-time U.S. fireworks manufacturers!

We are especially interested in locating items and/or information on the following manufacturers and distributors:

Victory Fireworks & Specialty Co.
Triumph Fusee & Fireworks Co.
Kent Manufacturing
Pain's Manhattan Beach Fireworks
NJ Fireworks Manufacturing
Keystone Fireworks Manufacturing
Rochester Fireworks Co.
Baltimore Fireworks & Specialty
Rozzi Fireworks (Tri-State Manufacturing)
Butler Brothers (NYC)

National Fireworks Co.
Havre de Gras Fireworks Co.
Unexcelled Fireworks Co.
Lloyd's Fireworks Co.
M. Backes Sons
Banner Fireworks Co.
Spencer Fireworks Co.
Essex Specialty Co.
Hitt Fireworks Co.
Others

Please contact us immediately if you think you have something we need. And remember, the items and catalogs that are worth cash today may end up in the trash tomorrow or in some future spring cleaning. So call or write today! If you have something we need, we will make an immediate cash offer; and we will make it worth your while to sell it to us! Please call us now at (201) 232-6100 with questions and offers.

Barry Zecker
Collectors' Exchange, Inc.
P.O. Box 1022
Mountainside, NJ 07092
(201) 232-6100 (8 am to 8 pm EST)

We Pay

Catalogs (from above firms & others)..........................**20.00-50.00 +**
Boxes (cardboard or wood) & Boxed Items.....................**5.00-50.00 +**
Packs...**up to 15.00**
Bricks (intact w/cellophane wraps)............................**up to 50.00**
Company Envelopes, Letters, Bills, Photos of Plants & Employees..**up to 20.00**
Other Items w/Fireworks Company Name Affixed..............**Write or Call**

Some of the most attractive throw-away paper art can be found on firecracker packs. The earlier labels of the 1920's through the 1930's are the ones that I seek.

They can often be found in old diaries or momento boxes. Here is how to tell the age of the labels:

Class Designations:
Class 1 Pre-1950: marked 'Made in China'
Class 2 1950-1954: marked 'Made in Macau'
Class 3 1955-1968: marked 'Made in Macau ICC Class C'
Class 4 1969-1972: marked 'Made in Macau ICC Class C' but with the addition of a box containing the word 'CAUTION'
Class 5 1973-1976: marked as above, but with 'Dot Class C' in place of ICC designation
Class 6 1977-Present: marked as above, but with the addition of '50mg. Maximum'
Exceptions:
Some Class 1 labels say 'Made in Hong Kong'
Some Class 6 labels say 'Made in China'
Firecrackers bigger than 1½″ may not say 'ICC' or 'DOT' or 'CAUTION'

Stuart Schneider
P.O. Box 64
Teaneck, NJ 07666
(201) 261-1983

We Pay

Class 1 Labels...5.00-75.00
Class 2 Labels through Class 4 Labels..........................50¢-20.00

FISHING TACKLE

Little did James Heddon know when he carved the first wooden lure many years ago that he would not only change the way fishing would be done from then on but would also unknowingly start one of the most interesting categories of collectibles today.

Collecting old fishing tackle has really caught on in the last few years and still hasn't reached it's peak. Old wooden lures are still the most popular items, but many other fishing-related items are also of interest to collectors.

I've tried to list a few of the items I will buy, but there are many more too numerous to mention. Please feel free to call any time. Prices listed are for items in excellent condition. I am also interested in many old fishing and hunting advertising items that are also too numerous to mention here. Please contact me about these items.

Randy Hilst
1221 Florence, Apt. 4
Pekin, IL 61554
(309) 346-2710

Lure	We Pay
Winchester	75.00
Charmer Minnow	75.00
Michigan Life Like	200.00
Oscar the Frog	65.00
Creek Chub Gar Minnow	75.00
Creek Chub Weed Bug	50.00
Creek Chub Beetle	30.00
Heddon Underwater Minnow	25.00
Heddon Lung Frog	20.00
Paw Paw Bullhead	35.00
Pflueger Kent Frog	65.00
Shakespeare Paddler	15.00
Shakespeare Waukazoo	65.00
Shakespeare Revolution	65.00
South Bend Whirl-Oreno	35.00
South Bend Plug Oreno	35.00
Garland Cork Head Minnow	40.00
Detroit Glass Minnow Tube	100.00

Related Items	We Pay
Lure Box, cardboard	1.00
Lure Box, wood	10.00
Orvis Glass Minnow Trap	30.00
Reel, Winchester	40.00
Reel, Meek	50.00
Reel, Gayle	50.00

We Pay

Bamboo Rod, Lenard...60.00
Bamboo Rod, Heddon..45.00
Catalog, Creek Chub 1936......................................20.00
Catalog, Heddon 1940...20.00
Catalog, Paw Paw 1945..20.00
Catalog, Shakespeare 1932.....................................25.00
Old Wooden Duck Calls..5.00

In the last ten to fifteen years lures have been highly collectible for many. As I am a collector of lures from many well-known companies, I am offering the highest prices for many of the old lures from the late 1800's to 1940. The lures must be in excellent-to-mint condition to merit the highest prices. Also add $1.00 to the lures that are in original boxes. There are other lures and companies that I am interested in that are not listed. Also, I will buy lures that are in less desirable condition, but these will command a much lower value. Contact me on other lures and companies that are not mentioned here.

Donald E. Morrow
9400 Knotty Pine Dr.
New Port Richey, FL 34654
(813) 856-1534

We Pay

Gee-Wiz Frog..15.00
Bing's Nemahbin Weedless.....................................100.00
Bite-Em Water Mole..20.00
The Charmer Minnow...100.00
Creek Chub Creek Bug Wiggler..................................35.00
Creek Chub Underwater Minnow 1800...........................100.00
Creek Chub Beetle 3800 Series..................................20.00
Creek Chub Sucker...50.00
Creek Chub Wee Dee..90.00
Creek Chub Gar Underwater.....................................60.00
Creek Chub Sarasota...70.00
Creek Chub Pikies..1.00
Croker Bait...120.00
Detroit Glass Tube...100.00
The Expert..50.00
Wilson 6-1 Wobbler..75.00
Heddon Dowagiac Underwater...................................150.00
Heddon Sloapnose 200...100.00
Heddon '0' '00' Series...65.00

We Pay

Heddon Yowser 195	45.00
Heddon Coast Minnow #1-2-3-4	65.00
Heddon Darting Zara	65.00
How's Vacuum Bait	35.00
Chippewa Bait	30.00
Kent Frog	120.00
Lanes Automatic Minnow	200.00
The Manistee	125.00
Michigan Life-Like	200.00
Miller's Reversible	200.00
Moonlight Lady Bug	125.00
Myers' Spellman	45.00
Pepper (wood baits only)	100.00
Flying Helgramite	1,000.00
Pflueger All-In-One	120.00
Shakespeare Evolution	120.00
Rhodes Mechanical Frog	80.00
Rotary Marvel	95.00
South Bend Whirl-Oreno	45.00
Truck Oreno	150.00
Smith Minnow	150.00
Wilcox	100.00
Winchester Indiana	150.00
Winchester Arms	100.00

I would like to buy old fishing items from the 1900's to the 1960's. Some of the older items I would like to find are listed below along with prices I will pay.

Randy Deerdoff
10222 Lafferty Oaks
Houston, TX 77013

We Pay

Lures: Heddon, Creele Club, Pflueger, South Bend (these are mainly wood, any shape)	50¢-20.00
Bamboo Fly Rods: any brand name (mainly 6-split, calutta cane)	5.00-150.00
Reels: any brand name	2.00-50.00
Tackle Boxes: wood only (must be very old)	5.00-40.00
Fish Hooks or Bobbers (any shape)	5¢-1.50

FLOUR AND SUGAR SACKS

Until near the end of the 19th century, flour was sold in bulk and in units of the standard barrel which weighed 196 lbs. The switch to decorated and proprietary cloth and (later) paper sacks would show weights reflecting this: e.g., 98 lbs., 49 lbs., 24 lbs., etc. During the 1940's, units went to a more standard 5, 10, 25, 50, 100 lbs., although there were still regional differences. As almost everyone needed flour and sugar and because (especially flour) competition was stiff and money short, sacks were more than just containers. They were meant to be reused as towels, pillowcases, drapes, etc. Many carried instructions on how to wash out the soluble inks for such uses. Some were printed with indelible inks, especially when they contained a pattern for a doll to be cut and stuffed after use. The following list is generally what I will pay for sacks. I want those in good condition with few tears, a compete design, and little spotting or damage due to aging.

Sacks Appeal©
98 Bryn Mawr Rd.
Winnipeg, Manitoba
Canada R3T 3P5

We Pay

Sea Island Sugar w/Doll Pattern	**15.00**
Flour Sacks w/Cutouts, large	**20.00**
Sleepy Eye Flour Sacks, large	**100.00 +**
Aunt Jemima Flour Sacks, early	**40.00**
Pictures of Indians on Sack, large	**20.00**
Comic Characters on Sack (Disney, etc.)	**30.00 +**
Paper Sacks of Most Types	**5.00-15.00**
Interesting Logo, but not pictorial	**5.00-18.00**
Black Characters, people on sack	**25.00**

Farm and other feed, seed, or coal sacks of cotton or linen only are wanted (no burlap). Also included in my want list are sacks for flour, sugar, etc. Sacks must be in good condition and not faded, with pictures as well as writing. Especially desired are ones with chickens, Indians, pigs, and those that are dated. I will pay from $1.00 to $5.00 each depending on condition, etc. If a sack is really unusual-- dated and with a picture--I will pay more.

W.A. Schroeder
1354 93rd Ave.
Kenosha, WI 53142

FLOW BLUE

Flow Blue was most widely produced from about 1840-1910. It is easily recognized by the intense cobalt blue color in its design, which many times is so 'blurred' that the pattern is almost obscure. During the earlier years, Flow Blue was manufactured using a heavy ironstone-bodied china. The most popular pattern themes were Oriental and English scenery. Many plates were twelve-sided, and serving pieces were very angular in basic shape. Tea cups were generally without handles, and the saucers were deep, like a small shallow bowl. The background color varied from white to robin's egg blue, especially on the underside of plates. Sometimes the pattern design was carried over to the rim beneath plates, soup bowls, and vegetable dishes. Approaching the turn of the century, the china had a more delicate weight as patterns were then applied to semi-porcelain. The basic shapes also evolved to a more rounded out and scalloped look. Floral and Art Nouveau patterns became more popular. Saucers were flatter, and teacups grew handles; sugar bowls and creamers shrank in size. There was a noticeable change in its overall look as more background color cobalt was left visible during the later period. The pattern name can be located on the underside of the piece; it is usually printed in large letters framed within the maker's trademark design or just above it. Not all pieces are marked.

I will buy all damaged pieces from the earlier period (1840-1880), including those not mentioned. Please note that miscellaneous items include sugar bowls, teapots, tureens, etc.

Barbara Amster
15 Bellevue Ave.
Bass River, MA 02664

We Pay

Creamers	20.00
Plates, 10½″	20.00
Plates, 7½″	9.00
Handleless Cups	15.00
Saucers	8.00
Flanged Soup Bowls	20.00
Platters	25.00-40.00
All Misc. Covers or Lids	5.00-13.00
All Misc. Bottoms Only	25.00-40.00

We will buy all pieces with old marks that are in good condition, although we will consider rare pieces with a small chip (no cracks). We pay good prices for good items; a photo would be helpful. Please list sizes and trademarks. Some of these are difficult to make out—a magnifier helps. Send this information together with information on condition (chips and/or stains), and we will reply promptly with our offer for each item. Please also remember to include a phone number where you can be reached during the day should we have questions. Thank you!

The Antique Place
1524 S. Glenstone
Springfield, MO 65804
(417) 887-3800

FOLDING RULES

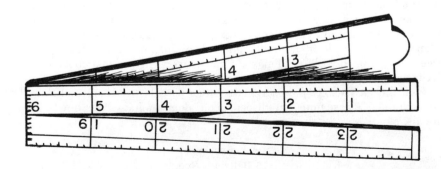

The Victorians were great inventors, enjoying the creation of variations on a theme; folding rules were no exception. A wide variety of rules were made to measure rope, timber, and the contents of barrels as well as for carpenters, engineers, machinists, and other craftsmen.

Rulers were made by many companies, but Stanley, Lufkin, and Belcher Bros. were the major American producers. Stanley, now a maker of a wide variety of tools and hardware, started as the Stanley Rule and Level Co. in the late 1850's. The main English manufacturer of rules was John Rabone & Sons.

We only buy rules that are in very good condition. Numbers should not be worn or faded, fittings should be complete and not bent, and wood should not be cracked or chipped. We also buy related items such as boxes or display cases. Write or inquire about any rules not listed.

John Goetz
P.O. Box 1570
Cedar Ridge, CA 95924

We Pay

E.M. Chapin #61	70.00
E.M. Chapin #74	70.00
Chapin-Stephens #61	7.00
Chapin-Stephens #62	15.00
Chapin-Stephens #036	75.00
Chapin-Stephens #36½	7.00
Chapin-Stephens #88	75.00
Chapin-Stephens #96½	15.00
Lufkin Rule/Level	30.00
Lufkin #8632	30.00
Rabone #1190	30.00
Rabone #1206	20.00
Rabone #1207	20.00
Rabone #1119	20.00
Stanley #1	15.00
Stanley #2	20.00
Stanley #3	20.00
Stanley #4	20.00
Stanley #12	20.00
Stanley #13	7.00
Stanley #16	75.00
Stanley #31	30.00
Stanley #38	50.00
Stanley #39	75.00
Stanley #40	50.00
Stanley #40½	50.00
Stanley #85	75.00
Stanley #86	75.00
Stanley #88	50.00

We Pay

Stanley #89	175.00
Stanley #92½	50.00
Stanley #95	150.00
Stanley #97	150.00
Stephens & Co. #036	70.00
Stephens & Co. #306, ivory	350.00
Stephens & Co. #66	20.00
Stephens & Co. #84	100.00
Stephens & Co. #89	20.00

FOLK ART TEXTILES

    Folk art textiles encompass any creative stitchery or loom techniques done by the average person, such as quilts and coverlets or hooked and braided rugs. Items in this category have become collectible as a true art form.

    Prices paid are for items in excellent condition without holes, tears, or stains. I will accept items in non-perfect condition at reduced prices. A color photo along with a complete description of items for sale will expedite a reply.

Heritage Antiques
516 S. Holland Ave.
Bellville, TX 77418
(409) 865-5618

We Pay

Bedspread, crochet	25.00 +
Bedspread, homespun	35.00 +
Camisole	2.00 +
Carpet, oriental	50.00 +
Counterpane, Marseilles	10.00 +
Coverlet, woven	50.00 +
Curtains, lace	5.00 +
Dress, homespun	10.00 +
Needlework Picture	5.00 +
Needlework Footstool	15.00 +
Needlework Fan	15.00 +
Needlework Hand Towel	1.00 +
Needle Lace	1.00 +
Needlepoint, miscellaneous	5.00 +
Petticoat, lace & ruffles	8.00 +
Pillow Shams	5.00 +
Pillow Cases, handwork	2.00 +
Purse, beaded	10.00 +
Quilt, pre-1920 pieced	50.00 +
Quilt, pre-1930 applique	50.00 +
Quilt, crazy, velvet & satin	60.00 +
Quilt, album, elaborate	100.00 +
Quilt, true crib size	50.00 +
Rug, hooked	15.00 +
Rug, crochet	5.00 +
Rug, rag	5.00 +
Sampler	35.00 +
Shawl, silk w/fringe	10.00 +
Shawl, paisley	35.00 +
Tablecloth, crochet	20.00 +
Table Linens, miscellaneous	5.00 +

FOUNTAIN PENS

Fountain pens produced between 1880 and 1945 are very collectible, as well as some produced later (such as Parker's Spanish Treasure pen). The most valuable pens are the major brands like Parker, Sheaffer, Waterman, Wahl-Eversharp, Conklin, and Swan. Pens commanding the best prices are those that are either very large, very fancy, or very rare.

I prefer very fancy and rare pens but will consider purchasing any high-quality pen that is in excellent condition and free from defects such as cracks, damage, or missing parts.

The following list reflects the current prices I pay for fountain pens. Some of these pens have identifying numbers stamped on the end of the holders. Prices are for pens in excellent condition. I have published a book on collectible fountain pens. Write for further information on the book or if you have fountain pens to sell.

Glen Bowen
2415 Villa Creek
Kingwood, TX 77339

We Pay

Parker #41 or #31 Sterling or Gold-Filled Filigree....................**50.00**
Parker #47 Pearl Sided w/Floral Design Gold-Filled Cap...............**75.00**
Parker #15 Pearl Sided w/Gold-Filled Filigree Cap....................**50.00**
Parker #45 Pearl Sided w/Gold-Filled Filigree Cap....................**50.00**
Parker #37 or #38 Gold-Filled or Sterling Snakes....................**750.00**
Parker #59 or #60 Gold-Filled or Sterling Indian Aztec Design.........**750.00**
Parker #58 Gold-Filled Partial Indian Aztec Design...................**100.00**
Parker #35 or #36 Gold-Filled or Sterling Floral Pattern...............**75.00**
Parker #52 or #53 Gold-Filled or Sterling Swastika Design.............**350.00**
Parker #39 or #54 Gold-Filled or Sterling Floral Pattern...............**100.00**
Parker #40 Gold-Filled or Solid Gold Floral Design..............**75.00-200.00**
Parker #43 or #44 Gold-Filled or Sterling Floral Design...............**50.00**
Parker #14 or #16 Gold-Filled or Sterling Filigree Design.............**50.00**
Parker #41 or #31 Gold-Filled or Sterling Filigree Design.............**75.00**
Parker #33 or #34 Gold-Filled or Sterling Overlay....................**50.00**
Parker #62 Gold-Filled Floral Engraved Pattern......................**50.00**
Waterman #452, #454, #0552, or #0554 Gold-Filled or Sterling.........**50.00**
Waterman #456, #458, #0556, or #0558 Gold-Filled or Sterling.........**75.00**

We Pay

Waterman #552, #554, #555, or #556 Gold Overlay	75.00-200.00
Waterman Ripple Pattern #7, #56, or #58	50.00-100.00
Waterman Ripple Pattern #52, #54, or #55	15.00-30.00
Waterman 100 Year Brown, Black, or Burgundy	20.00
Waterman 100 Year Blue, Yellow, Red, or Green Transparent	50.00
Waterman #20 Black, Red, or Red & Black Pattern	150.00
Waterman Patrician, Multicolored	75.00-100.00
Wahl-Eversharp Gold-Filled or Sterling #2, #3, #4, #5, or #6	15.00-75.00
Wahl-Eversharp Oversize in Various Colors, Roller Ball Clips	75.00
Wahl-Eversharp Oversize Doric (fluted sides) Various Colors	75.00
A.A. Waterman Gold-Filled or Sterling Overlay	25.00-100.00
Aiken-Lambert Gold-Filled or Sterling Overlay	15.00-75.00
Conklin Crescent Filler, Gold-Filled or Sterling	25.00-75.00
John Holland, Gold-Filled or Sterling Filigree	25.00-100.00
Paul Wirt Gold-Filled or Sterling Overlay or Filigree	25.00-75.00
Parker Duofold Sr. Blue or Yellow	50.00
Parker Duofold Sr. Red, Green, Black & Pearl, or Black	20.00

The first practical fountain pen was made by L.E. Waterman in 1884. Since that time many attractive, quality pens have been produced. The 'big four' among pen manufacturers are Waterman, Parker, Sheaffer, and Wahl-Eversharp. Prices vary from $1.00 to $1,500.00 (for the 1899 Parker Snake Pen), with most pens being worth $10.00 or less. The size of the pen is important—bigger is better, and condition counts for much of the value. A $100.00 pen with a gouge or hairline crack in the cap is worth only $40.00. The best way to offer pens is either to send the pens themselves or to Xerox them with a piece of white paper covering them.

Stuart Schneider
P.O. Box 64
Teaneck, NJ 07666
(201) 261-1983

Fountain pens, once a near necessity of life, are experiencing a rekindled interest by a few collectors. Several major companies produced quality pens in the United States at the turn of the century. In addition, a large number of small companies produced pens of various grades on a much smaller scale. Production and use of fountain pens declined sharply with the introduction of the ballpoint pen.

Condition is of primary importance in determining pen value. Pens with cracks or missing parts have little value, while pens in working order and free from defects have the highest. Some of the brands of pens we are looking for include: Parker,

LeBoeuf, John Holland, Wahl-Eversharp, Waterman, Dunn, Swan, Moore, Conklin, Mont Blanc, and Houston. We pay from $5.00 to $50.00 and up depending on the model and condition.

Andy Brenner
814 9th St.
Sheldon, IA 51201

Wanted: all solid silver and gold fountain pens for my personal collection. Retail prices are paid for pens in good working condition, undamaged, and complete. Ship with a price or for an offer.

Rich Hartzog
P.O. Box 4134 XW
Rockford, IL 61110

We Pay

Silver, pre-1935	**75.00-150.00 +**
Silver, post-1935	**45.00 to 75.00 +**
Gold (solid only, not plated)	**Ship for Offer**

FOX COATS

Fox coats, silver and red, as well as lynx and other long-haired furs are desired. Our clientele wants the elegance but not the price of new furs. We prefer coats that are in excellent condition. However, coats with imperfections will be considered. Please send photo, information, condition, price, and SASE.

Barbara N. Cohen Galleries
115 E. Main St.
Waterloo, NY 13165

FRAMES

Small frames for photographs or miniatures have become popular collectibles and decorator items. They were made in a fascinating array of materials: silver, brass, celluloid, wood, gold, stone, amber, tortoise shell, enamel, and leather, to name but a few. I am interested in frames under six inches with the folding easel on the back, with or without glass or picture, but the folding easel or flap must be intact. I might consider a repairable example. Send a description and SASE for reply. Please write or call for a quote. See examples given below for an indication of the prices I pay.

Carols Gallery
14455 Big Basin Way
Saratoga, CA 95070
(408) 867-7055 (Wed. through Sat. 11 am to 5 pm)

We Pay

Wood, carved, oval w/leaves, ca 1880, 4″	**15.00**
Brass, cast, gold plated, French, oval w/bow, ca 1890, 3″	**25.00**
Stone, malachite, held in brass frame, brass bow at top, 3″	**40. 00**
Cloisonne, enamel on brass, Chinese, ca 1890, 5″	**25.00**
Sterling Silver, stamped w/velvet back, ca 1920, 4″	**30.00**
Ivory, carved oval, ball feet, hook on top, Chinese, ca 1870, 3″	**50.00**

We Pay

Tortoise Shell, inlayed silver, oval, ca 1880, 2"........................50.00
Enamel on Silverplate, oval, USA, ca 1930, 2½".......................15.00
Enamel on Sterling, square, flowers, French, ca 1910, 1"..............30.00
Gold Plated, double, brass, English, ca 1890, 1"......................20.00
Sterling Silver, ornately cast, 3½"..................................55.00

FRANKLIN MINT ISSUES

Franklin Mint issues peaked in 1980, but they have been in a declining phase since then. In order to assist sellers of all Franklin Mint issues, I am giving below a rule-of-thumb buying guide; I will be glad to offer a quote on anything you may wish to sell.

Here are the options. Most of the sets wanted in art and dealing with art subjects will bring close to 'melt value.' States of the Union, Presidential, and others are worth 80%-85% of silver content. Gaming tokens of silver pay 85% of melt, and gold coins offer 10% above melt.

I buy all Franklin Mint issues and items from other private mints, as well as any other collectible in silver. Below are sample prices paid. If you have single items or other sets not mentioned here, I will quote you a price. Remember, silver prices change with the market. I buy all .925 sterling, .999 fine silver, complete sets, singles, 1-ounce bars, etc. All letters will be answered. Send offers.

AAACRC
P.O. Box 8061
Saddle Brook, NJ 07662

We Pay

American Art Treasures, sterling silver, 45mm, 100 Medals, Proof......800.00
Big Game Animals, sterling silver, 51mm, 20 Medals, Proof...........295.00
100 Greatest Masterpieces, gold on silver, 51mm, 100 Medals, Proof..1,650.00
Vatican Art Treasures, sterling silver, 45mm, 100 Medals, Proof.......850.00
History of Mankind, sterling silver, 51mm, 100 Medals, Proof........1,550.00

FRUIT JARS

I will buy fruit jars as listed. Jars must be in good condition with no cracks or bad stains and with the proper closures such as lids, clamps, etc. Some jars will be purchased at a reduced price without the proper closures. Please give descriptions and conditions of any other jars not listed here that you wish to sell.

Harry W. Fisher
Rt. 1, Box 197
Owensville, MO 65066

We Pay

Globe, aqua, pint	**10.00**
Globe, clear, any size	**10.00**
Globe, amber (brown), pint or ½-gal	**30.00**
Lightning, amber, pint	**20.00**
Lightning, green, any size	**30.00**
Lightning, aqua, ½-pint	**2.50**
Masons, any amber	**35.00**
Millville Atmospheric, aqua, pint	**15.00**
Millville Atmospheric, ½-pint	**32.00**
Millville Atmospheric, clear, any	**15.00**
Millville Improved, any	**25.00**
Princess	**6.00**
Perfection, aqua	**16.00**

We Pay

Lafayette	65.00
King, ½-gallon	5.00
King, ½-pint	6.00
Atlas E-Z Seal, amber	20.00
Canada Trademark N.S.E.W.	50.00
Jumbo Peanut Butter	1.00
Coronet	20.00
Royal, amber	32.00
The Dandy, amber	45.00
The Dandy, aqua, pint, or quart	20.00
Knowlton Vacuum	15.00
Fruit Keeper	18.00
Independent Jar (no lid OK)	20.00
Independent Jar, small pint (no lid OK)	25.00
Flaccus Bros.	30.00
Bee Hive	40.00
Clarke Fruit Jar Co.	25.00
Beaver, pint	20.00
The Darling	15.00

These Closures

We Pay

Metal Lid, F&J Bodine	5.00
Metal Lid, N. Whittelsey	5.00
Lightning Glass Lid, amber	2.50
Cast Iron Clamps (hold lid on)	3.00

I am wanting to buy blue or green pints or one-half gallon fruit jars. I will pay up to $3.00 each with tops. I would like jars other than Ball or Mason, as they are quite plentiful in Mississippi.

Betty Clark
Clark's Antiques
Rt. 2, Box 106
Houston, MS 38851

FURNITURE

We purchase cherrywood, oak, pine, and walnut antique furniture. We are especially seeking Victorian bedroom sets, sideboards, cylinder roll secretary-bookcases, marble-top tables, wardrobes, hall trees, and chests. All Eastlake-style pieces are also sought, plus turn of the century serpentine-front oak dressers, highboy chests, tall oak beds, sidy-by-side secretary-bookcases, all types and styles of desks, conference tables, early country cupboards, pie safes, jelly cabinets, corner cabinets, and step-back cabinets.

We also buy Fiesta ware and are seeking glassware as follows: Pattern Glass––Frosted Elephant, Jumbo; Carnival Glass––amethyst color, Singing Bird pattern.

Prices paid for furniture depend on condition; and all items will be considered regardless of condition. Glassware and Fiesta ware must be mint. Send photos, descriptions, and prices.

Plain & Fancy Antiques
239 S. Meridian
Newton, KS 67114
(316) 283-7009

For a brief period from 1900 to 1916, oak furniture in the Mission style (severely plain and rectilinear) was popular in this country. The best of it was handcrafted and well-made––an expression of the international Arts and Crafts movement that dominated much of the decorative arts in those years. The best Mission furniture

179

was designed and manufactured by Gustav Stickley (1857-1942) in Syracuse, New York. Other manufacturers included his brothers Albert, Charles, Leopold, and J. George. In East Aurora, New York, Elbert Hubbard (1856-1915) also produced bound books, furniture, and handmade household goods. Michigan manufacturer Charles Limbert rounded out the list of major producers.

We at 'Our Mission Antiques' purchase and sell desks, chairs, settees, etc. made by these major artisans. For assistance in the purchase or sale of Mission furniture call us. Remember, your mission is 'Our Mission Antiques.'

Leslie & Sydelle Sher
Our Mission Antiques
5210 Grange Hall Rd.
Holly, MI 48442
(313) 634-7612

GAMBLING
MEMORABILIA

I buy early gambling items in good-to-excellent condition. I am always looking for unusual items related to early gambling and gambling halls. Please forward descriptions, etc. for immediate reply.

R.E. White
7501 Grandview Ave.
Arvada, CO 80002

We Pay

Playing Card Mechanical Card Holdouts	200.00-800.00
Playing Card Trimmer, marked w/maker's name	100.00-500.00
Playing Card Trimmer, unmarked	100.00-300.00
Playing Card Corner Rounders, marked	300.00-600.00
Playing Card Corner Rounders, unmarked	200.00-400.00
Playing Card Dealing Boxes, metal only	200.00-800.00
Dice-Making Tools	100.00-500.00
Dice-Related Cheating Devices	300.00-500.00
Decks of Playing Cards, complete, pre-1890	50.00-100.00
Coin-Operated Trade Stimulators	100.00-500.00
Non-Coin-Operated Trade Stimulators	50.00-300.00
Faro Equipment	100.00-500.00
Keno Equipment, pre-1890	100.00-500.00
Dice Drops, wooden, pre-1920	50.00-100.00

In 1964 New Hampshire became the first state in modern history to initiate a lottery. Currently twenty-three states have lotteries, and several others are considering such games.

By constantly changing games to promote player interest and through advancements in technology, state lotteries have created huge varieties of tickets and related material. This has spawned a new collectible—the instant lottery ticket.

An instant ticket has an area that the player scratches off to see if he is an immediate winner. Prizes range from free tickets to thousands of dollars. In addition to this, however, the ticket also has a picture or design promoting the theme of the game. Past themes have included antique auto sets, zodiac designs, history, sports, holidays, and gambling gimmicks.

I will purchase your losing instant tickets. I am interested in single tickets or quantities, either past or current. Buying prices are determined by age and quantities. Please send information on what you have for sale.

William A. Pasquino
1824 Lyndon Ave.
Lancaster, PA 17602

I want to buy, sell, or trade old poker chips (ivory, clay, or casino, and tokens). No paper, plain, or plastic chips are wanted. I have two chip books for sale. Write or call for information.

Dale Syemour
11170 Mora Dr.
Los Altos, CA 94022

GARBAGE PAIL KIDS

Collector wants to buy Garbage Pail Kids gum cards. I am especially seeking cards from the first and second series.

Doug Bramlett
213 Belvin St.
Darlington, SC 29532-2105
(803) 393-7390 (nights & weekends)

GARDEN FURNISHINGS

Barbara N. Cohen is the site of The Historic James Russell Webster Mansion Inn. Garden furnishings are needed in order to complete the ambiance and whimsical feeling of our very special period gardens, as well as estates of others whom we supply. We are interested in statuary, urns, fountains, ornamental fences, gates, and related items. Please send photo, information, condition, price, and SASE.

Barbara N. Cohen Galleries
115 E. Main St.
Waterloo, NY 13165

GARDEN HOSE NOZZLES

Since the advent of the garden hose there have been garden hose nozzles. I buy all older brass and copper variations. I pay $1.00 each plus the postage or UPS. No inquiry needed. Check for payment sent day received.

Dale C. Schmidt
610 Howell Prairie Rd. SE
Salem, OR 97301
(503) 364-0499

GASOLINE PUMP GLOBES

Gasoline pump globes have been popular collectibles for many years. They once adorned local service-station pumps and were used on farms across the country. From 1914 through the 1950's, thousands of different oil companies used gasoline globes to advertise their gasoline, oil, and various other fuels. Today they are gone, except on the shelves of the people who collect them. There thousands of brands too numerous to mention, so I have chosen to list four general categories with an average price range. Generally more colorful globes or globes with airplanes, animals, or detailed graphics bring more than plain-looking ones. Please write or call, especially on special quotes for inserts only. I return all correspondence.

Scott Benjamin
7250 Franklin Ave. #216
Los Angeles, CA 90046
(213) 876-2056

We Pay

Plastic Body, glass insert.....................................**35.00-60.00**
Glass Body, glass insert.....................................**75.00-125.00**
Metal Body, glass insert.....................................**100.00-150.00**
One-Piece Glass, no insert...............................**250.00-1,200.00**

The automobile was an invention that had a great impact on Americans in the early 1900's. As years went by, autos became much more advanced and necessary. At the same time, the petroleum industry began its move toward supplying the fuel needed to power these autos. The first gas pumps were somewhat crude; but as time passed, the industry made the pumps more attractive and interesting. This was accomplished by several means, such as the manufacture of 'visible' gas pumps where one could actually see the gas that was being hand-pumped. Also, the various oil companies began using very brilliant and eye-catching advertising 'globes.' These globes, which were mostly made of glass, were generally located on top of the gas pump and displayed the company logo such as 'Standard Oil,' 'Texaco,' 'Ethyl,' etc. Usually these globes had a light inside them for advertising at night.

I have recently started a collection of these 'visible' gas pumps and the various globes that were used on these pumps. I will pay a fair price for any pumps, parts (nozzles, hoses, plates, etc.), and any globes. Prices also depend on condition.

Kent Blaine
P.O. Box 596
Winona, MS 38967

We Pay

Globes...**50.00 +**
Parts ....**5.00 +**

GOLD, GOLD-FILLED, SILVER

We buy all types of precious metals, including gold and silver coins, jewelry, and sterling silver.

Buck Fever Studio
Box 230
961 Country Club Rd.
Marion, VA 24354

We Pay

Eyeglasses or Sunglasses
    Marked 1/10 12K (must be all metal).............................**3.00**
    Marked 1/10 12K (w/plastic earpieces).........................**1.65**
    Marked 1/20 12K..**1.50**
Watch Cases, 25-year.......................................**Spot x .023**
Watch Cases, 20-year......................................**Spot x .0165**
Watch Cases, 10-year.......................................**Spot x .013**
Watch Bands, per ounce....................................**35¢-1.00**
R.G.P., per ounce...**50¢-1.00**
Gold-Plate, per ounce.......................................**5¢-50¢**
Unmarked Gold-Filled, per ounce...........................**50¢-2.50**
10K Gold-Filled..**Spot x .010**
12K Gold-Filled..**Spot x .013**
14K Gold-Filled..**Spot x .016**
10K..**Spot x .0195**
14K..**Spot x .0265**
16K..**Spot x .03**

We Pay

18K. . . . .**Spot x .33**
Sterling Silver Items. . . . .**85% Spot**
Silver Coins/War Nickels. . . . .**90% Spot**

We pay up to 100% of spot price for 12 through 24 karat gold and 90% of all silver in any form except electroplated. Send insured or registered mail for our offer. Include phone number if available.

Don Johnson
3808 Grand Ave. South
Minneapolis, MN 55409
(612) 824-1111

We will pay the highest prices for any of the items listed below. We will grade the item, advise you of our offer; and, if you should not accept, we will return your item intact and pay the freight both ways. We want any old broken jewelry, rings, watches, pendants, bracelets, brooches, any scrap gold or silver, old eyeglasses frames, or whathave you. Send for our offer. We will pay $7.00 each for any silver dollar minted prior to 1930.

B. Barn Antiques
515 E. Highway 66
P.O. Box 763
Tucumcari, NM 88401

GOLF MEMORABILIA

I am collecting old golf relics: all golf items before 1900, most items from 1900-1930, items from 1930-1960, unusual wood-shaft golf clubs, book, catalogs, and magazines. I also am interested in gadgetry used by retailers to sell golf clubs (items of this type was outlawed by the 'Rules of Golf' because they lacked uniformity). Also wanted are china, ceramic, pottery, and silver items (such as steins, tankards, pitchers, etc.) that are decorated with old golf scenes. The most desirable of these will carry quality trademarks such as Lenox, Weller, Spode, Royal Doulton, Dial O'Hare, etc. I also buy bronze statuary, old and unusual balls, bags, tees, old golf-ball molds, and other miscellaneous.

My serious collecting dates back twenty years. I obtained my first wood-shaft golf club at the age of six by bartering twenty golf balls with our local golf pro. I still cherish that club today. As a golfing family, we have won numerous amateur golf tournaments, and my children have had great success playing golf in high school as well as at the collegiate level. We collect rare, quality golf items. Let us hear from you!

Frank R. Zadra
Rt. 3, Box 3318
Spooner, WI 54801

We Pay		We Pay	
Lenox	300.00 +	Books, 1900-1929	10.00 +
Royal Doulton	125.00 +	Catalogues, pre-1928	10.00 +
Weller	150.00 +	Unusual Golf Clubs	25.00 +
Dial O'Hare	150.00 +	Rare Older Clubs	200.00 +
Bronzes	200.00 +	Gutty Ball Molds	100.00 +
Books, pre-1900	50.00 +	Miscellaneous Wanted	

Golf-ball markers have been made from most substances known to man. Hard rubber, plastic, pot metal, brass, silver, and even gold have been formed into small, easily-carried objects with which a golf ball's location on the green could be marked.

I collect all types of golf-ball markers with my greatest interest lying in those identifiable to a particular course, famous golfer, or tournament. Please write describing markers you have and the price you expect to receive for them.

Norman R. Boughton
1356 Buffalo Road
Rochester, NY 14624

Identifiable to: **We Pay**

Walter Hagen...10.00
Bobby Jones..10.00
Arnold Palmer...5.00
Jack Nickalus...5.00
U.S. Open Tournaments...1.50
Masters Tournaments...1.50
U.S. Amateur Tournaments..1.50
LPGA Championship...1.50
PGA Championship..1.50
Augusta National Course...1.00
Pebble Beach Course...1.00
Oak Hill, Rochester...1.50
Other Courses..50¢

Identifiable to Companies   **We Pay**

Plastic...10¢
Base Metals...50¢
Silver...3.00
Gold...5.00

HALLOWEEN

Born of Scotts and German traditions brought over by immigrants at the turn of the century, Halloween is the most truly American holiday. Jack-o'-lanterns, cats, witches, owls, vegetable people, ghosts, and trick-or-treaters are some of the motifs we are seeking to find in items such as candy containers, toys, lanterns, noisemakers, dolls, wall decorations, Bogie books, post cards, favors, and anything else Halloween-related that is fun, fantasy, and representative of the holiday. Good prices are paid for good pieces, much less for common or damaged items.

C.J. Russell
P.O. Box 499
Winchester, NH 03470

	We Pay
Dennison Bogie Book	10.00
Tin Noisemaker	2.00
Candy Container	10.00-300.00
Witch Ball	40.00+
Jack-O'-Lantern, tin, on stick w/paper insert	200.00
Crepe Paper Costume	15.00+
Jack-O'-Lantern (depends on size & features)	8.00-200.00

Halloween is the second leading holiday in collecting; Christmas, of course, is first. Germany started producing a large variety of Halloween party favors and decorations at the turn of the century. Japan and America followed in the late 1920's.

The most desirable items are made in Germany. The German characteristics are the purple German stamp, dull orange color (instead of bright orange), heavy composition materials, and comic faces. We buy German Halloween pieces and some Japan or American items if they are in excellent condition. Listed below are some of the items we buy. Please note that the jack-o'-lanterns must still have the original tissue-paper face intact.

John & Jenny Tarrant
67 May Valley
Fenton, MO 63026

We Pay

Papier-mache Jack-O'-Lantern.......................................**15.00**
Papier-mache Cat Lantern...**25.00**
Papier-mache Skull or Devil Lantern.............................**35.00**
Cardboard Jack-O'-Lantern...**10.00**
Cardboard Cat, Skull, or Devil.....................................**15.00**
German Composititon Lantern.......................................**55.00 +**
German Cardboard Lantern...**20.00**
German Cardboard Cat Lantern......................................**30.00**
German Cardboard Devil or Skull Lantern.......................**40.00**
Candy Containers:
    Papier-mache Cat, 3"..**10.00**
    Papier-mache Cat, 7"..**35.00**
    Papier-mache Owl, 3"..**10.00**
    Papier-mache Witch on Pumpkin, 7".....................**15.00**
    Composition Cat..**50.00 +**
    Composition Witch...**50.00 +**
    Composition Jack-O'-Lantern...............................**40.00 +**
    Composition Devil...**55.00 +**
    Composition Skull...**55.00 +**
    Composition Pumpkin Head Man...........................**55.00 +**
Wall Decorations:
    Cat Dressed in Clothes..**10.00**
    Pumpkin Dressed in Clothes.................................**10.00**
    Embossed Thick Cardboard..................................**10.00**
Crepe Paper Nut Cups...**.3.00**
Crepe Paper Pumpkin Figure...**20.00**
Crepe Paper-Dressed Spook Figure.................................**25.00**
Crepe Paper-Dressed Witch Figure.................................**25.00**
Crepe Paper-Dressed Pumpkin Figure.............................**25.00**
Early Halloween Game...**12.00**
Early Halloween Party Book..**10.00**
Early Halloween Dennison Bogie Book............................**20.00**

HATPINS AND HATPIN HOLDERS

Women wore hatpins as a decorative and functional device for a very short period of time from about 1850 through 1925. The history of the hatpin is a fascinating one of women's liberation and the influence of the great periods in art.

Many collectors of hatpins choose to specialize in one of the three great periods of the hatpin: Victorian, Art Nouveau, and Art Deco. Collectors also search for sterling silver, gold, and pins created by the greats—Faberge, Tiffany, and Lalique. Hatpin holders were made to hold the hatpins of the day. The holders were usually part of a dresser set, but today are often found alone. We buy large collections or just one hatpin or hatpin holder.

Joezane
715 Avalon Ct.
San Diego, CA 92109
(619) 488-8170

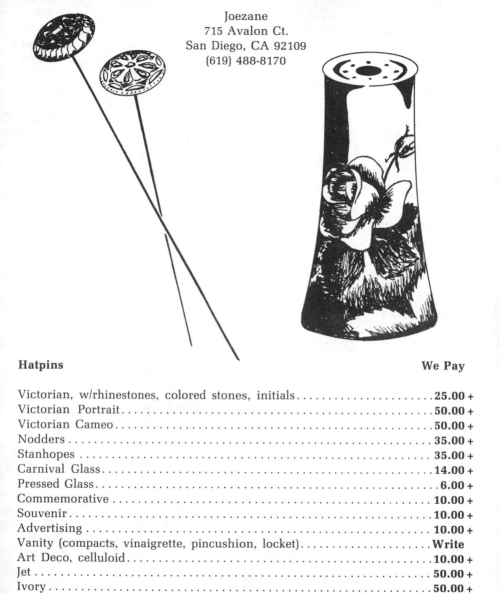

Hatpins

We Pay

Victorian, w/rhinestones, colored stones, initials	25.00 +
Victorian Portrait	50.00 +
Victorian Cameo	50.00 +
Nodders	35.00 +
Stanhopes	35.00 +
Carnival Glass	14.00 +
Pressed Glass	6.00 +
Commemorative	10.00 +
Souvenir	10.00 +
Advertising	10.00 +
Vanity (compacts, vinaigrette, pincushion, locket)	Write
Art Deco, celluloid	10.00 +
Jet	50.00 +
Ivory	50.00 +
Figurals, various materials	25.00 +
Art Nouveau Designs	15.00 +
Art Nouveau Sterling Figurals & Faces	30.00 +
Gold & Gemstone	50.00 +
Art Nouveau by Tiffany, Faberge, Lalique	Write

Hatpins and Hatpin Holders

Unger Brothers, sterling, signed.................................40.00+
Charles Horner, sterling...40.00+
Georg Jensen, sterling...40.00+
Kewpie...Write
Plique-a-Jour..Write
Shells (from the beach)..10.00+
Enamels..20.00+
Satsumas...45.00+

Holders   We Pay

R.S. Prussia..100.00+
R.S. Germany...40.00+
Rosenthal..50.00+
Pickard..85.00+
Belleek..65.00+
Bavaria..40.00+
Nippon...30.00+
Sterling Silver..65.00+
Silverplate..30.00+
Kewpie...Write
Figurals...Write
Schafer & Vater..75.00+
Carnival Glass..100.00+
Royal Bayreuth..100.00+

HATS

It is an historical fact that the hat is the true symbol of woman's emancipation. Adopting this masculine attire was their symbol of equality. Women were recognized and duly respected by the various hats they wore. A different hat was needed for the country, church social, motor car ride, afternoon wedding, and even for sleeping at night.

We buy all women's and children's hats that represent 'millinery madness'--large brims, small brims, feathered, flowered, or beaded--the crazier the better! We also purchase millinery supplies such as trims, ribbon, and ornaments. I will buy hats that need restoring and have a special liking for large straws.

Linda Hood
5828 Brentwood Trace
Brentwood, TN 37027

We Pay

Women & Children's Hats, large brim, pre-1900................**4.00-30.00**
Women & Children's Hats, small brim, pre-1900................**4.00-20.00**
Hats, 1900-1920..**4.00-18.00**
Hats, 1930-1950..**2.00-10.00**

HAWAIIANA

Since Captain Cook's first voyage to the Hawaiian Islands in 1778, tourists have been taking things of every conceivable nature home with them. From stone bowls to hula dolls, Hawaiian things have found their way to Alaska, Indiana, and other points east and west.

We're buying Hawaiiana. What have you? Ship for immediate cash offer or describe in first letter (a picture helps) for exact price quote. Typical prices for specific items are listed below. We prefer pre-1960's items in mint or near-mint condition for highest prices.

Cedric Felix
46 Market St.
Wailuku, HI 96793

We Pay

Artifacts, stone	10.00-5,000.00
Poi Pounders	100.00-1,000.00
Wooden Bowls	10.00-1,000.00
Post Cards	50¢+
Quilts	100.00-2,000.00
Coins	20.00-2,000.00
Tokens	1.00-800.00
License Plates	2.00-200.00
Matsun Items	5.00-50.00
Old Photos	1.00-100.00
Hula Items	5.00-150.00
Bottles	5.00-500.00
Badges	5.00-100.00
Maps	5.00-500.00
Autographs	5.00-250.00
Records	2.00-50.00
Stone Carvings	50.00-5,000.00
Wood Drums	200.00-2,500.00+
Feather Capes	1,000.00+
Photo Albums	20.00+
Scrapbooks	20.00-100.00
Documents & Deeds	10.00-150.00
Stock Certificates	1.00+
Statehood 1959	1.00+
Newspapers, through 1940's	1.00+
Oil Paintings	50.00-1,000.00
Whaling Items	10.00-500.00
Miscellaneous Items	**Name Your Price**

Today Hawaiian collectibles and vintage jewelry are becoming very popular. Pre-50's pieces are especially sought. The following are just a few of the specific items we would be interested in: vintage jewelry (fish pins, earrings, necklaces, and bracelets, along with palm trees, tropical flowers, and hula dancers), and Hawaiiana (menus, chalk and ceramic hula dancers, palm tree items, Arts Hawaii etched glass, TV lamps, tablecloths, scarves, and Hawaiian shirts)—all items pre-50's. We would prefer photos for inspection and will return if not interested. Prices are dependent upon particular merchandise; we buy mainly for resale.

Flamingos Hawaii, Inc.
75-5744 Alii Dr.
Kailua-Kona, HI 96740

HOLIDAYS AND CELEBRATIONS

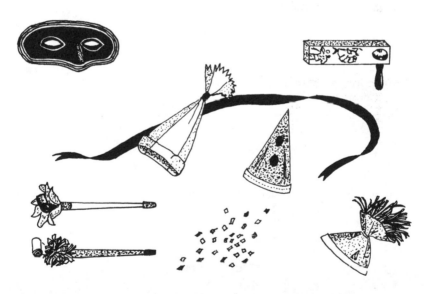

While Christmas ornaments grow in popularity on the secondary market, we collect ornaments and decorations for all celebrations (holiday and ceremonial)—from Valentines Day to Christmas, from christenings to weddings. Items wanted range from antique holiday candy containers to bridal magazines (1900 through 1970), from new Hallmark Christmas ornaments to Madame Alexander bridal dolls, from pinups of movie stars with holiday props to antique wedding photos, from 1950's Ginny dolls in Valentine dresses to baby dolls in christening gowns, from videos of old 50's sitcoms with a holiday theme or skit to videos or stills of famous weddings on screen or off, from Steiff white Easter Bunnies or Christmas reindeer to books on debutantes or Miss America, from antique Valentines to children's illustrated books on holidays, from an Irish leprechaun figures to Nancy Ann Storybook 1st Communion Dolls, from old Raphael Tuck Santa Claus post cards and books to Hallmark May Day maypole music boxes, from Anna Lee Uncle Sam dolls to bridal figures, etc., etc.

Ann Bergin
P.O. Box 105
Amherst, NH 03031

We Pay

Bridal Magazines	1.00
Madame Alexander Bridal Dolls	200.00
Wedding Books	10.00
Candy Containers	25.00 +
Hallmark Ornaments	25.00 +
Hollywood Pinup w/Holiday Props	2.50
Ginny Doll, nude, 1947-57	50.00
Ginny Doll Clothes, 1947-57	15.00
Steiff Easter Bunny	50.00
Steiff Reindeer	50.00
Antique Valentines	5.00
Antique Santa Claus Books	10.00
Nancy Ann Storybook Dolls	5.00
Anna Lee Character Dolls	10.00 +
Antique Post Cards	2.50

I want to buy Easter egg boxes for the annual collector Easter eggs for the years 1971, 1972, and 1977. These boxes are satin lined and hold the annual collector Easter egg that is put out by the Noritake Company each year at Easter time. The boxes must be in good condition.

Shirley Baumann
2109 Floyd Ave.
Iowa Falls, IA 50126
(515) 648-4051

I collect pre-1940 holiday cards and Christmas cards with patriotic-military themes of any age. Of particular interest are old post cards, cards, or letters mailed during the Chistmas season which have 'lick-and-stick' package stickers on them. These stickers are not to be confused with 'seals' put out by various charitable organizations. I pay $4.00 per one-hundred pre-1940 holiday cards and 25¢ each for Christmas cards with patriotic themes.

E.L. Sikinger
695 Greencrest St. NE
Salem, OR 97301

HOMER LAUGHLIN DINNERWARE

I am buying Homer Laughlin Mexican decaled dinnerware including these patterns: Mexicana, Hacienda, Conchita, Arizona, and Max-i-cana on Century, Nautalis, Yellowstone, Swing, Eggshell, or Kitchen Kraft shapes. Photos of some of the items are included in the Huxford's 6th edition *The Collector's Encyclopedia of Fiesta* book. Serenade pastel and Tango multi-colored dinnerware pieces are also wanted. See *The Collector's Encyclopedia of Fiesta* book for photos of these, too. Pieces should be in mint condition, free from chips and cracks, and decals should not be scratched or worn. Prices in the Huxford's book can be used as a guide, but some examples are listed below. Please write concerning any pieces you may have for sale to:

Robert Green
P.O. Box 222
San Anselmo, CA 94960

We Pay

Flat Soup, Serenade..**10.00**
Dinner Plate, Tango, 10″..**10.00**
Dinner Plate, Conchita, any shape, 10″............................**15.00**
Teapot, Hacienda..**10.00**
Butter Dish & Cover, Hacienda....................................**100.00**
Handled Cream Soup, Mexicana......................................**15.00**
Kitchen Kraft Fork, Spoon, Cake Server, Conchita.................**125.00**
Dinner Plate, Riviera, 10″..**20.00**

HORSE-RACING MEMORABILIA

I have been buying for over thirty years for my private collection. I am looking for programs from race tracks that are no longer in existence or programs that have 'name' horses such as Kentucky Derby programs prior to 1970. Also sought are older racing games, for which I will pay up to $500.00 depending on condition. Other items I am looking for are racing books, photos, tobacco cards, post cards, prints, plates, badges, passes, and other items related to thoroughbred horse racing. I would like to receive a complete description of items for sale and prefer to have the seller list the dollar amount they would like to receive. Any thoroughbred items considered.

Gary L. Medeiros
1319 Sayre St.
San Leandro, CA 94579

We Pay

Kentucky Derby Glasses, 1938-1955...........................**5.00-150.00**
Kentucky Derby Programs, pre-1955..............................**5.00 +**
Thoroughbred Programs, pre-1950................................**2.50 +**
Tobacco Cards...**50¢-4.00**
Post Cards...**25¢-10.00**
Thoroughbred Books..**2.00-300.00**
Thoroughbred Games, pre-1940..................................**15.00 +**
Thoroughbred Photos of Name Horses............................**2.00 +**
Offical Press Badges..**2.50-10.00**
Miscellaneous Paper Items...................................**50¢-50.00**

HULL
POTTERY

The Hull Pottery of Crooksville, Ohio, produced many fine examples of commercial pottery from the early 1900's to the late 1950's. Production from 1950 to the company's closing in 1986 centered on casual servingware items and floristware. Today Hull's delicate matte floral examples are widely collected, and most collectors demand mint examples. I also buy Hull items other than those listed below.

Brenda Roberts
Rt. 2
Marshall, MO 65340
(816) 886-8888

We Pay

Ash Tray, Parchment & Pine	50.00
Bank, figural cat, 11″	50.00
Basket, Open Rose, 10″	100.00
Basket, Woodland, 10″	100.00
Basket, Butterfly, 10″	50.00
Basket, Serenade, 12″	75.00
Basket, Wildflower No. Series	100.00
Basket, Bow Knot, 12 ″	200.00
Bookends, Orchid	200.00
Cookie Jar, Cinderella, Blossom	50.00
Cookie Jar, Vegetable	40.00
Cereal Ware, Delft, 15-pc set	500.00

We Pay

Double Cornucopia, Woodland.......................................95.00
Double Cornucopia, Water Lily....................................50.00
Ewer, Orchid, 13"...125.00
Ewer, Woodland, 13"...150.00
Ewer, Dogwood, 13"..150.00
Jardiniere, Bow Knot, 9"......................................150.00
Jardiniere, Iris, 9"..100.00
Lamp Base, Woodland, 13"......................................100.00
Lamp Base, Orchid...125.00
Lavabo, Butterfly, w/hanger....................................50.00
Nested Bowls, Vegetable, 5" through 9".........................45.00
Pitcher, Poppy, 13"...150.00
Pitcher, Bow Knot, 13"..175.00
Pitcher, Rosella, 9"...65.00
Pitcher, Serenade, 13"...95.00
Planter, Open Rose, mermaid...................................125.00
Plaque, advertising, 5x11"....................................500.00
Plaque, Red Riding Hood.......................................500.00
Vase, Wildflower, 15"...100.00
Vase, Tropicana, 14"...90.00
Vase, Iris, 16"...150.00
Tile, decorated, 4x4" or 3x6"..................................25.00

The Hull Pottery was started in 1905 in Crooksville, Ohio, and over the next eighty years produced hundreds of different pieces of stoneware, art pottery and kitchenware.

From the 1930's through the 1950's Hull produced their most famous line of art pottery vases, jardinieres, baskets, planters, and ewers. Most famous of these are the Tulip, Bow-Knot, Iris, Dogwood, Orchid, Poppy, and Calla Lily lines in pastel shades with an attractive matte finish.

Later in the 1950's, they also produced numerous glossy novelty planters as well as glossy Woodland and Magnolia art pottery. Hull is famous for their Little Red Riding Hood line of cookie jars, creamers, and various other kitchen items. They continued to produce high-gloss items into the 1960's such as Ebb Tide, Parchment and Pine, banks, and all types of kitchenware and florist items. The firm closed in 1986. I am also interested in lines of Hull pottery other than the ones listed. Write or call for prices.

D&M Collectibles
3714 Lexington Rd.
Michigan City, IN 46360
(219) 879-0409 (evenings)

Calla Lily	We Pay
Vase	10.00-35.00
Ewer	35.00 +

Tulip	We Pay
Vase, small	10.00-15.00
Vase, large	20.00-50.00
Ewer, large	50.00 +

Orchid	We Pay
Bookends	100.00-175.00
Ewer, large	75.00 +
Vase, small	10.00-15.00
Vase, large	20.00-75.00
Lamp Vase	75.00-125.00

Iris	We Pay
Vase, small	10.00-15.00
Vase, large	15.00-50.00 +
Ewer, large	75.00-125.00

Dogwood	We Pay
Vase, small	15.00-25.00
Vase, large	25.00-50.00
Ewer, large	125.00-175.00

Poppy	We Pay
Vase, small	15.00-25.00
Vase, large	25.00-100.00
Ewer, large	125.00-175.00
Wall Pocket	50.00-75.00
Basket	100.00-125.00

Open Rose	We Pay
Vase, small	10.00-15.00
Vase, large	20.00-40.00
Ewer, large	100.00-150.00
Lamp Vase	75.00-100.00
Basket	50.00-100.00

Water Lily	We Pay
Vase, small	10.00-12.00
Vase, large	15.00-30.00
Basket	50.00-75.00

Bow-Knot	We Pay
Vase, small	20.00-30.00
Vase, large	50.00-100.00
Basket	125.00-200.00
Ewer, large	200.00 +
Jardiniere, large	175.00 +
Wall Pocket	20.00-50.00
Advertising Plaque	300.00 +

HUMMELS

When most people hear the name 'Hummel,' they think of small porcelain figurines of children and animals; but there are many other types of Hummels—plates, bells, clocks, lamps, ash trays, bookends, candle holders, candy boxes, fonts, music boxes, porcelain dolls, wall plaques, and wall vases. All were created from the artwork of Sister M.I. Hummel.

Berta Hummel was born in Lower Bavaria, Germany, in 1909; she entered the convent in 1931. Franz Goebel asked the convent for permission to convert her sketches of sparkling children and serene religious figures into three-dimensional form.

This marked the beginning of a relationship between Sister Maria Innocentia, the convent, and W. Goebel that continues today, long after her death in 1946.

Every Hummel item is marked on the base 'M.I. Hummel' and on the bottom with the Goebel mark. The Goebel crown mark was used from 1935-1941, the full bee mark from 1941-1955, the stylized bee from 1955-1968, the three-line mark from 1968-1971, the one-line Goebel with the stylized bee above the 'e' from 1971-1979, and the current Goebel mark.

We purchase and sell all types of Hummel products. Rarity, general condition, and Goebel mark on the bottom of the piece determine its price. We also purchase broken and damaged figurines. Please call or write us.

Cindy Oakes
34025 W. 6 Mile
Livonia, MI 48152

We Pay

Apple Tree Boy or Girl, Hum 141/3/0 or Hum 142/3/0, Current Mark....	**85.00**
Bookworm, Hum 8, Current Mark	**135.00**
Chick Girl, Hum 57/2/0, Current Mark	**135.00**
Doctor, Hum 127, Current Mark	**90.00**
Goose Girl, Hum 47/3/0, Current Mark	**105.00**
Happy Birthday, Hum 176/0, Current Mark	**140.00**
Just Fishing, Hum 373, Current Mark	**135.00**
Little Nurse, Hum 376, Current Mark	**150.00**
Meditation, Hum 13/0, Current Mark	**150.00**
On Holiday, Hum 350, Current Mark	**120.00**
Postman, Hum 119, Current Mark	**125.00**
Figurine Price Comparison of Different Marks:	
Merry Wanderer, Hum 7/11, Crown Mark, 8″	**1,500.00-2,000.00**
Merry Wanderer, Hum 7/11, Full Bee, 8″	**1,000.00-1,500.00**
Merry Wanderer, Hum 7/11, Stylized Bee, 8″	**750.00-850.00**
Merry Wanderer, Hum 7/11, Three-Line, 8″	**650.00-750.00**
Merry Wanderer, Hum 7/11, Goebel w/Bee, 8″	**600.00-750.00**
Merry Wanderer, Hum 7/11, Current Mark, 8″	**600.00**

'M.I.Hummel' figures have been collected and given as gifts since 1935. These delightful hand-painted porcelain figurines of children have captured the hearts of young and old alike. They are carefully handcrafted by skilled artisans of the W. Goebel Porzellanfabrik Company of Rodental, West Germany, and are based on the original art work of Sister Maria Innocentia Hummel. These charming figurines can easily be identified by looking for the 'M.I.Hummel' signature that almost always appears on the base. The Goebel Company trademark of a bumblebee within the letter 'V' will also appear on the bottom part of most figures. Originally selling for less than $10.00 each, some of these figurines are now worth $500.00

or more if they are in good condition. An incised number on the bottom of the base also helps identify the figurine as a genuine Hummel. We are offering to buy your Hummel figurines acquired before 1957 at the following prices.

Col. Gerard Ham
Appraiser & Auctioneer
P.O.Box 405
Freehold, NJ 07728
(201) 780-1342

We Pay

Mother's Darling, Hum 175	**100.00**
Spring Cheer, Hum 72	**60.00**
Madonna Plaque, Hum 48/V	**500.00**
Joyous News, Hum 27/3	**600.00**
Forest Shrine, Hum 183	**400.00**
Birthday Serenade, Hum 218/0	**250.00**
Swaying Lullaby Plaque, Hum 165	**300.00**
Begging His Share, Hum 9	**125.00**
Hello, Hum 124	**75.00**
Adoration w/Bird, Hum 105	**1,000.00**
Auf Wiedersehen (Boy w/Hat), Hum 153	**600.00**
Whitsuntide, Hum 163	**450.00**
The Skier, Hum 359	**100.00**
Good Shepherd, Hum 42/I	**1,000.00**
Latest News, Hum 184	**150.00**
Stormy Weather, Hum 71	**200.00**
Signs of Spring, Hum 203/2/0	**200.00**
Umbrella Girl, Hum 152 B	**250.00**
Chimney Sweep, Hum 12	**35.00**
Waiter, Hum 154	**125.00**
Girl w/Frog, Hum 219/2/0	**1,000.00**
Kiss Me (Doll w/Socks), Hum 311	**150.00**
International Hummel Children, Hum 809 to Hum 968, each	**1,500.00**

I am very interested in buying any Hummel figurines with marks older than the current mark. They must be in good condition. These can be any size, but I'm mostly looking for 4½″ through 6″ sizes. I am also interested in some of the limited editions and club pieces. I would like to find a Pleasant Journey for under $300.00 as well as Chapel Time.

Audrey Domenick
7735 E. Jefferson Place
Denver, CO 80237
(303) 779-5221

HUNTING AND FISHING

Wanted: hunting, fishing, trapping, guide license, and pin-back buttons. The buying prices listed are for buttons in good-to-excellent condition. Buttons with stains, cracks, or other damage may be purchased at reduced prices depending on the extent of damage. Those from certain southern states (as South Carolina, Florida, Georgia, and Mississippi), and Ohio will bring the highest prices. Buttons with birds, fish, or animals also bring better prices.

James C. Case
Box 1076
Corning, NY 14830
(607) 962-2504

NY License Buttons	Resident H,F,T, or combination	Non-Resident	Resident Deer
1917	30.00-70.00	75.00-150.00	
1918-1925	5.00-15.00	25.00-75.00	
1926-1941	2.00-6.00	15.00-100.00	8.00-25.00
1927 Deer		35.00-50.00	100.00-200.00
Trapping:			
1940-1941	100.00-150.00	100.00-300.00	
Paper License:			
1905-1907		50.00-300.00	
1908-1916	3.00-25.00	25.00-50.00	

NY license buttons	Alien	Guide
1917	200.00-400.00	50.00-100.00
1918-1925	200.00-300.00	40.00-75.00
1926-1941	100.00-300.00	25.00-60.00
1927 deer	200.00-400.00	
Trapping:		
1940 & 1941	200.00-400.00	
Paper license		
1905-1907	100.00-300.00	
1908-1916	25.00-100.00	

PA Fishing buttons	Resident	Non-resident	3-5 day tourist
1923	40.00-75.00	100.00-200,00	
1924-1927	15.00-40.00	40.00-75.00	
1928-1934	5.00-12.00	15.00-35.00	20.00-40.00
1935-1940	2.00-4.00	10.00-25.00	15.00-30.00
1941-1959	1.00-3.00	4.00-15.00	4.00-15.00

PA Hunting backtags	Resident	Non-resident	Deer & special issue
1901-1912		150.00-300.00	
1913	100.00-200.00	150.00-300.00	
1914-1923	20.00-75.00	30.00-100.00	30.00-100.00
1924	15.00-40.00	40.00-75.00	20.00-50.00
1925-1928	8.00-15.00	20.00-40.00	10.00-35.00
1929-1937	3.00-15.00	10.00-30.00	10.00-25.00
1938-1941	2.00-3.00	6.00-15.00	3.00-10.00

Other state hunting,fishing pinbacks	Resident H,F, or combination	Non-resident or alien
1890-1905	25.00-100.00	30.00-100.00
1906-1918	25.00-75.00	30.00-75.00
1919-1927	10.00-30.00	15.00-45.00
1928-1940	5.00-25.00	7.00-40.00
1941-1946	2.00-20.00	5.00-30.00

Other state hunting, fishing pinbacks	Resident deer/trap or guide	Non-resident or alien deer/trapping
1890-1905	25.00-100.00	40.00-100.00
1906-1918	25.00-75.00	25.00-100.00
1919-1927	15.00-50.00	20.00-75.00
1928-1940	5.00-25.00	10.00-50.00
1941-1946	3.00-20.00	5.00-25.00

INDIAN ARTIFACTS

American Indian artifacts from the prehistoric era have long been in demand, and many new collectors have entered the field in recent years. In the Midwest, the major collectible categories are flint, stone, and slate, with flint artifacts the most common and slate artifacts the most scarce. Flint includes points, drills, and knives, while stone includes axes, celts (ungrooved axes), and various tools like adzes and gouges. Slate objects include the rare birdstones, Atl-atl weights and/or bannerstones, pendants, and gorgets.

While size and material are of importance and artifact types are much in demand, the major consideration is condition. This is because many artifacts were broken or damaged in use, and farming equipment adds to the destruction. This in turn decreases artistic value; complete artifacts are in short, the most valuable.

The following artifact types are being sought, and preference is given to those from Ohio and neighboring states. All items must be old and authentic, and no modern reproductions are desired. Since prehistoric American Indian artifacts are all different, no exact price can be given; so as close a range as possible is provided here. Entire collections are now being purchased.

Lar Hothem
P.O. Box 458
Lancaster, OH 43130

Stone	We Pay
Axes, ¾ groove	5.00-50.00
Axes, full groove	5.00-30.00
Axes, trophy type	50.00-100.00
Celts	2.00-30.00
Adzes, Adena	5.00-30.00
Adzes, ¾ groove	5.00-30.00
Celts, Hematite	2.00-5.00

Slate	We Pay
Pendants	5.00-50.00
Gorgets	1.00-50.00
Birdstones	Write
Atl-atl Weights	10.00-75.00
Bannerstones	Write
Effigy Stones	10.00-50.00

Flint	We Pay
Birdpoints	1.00-4.00
Triangles	1.00-7.00
Eastern Clovis	10.00-100.00
Lanceolates	10.00-100.00
Bifurcates	3.00-20.00
Paleo Unifaces	1.00-10.00
Snubnose Scrapers	1.00-2.00
Archaic Types	3.00-50.00
Hopewell	2.00-20.00
Adena	2.00-20.00
Drills, T-top	5.00-15.00
Drills, Pin	2.00-10.00

This is a broad term for **arts and crafts** produced by the North American Indians. I specialize in the Pueblo Indians of the Southwest and Western Plains. I do not purchase stone items such as arrowheads, axes, etc. Today there is a resurgence of interest in the American Indian––his way of life, his history, his culture, and his artifacts. It is important to respect his culture––past and present. We must avoid certain items related to secret ceremonies (Hopi masks and religious articles and feathered items of all tribes). Therefore in offering your items for sale please take this into consideration. Perhaps a museum is best suited for certain items. You may want to consult Lar Hothem's book, North American Indian Artifacts.

John W. Barry
Indian Rock Arts
P.O. Box 583
Davis, CA 95617
(916) 758-2561

We Pay

California Baskets	25.00-2,000.00
Southwest Baskets	75.00-300.00
Pueblo Pottery	25.00-500.00
Pueblo Paintings	50.00-300.00
Hopi Katchinas (pre-1950)	125.00-400.00
Drums (pre-1940)	100.00-200.00
Indian Photographs	3.00-200.00
Indian Books	5.00-50.00
Northwest Coast Carvings	50.00-500.00
Bows & Arrows (pre-1900)	100.00-500.00

Fascination with Indian artifacts often comes from cowboy and Indian culture-related movies and TV shows, for instance, 'Indian Summer.' Most artifacts are made from natural materials (plants or minerals), and each tool, weapon, ornament, etc. is unique and of excellent quality. American Indian artifacts are even collected and appreciated in Europe. My interest is in both pre-historic and historic items. Other items than those listed below will also be considered. Please send pictures.

World City Inc.
6935 James Ave. South
Minneapolis, MN 55423

We Pay

Beaded Items	5.00-500.00
Pottery	10.00-1,000.00
Rugs	15.00-1,500.00

Indian Artifacts

The Pueblo Indians of Arizona and New Mexico are known for their artistic abilities, especially pottery. Sometime around 700 A.D. ancestors of the present day Pueblo Indians began to farm, giving up their hunter-gatherer life style. Within a few hundred years they were making beautifully decorated pottery for trade and ceremonies. Even their plain, undecorated pottery was expertly executed. This tradition survives to this day at known villages such as the Hopi Polacca, Santo Domingo, Zia, San Ildefonso, Cochiti, Santa Clara, and others.

We buy all types of Pueblo pottery from the Southwest made during historic times. The prices below are for pottery in good condition. Value varies depending on condition, size, origin, documentation, design, aesthetics, and market demand. We especially want pottery made before 1940. You may want to consult Lar Hothem's book, *North American Indian Artifacts*, and John Barry's book, *American Indian Pottery*.

John W. Barry
Indian Rock Arts
P.O. Box 583
Davis, CA 95617
(916) 758-2561

We Pay

Black Polished Jars & Bowls	**25.00-500.00**
Multi-Colored Jars & Bowls	**20.00-500.00**
Undecorated Gray or Brown Jars	**10.00-75.00**
Storyteller Figurines	**10.00-200.00**
Pottery, Signed by:	
Maria Martinez or Lucy Lewis	**100.00-1,200.00**
Margaret Tafoya or Marie Chino	**100.00-1,200.00**

The Skookum doll was manufactured and distributed by the H.H. Tammen and Arrow Novelty Company from 1914 to about 1950. Usually paper labels reading 'Trademark registered/Skookum (Bully good) Indian/U.S.A./patented' are afixed to the soles of the feet. Later dolls have plastic moccasins, and the mark is imprinted there. The dolls vary in size from 6″ to 36″. Early doll heads were made of dried apples and composition; later heads are plastic, and wigs are usually horsehair. Bodies are built of straw and legs are wooden. A blanket is always folded around the body to indicate arms. The earliest dolls have leather boots; felt eventually replaced leather, after which their boots were made of plastic. Skookums almost always look to the right, and many wear a necklace of glass beads. I am looking for large Skookum dolls. They must be in good condition.

Donna McMenamin
5001 Woodway #1002
Houston, TX 77056

We Pay

24″ Man or Woman..**100.00**
36″ Man or Woman..**150.00**

IRONS

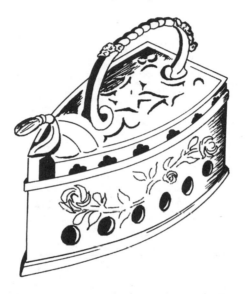

Antique pressing irons come in great variety: some plain, and some elaborate. If it was used for ironing, I am a buyer. Some types to look for are box irons, charcoal irons, gasoline irons, natural gasoline irons, fluting irons, boxed sets, and iron-related accessories. The most common iron is the flatiron. Even these are desirable if they have interesting handles or decorations.

I can't use broken, repaired, or heavily rusted pieces. I do not buy trivets or large tailor irons. These sample prices are for irons in fine condition.

Non-electric toy irons are especially interesting. Send sole tracings of little irons. On all offerings, fully describe markings, handle shape, and type of iron. Photos are always helpful. I reply to every offer accompanied by a stamped self-addressed envelope. Tell me the price and condition. I will buy one iron or a collection.

Carol Walker
The Iron Lady
100 NE 5th St.
Waelder, TX 78959
(512) 665-7166

We Pay

Art Deco Electric Iron..**20.00 +**
Saunders 'Silver Streak' Pyrex Electric Iron......................**200.00**
Manville Crank Fluter..**175.00**
Old Toy Swan Iron..**50.00**
Swan Iron, 5"..**175.00**
Hatter's Iron..**35.00 +**
Enterprise Promotional Iron, ¾".................................**125.00**
Flip-Over Oil-Fired Iron...**100.00**
Slant-Handle Gasoline Iron w/Pump in Handle......................**75.00**
Miniature Tailor Iron..**50.00 +**
Eagle Crank Fluter w/3¼" Rollers................................**150.00**
Dion Rocking Fluter..**200.00**
Combination Sadiron & Fluter.....................................**70.00**
Elgin Rocking Fluter...**75.00**
Henry A. Doty Fluter...**65.00**
Howell's Wave Fluter...**90.00**
Crown Plaiter..**75.00**
Green Coleman Gasoline Iron......................................**40.00**
Red Coleman Gasoline Iron..**60.00**
M.A.B. Cook Polisher...**70.00**
Boxed Set of Irons...**100.00 +**
Soapstone Iron...**60.00**
W.M. Ferris Wire-Handle Iron.....................................**50.00**
Iron Heated on Gas Jet...**55.00**

JEWELRY

I am collecting 1930's through 1950's rhinestone jewelry. All stones must be bright, 'alive,' with none missing. Pieces do not have to be backmarked, but I am looking for quality designs and sets. I prefer clear, pink, purple-amethyst, and black.

I am buying Victorian jewelry to the 1920's—rolled gold, gold-filled, Art Nouveau sets, or individual pieces. Condition can be good to medium since I do minor replacements of clasps, links, etc.

I want sterling silver puff heart charms found on bracelets from 1900 to 1940 and lockets that are gold-filled, rolled gold, or silver. I also want white gold Deco filigree rings from 1890 to 1920 with small a diamond (or diamonds) or other original stones. I will buy by the piece, a full collection, or stock from a retiring dealer.

Betty Rundell
Rt. 1, Box 444
Leander, TX 78641

We are currently buying vintage jewelry circa 1850 through 1940. We are looking for all types in good-to-mint condition in gold, gold-filled, and sterling to 800 silver. Pieces may be with or without precious or semi-precious stones or have enamelwork. In addition, we also buy a wide range of quality costume jewelry such as Bakelite, jet, amber, etc. These pieces may be signed or unsigned.

We pay top, fair-market dealer prices for everything we buy. We have been buying through the mail successfully for over fifteen years from thousands of happy sellers. Many are served on a repeat basis. Please write with confidence to:

Ancient Arthur
111 Parkway
Cleveland, MS 38732

As a professional weed scientist, I have long been fascinated by plants, particularly thistles. When I began attending antique shows and flea markets, I found that a wide variety of items including glassware, china, utensils, and pottery were to be found bearing a thistle motif. What really caught my interest was jewelry in the shape of thistles!

I have since learned that this motif is particularly popular in Scotland but it has also been used by many American companies including Trifari and Coro. Thistle-shaped pieces can be found as pins, brooches, pendants, and earrings in a wide variety of materials including stone, tin, sterling, plastic, Bakelite, enamel, and in many combinations. For my interest, condition is more important than intrinsic value.

The prices listed give a general idea of what I have paid—but who knows what else is out there. Feel free to send items priced or a 'make-offer' basis. These prices are for jewelry shaped like thistles.

Richard Old
316 Harrison
Pullman, WA 99163

	We Pay		We Pay
Plastic	1.00-5.00	Sterling, small	5.00-10.00
Tin	1.00-5.00	Sterling, large	10.00 +
Bakelite	3.00-8.00	Glass 'Stones'	10.00 +
Enamel	8.00 +	Semi-Precious Stones	20.00 +

I am looking to by a baroque pearl ring, by artist Peter Unger, who made and sold these rings at a show in Cocoa, Florida. Baroque pearls are 'bumpy' in texture and iridescent or white in color. Unger's rings have a silver Art Nouveau setting, and the pearl looks as though it is nestled in a flower similar to a lily. I want a rather large ring––at least an inch in length. I can use sizes 6½ through 7½. For one like this, I will pay $80.00. Call me collect after 6 p.m., or leave me your number to call back.

Doris J. Reissig
(305) 724-2375

Like most women, I love gold and silver jewelry––especially if enameled. In fact, I love all enameled items in gold and silver. My favorite subjects are pretty ladies, golfers, tennis players, cats, dogs, and horses. Of course, any spectacular piece of jewelry will be cherished. When writing about items for sale, please describe completely as to condition, etc. A photo is helpful. Items must be priced in first letter. Listed below are pieces I wish to buy with prices I will pay.

Lenore Monleon
33 Fifth Ave.
New York, NY 10003

	We Pay
Sterling Pin, Russian wolfhound, 1½″	30.00
Sterling Match Safe, enameled golfer in knickers, loop to wear on chain	50.00

14K Gold Pin, round w/enameled kitten **60.00**
Cigarette Case, w/nude dancer in garden **75.00**

We are buying butterfly pins or brooches, preferring jeweled pins labeled with the maker's name such as Trifari, Weiss, Eisenberg, etc. However, enameled, cloisonne, filigree, and metal butterfly pins are also solicited. We prefer photos or pictures produced with copying machines found at your local library or post office. Please send details as to size, condition, asking price, etc.

D.M. Diabo
19953 Great Oaks Circle S.
Mt. Clemens, MI 48043

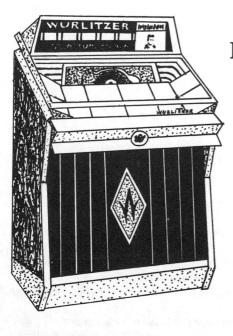

JUKE BOXES

Wurlitzer juke boxes made from 1939 through 1948 are the most valuable juke boxes around. These were twenty-four selection machines, designed to play 78 RPM records. In 1950 Seeburg became the more desirable because it could play one-hundred selections and was designed to use the 45 RPM record. From 1950 to 1965 Seeburg was king.

A newsletter for juke box collectors (Juke Box Collector, RR#5, Box CD, Des Moines, Iowa 50317) is published each month for the purpose of bringing collectors together to buy, sell, and trade machines, parts, and gossip. A sample copy is $3.00, and a one-year's subscription is $24.00.

Listed are the items that I am looking for and the prices I will pay. If you have other juke boxes, please send a listing and I will contact you if I am interested. The prices listed are for juke boxes in good condition.

Rick Botts
2545 SE 60th Ct.
Des Moines, IA 50317

We Pay		We Pay	
Wurlitzer 500	500.00	Wurlitzer 1100	1,500.00
Wurlitzer 600	600.00	Wurlitzer P-10	600.00
Wurlitzer 700	700.00	Rock-Ola 1422	700.00
Wurlitzer 800	900.00	Rock-Ola 1426	800.00
Wurlitzer 750	1,000.00	Rock-Ola 1428	600.00
Wurlitzer 780	1,000.00	Seeburg M100A	400.00
Wurlitzer 850	3,000.00	Seeburg M100B	450.00
Wurlitzer 950	4,000.00	Seeburg M100C	500.00
Wurlitzer 1015	2,500.00	Seeburg M100W	400.00
Wurlitzer 1080	1,500.00	Wurlitzer 42	1,500.00

KANSAS

For a short time from the late 1800's to around 1912, there were many glass and pottery plants in the area of south-east Kansas. Abundant natural gas (which began to run out by 1912) attracted two well-known fruit jar producers (Mason and Ball) to the Coffeyville area. Other glass plants (whose products are unknown today) also located there, as well as several window-glass plants. A few of the products known to have been produced in the area are listed below. Also listed are sample miniature bricks which were put out by as many as a dozen or so different brick and tile plants.

Here as everywhere else in the early days of the United States, a popular way for a merchant to advertise was to sell or give away a ceramic or glass souvenir featuring a view of a local park, a building, or a special event to visitors and local customers as well. Most of these plates, vases, jugs, etc. were made in Germany and England, as were view post cards and other items. Some souvenirs carried the message 'souvenir of (name of town, state).' We buy these as well as similar items with street names, buildings, etc. found on them. We also want post cards, calendars, or any advertising material.

214

Listed below are glass, pottery, souvenir, advertising, and related items we buy. We will buy other items as well as damaged pieces if contacted for prices. Please note that my home town, Dearing, may be spelled Deering.

Billy & Jeane Jones
P.O. Box 82
Dearing, KS 67340
(316) 948-6389

We Pay

Premium Glass Fruit Jar, Coffeyville, KS, pint or quart	7.00
Premium Glass Fruit Jar, Coffeyville, KS, ½-gallon	8.00
Premium Glass Fruit Jar, Coffeyville, KS, 1-gallon	20.00
Premium (Plain) Fruit Jar	5.00
Premium 'Improved' Jar	8.00
Premium Lid w/Coffeyville	3.00
Premium Wire Clip	2.00
Premium Magazine Ads, Etc.	1.00
Lace Edge Glass Plate, w/'Premium Jar,' 7"	25.00
Lace Edge Glass Plate, w/'Ball Jar,' 7"	35.00
Lace Edge Glass Plate, w/'Pioneer Glass,' 7"	20.00
Ball, The Mason, or Premium Wooden Boxes	10.00
Coffeyville, Independence, Cherryvale, Buffalo, Etc., Miniature Bricks	10.00
Any Tin or Cardboard Advertising Signs	Write
Stoneware Jug, bottom incised 'Made in Coffeyville' brown	25.00
Stoneware Crock or Churn, bottom incised 'Made in Coffeyville', brown	20.00
Terraco O.&H. Coffeyville, KS; Pitcher, brown pottery	15.00
Coffeyville Pottery & Clay Co. Miniature Jug	25.00
Coffeyville Pottery & Clay Co. Crock, Churn, or Jug, smaller than 4-gal	18.00
Coffeyville Pottery & Clay Co. Crock, Churn, or Jug, 4-gallon or larger	12.00
Coffeyville Stoneware Co. Minature Jug	25.00
Coffeyville Stoneware Co. Crock, Churn, or Jug, smaller than 3-gallon	15.00
Coffeyville Stoneware Co. Crock, Churn, or Jug, 3-gallon or larger	12.00
Any Stoneware w/Sponge Decoration, Advertising	Write
Magazine Ads, Etc.	1.00
Advertising Signs, tin, cardboard, paper	Write
Large Pictures, Post Cards	Write
Calendar Plate, Dearing or Deering, early 1900's	20.00
Calendar Plate, Coffeyville, Independence, early 1900's	10.00
Calendar Plate, Jefferson, Tyro, Chanute, early 1900's	15.00
Calendar Plate, Caney, Wayside, early 1900's	12.00
Calendar Plate, Parsons, Oswego, Altamont, early 1900's	10.00
Calendar Plate, Mound Valley, early 1900's	10.00
Calendar Plate, Dearing or Deering, scenic view, early 1900's	10.00
Calendar Plate, towns as listed above, early 1900's	5.00
Vases, Jugs, etc., towns as listed above, Dearing	10.00
Vases, Jugs, etc., other south-east KS cities	5.00

We Pay

Heisey Custard or Other Glass Souvenir Items, Dearing............... **20.00**
Dearing Marked Smelter Ash Tray.................................. **10.00**
Dearing Marked Smelter Picture.................................... **5.00**
Dearing Marked White's Amusement Park Plate.................... **10.00**
Dearing Marked Ruby-Stained Toothpick.......................... **15.00**
Dearing Marked Items, other than mentioned above................ **Write**
View Post Cards, Dearing, early 1900's........................... **4.00**
View Post Cards, Coffeyville, Chanute............................ **2.00**
View Post Cards, other south-east KS towns....................... **1.00**
Calendars, Dearing... **5.00**
Calendar, other towns.. **3.00**
Sterling Spoons, Dearing... **20.00**
Sterling Spoons, other south-east KS cities....................... **Write**
Carlton Hall Bottle Caps... **15¢**
Advertising Signs, Tokens, Etc................................... **Write**

KNIVES

During America's frontier years, the knife was the prized possession and constant companion of the migrating settlers. By the early 1900's, there were over two thousand knife manufacturers in America. Today only a handful remain. One of the important criteria collectors look for is a stamp on the blade that identifies it as having been made by a knife manufacturer no longer in business.

Pocket knives come in many sizes, shapes, styles, and handle materials. Today this variety and a relatively low price make the pocket knife a fascinating collectible. Pocket knife collectors now number in the thousands.

Not all old pocket knives are valuable. Quality, condition, maker, size, pattern, and handle material are all factors to be considered. Pocket knives are graded from mint condition. Therefore, sharpening them only reduces their value.

The following price list is reflective of prices now being paid by me for various brand names and handle materials in undamaged, excellent condition. I will buy other brands not listed as well as damaged items if you contact me for prices. I buy single items and entire collections.

Bill Campesi
Box 140
Merrick, NY 11566

We Pay

Remington	5.00-75.00
Remington 'Bullet Shield'	5.00-400.00
Winchester	5.00-150.00
Schrade	3.00-30.00
Schrade Cutlery Co. & Walden	5.00-45.00
Ulster	3.00-30.00
Utica	3.00-25.00
Imperial	4.00-40.00
Cattaraugus	5.00-40.00
Ka-Bar	5.00-150.00
Kara-Bar 'Dog's Head Shield'	10.00-250.00
Case (various markings)	5.00-125.00
Pocket Knife w/Second Blade in Shape of a Small Hatchet or Meat Cleaver	25.00-250.00
Keen-Kutter	4.00-35.00
E.C. Simmons, Keen-Kutter	5.00-60.00
Marbles	10.00-275.00
Canton	5.00-40.00
Novelty	5.00-40.00
Boker, U.S.A.	4.00-35.00
Boker, Germany	4.00-30.00
Challenge	5.00-45.00
Golden Rule	5.00-50.00
Bridge	5.00-50.00
I.X.L.	5.00-60.00
Advertising Items	**Will Quote Price**
Any Over-Sized Cutlery Items	50.00-500.00

I have been collector of pocket knives since 1972. I also collect related items —razors, books, daggers, hunting knives, and anything relating to knives such as swords. I belong to the leading National Knife & Collectors Association (the biggest knife club around) whose members number eighteen thousand at last count. My knives must be in A-1 shape. I buy sell, trade, and keep some for a collection. I am mostly intested in U.S., English, and German knives. The two magazines I take are *Knife World* and *The Blade*. I buy knives at flea markets, garage sales, and from want ads in hobby magazines. I also give advice to anyone who writes. Lots of brands have little value. The popular brands to collect are Remington, Boker, Winchester, Russell, Western, Marbles, Ka-Bar, I.X.L., Wm. Rogers, Wade & Butcher, Holly, and Miller. Lots of unnamed brands are in demand. As a knife collector, buyer, or trader it is necessary to own and study up-to-date research books and to attend knife shows throughout the United States.

Machairologist
Gerald A. Shaw
1928 Causton Bluff Rd.
Savannah, GA 31404

LABELS

We buy all pre-1910 labels, especially cigar box and fruit crate labels. We are paying very attractive prices for sample labels, sample books, or lithographer's proofs of cigar box labels. We will pay over $1,000.00 for the largest hard-bound box-maker's sample books. We also buy cigar labels of the more plentiful variety. Please send a sample along with the quantity that is available.

We buy pictorial cigar bands––especially band collections and sample band books. We are paying very interesting prices for complete pre-1910 sets.

We buy all pre-1910 fruit crate labels; in particular, citrus labels from California and Florida. Sample books and collections are actively sought; we will pay high prices in order to obtain them. We also purchase related ephemera dealing with the early citrus industry (invoices, maps, promotional items, advertising cards, and post cards) .

Firecracker labels and related ephemera are wanted. We are buying only pre-1910 American cigarette cards. As a rule of thumb, any card 2½″ x 3″ was made after 1910 and is of no interest. Also we are buying can labels, other graphically pleasing labels, foreign coins, tokens, currency, match safes, cigar cutters, stocks and bonds (especially those made by lithographers who made labels, write for list), baggage labels (airline, ships, hotels), Cinderella posters, advertising stamps, credit cards, Victorian scrapbooks, die-cuts, and trade cards.

If you have any of the items mentioned, please contact us before you sell. Obtain other estimates, but for the best price contact Cerebro. Please send items for sale securely packaged and insured or by registered mail. If you prefer not to send items, please send a photocopy and description of any damage. We will travel to inspect large estates. Cash is always available. References are available upon request.

Cerebro
David & Barbara Freiberg
P.O. Box 1221
Lancaster, PA 17603
(717) 656-7875

Cigar Bands   **We Pay**

Presidential Sets...**40.00 +**
Playing Cards Set..**100.00 +**
Flags of the World, ea...**1.00**

Cigar Labels   **We Pay**

Lime Hilm Club..**50.00**
Champions...**250.00**
Sample Books...**25.00-2,500.00 +**
Foreign Coins, per lb...**3.00**

LALIQUE

We are interested in purchasing vases and perfume bottles made by Lalique. We are especially interested in the older pieces, pre-1940, made by Rene Lalique, but we will consider modern pieces, as well. Listed are some sample buying prices.

Randall B. Monsen
P.O. Box 1503
Arlington, VA 22210

We Pay

Perfume Bottle, Le Jade	**1,200.00**
Perfume Bottle, Epines	**300.00**
Perfume Bottle, Camille, blue	**800.00**
Perfume Bottle, Panier de Roses, frosted	**450.00**
Perfume Bottle, Pan	**650.00**
Vase, Serpent	**2,500.00**
Vase, Aras	**850.00**
Vase, Pierrefonds	**2,000.00**
Vase, Rouces	**650.00**
Vase, Ceylan	**1,250.00**

Lalique, crystal from France, was made from 1902 to the present day. The majority of pieces produced had Art Deco motifs and were either partially or totally frosted. Popular themes are female nudes and flowers.

We pay according to age and condition. Please send photo or complete description for instant quote from private collector.

C.T. Peters, Inc.
P.O. Box 2120
Red Bank, NJ 07701

LAMP SHADES AND FRAMES

Holophane crystal glass lamp shades have been made in Newark, Ohio, since 1896. We are particularly looking for those made for home use, but we buy the industrials, as well. The shades can be either frosted or clear and come in a variety of fitter sizes from 1⅝" to 5⅝". Most are signed 'Holophane.' Some carried a paper label. Many other manufacturers made similar shades. Gill, Franklin, Wellington, Gillander, Pagoda, and Magian are but a few. We will buy shades from any of these companies.

At the time of writing, these are average prices for shades in at least very good condition. We will purchase one through one thousand pieces. We also buy old fixtures and lamps. Please contact me for current needs and prices.

Dan Johnson
7 S. Orleans Rd. Rte. 28
Orleans, MA 02653
(617) 255-8513

1⅝″ Fitter Size, without fitter...**5.00**
3¼″ Fitter Size, Holophane E9 or larger...........................**75.00**

I want to buy brass lamp frames with brass fonts for 10″ or 14″ hanging lamps (aka swinging lamps or parlor lamps). These lamps were popular in the Victorian era, but their popularity declined with the use of electrical power. The upper rim held a glass shade whose diameter was either 10″ or 14″, and often it was hung with glass prisms. The lower carriage held a font for coal oil. Sometimes both the upper rim and the lower carriage were decorated with colored jewels or fancy metalwork.

I will pay up to $300.00 for a nice old brass lamp frame. Please send a photo of the frame and your asking price.

Juanita Wilkins
P.O. Box 1884
Lima, OH 45802
(419) 227-2163

I want to buy lamps and lamp parts. I offer lamp services such as repair and wiring, brass and metal refurbishing, shade repairing, converting to electric, replacement of all missing lamp parts, lamps made from all items, etc. I pay top prices for kerosene lamps and parts. Write or telephone concerning what you have for sale.

E.W. Pyfer
218 N. Foley Ave.
Freeport, IL 61032
(815) 232 8968

LAMPS

I published my book on Aladdin kerosene lamps in 1971 and one on Aladdin electric lamps in 1987. Aladdin kerosene lamps were first sold in 1908 and electric lamps were made from 1930 to 1956. Both the kerosene and electric Aladdins are highly collectible. I am particularly seeking the following kerosene lamps which sold from 1909 to 1914 and will pay the highest prices for them. Prices are for Aladdin electric lamps in original condition—no chips or damage.

J.W. Courter
Rt. 1
Simpson, IL 62985
(618) 949-3884

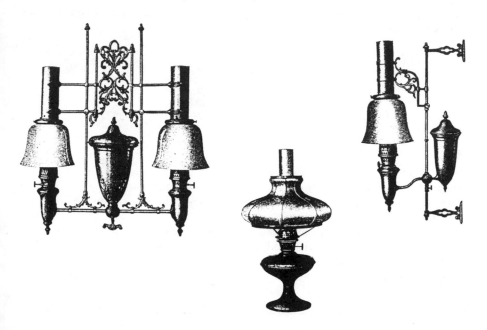

We Pay

G-16 Figurine, clear or Alacite...............................	**150.00-200.00**
G-16 Figurine, color.......................................	**300.00-400.00**
G-77 Figurine, clear.......................................	**300.00-400.00**
G-130 Figurine, clear......................................	**300.00-400.00**
G-130 Figurine, color......................................	**600.00-800.00**
Aladdin Dealer Signs.......................................	**25.00-50.00**
Aladdin Advertising Posters, Signs, Banners................	**25.00-75.00**
Aladdin Catalog on Electric Lamps, pre-1937................	**50.00-100.00**
Pleated Paper Shades for Electric Lamps....................	**25.00-75.00**
Angle Lamps (table model, student type)...................	**300.00-400.00**
Angle Lamps, colored chimneys.............................	**100.00-200.00**
Angle Lamp, etched chimneys...............................	**50.00-60.00**
Original Catalogs...	**50.00-75.00**
Old Advertising Posters, Signs............................	**50.00-60.00**

Early American lamps have become a favorite of antique collectors. Betty lamps were used in the time of the pharoahs. Roman soldiers carried iron cruises. Our own pioneers used them in their covered wagons. On American frontiers, candles were the preferred light but often took too much time to make. The Betty lamp could use any kind of oil or grease. Often bear grease was used, and it smelled to high heaven. Wicks of braided grass could be burned. Ordinarily the lamp was made of iron, but it could also be made of tin, brass, or any other convenient metal. My shop is named 'The Betty Lamp' and is located in the mining country of the high Rockies. I buy all kinds of primitive lighting devices used before 1850 when kerosene lamps became common sources of light.

Betty Schoon
The Betty Lamp
Box 1038
Georgetown, CO 80444

We Pay

Betty Lamp, wrought iron, pear-shaped, curved handle, sliding top......**50.00**
Double Cruises, same as above, w/2nd pan beneath top one...........**75.00**
Sticking Tommies, candle holders of wrought iron, shaped w/point to
    stick into wood..**45.00**
Miner's Carbide Lamps, usually brass, w/reflector & hook
    handle to hook onto front of miner's hat........................**30.00**
All Kinds of Oil or Grease Burning Lamps (skaters, loom, lace makers,
    peg, kettle, Argand, whale oil)...........................**25.00-250.00**

Although Thomas A. Edison invented the electric lamp in 1879, it was not until two or three decades later that electric lamps replaced kerosene lamps. From about 1910, Aladdin lamps with a mantle became a mainstay of rural America. Gaslight, introduced in the early nineteenth century, was used mainly in homes of the wealthy and public places until the early twentieth century. Most fixtures were wall or ceiling mounted, although some table models were also used. Top of the line lamps were made by Pairpoint, Tiffany, Bradley & Hubbard, and Handel.

Daniel Batchelor
R.D. #3, Box 10
Oswego, NY 13126
(315) 342-1511

We Pay

Pairpoint, 13" diameter dome shade, engraved base, 21"...........**1,750.00**
Tiffany, 14½" Arabian, deep blue lustered glass, LCT Favrile base,
    marked L.C. Tiffany.......................................**3,400.00**

Bradley & Hubbard, 15″ diameter shade, panel lamp.................**325.00**
Handel, 18″ diameter dome, chipped ice shade, reverse painted, 24″..**2,300.00**

Fluid-burning lighting devices of 1850 through 1930 are still popular decorating items in modern homes of nearly all styles and decor. These items were made by such companies as Rochester, Aladdin, Miller, Plume & Atwood, Bradley & Hubbard, etc. When properly restored, they are quite attractive and can even result in a love affair with old lighting, but don't tell my wife.

Send me your tired, your poor huddled masses (lamps and parts). We buy and restore all manner of antique lighting devices in almost any condition—from single items to entire collections. We can repair most any device, therefore old parts are needed for the following common and unique lamp types: brass and nickel table, hanging, angle, Hitchcock, piano, student, etc. Particularly desired are lamps and lamp parts in the rough. Prices will vary according to condition, scarcity, completeness, whether electrified or in original (oil burning) condition, and if a single item or a quantity is bought. Stress cracks in the brass lower the price considerably. Call or write to me for a price quote on unique types of lamps such as angle, student, piano, Harvard, Betty, etc., or parts such as smoke bells, filler caps, ceiling hooks, prisms, or other hardware.

Richard & Barbara Dudley
1412 Forest Lane
Woodbridge, VA 22191
(703) 491-2878

We Pay

Brass/Nickel Table Lamp..................................**5.00-30.00**
Brass/Nickel Table Lamp (embossed)......................**20.00-40.00**
Burners Center Draft.......................................**5.00-15.00**
Burners Flat Wick..**3.00-10.00**
Hanging 'L' Frame...**15.00-40.00**
Hanging 'L' Frame w/14″ Ring.............................**25.00-70.00**
Hanging 'L' Pressed Font..................................**15.00-30.00**
Hanging 'L' Ceiling Extender..............................**20.00-35.00**
Shades 7″, 10″, or 14″ Opal...............................**10.00-35.00**
Shades 7″, 10″, or 14″ Decor..............................**20.00-75.00**
Chimney (fancy) **2.00-10.00**

I want to buy miniature oil lamps. I am looking for old, colored glass night lamps for resale with burners, chimneys, and wicks to burn kerosene, and matching colored glass shades, as pictured in Ruth Smith's *Miniature Lamps*, books I and II. I also need clear glass lamps with names such as Little Harry, Little Favorite, Little Crown, or Wonder embossed on the front. These measure about 2″ high and have 1″ milk glass chimneys. Return privilege is essential. Please include SASE for reply.

Ann McDonald
Box 7321
Arlington, VA 22207

LICENSE PLATES

I collect cast aluminum license plate attachments also known as crests, piggy backs, and add-ons. These attachments were made of a heavy sand-cast aluminum. The purpose of these crests was largely promotional. They were sold for about fifty-nine cents in all tourist meccas. Florida must have been like heaven for the traveling salesman who wrote orders for these crests. It seems every city and beach in Florida had a crest boasting its name and slogan. Examples would be: 'Miami Beach,' 'Land of Sunshine' or 'World's Playground.' They all seemed to have adornments flanking both sides of the name, for instance, Florida with a palm tree on one side and a sailfish on the other.

I have sufficient 'Miami,' 'Miami Beach,' and 'Florida.' I want license attachments from other Florida cities, towns, and beaches, as well as cities and towns from other states. I am paying $10.00 to $25.00 depending on rarity and condition. I will also consider broken ones if reparable. Please contact me for prices.

Edward Foley
227 Union Ave.
Pittsburgh, PA 15202

The specific keychain license plates I am seeking are painted brass with 'B.F. Goodrich' or 'Goodrich Tires & Batteries' embossed on the reverse side. They are approximately 1½″ x ⅝″, not to be confused with the smaller type in a metal case that was mailed to vehicle owners from 1942 through 1971 by the Disabled Vets for the purpose of soliciting donations. B.F. Goodrich tags were available for 10¢ apiece through promotions held in their stores from 1942 through 1971. Although 10¢ sounds insignificant today, the depression syndrome still hung on, and many people would not freely spend a dime on a keychain license plate.

I am seeking B.F. Goodrich tags from all states for my collection. Prices paid for them vary depending on paint, condition, and rarity (tags from lesser-populated states are scarce). Price guides frequently value these at $15.00 to $20.00 each. Please inquire as to prices paid for specific states and conditions.

Edward Foley
227 Union Ave.
Pittsburgh, PA 15202
(412) 761-0685

LIGHT BULBS

I buy unusual light bulbs. Some of the types I prefer are are described in the following text. Neon bulbs have a design inside a clear glass bulb which glows in color (or colors) when lit. Of the Christmas bulb variety, I buy figurals, bubble lights, and matchless stars (plastic or glass prisms that completely enclose a bulb). Another type of bulb I want to buy is of colored glass with a tip on the top round end and/or with a carbon filament (one to four large filament loops). I want no coated glass (these usually show scratches when held to the light), auto, or industrial bulbs.

I also seek electrified displays such as hardware store stands and artificial Christmas trees––anything with sockets that I can use to display lighted bulbs.

Please write if you think you may have something. Include a photo or sketch and price. Thank you.

Joseph R. Kimbell
29-A Rivoli St.
San Francisco, CA 94117

LINENS

We are currently buying quality vintage linens of all types (natural fibers only) circa 1850 through 1939. We prefer items in whites or ecru with lots of handwork or lace in good-to-mint condition. No colored embroidery or items with holes are acceptable; however, we will accept items with age stains. We pay top dealer prices for all items. We love items in Battenburg, Normandy, Pointe de Venice, Duchesse, drawnwork, cutwork, Nandutti, Brussels laces, etc.

We have been buying through the mail successfully for over fifteen years from thousands of happy sellers. Many we deal with on a repeat basis. Please write with confidence.

Ancient Arthur
111 Parkway
Cleveland, MS 38732

Lace, linens, and needlework represent the styles and tastes of days gone by as much as furniture, jewelry, or clothing. Popular collectibles today, these beautiful 'labors of love' from days past can be pressed into service again, displayed as a collection, or adapted to items of feminine apparel and home decor.

From homespun to satin, from cross-stitch to tatting, the adornment of clothing and items for the home made––and still make––life 'more beautiful.' Anyone who does handiwork knows and appreciates the hours and expertise put into these beauties.

It would be difficult to list the many types of handiwork sought. Prices are based on very good or easily-repaired condition for a piece of average size. Please contact us for prices where the item is either not listed or is in seriously damaged condition. Add $1.00 if item is in original box.

Sam & Jan Spencer
3671 E. Highland
Highland, CA 92346
(714) 864-3662

We Pay

Aprons, handmade, w/crochet	2.00-15.00
Victorian Aprons, handmade	2.00-15.00
Bedspreads & Coverlets, Battenburg	50.00+
Bedspreads & Coverlets, crochet	15.00-75.00
Christening Gowns & Caps, tucks, lace inserts	up to 20.00
Christening Gowns & Caps, & Slips, ornate	up to 40.00
Christening Caps	1.00-10.00
Collars & Cuffs, w/handmade lace	2.00-25.00
Collars & Cuffs, w/embroidery	1.00-10.00
Crib Covers & Quilts	25.00-65.00
Doilies, crochet	25¢-3.00
Doilies, Battenburg	3.00+
Doilies, knit	25¢-3.00
Doilies, filet crochet	50¢-5.00
Doilies, tatting	1.00-10.00
Gloves, crochet	50¢-5.00
Handkerchiefs, w/embroidery	25¢-2.00
Handkerchiefs, w/crochet	50¢-4.00
Handkerchiefs, w/tatting	1.00-10.00
Handkerchiefs, w/figures	25¢-2.00
Napkins, damask	25¢-2.00
Napkins, w/crochet trim	50¢-3.00
Napkins, w/embroidery	25¢-2.00
Napkins, w/tatting, fancy	1.00-5.00
Petticoats (women's or girls')	1.00-15.00
Pillowcases, w/crochet trim	1.00-5.00
Pillowcases, w/tatting	2.00-10.00
Pillowcases, w/embroidery	50¢-5.00

We Pay

Quilts	Depends on Patterns, Colors
Scarves & Runners, Battenburg	5.00-40.00
Scarves & Runners, crochet	2.00-20.00
Scarves & Runners, embroidery	1.00-10.00
Scarves & Runners, tatting	5.00-40.00
Tablecloths, Battenburg	25.00-100.00
Tablecloths, crochet	15.00-75.00
Tablecloths, w/embroidery	5.00-50.00
Tablecloths, w/cutwork	5.00-50.00
Show Towels, w/drawnwork	50¢-7.00
Show Towels, w/crochet	50¢-7.00
Show Towels, w/embroidery	50¢-6.00

We wish to purchase linens of exceptional quality with as much handwork as possible. Unusual pieces are desired, such as button-back pillow shams, baby pillow shams, fancy tablecloths, napkins, fancy white hankies, English christening gowns, bonnets, etc. Please send a description and photo if possible. Prices paid depend on condition. No holes or tears can be accepted.

Linda & Ken Ketterling
3202 E. Lincolnshire
Toledo, OH 43606

We Pay

Continental Shams, lace trim, pair	50.00+
English Night Dress Case, embroidery & cutwork	20.00-40.00
Christening Gown, pintucks & eyelet	30.00+
Madeira Teacloth	15.00-25.00
Wedding Hanky, handmade Battenburg lace trim	15.00-25.00

I buy good quality lace and bed and table linens. All kinds of laces interest me except heavy crochet. I don't want things with rips or holes, but stains don't bother me as I can safely and professionally clean them. Price ranges are listed, but exact prices depend upon size and workmanship. All letters enclosing a LSASE will be answered. I will buy by the piece or box lot. Damaged pieces will be considered at the lower prices if repairable.

Pahaka September
19 Fox Hill
Saddle River, NJ 07458

We Pay

Lace Curtains, older	10.00-75.00
Lace Bedspreads	10.00-75.00
Pillow Shams, large	5.00-35.00
Pillow Cases, w/handiwork	3.00-15.00
Baby Pillowcases	3.00-15.00
Sheets, fancy	5.00-45.00
Sheet & Pillowcase Sets	15.00-50.00
Tablecloths, fancy	10.00-75.00
Napkins, ea.	1.00-5.00
Towels, fancy	1.00-7.00
Runners, fancy	4.00-20.00
Other Linens	3.00 +
Needlework Pictures	5.00-50.00
Lace Yardage	Write
Lace Collars	4.00-75.00
Bridal Veils & Headpieces (1880-1930's)	10.00-50.00
Hankies	1.00-20.00

LITHOPHANES

Lithophanes are porcelain transparencies which reveal their detailed three-dimensional pictures only when they are lighted up from behind. There were many sizes, shapes, and usages for these during the Victorian period. Some were hung in windows for the sun to shine through. Others were used as lamp shades for night lights, table lamps, floor lamps, fairy lights, or hall lights. More were used in souvenir cups and saucers, steins, tea cups, and complexion fans. Some were colored but most were simply pure white porcelain, and only the shading created by the varying thickness of the porcelain revealed the picture.

Mr. Laurel G. Blair
P.O. Box 4557
Toledo, OH 43620

We Pay

Plaques, 4x5″	70.00
Plaques, 9x10″	150.00
4-Sided Shades	280.00
5-Sided Shades	450.00
Single Cast Shades, small	200.00
Single Cast Shades, medium	450.00
Single Cast Shades, large	700.00
Fairy Lights	300.00

Lithophanes, Berlin transparencies, look like a piece of bisque. When one is held to the light, the picture it contains becomes apparent. Sometimes lithophanes are found in tea sets, lamp shades, saki glasses, or beer steins. I am interested in all pieces except the cups and steins.

Donald Gorlick
P.O. Box 24541
Seattle, WA 98124

LITTLE GOLDEN BOOKS

Older Little Golden Books are becoming popular collectibles. They were originally published in 1942 for 25¢ and are currently selling for under $1.00. The original editions were published with dust jackets and contained forty-two pages. The bindings on the books vary according to the book's age. Earlier books had a blue or golden binding, while the later books have a silver spine.

The books range in number from 1 to 600. The series of numbers from 100 to 200 have two books (different titles) per number. There is also a Disney series from 1 to 140, indicated by a 'D' in front of the number, many of which were put out by the Mickey Mouse Club. In addition, an 'A' or activity series exists numbered from A1 through A52.

The edition of the books can be determined by a letter (A to Z) on the bottom right-hand side of the book's last page. The books usually range in price from $3.00 to $7.00 depending on edition and condition.

Gloria Flager
1330 Elser Dr. S.E.
Salem, OR 97302

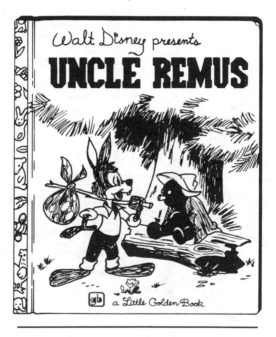

Little Golden Books seem to have a place in almost everyone's childhood memories. The first Little Golden Books were printed in 1942 by Simon and Schuster. Approximately the first thirty-five books were published with a blue binding and a dust cover. No cover price was printed on these books until later when a book with a brown binding printed with a cover price of 25¢ was produced. Next to follow was the familiar gold binding and prices that gradually increased from 29¢ to 39¢ to 49¢, etc. The edition/printing of each book is shown in one of two possible places—on the first page of the book or on the last page in the lower right corner next to the spine. (A meaning 1st, B meaning 2nd, etc.)

I collect all the Little Golden Books with a cover price of 25¢, 29¢, or older—also the 39¢, 49¢, etc. books that may be a 1st printing. All books must be in at least good condition with all pages and covers intact. Some titles are harder to find and are therefore worth more than others. Prices vary from $2.00 to $10.00 and higher depending on title, condition, edition, dust covers, etc.

Laura Fadem
6116 S. Gary Ave.
Tulsa, OK 74136

MAGAZINES

When the now immortal film classic *The Wizard of Oz* was first released back in 1939, the people at Metro-Goldwyn-Mayer Studios set out to launch one of the most extensive publicity campaigns ever. A major part of the plan to exploit the movie included an unprecedented amount of magazine and newspaper coverage. This meant that during the fall of 1939 the general public was saturated with *The Wizard of Oz* magazine stories, features, photo spreads, color rotogravure sections, comic strips, full-page color advertisements, full-page two-tone advertisements, and countless reviews along with other items.

Because I am a collector of all kinds of *The Wizard of Oz* memorabilia, I am trying to buy as much of this beautiful magazine and newspaper material as I can find. Please let me know if you can help me obtain any 1939 magazines or newspapers featuring *The Wizard of Oz* such as the following:

The American, September 1939
American Boy, September 1939
Boys' Life, August or September 1939
Cosmopolitan, September 1939
Good Housekeeping, August or September 1939
Harper's Bazaar, August 1939
Liberty, September 23, 1939
Look, August 15, 1939
MGM Studio News, August 14, 1939
Motion Picture, August 1939
Movie Story, August 1939
Movies, August 1939
Newsweek, August 21, 1939
Pathfinder, August 26, 1939
Photoplay Studies, circa August 1939
Redbook, September 1939
Saturday Evening Post, August 26, 1939
St. Nicholas, August 1939
Screen Guide, September 1939
Screen Romances, August 1939
Screen Stories, January 1957
Screenland, August 1939
Silver Screen, August 1939
Song Hits, October, November, or December 1939
Time, August 21, 1939
Woman's Home Companion, September 1939

Most of all I am looking for *Movie Life*, August 1939, with a cover photo of Judy Garland as 'Dorothy' and *Minicam*, August 1939, with a cover photo of Ray Bolger as 'Scarecrow.'

Jay Scarfone
985 Parma Center Rd.
Hilton, NY 14468

I am a pulp magazine collector who will pay top prices for issues of *The Spider, The Shadow, Doc Savage, Operator #5, Secret Agent X, Captain Satan, Captain Zero, The Skipper, The Whisperer, The Wizard, The Scorpion, The Octopus, Bill Barnes Air Adventurer, Dusty Ayres and His Battle Birds, G-8 and His Battle Aces, Flying Aces, Dare-Devil Aces, Wings, Black Mask Detective, Dime Detective, Phantom Detective, Black Hood Detective, Red Hood Detective, Ace Mystery, Dime Mystery, Horror Stories, Terror Tales, Weird Tales, Adventure, Argosy All-Story*, many other air-war, hero, character, mystery, and miscellaneous. This is a hobby with me. Write for bid before you decide to sell, or call me collect. Thank you. All offers will bring response.

Jack Deveny
6805 Cheyenne Trail
Edina, MN 55435-1158
(612) 941-2457

I have been collecting *Etude Music Magazine* for nearly thirty years and have most issues in near-mint to mint condition from 1889 through 1957. I am in search of certain first issues in near-mint to mint condition to upgrade conditions of other issues I already have from this period. I will pay $100.00 each for October, November, or December 1883 issues of *Etude Music Magazine* in near-mint to mint condition. I will pay the following for issues in near-mint to mint condition.

Ervin Erickson
1211 N. 18th St.
Bismarck, ND 58501

We Pay

		We Pay
1884,	12 issues, ea	50.00
1885,	12 issues, ea	40.00
1886,	12 issues, ea	30.00
1887,	12 issues, ea	25.00
1888,	12 issues, ea	25.00
1889,	12 issues, ea	8.00
1890,	12 issues, ea	8.00
1891,	12 issues, ea	8.00
1892,	12 issues, ea	7.00
1893,	Jan., Feb., June, July, Dec., ea	7.00
1894,	Jan., June, July, Dec., ea	7.00
1895,	Jan., April, ea	7.00
1896,	March, April, Sept., Oct., ea	6.00
1898,	Jan., Feb., May, July, Dec., ea	6.00
1899,	March, April, May, June, Oct., Dec., ea	6.00
1900,	Jan., Feb., March, Sept., Oct., ea	6.00
1901,	12 issues, ea	3.00
1902,	12 issues, ea	3.00
1903,	12 issues, ea	3.00
1904,	Jan., Feb., March, June, Sept., Oct., ea	3.00
1905,	Jan., Feb., April, Oct., ea	4.00
1906,	Jan., Feb., March, May, July, Aug., Nov., ea	4.00
1907,	Jan., ea	10.00

1907, Feb., March, June, Aug., Nov., Dec., ea.........................**4.00**
1908, Jan., June, Aug., ea...**3.00**
1909, Feb., March, April, May, July, Aug., Sept., Dec., ea..............**3.00**
1910, 12 issues, ea..**3.00**
1911, Dec., ea...**4.00**
1912, Feb., April, July, ea..**3.00**
1913, April, Dec., ea..**3.00**
1914, Jan., May, Nov., ea..**3.00**
1915, June, ea...**6.00**
1916, April, May, Sept., Oct., ea......................................**3.00**
1916, Dec., ea...**5.00**
1917, Jan., ea..**10.00**
1917, Feb. through Dec., ea..**3.00**
1918, July, ea...**3.00**
1919, April, Oct., Nov., Dec., ea......................................**3.00**
1920, March, July, Sept., Oct., ea.....................................**3.00**
1921, Feb., April, July, Sept., ea.....................................**3.00**
1922, June, July, Oct., Dec., ea.......................................**3.00**
1923, Jan., Dec., ea...**3.00**
1923, April, Oct., ea..**5.00**
1924, Jan., April, Sept., Oct., Nov., Dec., ea.........................**3.00**
1925, 12 issues, ea..**3.00**
1926, March, April, June, July, Dec., ea...............................**3.00**
1927, Jan., July, ea...**3.00**
1930, Dec., ea...**3.00**
1931, Jan., ea...**3.00**
1934, Aug., Sept., ea..**3.00**

Prices listed are for magazines in fine or better condition. Tape, stains, creases, wear, etc. greatly depreciate the value of paper items. I will buy any quantity as long as they are in nice condition and complete. Interest in magazines seems to be growing with each year. I am interested in many magazines from the 1800's through the 1950's. If you have any magazines that are listed below or any nice lot of magazines, please contact me. This is just a sample of some of the things that I buy. You can either ship items for immediate payment or, if you prefer, write or call first. I am a serious buyer, and I'm always interested in nice material. If you have any questions, please write or call. Thanks.

Bob Havey
Box 3
W. Sullivan, ME 04689
(207) 422-3083

Magazines

Movie Magazine, ca 1920's...3.00
Movie Magazine, ca 1930's...5.00
Movie Magazine, 1940-1944...3.00
Movie Magazine, 1945-1949...2.50
Movie Magazine, 1950-1956...1.50
Movie Radio Guide, 1940's...2.00
Ladies' Home Journal, 1910's......................................6.00
Ladies' Home Journal, 1920's......................................5.00
Woman's Home Companion, 1910's....................................6.00
Woman's Home Companion, 1920's....................................3.00
Vogue, 1910-1929..7.00
Vogue, 1930's...3.00
Vanity Fair, 1910-1929..7.00
Vanity Fair, 1930's...3.00
Harper's Bazaar, 1910-1929..7.00
Harper's Bazaar, 1930's...3.00
Pictorial Review, 1910's..6.00
Pictorial Review, 1920's..3.00
Pictorial Review, 1930-1933.......................................2.50
Delineator, 1910's..5.00
Delineator, 1920's..3.00
Esquire, w/Varga fold-outs, 1940's................................8.00
Esquire, other pre-1946...2.50
Movie Western Magazine...15.00
TV Western Magazine, 1950's.......................................8.00
Saturday Evening Post, 1910-1929..................................3.00
Saturday Evening Post, 1930's.....................................1.25
Boy's Life, pre-1940..2.50
Cosmopolitan, 1900-1920...2.00
Cosmopolitan, 1921-1932...3.00
Good Housekeeping, 1900-1920......................................2.00
Good Housekeeping, 1921-1932......................................3.00
Good Housekeeping, 1933-1949......................................1.00
McCall's, 1910's..2.50
McCall's, 1920's..3.00
Mickey Mouse Magazine, 1930's-1940...............................15.00
Pulps, 1910's-1930's
    horror ....5.00 +
    mystery ....4.00 +
    weird ....4.00 +
    detective ....2.00 +
    western ....1.00 +
    science fiction ....3.00 +

I want to buy old magazines from 1800 to 1930. I am paying 50¢ to $10.00 each, depending on condition and date of issue. I am looking for magazines such as *Saturday Evening Post, Life, Look, Modern Priscilla, Ladies' Home Journal, Silver Screen, Harper's Weekly, Harper's Bazaar, Movie Story, Movie Stars' Parade, Motion Picture, Hollywood, The Farmer's Wife, The Flapper, The Brown Book, Boys' Life*, etc.

Sharon Hood
46060 Warren
Canton, MI 48187

Magazines I am looking for feature these shows: The Untouchables, Maverick, Bonanza, The Saint, The Man from U.N.C.L.E., The Avengers, Batman, The Monkees, The Invaders, Dark Shadows, and many more. I am also looking for magazines such as *Famous Monsters of Filmland, Yank, TV Guide, Movie Mirror, Photoplay, Esquire, Playboy*, and many others. Magazines must be in very good or better condition, as this will determine the price. My buying prices range from 50¢ to $3.00 an issue. Please write and give descriptions of items.

Rick Nosker
8519 E. Sheridan
Scottsdale, AZ 85257

We buy old magazines from 1915 through 1926. These include such magazines as *Ladies' Home Journal, Woman's Home Companion, The Delineator, Pictorial Review, Good Housekeeping*, and others. Coverless issues are acceptable if contents are complete. Please state condition, price, and date of each issue.

Carol J. Beattie
3374 Ver Bunker Ave.
Port Edwards, WI 54469
(715) 887-3497

I am looking for issues #1 through #50 of *Rolling Stone Magazine*. I will pay $10.00 and up per issue. These must be complete and in very good condition.

Ray Peters
4174 Springdale Rd.
Stow, OH 44224

239

Magazines

I want to buy pre-1950's fashion magazines. I will pay $2.50 to $4.00 each for *Vogue* and $1.00 to $3.00 each for *McCall's*. I am also looking for other magazines.

Beatrix Brockerman
730 W. Gaines St.
Tallahassee, FL 32304

Wanted: *Playboy* from before 1960. I pay more for 1954 issues—$10.00 each and up—and $3.00 to $7.00 for those on up to 1956. I pay $1.00 to $3.00 each for any printed after 1956. Nudist books and magazines (such as *Sunbathing*) dated 1965 or before are worth $1.00 each. For movie magazines prior to 1960, I will pay $1.00 to $2.00. I will pay $2.00 to $3.00 for issues from the 40's and $3.00 to $5.00 for those from the 30's—depending on the cover and condition. *Rolling Stone Magazines* dated prior to 1980 are also sought. I will pay 50¢ to $3.00 each for certain issues. For *Movie Magazines* with Monroe covers, I will pay $4.00 for each copy dated before 1960. I buy *Teen Magazine* with dates prior to 1962; I pay $1.00 to $2.00 each for these. I'll pay $3.00 to $5.00 each for *Esquire* printed before 1945. For *Fortune* magazines from before 1940, I pay $2.00 to $4.00 each. I pay $2.00 to $10.00 each for baseball yearbooks by team and *Street-Smith* that were published before 1970, depending on the year issued. Many other magazines are wanted, as well. They must be fine condition with no clipped or missing pages or any major damage.

Glen Arvin
Box 53
Celestine, IN 47521

MAJOLICA

We are interested in buying unusual and top-quality items—preferably without chips or cracks. Prices paid depend on the rarity of the piece. We particularly want English majolica but also buy good American pieces. Please send description and photo, if possible. All letters will be answered.

Linda & Ken Ketterling
3202 E. Lincolnshire
Toledo, OH 43606

We Pay

Minton Shell & Seaweed Oyster Plate........................**125.00-175.00**
Etruscan Cauliflower Plate, 9″..............................**65.00-80.00**
George Jones Strawberry Server...............................**300.00+**

MAPS

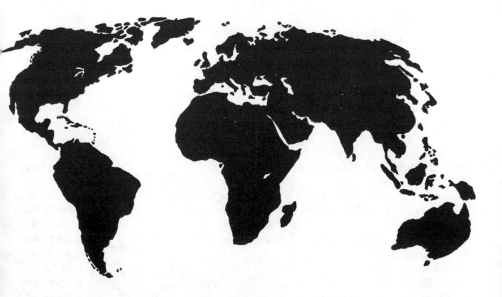

Maps

Maps are one of the most popular types of paper collectibles. They are sought after for many reasons. Some collectors appreciate the beautiful artwork and intricate etchings on the very early maps and purchase them for decorative purposes. Other collectors seek all maps depicting a specific geographic area and want representative examples of all time periods showing changes to that area (i.e., additional information resulting from exploration, political boundary changes, or just natural increase of settlement).

I buy all old maps and atlases, specializing in the western United States, for my personal collection and for resale. The list that follows is only a very general guide to prices I pay. Rare and early maps command much higher prices. As with most collectibles, condition is as important a factor as subject matter when trying to determine value. Bear in mind that condition will contribute to the value of any item. Prices listed are for maps in fine condition. Poor material will bring less; pristine material will bring more, and damaged may be worth nothing. Other determining factors include rarity, date, size, coloring, publisher, cartographic accuracy, historic importance, and general attractiveness. It is best to send a description or photocopy to get a definite quote.

Dennis B. Goreham
1539 East, 4070 South
Salt Lake City, UT 84124

Pre-1850 Maps   We Pay

Western U.S. Individual States & Territories	20.00-50.00
Eastern U.S. Individual States & Territories	10.00-35.00
Western U.S. Groups of States & Territories	20.00-45.00
Eastern U.S. Groups of States & Territories	10.00-25.00
Entire U.S.	20.00-70.00
European Countries	5.00-25.00
Other Countries	5.00-20.00
North American Continent	15.00-50.00
Other Continents	10.00-30.00
U.S. Cities & Counties	10.00-40.00
Foreign Cities & Counties	5.00-20.00
World or Hemisphere (either)	10.00-70.00

1850 through 1900 Maps   We Pay

Western U.S. Individual States & Territories	5.00-25.00
Eastern U.S. Individual States & Territories	5.00-20.00
Western U.S. Groups of States & Territories	5.00-25.00
Eastern U.S. Groups of States & Territories	5.00-15.00
Entire U.S.	5.00-25.00
European Countries	5.00-10.00
Other Countries	3.00-10.00
North American Continent	5.00-20.00

We Pay

Other Continents...5.00-15.00
U.S. Cities & Counties.......................................5.00-25.00
Foreign Cities & Counties....................................3.00-10.00
World or Hemisphere (either)..................................5.00-20.00

MARBLES

Marbles have been used as toys since the days of the Romans. The oldest examples are made of clay and stone. The most collectible marbles are handmade glass marbles produced primarily in Germany between 1870 and 1920. Glass marbles range in color from clear to various shades of green, blue, or amber, with opacity varying from clear to transparent to completely opaque. These marbles have surface or internal decoration of threads or bands of colored glass. Others have bands of gold-like lutz or flecks of silvery mica. Sulphide marbles contain figures of animals, people, or other items. All handmade marbles have a characteristic pontil mark that occurs during manufacture.

We will buy marbles that are in mint condition—free of chips, cracks, and haze. We will consider marbles of rarer types in less-than-mint condition. We also buy marble-related pictures, games, post cards, advertisements, etc. Contact us for prices not listed. Listings are for marbles 1″ in diameter. Prices are higher for larger examples and less for smaller sizes. Please note sulphide prices are for 1½″ size.

Thomas Baxter
P.O. Box 677
Wheatley Heights, NY 11798
(516) 454-9067 (evenings)
(516) 293-2576 (leave message 24 hrs.)

Marbles

Lutz	We Pay
Indian	1,000.00
Black Glass	300.00
Ribbon	250.00
Onion	200.00
Opaque	20.00
Colored Glass	150.00
Clear Glass	100.00

Swirl	We Pay
Latticino	15.00
Solid Core	20.00
Divided Core	5.00
Colored Glass	20.00
Ribbon Core	25.00
Coreless	15.00
Coreless Colored	20.00

Indian	We Pay
Blue Bands	75.00
Colored Bands	150.00

Others	We Pay
Onion	50.00
Onion w/Mica	75.00
Peppermint	100.00
Peppermint w/Mica	1,100.00
Opaque	25.00
Opaque Banded	10.00
Cleary	25.00
Mica, red	500.00
Mica, black	250.00
Mica, other color	30.00
Agate, stone	20.00
Clambroth	150.00
Steelie, hollow w/X	20.00
Sulphide w/Animals	70.00
Sulphide	
Colored Glass	1,000.00
Colored Figure	1,000.00
Slag, single pontil	50.00
Akro Agate,	
machine-made	5.00
Corkscrew,	
machine-made	5.00

Marbles have been made for over one hundred years throughout the world. Today nearly every home has marbles stashed somewhere. Occasionally, individuals come across old, highly collectible marbles ranging upwards in value to $500.00.

We are especially interested in buying these types of marbles: Lutz, Indian swirls, clambroths, and comic marbles, with general interest in all other collectible marbles. We will purchase individual marbles, collections, marble literature, and marble advertising material. We welcome photos, descriptions, or product previews. We will familiarize you with a published market value of what we will pay.

Bob Hanson
Rt. 1, Box 222
Wapato, WA 98951
(509) 848-2345

I want to buy marbles--sulphides, swirls, and agates. Please call.

Bill Sweet
14 Diana Dr.
Rumford, RI 02916
(401) 434-4548

MATCH COVERS

Match cover collecting is the second most popular collecting hobby in America (second to stamps). As an advertising medium, matchbooks have been used since the early 1900's by businesses trying to get their message across to the public. Match covers and matchbooks are usually collected in mint condition (the striker never having been struck by the match); however, pre-WWII covers are collected in any condition.

I am buying collections of match covers or matchbooks that are pre-1960 (the striker is on the front of these, not the back). Condition is important and is reflected in the price. I am buying in any quantity--from one hundred to one hundred thousand. Also wanted are any items from the match industry (salesmen's sample books, invoices, bills, catalogues, etc.). Prices paid for neatly-kept and full Beach match cover albums range from $12.00 to $50.00 depending on content. Prices paid for 1939 World's Fair full books or match covers range from 25¢ to $2.00. Please send a brief description.

Bill Retskin
3417 Clayborne Ave.
Alexandria, VA 22306-1410
(703) 768-3932

MATCH SAFES

Since 1961 I have written articles on pocket match safes. I am always hunting for those in the shape of animals, people, and objects. Enamels are my specialty, along with sterling Art Nouveau match safes and cigarette cases. All match safes have hinged lids and a groove on the bottom used to strike the match. The purpose for the lid was to keep matches safe so they wouldn't catch fire by accident, thus giving them their name. Later, safety matches came into existence and match safes were no longer needed.

Listed below are match safes I am seeking. If you have others, please write, giving a complete description. Please note condition and your asking price in the first letter. A photo is preferred.

Lenore Monleon
33 Fifth Ave.
New York, NY 10003

We Pay

Figural Frog	**15.00**
Enamel on Silver w/Nude	**35.00**
Embossed Picture, 14K gold	**60.00**
Embossed Picture, sterling	**15.00**
Advertising	**5.00**
Art Nouveau Lady, sterling	**17.00**

We Pay

Porcelain **20.00**
Cigarette Case, lady w/flowing hair, enamel on silver **35.00**

    Match strikers and match safes are tiny pocket-sized containers for matches which were used before the safety match was invented. These little treasures always have a striker on them––usually on the side or bottom.

    Universally popular in the 19th century, these tiny boxes were made of many materials (brass, silver, steel, pewter, tortoise-shell, leather,ivory, etc.) and were fashioned into a wide variety of shapes (horn beetles, tortoises, owls, hogs, dogs, books, profiles of people, musical instruments, etc.). These whimsical objects were often given as keepsakes and souvenirs.

    We buy match safes and any other type of figural or unusual boxes and containers, including enamels. Condition is all important, and price range is wide and depends on the item. We will pay your asking price when feasible. Do not hesitate to write, but please include a SASE for your reply.

Betty Bird
107 Ida St.
Mount Shasta, CA 96067

MECHANICAL ADVERTISING PENCILS

Mechanical advertising pencils have been used by advertisers since the 1920's to get their message to their customers. In general, the erasers and leads have not withstood the test of time, but many of the pencils themselves have remained in collector's condition.

I am buying pre-1965 collections of mechanical advertising pencils, bullet pencils, and ball-bat pencils that are in excellent condition and colorful in design, and mechanical pencils with figural or mechanical caps. Government pencils or cheap commerical pencils are not wanted. Broken or worn pencils can only be used for parts, and value is greatly reduced.

Bill Retskin
3417 Clayborne Ave.
Alexandria, VA 22306-1410
(703) 768-3932

We Pay

Colorful, Mechanical Advertising Pencils.........................50¢-2.00
Colorful, Fully-Addressed Bullet Pencils..........................25¢-1.50
Ball-Bat Mechanical Pencils from Teams........................1.00-3.00

MEDICAL MEMORABILIA

I purchase all sorts of pre-1900 medical and scientific instruments. In the medical line, I am particularly interested in surgical instruments with ebony or ivory handles––individual pieces or cased sets. Civil War era medical items such as surgical sets, uniforms, manuals, etc. are eagerly sought.

The scientific instruments which I look for are brass microscopes and telescopes, celestial and terrestrial globes, and other well-made instruments of brass, mahogany, etc.

Alex Peck
Antique Scientifica
P.O. Box 710
Charleston, IL 61920
(217) 348-1009

Wanted: medical and surgical instruments or books on all areas (ophthalmology, neurosurgery, urology, orthopedics, plastic surgery, E.N.T., etc.). I am seeking pre-1900 instruments, one or an operating room full! Please send a photo. You will receive an immediate reply.

Norman B. Meadow, M.D., F.A.C.S.
225 E. 64th St.
New York, NY 10021

Serious collector and researcher wants to buy old medical quack gadgets and old electrotherapeutic devices which shock, buzz, or light up to serve as a cure-all. They date from the 1800's to the early 1900's. Many were built into fancy wooden boxes with dials, wires, hand-held electrodes, spark coils, and levers. Others were in the form of belts, gloves, brushes, pendants, and short pipes. Specific examples with names are: paired, pointed metal rods 3″ long stamped 'Perkins'; Abrams' black boxes; Ruth Drown's suitcase treatment device; and Davis & Kidder magneto electric device. Steel-plated pipes with wires leading from them were also made bearing names such as Oxhealer, Oxapathor, Oxgenator, Oxgenor King, Oxydonor, or Farador; wooden boxes with spark coils and a dry cell or a battery were named Williams, Englemann, Waite & Bartlett, Chloride of Silver, or Florence. No hand-held violet ray or Electreat devices are wanted. Collector also wants any literature on medical quackery and electrotherapeutics. Please identify items by name; illustrate, describe, and price.

Ed Keller
1205 Imperial Dr.
Pittsburg, KS 66762

MILITARIA

Militaria related to the Foreign Legion is my major collecting interest. However, the 'mystique' of pre-war China and the Shanghai International Settlement has prompted me to seek all items related to the U.S. Marines (Shanghai, Peking, etc.); the 15th Infantry (Tientsin); the Asiatic Fleet; the Shanghai Volunteer Corps, Police, etc.; the French and White Russian Forces (China); the Chinese Maritime Customs Service; the Chinese Warlords; the Soldiers of Fortune; Devils Island; the International Brigades (Spain); and the Chaco War (Bolivia vs. Paraguay), to round out my collecting interests. The following list constitutes average prices paid for good-or-better condition items.

G. Christian
3849 Bailey Ave.
Bronx, NY 10463

We Pay

Badges **10.00**
Certificates **25.00**
Guidons, Etc. **50.00**
Headdress **25.00**
Naval Cap Ribbons **10.00**
Military Kukris **50.00**

We Pay

Regimental Histories & Cruise Books.............................**25.00**
British Colonial Shooting Medals..................................**25.00**
School Attendance & Animal Rescue Medals.......................**10.00**
Truant Officer Badges...**25.00**

We buy the following items. The better the condition, the higher the price. (Condition of ribbons is not important.) Army, Navy, and Marine Corps medals should have a number stamped in the lower rim. All offers answered.

Carl Sciortino, Militaria
Box 6424
Scottsdale, AZ 85261

We Pay

Army Medal w/No...**15.00-20.00**
Navy Medal w/No...**20.00-25.00**
Marine Corps Medal w/No...................................**25.00-35.00**
WWI City & State Medal.....................................**8.00-10.00**
Civil War City & State Medal...............................**15.00-20.00**
Mexican War, 1846-8, Shields & Medals.....................**35.00-50.00**
Philippine Insurrection Medal..............................**15.00-20.00**
Boxer Rebellion Medal, China 1900-1901....................**18.00-25.00**
Indian War Veteran Medal...................................**18.00-25.00**
WWI Collar Disk, bronze.....................................**2.00-5.00**
WWI Patches...**5.00-6.00**
Aviation Wings, sterling...................................**12.00-30.00**
Shako Plates, large insignia...............................**10.00-20.00**
Combat Knives
    K-Bar..**8.00-12.00**
    MK-3..**15.00-20.00**
    Everitt...**25.00-30.00**
    Case..**25.00-30.00**
    'F-S'...**15.00-18.00**
Unit Histories: Spanish Amer. thru Vietnam, all service branches...**8.00-15.00**

U.S. Marine Corps memorabilia is wanted by collector, especially recruiting posters, books, photos, sheet music, belt buckles, cigarette lighters, steins and mugs, toy soldiers, trucks, planes, etc. Also wanted are documents and autographs, artwork, post cards, trench art, bronzes, novelty items, and John Phillip Sousa memorabilia.

Dick Weisler
53-07 213th St.
Bayside, NY 11364
(718) 626-7110 (office)
(718) 428-9829 (home)

We buy German, U.S., and Japanese military items of WWI, WWII, and Vietnam. Check your attics, closets, barns, and cellars for helmets, badges, uniforms, medals, hats, flags, documents, photos, field gear, swords, and daggers. Please ship for our same-day offer. We pay postage both ways if we can't come to terms on a value. We must see them to price them. Given below is a sample listing for buying WWII German items. Let us hear from you!

Ron Gordon
San Juan Precious Metals Corp.
4818 San Juan Ave.
Jacksonville, FL 32210-3232

We Pay		**We Pay**
Helmets **10.00-500.00**	Swords **15.00-250.00**	
Hats **10.00-750.00**	Uniforms **30.00-400.00**	
Flags **15.00-2,500.00**	Documents **5.00-200.00**	
Daggers **10.00-600.00**	Badges **2.00-600.00**	

MONTANA COLLECTIBLES

Residents of Montana are very proud of their rugged state, and most would never want to live anywhere else despite the cold winters and empty spaces. These two factors seem to produce a friendliness and a sense of strength and pride which seem to spill over into the collecting field. Because this area of our country was not settled until the late 1800's and the population was and remained for some time very small, the amount of historical material related to Montana is very scarce; handmade or early manufactured items are in very small supply when compared to cities like Milwaukee, Wisconsin, for instance, where collectors interested in finding state-related memorabilia find abundant examples of advertising items due to the fact that there were many, many breweries operating there in the late 1890s. Because

Montana items are harder to find, as a general rule, they bring higher prices.

I buy anything produced before 1930 made in or marked Montana. I buy calendars, advertising trays, photographs, post cards, letterheads, history books, tokens, trade cards, frontiersmen's relics, small souvenirs, advertising mirrors, etc., etc.

Tim Gordon
2700 Eaton St.
Missoula, MT 59801

MOVIE MEMORABILIA

Although movie posters have been around since the turn of the century, only since about 1965 have they been collected at all. In the past five years, however, more people than ever before have taken an interest in them and have joined ranks with other collectors. Movie posters come in various sizes such as 11" x 14" (lobby cards), 14" x 36" (inserts), and 22" x 28" and 27" x 41" (one-sheets). They are colorful, and the artwork, especially from the 1930's, is outstanding.

I buy all sizes. Prices I'll pay will vary according to year, title, star, and condition––also whether it is original or a reissue. Current posters and lobby cards have little value.

Gene Arnold
2234 South Blvd.
Houston, TX 77098

Movie Memorabilia

Lobby Cards   We Pay

Casablanca...250.00
Gone with the Wind.......................................200.00
The Broadway Melody......................................75.00
The Jazz Singer, 1927....................................300.00
Tarzan's New York Adventure...............................50.00
Sherlock Holmes...35.00
Charlie Chan (Oland)......................................30.00
Charlie Chan (Toler)......................................15.00
Tom Mix...15.00
You Can't Take It with You................................30.00
Mutiny on the Bounty......................................75.00

Posters   We Pay

Marx Brothers..250.00
W.C. Fields..250.00
Mae West...250.00
Laurel & Hardy...250.00
Citizen Kane...350.00
Shane...50.00
Marilyn Monroe..35.00
The Searchers...35.00
Stagecoach (John Wayne)..................................250.00
Captain Marvel...100.00
Superman...100.00

I want to buy **Janet Lynn** memorabilia. I seek books, magazines, pictures, articles, etc. Material desired is from 1970 to the present. Please state price and condition.

Albert Gerard
Box 97
Lafayette, OR 97127

I collect almost anything relating to **Marilyn Monroe** (no dolls) that is reasonably priced--movies, posters, bedding, magazines, records, sheet music, jewelry, stationery, paper dolls, post cards, hangers, photos, cups, buttons, pillows, and any 1950's clothing in good condition with her trademark on the label. 1983 clothing with estate label is not as highly sought after, though it depends on what the item is. What do you have? Please describe item, condition, and price.

Lynn MacCarroll
4970 Palmyra
Las Vegas, NV 89102
(702) 871-9383

I want **Marilyn Monroe** cover *TV Guides*. I will pay $50.00 for a 1953 cover. I will pay $5.00 for movie tie-in paperbacks (no Misfits wanted). 1950's mini-magazines with Marilyn covers are worth $5.00 to $10.00 each. A 1953 hard-back book with a dust jacket photo of Marilyn will bring $50.00. For 1940's magazines with Marilyn covers, I will pay $25.00 to $50.00. Higher prices are paid for *Salute*, *Personal Romances*, and certain *Laffs* magazines. I will pay $25.00 for Vol. 1, No. 1, larger-type magazines with Marilyn covers up to 1952. I want all Marilyn magazines issued prior to 1962; I pay $10.00 to $25.00 each for these. I want movie posters or other related items. I pay $25.00 to $75.00 for life-size posters. Any other unusual Marilyn Monroe-type collectible is also wanted. Please describe condition accurately.

Glen Arvin
Box 53
Celestine, IN 47521

I want to buy anything reasonably priced pertaining to **Natalie Wood**—books, magazines, paper dolls, posters, records, photos, buttons, ads, autographs, films, cups, jewelry, etc. What do you have? Please describe the item, its condition, and price. Thank you.

Lynn MacCarroll
4970 Palmyra
Las Vegas, NV 89102
(702) 871-9383

I collect silent movie items of all sizes, materials, and categories. Such items include posters, lobby cards, press books, programs, stills, paper dolls, sheet music, spoons (except Oneida), figurines, games, pin-backs, puzzles, medals, tins, novelty items, clothes hangers, etc. All items must have an image or some other connection to silent movies or movie stars. Also wanted are poster frames, signs, fixtures, decorations, ticket booths, marquees, theater projectors, slide projectors and slides, or any other commercial equipment from old movie theaters. I will return all postage whether or not I buy items. I will return all calls left on my answering machine if I'm not in.

Dick Davis
9500 Old Georgetown Rd.
Bethesda, MD 20814-1724
(301) 530-5904

We Pay

Roger Bros. Spoons..**20.00**
Athens Silver Co. Spoons......................................**30.00**
Star Player Photo Plates......................................**30.00**
Our Gang Plates...**25.00**

I want to buy movie and book trade publications. Unlike book and magazine publications printed for the fan and general consumer, trade publications were printed strictly for movie theater owners and operators. These publications were written for people working in the movie industry to give them a 'progress report' and other general information without the usual fan-type publication frills. However, many of these trade publications were used to 'sell' the theater owners on what the various movie studios had to offer in the way of features, shorts, etc. Unlike the general advertising material the public would see—posters, lobby cards, etc. —this material was used specifically to persuade the theater owners to buy or book a specific movie studio's product. This type of material is easy to recognize as it speaks to the theatre owner directly and refers to the public as his business, customers, or by some similar term.

I will buy all related material, studio preview ad books, and annuals from all studios (MGM, Universal, Paramount, etc.). Some trade magazine titles are listed below.

Exhibitors Herald World
Moving Picture World
Motion Picture News
The Exhibitor
Exhibitors Herald
Film Daily Yearbook
Greater Amusements
Hollywood Filmograph
Hollywood Vagabond

Inside Facts
Motion Pictures Today
National Exhibitor
Show-World
Lion's Roar
R.K.O. Flash
Columbia Mirror
Your Lucky Star
New Show World

Universal White List   Paramount's Birthday Jubilee
Parade of Hits   Paramount Pictures 15th Birthday Group

George Reed
5239 Howland St.
Philadelphia, PA 19124
(215) 743-5201

MULBERRY WARE

Mulberry ware was manufactured from about 1835 until about 1855. It is closely related to the earlier Flow Blue china in design, shape, and patterns, since Flow Blue manufacturers also produced Mulberry ware. It is readily identified by its unique coloring which ranges from sepia brown to dark brownish-black. Many pieces have a blurred look, sometimes making the details of the pattern somewhat obscure. The body of this china has a heavy ironstone feel and a gray-white tint. A majority of the plates are twelve-sided and paneled; they normally have of an outer rim decoration with a scenic design in the center. Oriental and English themes are most often seen; floral patterns are less abundant. The pattern name is located on the underside of the piece, usually in large printed letters framed within the marker's trademark. Not all items were marked. In addition to dinner sets and tea services, there were also chamber sets which included such pieces as washbowl and pitchers, soap dishes, chamber pots, hair receivers, footbaths, and toothbrush boxes. Nearly all pieces of Mulberry ware were made for the purpose of serving food and beverages or were useful in the aid of personal hygiene. There are very few exceptions. I will buy other pieces not mentioned and all damaged items at adjusted prices.

Barbara Amster
15 Bellevue Ave.
Bass River, MA 02664

We Pay

Dinner Plates, 10½″	**28.00**
Plates, 7½″	**14.00**
Flanged Soup Bowls	**24.00**
Creamers	**45.00**
Sugar Bowls	**45.00**
Handleless Cups	**10.00**
Saucers	**5.00**
Cups & Saucers	**22.50**
All Miscellaneous (sugar bowl, teapot, tureen, etc.) Covers or Lids	**5.00-13.00**
All Miscellaneous (sugar bowl, teapot, vegetable dish) Bottoms	**25.00-40.00**

MUSIC BOXES

There are many types of music boxes in forms ranging from dolls, birds, carriages, and horses covering musical movements to large stationary boxes. Music boxes were first made in the late 18th century by Swiss watchmakers and were produced in both disk and cylinder models.

The cylinder is studded with tiny projections; as the cylinder turns, these projections lift the tuned teeth in the 'music comb,' and a melody results. The value of the instrument depends upon the length of the cylinder and the quality of the workmanship. Bells, mechanical birds, and porcelain dolls increase the value of the unit.

Disk-type music boxes utilize interchangeable steel disks with projecting studs, which by means of an intervening 'star wheel' cause a music comb to play. There are many different variations and mechanisms. Most were made in Germany, but some were produced in the United States. Among the most popular are Polyphon, Symphonion, Regina, and Thorne.

We purchase all types of music boxes, large and small. Prices are for music boxes in fine condition, playing properly, with cabinets or cases in well-preserved condition. In all instances, non-playing music boxes (those with broken parts and damaged cases) sell for much less. On the other hand, examples in ornate cases and with bisque dolls often will command more. Please write us.

Cindy Oakes
34025 W. 6 Mile
Livonia, MI 48152

We Pay

Music Box, key-wind, 2-tune 4″ cylinder, 1840's, 3½x4x8½″ **800.00**
Disk Thorne Music Box, 20 interchangeable disks **300.00**
Disk Regina Music Box, 15½″ **200.00**
Music Box, German bisque doll movement **750.00**
Music Box, Jumeau doll movement **1,000.00**

MUSICAL INSTRUMENTS

The banjos, mandolins, and guitars made in America between 1833 and 1969 comprise the field called 'vintage fretted instruments.' Brands which are desired in additon to Gibson (guitars, banjos, and mandolins) and C.F. Martin (guitars and mandolins) are guitars by Dobro, National, D'Angelico, Stromberg, Fender, and Euphonon. Brands of mandolins which are desirable (besides Gibson) are Washburn, Lyon & Healy, Martin, Fender, and D'Angelico. Brands of banjos sought by dealers are Gibson Mastertone, B&D Silverbell, Epiphone, Paramount, Vega, Fairbanks, S.S. Stewart, Lyon & Healy, Washburn, and Stromberg.

We have been in business since 1971, and ours is the only company of its kind which is continuously recommended for appraisals and sales by both the major companies—Gibson, Inc. of Kalamozoo, Michigan; and C.F. Martin Guitar of Nazareth, Pennsylvania. Written appraisals are available for a fee of $35.00. Please include neck block information, the width of the body at the widest part, a brief description of condition (noting wear), previously-made or needed repairs, missing or replaced parts, and whether or not the instrument has a hard-shell (wooden) case. Sellers are also invited to call collect.

Stanley M. Jay, President
Mandolin Bros. Ltd.
629 Forest Ave.
Staten Island, NY 10310
(718) 981-3226

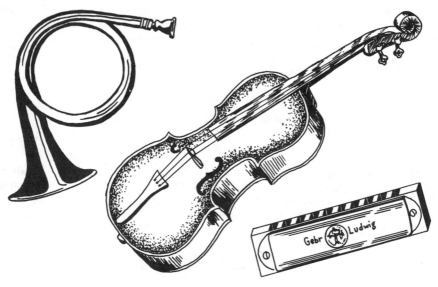

We Pay

1930 Gibson Mastertone Tenor Banjo, TB-3, maple neck & resonator...**500.00**

1925 B&D Silverbell No. 1 Tenor Banjo, maple resonator..............**300.00**

1915 Fairbanks or Vega Whyte Laydie No. 2 Five-String Banjo.........**500.00**

1899 S.S. Stewart Five-String Banjo................................**175.00**

1928 Epiphone Deluxe Tenor Banjo, gold-plated metal parts...........**700.00**

1935 Gibson Mastertone TB-6 Tenor Banjo, fancy, gold plated........**1,000.00**

1915 Gibson Style A Mandolin (pear-shaped, not fancy), natural, brown, or black top finish...**250.00**

1919 Gibson Style F-4 Mandolin (Florentine w/scrolls), red finish, oval soundhole **700.00**

1916 Gibson Mandola, medium-size A-style body, oval soundhole.......**300.00**

We Pay

1920 Gibson Eight-String Mando-Cello, K-1, large body..............350.00
1924 Gibson Style F-5 Mandolin, dark sunburst finish, f-holes........2,000.00
1959 Gibson Style F-5 mandolin, red sunburst finish, f-holes...........900.00
1920 Martin Style 0-18 Guitar, small body, mahogany back & sides.....250.00
1935 Martin Style 000-28 Guitar, medium body, rosewood bk & sides.1,000.00
1940 Martin Style D-28 Guitar, large body, rosewood back & sides.....1500.00
1965 Martin Style D-28 Guitar, large body, rosewood back & sides......700.00
1972 Martin Style 00-21 Guitar, small body, rosewood back & sides.....350.00

There are two main categories of violins: handcrafted and factory manufactured. Each category then breaks down into two parts of their own: handcrafted
by well-schooled professionals or amateurs, and factory violins made by quality-
controlled manufacturers or cheaply-made low-grade violins. In both categories,
the professional handcrafted and the quality-controlled factory violins are the better instruments and are valuable, good investments for a buyer. In most cases, the
amateur violins are poorly constructed. Inferior materials and finishes make them
undesirable because of appearance and poor sounding. Low-grade factory violins
are almost always a cheap reproduction of Stradivarius or other past master-makers
with facsimiled labels inside. These, too, have little value due to appearance and
poor sounding

We are interested in purchasing quality, handcrafted violins as well as quality,
factory-made violins.

Providence Violin Shop
1279 N. Main St.
Providence, RI 02904

We Pay

American Violins.......................................**up to 1,000.00**
German Violins...**up to 2,000.00**
French Violins...**up to 3,000.00**
Italian 19th & 20th Century Violins........................**up to 15,000.00**

NAPOLEONIC MEMORABILIA

There is presently a growing awareness of the influence that Napoleonic France
had upon all aspects of late 18th and early 19th century Europe. There is an ever-

increasing demand for all materials related not only to Napoleon himself but also to those who were with his contemporaries, whether in France or not. Napoleon's efforts to consolidate a European empire under a unified political, military, and economic system created a wealth of material attractive to those who are as yet piecing together the puzzle shapes of empirical forces that still affect us today.

Thus importance is placed upon much material of the period from 1769 to 1869 that might not be considered related to that illustrious name by those not familiar with European history. Let us describe how important that letter, document, diary, map, book, etc. is to us. As space will not allow for expansive lists, let a phone call complete it for you.

James Hilty
216 S. Broad St.
Holly, MI 48442
(313) 634-1400

We Pay

Letters **500.00-2,500.00**
Diaries . . . . **500.00 +**
Maps . . . . **up to 2,000.00**
Documents **25.00-3,500.00**
Books **10.00-200.00**

NEW ORLEANS
MARDI GRAS

The New Orleans celebration of Mardi Gras, born in its present-day form in 1857, has produced countless numbers of paper collectibles. Lavish invitations to 'tableau balls' (many of which were produced in Paris) were issued by carnival organizations during the Gilded Age of Mardi Gras which ended prior to World War I. Parading groups, called krewes, (among the most popular were Rex, Comus, Momus, Proteus) also produced newspaper supplements, or carnival bulletins. Each float in the parade was depicted in these elaborate 28″ x 44″ fold-out chromolithographs which sold on New Orleans street corners for only a dime.

As publisher of the annual *New Orleans Mardi Gras Guide*, we collect virtually any item that mentions the carnival season in New Orleans. Of particular interest is 19th century material: black and white photos, post cards, periodical articles, illustrated features from *Harper's*, *Leslie's*, etc. This is only a starter list, so please advise if you have other items.

Arthur Hardy
P.O. Box 8058
New Orleans, LA 70182

Ball Invitations	We Pay
1857-1875	60.00
1876-1899	35.00
1900-1920	25.00
1921-1949	15.00

Carnival Bulletins (Parade Papers)	We Pay
Pre-1900	80.00
1900-1920	35.00
1921-1950	25.00

Illustrated Features (Leslie's, Harper's, etc.)	We Pay
Pre-1900	25.00

Post Cards	We Pay
Pre-1900	25.00
Post-1900	5.00

Photos	We Pay
Black & White	10.00
Pre-WWI	7.50
Pre-WWII	5.00

Magazines, Newspapers Periodical Articles Railroad Brochures	We Pay
Pre-1900	15.00
Post-1900	10.00

NEWSPAPERS

The Kurdish Program, Cultural Survival, Inc., is a private non-profit organization which operates a Kurdish Library seeking newspapers and memorabilia relating to the culture, archaeology, geography, and history of the Kurdish people of the Middle or Near East. Publications related to the following would be of interest: Ottoman Empire, Babylonia, Median Empire, Turkey, Iraq, Iran, Syria, as is material on Saladin and the Crusades. We also collect books on the geo-political or regional interests of European countries, the United States, and the Soviet Union as they relate to the Middle East. The geographical area of our interest falls into such places as Southeastern Turkey (Anatolia), Northern Iraq, Northern Syria, and Western Iran.

Please send description and price list, or we will be happy to make you an offer.

The Kurdish Program
Cultural Survival, Inc.
1133 Ave. of the Americas
New York, NY 10036
(212) 764-1133

I want to buy newsboy carrier addresses from 1736 through 1936. These may be any form––broadside, pamphlet, newspaper, etc.

Don E. Burnett
P.O. Box 178
East Greenwich, RI 02818

NIGHT LIGHTS

There are numerous shapes of glass night lights that were made by various lamp manufacturers. Shapes include parrots, lovebirds, monkeys, owls, rabbits, dogs, Santa Clauses, and others. These were screwed onto black glass bases. We will pay a fair market price for any or all of these items. We want old glass night lights only —no ceramic or pottery items, no new items, please.

Wesley & Betty Strain
(314) 524-5608

NIPPON

I am wanting to buy cups to match a lemonade pitcher that is cream color with purple violets. They have a china E-OH mark.

Ray Richardson
P.O. Box 292
St. Paul, VA 24283-0292

OCCUPIED JAPAN

Figurines made in Japan from the beginning of the U.S. occupation at the end of World War II until the spring of 1952 were exported from Japan to the United States. Now they have become collectors' items.

I collect only the figurines—no plates, cups, fans, or metal objects. My primary figurine interests are Scottie dogs, shelf sitters, ethnic figurines, and mermaids.

Most collectors of Occupied Japan figurines have Gene Florence's *The Collector's Encyclopedia of Occupied Japan Collectibles*, Volumes 1, 2, and 3. I have given reference to the edition and page number of these price guides so that the pieces I'm interested in will be easier to identify. I want only pieces without cracks or defects of any kind.

Linda Trew
9015 Lake Braddock Dr.
Burke, VA 22015-2132
(703) 978-9793

Second Series   **We Pay**

Woebegone Horse, p.6...11.00
Elephant, p.6...9.00
Bees, set, p.6..20.00
Scotties, celluloid, p.6.......................................7.00
Scotties, rubber, p.8..8.00

We Pay

Penguin, p.8..**7.00**
Dog w/Ribbon, p.8...**8.00**
Any Dog, row 4, p.8.......................................**6.00**
Duck, humanoid, p.8.......................................**12.50**
Mermaid, p.36...**17.00**
Soldiers, p.48..**6.00**
Negro Outhouse, p.48......................................**15.00**
Dog & Hat, p.56...**6.00**
Scottie Dog, p.56...**6.00**
Fat Boy, p.56...**12.00**
Tearful Girl, p.56..**12.00**
Spotted Dog, p.72...**6.00**
Scottie Dog, p.72...**6.00**
Dutch Children Holder, p.90...............................**22.00**
Any Shelf Sitter, p.100.............................**Top Dollar**
Negro Match Holder, p.102.................................**20.00**
Horned Bugle-Boy Devil, p.112.............................**20.00**
Grampa w/Bug, p.112.......................................**12.00**
Old Oriental, p.111.......................................**12.00**

Third Series

We Pay

Butterfly Babe, p.9.......................................**20.00**
Nude on Sea Horse, p.9....................................**20.00**
Scotties, 3 white, p.9....................................**7.00**
Scotties, 3 black, p.9....................................**7.00**
Dogs in Basket, 3¼", p.9..................................**7.50**
Dog w/Lamp, p.9...**4.00**
Puppies in Basket, 2½", p.9...............................**14.00**
Ladybugs, set of 3, p.9...................................**20.00**
Boy w/Dog, 4¾", p.32......................................**12.00**
Girl w/Dog, 4¼", p.32.....................................**11.00**
Newsboy, p.32...**13.00**
Boy w/Dog, 4⅛", p.32......................................**15.00**
Violin Player, p.32.......................................**13.00**
Indian Squaw, 4½", p. 58..................................**13.00**
Balloon Lady, 5½", p.58...................................**40.00**
Indian w/Papoose, red, 5½", p.58..........................**20.00**
Indian Planter, 3", p.58..................................**10.00**
Indian Squaw, red, 6", p.58...............................**20.00**
Buddha, embossed mark, 5½", p.58..........................**23.00**
Incense Burner, red, 4", p.58.............................**20.00**
Dancer, green, 5", p.58...................................**23.00**
Black Shoe Shine Boy, red, 5½", p.58......................**45.00**
Dutch Water Girl, 4", p.58................................**13.00**
Dutch Girl w/Milk Can, red, 6", p.58......................**23.00**

We Pay

Dutch Children, 3″, p.58	13.00
Eskimos 3″ & 2¾″, p.58	15.00
Indian Water Boy, red, 4″, p.58	12.00
Indian, red, 3″, p.58	10.00
Spanish Guitar Player, 4¼″, p.58	10.00
Martian (?), 3″, p.58	30.00
Couple at Piano, 4″, p.60	23.00
Triple, 3″, p.60	15.00
Romantic Couple, 4″	23.00
Couple, Canadian, 4¼″, p.60	20.00
Couple, 4″, p.60	15.00
1st & 4th Serenading Couple, 5¼″ & 5⅛″, p.60	20.00
Coach et. al., 5¾″, 5⅛″	60.00
Serenading Couple, Black, 4¼″, p.60	18.00
Triple Couple w/Piano, 3¾″, p.60	25.00
Couple Waiting for Rain, 5½″, p.60	25.00
2nd & 3rd Couples, 5½″ & 5¼″, p.60	20.00
4th, 5th, & 6th Couples, 4¼″ to 3¾″, p.60	15.00
Couple, 4½″, p.60	17.00
1st, 3rd, & 4th Couples; 3rd marked 'ST,' 6⅞″ to 6⅜″, p.60	35.00
Musicians, 7x7⅞″, p.60	50.00
Villain & Captive, blue, 7½″, p.60	50.00
Clown, 4″, p.88	12.00
Mermaid, bisque, 3½″, p.92	25.00
Duck Held by Child, 4″, p.96	16.00
Monkey Clown, p.98	12.00
Dog w/Shoe, p.98	8.00
Dog, 4th row, 4¾″ p.98	16.00
Boy at Cactus, p.98	9.00
Girl w/White Dress, p.98	18.00
Bulldog, p.128	15.00
Tumbled Ice Skater 'Ardalt,' p.128	15.00
Frog, bisque, 29¢, 4½″, p.128	15.00

OCEAN LINERS

With the turn of the century and the advent of new forms of sea travel and luxury on the high seas, great ocean liners such as the Titanic, the Olympic, the Queen Mary, the Elizabeth, and the U.S.S. United States came into being. They all claimed to be the fastest and to have the ultimate in gracious accommodations.

These vestiges of the past are part of our heritage, and items related pictorially or otherwise are part of our collecting interest. We are anxious to obtain any items related to sea travel prior to 1940. I am looking for items from the following categories.

E.S. Radcliffe
3732 Colonial Lane SE
Port Orchard, WA 98366

We Pay

Ship Cards	2.00-10.00
Menus	1.00-10.00
Baggage Labels	1.00-5.00
Souvenirs	2.00 +
Flatware	2.00-10.00
Dinnerware	3.00-15.00
Travel Brochures	2.00-10.00
Travel Posters	10.00 +
Silverplate	10.00 +
Linens	3.00-10.00
Pictures	1.00 +
Candy Tins	7.00-12.00
Ship Models	5.00 +
Ship Toys	5.00 +
Books	2.00 +
Passport Covers	3.00-8.00
Pins	5.00-12.00

	We Pay
Tickets	5.00-10.00
Match Covers	1.00-5.00
Match Boxes	1.00-5.00
Ash Trays	2.00-10.00
Badges	5.00 +
Medals	5.00 +

OHIO MEMORABILIA

I would like to purchase all memorabilia from Bellevue, Ohio, including post cards (I love the real photo type), photographs, souvenir pieces, advertising material, etc., etc. Bellevue is located about halfway between Toledo and Cleveland, Ohio.

The Union Bank of Bellevue is given as reference. I prefer the seller to price his items, but I will make offers. I ask for an accurate description, a statement of condition, and the age of the item offered. All letters will receive a reply. Hope to hear from you soon!

Katherine Hansard
644 Shumaker Dr.
Bellevue, OH 44811

OIL
PAINTINGS

We are looking for oil paintings by American and European artists from the 16th through the 20th centuries in almost any condition and size--small, medium, and large. We do not usually buy extra large paintings. Call any day of the week until 9:00 p.m.

Don Johnson
3808 Grand Ave. South
Minneapolis, MN 55409
(612) 824-1111

OLD IVORY
CHINA

Old Ivory China is usually marked 'Silesia' under a blue fleur-de-lis, 'OHME' over a red shield, and 'Old Ivory' with a pattern number (i.e., #15 or XV). The china always has an ivory background, flowers, and trim all around the outside edge, which is usually done in brown. Some pieces carry no mark at all.

I will buy almost any piece in the patterns listed below, or I will buy complete table services. I will also buy patterns other than those listed and some unmarked pieces, as well. I do not want any pieces with a pattern number lower than #12 or XII. Please call or write, listing items and prices.

Juanita Wilkins
P.O. Box 1884
Lima, OH 45802
(419) 227-2163

We Pay

#15 or XV Chocolate Cup Saucers or Demitasse Saucers.............**15.00**
#63 Teacup Saucers...**15.00**
#15 or XV Gravy Boat..**175.00**
#15 or XV Sugar Shaker..**110.00**
#15 or XV Teapot..**150.00**
For pattern #'s #17 or XVII, #22 or XXII, #40 or XL, #63, #12 or XII, or any
   pattern with pink, orange, peach flowers:
    Dinner Plate...................................**up to 100.00**
    Toothpick Holder...............................**up to 100.00**
    Gravy Boat.....................................**up to 175.00**
    Cracker Jar, Biscuit Jar.......................**up to 225.00**
    Teapot, Demitasse Pot..........................**up to 150.00**
    Chocolate Pot..................................**up to 200.00**
    Chocolate Set..................................**up to 550.00**
    Water Pitcher..................................**up to 275.00**
    Covered Tureen.................................**up to 300.00**
    Shaving Mug....................................**up to 150.00**
    Mustache Cup & Saucer..........................**up to 125.00**
    Mustard Pot....................................**up to 100.00**
    Egg Cup..**up to 60.00**

OLYMPIC GAMES

ORIENTAL RUGS

The oriental rug market consists of rugs and carpets from about 1875 to the present. It is impossible to give an accurate value because of the variation in the quality of a rug. As an example, a Persian Sarouk rug circa 1920-1930 may have five to six different knot counts, ranging from one hundred fifty to three hundred per square inch. An eighteen square foot rug in very fine condition would bring you $300.00 to $500.00.

Given as further examples and depending on condition, a Persian Sarouk 9 x 12 ft. rug would be $700.00 to $1,400.00; a Persian Kashan 9 x 12 ft. rug would be $1,000.00 to $2,000.00; a Chinese Peking 9 x 12 ft. rug would be $500.00 to $1,000.00; and a Chinese Nichols 9 x 12 ft. rug would be $400.00 to $800.00.

Please send a photograph for a more accurate evaluation. An immediate response will be given.

Calling House Antiques
19565 W. 9 Mile
Southfield, MI 48075

OUTHOUSES

I collect items relating to outhouses, such as post cards, books, old photographs, plans, catalogs, models, etc. Please see list for prices.

J.W. Courter
Rt. 1
Simpson, IL 62985
(618) 949-3884

	We Pay		We Pay
Post Cards	50¢-1.00	Catalogs	2.00-5.00
Books	2.00-3.00	Models	5.00-10.00
Old Photographs	2.00-3.00	Toys or Other Items	5.00-10.00
Plans	3.00-4.00	Fine Ceramics	10.00-25.00

PAP BOATS

Before the modern-day baby bottle or straws as we know them, infants or invalids were often fed from ironstone, china, or silver feeders. They were most popular in the 18th or 19th centuries in Europe; many of them were hand-painted or highly embossed. They were produced by Haviland and many other companies in the Meissen and Staffordshire areas.

Hand-feeding was not well accepted in colonial America for some time until mothers found that chamois, sponge, or leather nipples over the spout of the feeder allowed babes (as well as invalids) to suckle milk from them, drawing nourishment from the 'pap' or gruel that was made from bread, water, sugar, beer, or wine. They were used until the 1950's in the U.S.A. and England; these were often made of enamelware. Most frequently-found shapes were similar to an Aladdin lamp or gravy boat; there was also a teapot style with the spout emerging from the inside.

Pat Van Gaabeek
631 Randolph
Topeka, KS 66606

PAPER

I am buying just about everything and anything in the way of old printed paper. I am particularly interested in Confederate or any other old paper money, old bank checks, financial documents, etc. I also buy older books on coins and currency, and old stocks and bonds. When available, I'll buy in large lots.

Checks with vignettes (engravings) of people, buildings, trains, animals, etc. are usually worth $1.00 to $20.00. Confederate currency starts at $2.00 each for common examples and goes up to $50.00 for the better notes. Most paper items in my field of interest need to be dated prior to 1900 to be considered collectible.

Bob Pyne
P.O. Box 149064
Orlando, FL 32814

PAPER DOLLS

Paper dolls probably reached the height of their popularity in the late 1940's and the early 1950's due in many ways to the popularity of Hollywood and its film stars. With the advent of television and other more sophisticated ways to capture the imagination, interest in this amusing art form began to wane.

We are assembling a collection of these somewhat neglected, later works dating from the late 1950's to the present. We will buy out-of-print, uncut, mint-condition sets, as well as single- and double-page novelties from periodicals. Prices may vary due to stains, torn corners, markings, etc. Below is a representative list of titles and the prices we will pay for them. In addition to this, we are looking for any foreign titles (published in the past or present) as well as any quality one-of-a-kind or limited-edition artist sets, if you contact us for prices.

Keith O. Henderson
23 SW 22nd St. #1G
New York City, NY 10011

We Pay

Saafield, #1330 Mother & Daughter, 1962	**20.00**
Saafield, #4218 Susan Dey as Laura Partridge, 1972	**20.00**
Saafield, #4425 Evelyn Rudy, 1958	**40.00**
Saafield, #9619 Once Upon a Wedding Day, 1964	**18.00**
Saafield, #4445 Little Women, 1960	**28.00**
Merrill, #2968 Little Miss Christmas & Holly Belle, 1965	**18.00**
Merrill, #2580 The Heavenly Blue Wedding, 1955	**25.00**

We Pay

Merrill, #M3480 Vivien Leigh, 1980 . . . . **Negotiable**
Blaise, #1000 Cleopatra, 1963 . . . . **45.00**
Wolfpit, #? Love Paper Dolls, 1975 . . . . **10.00**
Hobby House Press, American Colonial Brides, 1980 . . . . **6.00**
Magic Wand Corp., #114 Bewitched, 1965 . . . . **40.00**
Merry Mfg., #6402 The Bride of Frankenstein, 1964 . . . . **18.00**
Paper Palace, Victoria, 1981 . . . . **10.00**
Platt & Munk Co., #245 Williamsburg Colonial Dolls, 1967 . . . . **30.00**
Pedigree Books, Princess Diana Book of Fashion, 1982 . . . . **8.00**
Stecher Lithographic Co., #175 Patty's Party, date? **6.00**
Transogram Toys, #3456 Angela Cartwright, 1960 . . . . **23.00**
Troubador Press, Gorey Cats, 1982 . . . . **10.00**
Toy Factory, #107 Vinnie Barbarino, 1977 . . . . **12.00**
Whitman, #1978 Miss America, 1973 . . . . **10.00**
Ainsley Worrell, Dottie West, 1973 . . . . **20.00**
McCall's Magazine, Betsy McCall, single uncut sheet **2.00-6.00**
Marvel Comics, Millie the Model, single uncut sheet **2.00-5.00**
Archie Comics, Katy Keene, single uncut sheet **2.00-5.00**
Doll Reader, double uncut sheet **3.00**
American Greeting Card, Holly Hobby, 1976 . . . . **4.00**
Time Magazine, Henry Kissinger Cartoon, March 1974 . . . . **2.00**

Collector-dealer wants to buy any quantity of pre-1960 paper dolls––cut or uncut, sorted or unsorted. Types (cut-outs, press-outs, punch-outs) wanted are: celebrity, antique, babies, children, animals, military, glamour, Disney, fictional characters, magazine sheets, and newspaper comic-strip paper dolls. Please give price and describe condition. All offers are appreciated. I give an immediate reply.

Paperdolls Wanted
Sharon Rogers, Dept. L
1813 Junius
Fort Worth, TX 76103

I buy uncut paper doll books from the 1950's through the 1970's––celebrity and non-celebrity. I pay according to condition and rarity.

Shirley Harwood
P.O. Box 33454
Granada Hills, CA 91344

PAPERWEIGHTS

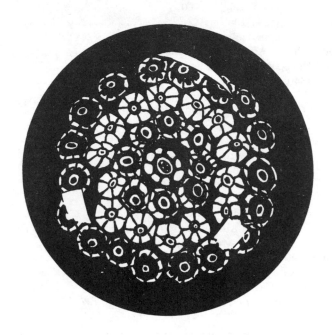

We will buy antique and contemporary American or European glass paperweights. Prices depend on condition, rarity, and beauty, as well as the maker. They often range from $20.00 to more than $1,000.00. Generally, weights which are internally signed and/or dated will be more valuable than those which are not. Also, weights with millefiori canes in excellent condition are more acceptable. Please send description or photos or call me toll-free at 1-800-524-0576.

Warren Abrams
33 Miriam Dr.
P.O. Box 717
Matawan, NJ 07747
(800) 524-0576

PATTERN GLASS

I would like to buy single pieces of table sets (creamers, sugar bowls, spooners, and covered butter dishes), celery vases, relish dishes, and toothpick holders in the following patterns: Block & Honeycomb, Budded Ivy, Flower Medallion, Flower Pot, Hummingbird, King's Crown, Ribbed Palm, Sprig, Stippled Ivy, and Viking.

Mrs. V.R. Lewis
Rt. 1, Box 102
Stafford, KS 67578

Pattern glass mugs were very popular during the mid-1800's until the early 1900's. Often given as gifts to children, these mugs sometimes had a pattern depicting a nursery rhyme, an animal, or a bird. Toward the late 1800's and early 1900's, they gained wide popularity as souvenirs of visits to various towns and expositions throughout the country.

Mugs were produced in hundreds of patterns from geometrics to historical designs. Although clear glass was the standard, they were produced in as many colors as the glassmakers could devise. After the turn of the century, they were also produced in carnival glass and custard glass.

Being an advanced collector of pattern glass mugs from the early 1800's to the 1930's, I am interested in purchasing one piece or entire collections. I am willing to pay the following prices for perfect specimens.

Brent Godlewski
8320 NW 44th Ct.
Lauderhill, FL 33351
(305) 741-5673

We Pay

Hand Blown, pre-1840	75.00 +
Pressed w/Applied Handles	25.00 +
Flint	40.00 +
Purple Slag	60.00 +
Carmel Slag	30.00 +
Greentown	20.00 +
Custard	30.00 +
Carvival, marigold	20.00 +
Carnival, colored	35.00 +
Historicals	25.00 +
Nursery Rhymes	20.00 +
Geometrics	5.00 +
Advertising	20.00 +

Sometimes this pattern is called Dahlia, though its proper name is Stippled Dahlia. It is listed in Alice Hulett Metz's first book as #686. Made in the 1880's of non-flint glass, it was produced in clear as well as many colors--yellow, amber, blue, and apple green. I buy items in good condition only--no cracks or chips.

Lee Kramer
3725 Huaco Lane
Waco, TX 76710
(817) 753-4469

We Pay		We Pay	
Plate, round, 7"	20.00	Wine	35.00
Water Goblet, tall	35.00	Egg Cup	25.00
Cordial	35.00	Mug	25.00

PERFUME BOTTLES

We buy all kinds of perfume bottles; contact us for specifics. We are especially interested in commercial types with their original labels. Many often have residue of original perfume in them. There are hundreds of different makers, but some of the more common are: Guerlain, Nina Ricci, Worth, Coty, Vigny, Babani, Molinard, Roger & Gallet, Elizabeth Arden, Lucien Lelong, Schiaparelli, Robj, Dior, Corday, and there are many others. Examples contained in their original boxes are especially wanted.

We are also interested in a second type, the Czechoslovakian cut glass perfumes that were imported in quantity in the 1930's. These should have an acid-etched stamp on the bottom that reads 'Made in Czechoslovakia.' Listed are some sample buying prices.

Randall B. Monsen
P.O. Box 1503
Arlington, VA 22210
(703) 938-2129

We Pay

Elizabeth Arden 'It's You'..250.00
Elizabeth Arden 'Blue Grass'.......................................25.00
Lucien Lelong 'Impromptu'..50.00
Lucien Lelong 'Opening Night'....................................150.00
Schiaparelli 'Sleeping' Baccarat..................................150.00
Czechoslovakian, blue cut glass w/lovebirds.................50.00
Czechoslovakian, tall, yellow cut glass, dancer in stopper.............75.00
Czechoslovakian, small, clear, red diamond stopper.................40.00

PHOENIX GLASS

I am researching the Phoenix Glass Company of Monaca, Pennsylvania, in an effort to write a detailed and accurate history of the company since its beginning in 1880. Over the years, Phoenix has produced a wide variety of utilitarian and decorative glassware including Webb-style art glass, colored cut glass, hand-decorated oil lamps, hotel and bar ware, gas and electric light shades, and the line of 'sculptured' vases, bowls, etc., for which they are best known. I am especially hunting original company catalogues and advertising brochures, magazine ads showing glassware, unusual pieces, and related items such as post cards of Monaca. I'd like to hear from retired workers and other people who are willing to share their knowledge and love of Phoenix glass with me. Mini-biographies of 'the Phoenix family' will be included in my book.

The price I can pay for an item varies, depending on the pattern, color, and condition of each piece. Please price and fully describe each item. Photos are helpful. I answer all letters.

Kathy Kelly
1621 Princess Ave.
Pittsburgh, PA 15216
(412) 561-3379

PHOTOGRAPH NEGATIVES

I am looking for high-quality photographic negatives that were made before 1960. I am interested in negatives relating to obsolete forms of transportation such as railroading, propeller-driven aircraft, steamships, sailing ships, canals, automobiles, trucks, and busses prior to World War II, military vehicles, streetcars, trolleys, inclines, horse-drawn vehicles, and steam-powered industrial or farming equipment.

I am especially interested in railroading negatives of all types. Examples of these would depict steam locomotives, early diesel locomotives, electric locomotives, 'name' passenger trains, early passenger coaches, special equipment (snow plows, pile drivers, cranes, etc.), terminals, depots and stations, bridges and trestles, work crews, train crews, cabooses, publicity shots, 1949 Chicago Railroad Fair, builders' photos, shops, wrecks, and railroad officials.

I would also be interested in pre-World War II negatives pertaining to architecture, cities, bridges, landscapes, people, rivers and dams, professional athletic teams and stadiums, and newsworthy events––politics, wars, fires, floods, etc.

Any format (size) negatives will be considered, but I am most interested in larger sizes such as 620, 120, and 127 in roll films and 2¼" x 3¼", 4" x 5", and 5" x 7" in sheet film. Glass plates will also be acceptable. The negatives must be of high quality, properly exposed, in sharp focus, and undamaged.

The prices I will pay will be dependent on the subject matter, quality, and negative size. Examples are given below.

Don Culver
3083 Balsam
Edgewood, KY 41017

We Pay

Steam Locomotives	5.00
Early Diesel Locomotives	3.00
Electric Locomotives	4.00
Railroad Equipment	2.00
'Name' Passenger Trains	7.50
Bridges & Trestles	2.00
Cabooses	3.00
1949 Chicago Railroad Fair	5.00
Wrecks	5.00
Steam Ships	5.00
Sailing Ships	7.50
Propeller Aircraft	4.00
Military Propeller Aircraft	8.00
Early Autos, Trucks, & Busses	2.00
Streetcars & Trolleys	2.00
Inclines	5.00
Horse-Drawn Vehicles	3.00
Bridges	2.00
Major News Events	5.00

PHOTOGRAPHS

I will buy nearly all old photographs circa 1860 to 1930 from the United States, Canada, or Japan. They may be loose or in albums. I prefer the older ones, of course. These are usually mounted on a piece of stiff cardboard. Rather than just portrait photographs, I prefer those showing people at occupations, street scenes, buildings, stores, and businesses (interiors or exteriors). The prices I pay reflect the clarity of the photograph as well as the condition. When responding, please either send photocopies with asking price, or send the items themselves for an offer and immediate payment. Please use U.S. insured mail. Here are some examples of what I'm looking for, but note that my collecting interests are vast!

Joseph F. Loccisano
Box 5301
Lancaster, PA 17601
(717) 560-0639

We Pay

Interior of 1906 Gambling Casino	35.00
Interior of 1910 Barber Shop	20.00
Interior of 1915 Toy Store	20.00
Exterior of 1897 Shoe Store	15.00
Exterior of 1888 Cigar Store	18.00
Exterior of 1897 Lumber Company	19.00

PIE BIRDS

Pie Birds

These attractive little figures are being very widely collected. Some are imported, but most are American. Pie birds are also called pie vents. Most are ceramic. They were used in the 1920's and 1930's. They were placed in the middle of a pie while it baked; when the pie liquids began to boil, they were contained in the hollow cavity of the pie bird. This kept the pie from boiling over. As the pie cooled, the liquids drained back into the pie. Although the term 'bird' is used, they came in different types of figures and sizes as listed below.

Keep in mind that the blackbird (American) has been reproduced. It was sold in numerous department stores in the early 1980's. It was packed in a black box with a stringed tag around its neck. Note the lower price it commands. All pie birds should be in good condition without chips or cracks. I will buy others than those listed. Examples with slight damage would be considered at a somewhat lower price.

Hicker' Nut Hill Antiques
c/o Genie Prather
Rt. 2, Box 532-Y
Tyler, TX 75704

We Pay

Blackbird (England)	4.00
Black Mammy or Chef	10.00
Blackbird	2.50
Benny the Baker, 5"	6.00
Benny the Baker, w/original box & crimper, 5"	10.00
Bird, gray	3.50
Chick, pink or blue trim	4.00
Duck, various colors	4.00
Goose, various colors	4.00
Elephant, tri-color	5.00
Bird, turquoise & white	4.00
Bird, pink & burgundy	4.00
Bird, singing, brass	12.00
Pillsbury Premium	6.00
Peacock, blue & green, 4½"	10.00
Steam Whistle	10.00
Rooster, various colors	5.00
Bird, yellow, 3¼"	3.00
Blackbird (Scotland), 4"	3.00
Blackbird, white vest, 2-piece, w/original box	8.00
Black Chef w/Spoon	10.00
Bluebird	4.00
Duckling, long neck, yellow, 5"	3.00
Mammy w/hands out, brown & pink	10.00
Chick, cream w/pink & gray, 5½"	4.00
Elephant, gray	6.00
Rooster, Blue Willow	10.00

	We Pay
Bird, gray & yellow	3.00
Bird, light brown, 4¼"	3.00
Elephant, seated, pink, 4"	8.00

PLUMBING AND BATH

Indoor plumbing came into popular use just before the turn of the century (in some areas of the country a bit later). Early fixtures in the Victorian era reflected the embellishment of that era in embossed toilets and sinks. An early bath might include a high-boy oak toilet with a pull-chain pedestal sink, or a fluted column or marble sink with wall-mounted brackets or an iron pedestal. Tubs sometimes had an ornate clawfoot design; others filled and drained from the center rather than from the end.

Hygienic health sanitariums of that era incorporated water therapy in their treatments by using sitz baths in a low tub (shaped like a chair), foot tubs, and rib cage needle showers. I am seeking early plumbing fixtures such as those listed below. Because refinishing is possible for some old fixtures, condition is not important. I can arrange pickup of heavy items. We are seeking ornate and unusual bath items other than those listed here, as well.

Dan & Elaine Kelley
SRB Box 397
Franklin, LA 70538
(318) 867-4405

We Pay

Center-Fill & Drain Tubs	75.00-100.00
Pedestal Sinks, oval	50.00-75.00
Marble Sinks	50.00-65.00
Shower Tub on Legs	30.00-45.00
Tub, 4 ft.	25.00
Tub, 6-6½ ft.	75.00
Toilet, embossed	25.00
Sink, embossed, wall-hung	20.00
Wrap-Around Shower	25.00-50.00
Shower Head, porcelain	10.00
Shower Head, brass	2.00-4.00
Mixer Faucets, porcelain handle	10.00-15.00
Tub Faucets, porcelain handle	5.00-10.00
Cross Handles, porcelain, pair	4.00-8.00
Single Handles	2.00-4.00
Porcelain Inserts, marked H or C	50¢
Ornate Tub Legs, set	7.00-10.00
Toilet, oak	15.00-25.00
Soap Dishes, over tub	3.00-5.00
Brush & Tumbler Holders, brass	5.00-7.00
Medicine Cabinets, early	Varies
Sink Brackets, brass, pair	10.00-15.00
Sink Brackets, iron, pair	2.00-4.00
Paper Holders, brass	2.00-4.00

PORTRAIT MINIATURES

American, English, Continental, Oriental, and Mid-East portrait miniatures from the 17th century through the early 20th century have been hand-painted in oils, watercolors, and tempera on surfaces such as ivory, parchment, wood or metal panels, and canvas materials. I buy these items in good-to-slightly-damaged condition. Sizes range from 1″ to 10″ tall and may be oval or rectangular in shape. Some areas of the world portray the subject by incorporating a background that suggests or pertains to that person's reputation or life style. As in all original art, values of items in this category differ dramatically depending on artist, age of item, condition, rarity, and quality. Please contact me by calling direct or by sending photos of the items (or the actual items themselves) for evaluation.

Lester E. Sender
3482 Lee
Shaker Heights, OH 44120

POSTAL ARTIFACTS

There is a wide spectrum of postal artifacts which includes obsolete items that were issued and used by the Post Office Department or U.S. Postal Service. Most of these were marked 'Property of the Post Office Department' or had similar wording to that effect. Some of the major categories are listed below with price ranges. As with most historical objects, the price will vary depending upon age, condition, usage, and origin. Prices quoted are for USA artifacts; those from other countries may command an additional premium. For example, Canadian artifacts in each of these categories are generally scarcer than their USA counterparts. This is not true across the board, however, as in the case of street letter boxes from Great Britain. These have been imported in abundance, so they may be priced equal to or less than USA letter boxes. For specific items, please write to the Railway Mail Service Library with a complete description. Also include a LSASE with 45¢ postage affixed for a detailed seven-page illustrated want list.

Railway Mail Service Library
18 E. Rosemont Ave.
Alexandria, VA 22301-2325

We Pay

Street Letter Boxes....................................50.00-250.00
Badges...5.00-100.00
U.S. Mail Locks w/Keys.................................5.00-100.00
Coat or Vest Buttons.....................................50¢-5.00
Uniform Patches.......................................1.00-10.00
Glass Paperweights....................................5.00-50.00
Glass Inkwells.......................................10.00-60.00
Balance Beam Scales.................................25.00-100.00
General Schemes.......................................3.00-100.00
Schedules of Routes...................................3.00-40.00
Post Route Maps.......................................2.00-35.00
Annual Reports..5.00-50.00
Other Post Office Books...............................5.00-50.00
Steel Postmarking Handstamps........................25.00-200.00
Other Wood, Steel, or Brass Handstamps; Other Marking Devices.10.00-100.00
Rubber Handstamps......................................25¢-10.00
Cancelling Machines.................................50.00-250.00
Cancelling Machine Ring Dies.........................10.00-50.00
Cancelling Die Hubs..................................25.00-75.00
Steel Date Type Sets.................................10.00-30.00
Instruction, Repair Manuals, or Cancelling Machine Catalogs.....10.00-50.00
Postal Clerk Uniforms................................25.00-50.00
Early Mail Pouches or Sacks..........................10.00-25.00
Lead Sealer Presses..................................15.00-40.00
Lock Box Door Fronts..................................2.00-50.00
Postal Guides...5.00-50.00

POST CARDS

The last several years have seen a revival in the collecting of picture post cards, a fad which was popular during the turn of the century. The subject matter ranges from local scenes to popular topics such as early transportation, greetings, and social history that has influenced today's society. The pictorial history they preserved gives us great insight into events, history, lost buildings, and views that were commonplace both in the United States and in foreign countries during the height of the post card-collecting period (1895 through WWI).

Post cards can be valued from five cents for common holiday greeting post cards to several dollars for real photo-picture cards depicting early department store interiors, political history, etc.

In evaluating post cards, the subject matter as well as the card's condition is a factor in the pricing structure. I have listed below the average values of certain types of cards, but these values are only an indication. Cards may be worth more or less depending on their quality, condition, and image. I am interested in purchasing all post cards and will pay according to the guidelines as previously stated.

S. Dobres
110 E. Lexington Street
Baltimore, MD 21202

We Pay

Photo-Picture Interiors	3.00
Political	5.00
Ships	1.00
Advertising	2.00
Busy Street Scenes	50¢
Buildings	25¢
Judaica-Comic Type	8.00
Synagogues	2.00
Suffragette	10.00
Kewpies	12.00
Campbell's Kids	10.00
Silk Santas	12.00
Miscellaneous Santas	2.00
Hold-To-Light Santas	25.00
Columbian Expos	5.00
Cotton States Expos	50.00
California Mid-Winter Expos	50.00
Pan American Expos	3.00

We Pay

Major League Baseball Players, pre-1940	10.00
Major League Ball Parks, pre-1940	3.00
Military	1.00
Art Nouveau	10.00
Other Signed Art	3.00
Small Non-European Foreign Countries	1.00
Hawaii	1.00
Alaska	1.00
Railway Depots	1.00
Mechanicals	5.00

Post cards with pictures are perhaps one of the most intriguing of all collectibles, since they cover every conceivable topic. The collecting craze became popular in the United States during the Columbian Expo in Chicago in 1892 and 1893—post cards were sold via vending machines in packets of ten. It was fun to send a 'wish you were here, I am' type message. Publishers in turn saw that this was a viable commodity and literally millions of cards were published.

It is most important that post cards be in near-perfect condition—no bends, tears, creases, cancel marks, or blemishes. It does not matter if they are used or unused. Prices listed are just a sampling of the many categories I need. Single cards as well as large collections are wanted.

Sally S. Carver
179 South St.
Chestnut Hill, MA 02167

We Pay

Hold-To-Lights	15.00-25.00
Hold-To-Lights w/Santas	50.00-80.00
Mascerated Money	75.00+
Any Pre-1900 Exposition	10.00-500.00
Cars w/Full-Length Santas in Robes	8.00+
Small Town Railroad Depots	2.50
Small Town Railroad Depots on Photos	4.00-5.00
Labor Cards by Lounsbury	100.00
Groundhog Day Cards by Henderson Litho (HH)	100.00
Rock Island Railroad by Rose O'Neill	50.00
Hamilton King Coca-Cola	350.00
Real Photos of Store or Barber Shop Interiors	10.00+
Real Photos of Horse-Drawn Ice Trucks, Hearses	10.00+
Pan-American Expo, 6x9″	75.00
St. Louis Expo, 6x9″	75.00

We Pay

St. Louis Expo 1904 Hold-To-Light, 6x9″ **100.00**
Campbell Kids Advertising, No. 4 (& higher nos.) **25.00**
Sleepy Eye Flour (many advertising series wanted) **50.00**
Louis Wain Cat, signed **25.00**
Halloween by Winsch **15.00-25.00**
Mechanical Disk by Ellen Clapsaddle **20.00**
Paper Dolls by Tuck **40.00-50.00**
Suffragettes **10.00-18.00**
Autographed Baseball Pictures **5.00-20.00**

For as long as post cards have been printed and sold, there have been views of post offices. The attraction to the post card printer was that there was a post office in every community of significance; it was the federal presence at a personal service level. Before the phone, it was the focal point of communication with the outside world. Money orders were bought here to pay for mail-order catalog purchases. Aliens had to register their addresses here once a year; neighbors met each and every day to chat, even if there was no mail to be picked up or posted. Such a focal point of the village, town, or city was the post office, the ideal subject for a post card which for many years was a popular mode of writing.

Aside from local residents who often took pride in sending a picture of their local post office, these views were also popular among early post card collectors. There were units of post card clubs whose members specialized in them. Fortunately for collectors today, many of those people built large collections so that post office views are very abundant, especially from the large cities. The Railway Mail Service Library will buy any post office-view post cards at the following prices. Also, if you have more than one hundred post office views, I will discuss a group price to avoid the time and effort of evaluating each card individually. I accept any quantity of views, but I will purchase no more than five of any identical cards in one transaction. However, I will buy an unlimited number of cards of the same post office if they are different views by various manufacturers. Deduct five cents for used post cards missing their postage stamps. I will pay a premium of ten cents per card for any small town post office other than those described as 'smallest post office.' I will pay a fifty-cent premium for any interior post office view showing the sorting area (not the post office lobby) or one showing a railway or highway post office close-up (not as a part of a train). I will trade duplicate cards at the values shown below for any post office-view card you have of equal value. I do not purchase any unused linen post cards produced by the Asheville Post Card Company. I will buy used views.

Railway Mail Service Library
18 E. Rosemont Ave.
Alexandria, VA 22301-2325

Post Cards

	We Pay	
	Used	Unused
Chromes, 1950's & later	10¢	15¢
Linens, 1930's to 1950's	10¢	15¢
Monocolor (black & white), undivided back	25¢	30¢
Monocolor, divided back, no border	20¢	25¢
Monocolor, divided back, w/border	15¢	20¢
Multi-Color, undivided back	50¢	60¢
Multi-Color, divided back, no border	40¢	50¢
Multi-Color, divided back, w/border	30¢	40¢
Real Photo (on photo paper), undivided back	1.00	1.25
Real Photo, divided back	75¢	1.00

We want to purchase pre-1920 post cards, both U.S. and foreign, in many varieties. Cards that we especially need are those in excellent condition that show 'Beautiful Women and Beautiful Children,' and artist-signed cards of all types: including women, children, animals, comics, military, transportation, etc. We are interested in duplicate lots,especially large quantities. Remainders of old distributors' or store stock are also wanted.

Cards may be used or unused, but it is very important that they be in fine condition with no bends, tears, bad corners, or dirt. No writing or cancellations on the front, please. Listed below are some of the prices I will pay for certain cards.

Mashburn Cards
P.O. Box 609
Enka, NC 28728
(704) 667-1427

Beautiful Ladies (no couples or lovers) Signed　　　　　　　　　　**We Pay**

C.W. Barber	2.50
Court Barber	2.50
James M. Flagg	3.00
C.D. Gibson	3.00
C. Allen Gilbert	2.00
W. Haskell Coffin	2.00
R. Ford Harbor	2.50
Lou Mayer	2.50
Will Grefe	2.50
Alice L. Fidler	2.50
Alice Fidler Lemunyan	2.50
The Kinneys	2.50
Stanlaws	3.00
R. Kirchner	20.00 +
A. Mucha	30.00 +
T. Corbella	3.00

We Pay

Nanni	3.50
Guerzoni	3.00
Busi	3.50
Mauzan	3.00
Colombo	2.50
Bompard	2.50
Barribal	3.00
Chiostri	3.00
Usabal	2.50
Boileau	4.00
Harrison Fisher	4.00
C. Underwood	2.50
Henry Hutt	2.50
Coles Phillips	3.50
Others, signed	1.00 +

Beautiful Children Signed   **We Pay**

K. Feiertag	2.50
F.B. Pease	2.00
Agnes Richardson	3.00
Grace Weiderseim	7.50
Grace Drayton	7.50
W. Fialkowski	2.50
Frances Brundage	3.00
Mary Ellen George	3.50
Florence Upton	4.00
M.G. Hays	3.00
Grace Marcellus	3.00
H.B.G.	3.50
Helen Clapsaddle	3.50
Ethel Parkinson	3.00
M. Sowerby	3.00

I am very much interested in buying post cards from the Ocean City and Berlin, Maryland, areas. I would prefer the post cards to date from the early 1900's through the 1940's. I will pay from $1.00 to $3.00 each depending on whether or not I have them in my collection. Please send me a list of the post cards that you have, so I can compare it with mine.

Mrs. Cathy Hastings
Rt. 3, Box 617
Berlin, MD 21811

Post Cards

I want to buy pre-1930 post cards of Kansas and Oklahoma showing street scenes and buildings—no parks, rivers, bridges, statues, or trees. Also '101 ranch cards' are wanted. We pay postage.

Chester Ashby
2232 E. Maple
Enid, OK 73701-4613

Propaganda post cards of the WWII era are my special interest. The prices I'm willing to pay for the right material are well beyond 'competitive' as the following will indicate. I will consider material from all of the belligerent nations of the conflict (primarily Germany, Italy, Japan, the USSR, and the United States), but I might also be interested in other countries if the post cards represent political, racial, or nationalistic propaganda that is common to the themes of the 1930's to 1940's. The nature of the message is often as important to me as the visual impact of the post card representation itself. Where possible, however, I prefer the items to be pictorial. I also prefer them to be in color and postally used, but these are not absolute criteria.

I can provide references from fellow collectors and dealers throughout the world. Please contact me in writing or try to reach me by phone before 9:00 a.m. or after 5:00 p.m EST. I'm looking forward to hearing from you.

Dr. James B. Kahn
Route 107
121 Raymond Rd.
Deerfield, NH 03037-1599
(603) 463-7105

We Pay

Nuremburg Party Day Rally Cards...........................**up to 300.00**
Tag der Wehrmacht Stalingrad Cards.............................**875.00**
Italian SS Images by Boccasile.............................**up to 350.00**
Russian Anti-Fascist Propaganda...........................**40.00-60.00**

Post cards from Old Sleepy Eye down to views of churches make a wonderful collection. Having collected post cards for twenty years, we now specialize in Old Sleepy Eye, Indians, and Prairie du Chien, Wisconsin, cards. Historic Prairie du Chien is the second-oldest city in Wisconsin and was neutral ground—most Indian rendezvous were here. We pay the following prices for post cards and Prairie du Chien souvenirs.

Bob & Jan Check
115 S. Dousman St.
Prairie du Chien, WI 53821
(608) 326-6014

Post Cards   **We Pay**

Old Sleepy Eye, mint...**30.00**
Old Sleepy Eye, worn...**15.00**
Indians, black & white..**3.00**
Indians, color...**1.00**
Prairie du Chien, WI..**3.00**
Prairie du Chien Schools...**50¢**

Souvenirs of Prairie du Chien   **We Pay**

Made of China...**8.00**
Made of Glass...**5.00**
Made of Wood...**3.00**
Books ....**Call**

POTTERY

On the crest of a ridge on Sand Mountain in Alabama, a group of potters turned out work over a span of sixty years ranging from the 1850's to the time of World War I. These are unknown potters, but to me their work is of importance as they represent four generations of my family. Their pottery will be marked T.J. Henry, E.T. Belcher, E.E. McPherson, or simply by initials with D.S. ALA.

Forms seen so far include jugs from one to six gallons, churns and storage jars in various sizes, pitchers, bowls (the straight-sided 'milk pan' form), preserve jars (with or without handles), two-handled bean pots, and a one-handled bean pot type designed to hold syrup or honey. We will buy items in good condition as well as damaged items. We will pay $25.00 and up (according to size and condition) or your reasonable price.

Charles & Gail N. Turk
Rt. 8, Box 52-A
Boaz, AL 35957
(205) 593-3766

I am very interested in unusual, old crockery pieces including spongeware, spatterware, and gray or brown pieces with bluebirds, flowers, or other designs. All prices considered.

Mrs. Wm. H. Lidey
2109 Sunland Ave.
Las Vegas, NV 89106
(702) 383-4009

I want to buy items from the California Mission Potteries of the 1920's to the 1950's. These include Bauer, Catalina Island, and California hand-decorated tiles.

Barbara Jean Hayes
Calico Cat Antiques
1629 W. Washington Blvd.
Venice, CA 90291

PRINTS

We are buying old color prints, pictures, calendars, trade cards, and illustrated books published before 1930. We are especially interested in prints by the following companies and artists:

Maude Humphrey	H.C. Plumb	Paul DeLongpre
Francis Brundage	Harry Roseland	C.L. Vandenburg
Arthur Elsley	Zula Kenyon	A.W. Adams
C. Burton Barber	Louis Icart	Others
Pears Soap		

Please include description, condition, and a photo if possible. All photos will be returned. We will consider complete collections.

Gallery Graphics Inc.
P.O. Box 502
Noel, MO 64854
(417) 475-6367

We buy old, framable color prints of children, animals, and beautiful girls by artists such as Jessica Wilcox Smith, Zula Kenyon, Annie Benson Muller, Charlotte Becker, Bessie Pease Gutmann, Mabel Rollins Harris, and Adelaide Hiebel. We are also interested in buying pin-up prints and calendars by artists such as Vargas, Petty, Armstrong, Pressler, Mozert, Moran, De Vorss, Erbit, and others. Some specific prints being sought are: *Spring Song*, *The Lone Wolf*, *Found*, *Can't You Talk*, *Boy with Rabbit*, and *Saved*. All items must be in very good condition. Please state the artist, title, size, condition, and price.

Carol J. Beattie
3374 Ver Bunker Ave.
Port Edwards, WI 54469
(715) 887-3497

PUZZLES

Wanted: mechanical puzzles; paper puzzles; puzzle locks and trick-opening devices; puzzle jugs and trick pottery of all types; puzzle trade cards; Sam Loyd puzzles and articles; puzzle books, booklets, and articles; hidden-figure pictures; optical illusions; and Rebus pictures and cards. Please send a photo, photocopy, or complete description and price. No jigsaw puzzles are wanted.

Jerry Slocum
P.O. Box 1635
Beverly Hills, CA 90213

PYROGRAPHY

Literally, pyrography means fire-writing. For our purposes, it indicates those wooden, leather, and velvet items which were decorated by a burning pen. Sometimes pyrography is known as Flemish art or 'burnt wood.' From the period of 1895 to 1911, pyrography was popular among men and women. Wooden boxes, plaques, furniture, and house novelties were decorated with a wood-burning pen; hand-painted details were sometimes added, as well. Major companies selling burning tools and wooden objects were Thayer & Chandler, Flemish Art Co., F.W. Weber & Co., F.F. Rick & Co., and Sears & Roebuck. These companies borrowed designs and patterns from each other. Many of them imported burning tools from Europe.

Pyrography boxes gave way to mass-produced, stenciled boxes from candy and gift companies. Many of these boxes were lighter in weight and were never burned or painted by hand. These pieces have less value. Other pyrography pieces were produced by professional artists working for the companies which manufactured and sold the burning tools and wooden items.

We buy quality pyrography items such as plaques and furniture; we prefer the more unique examples. We have a special interest in company catalogs, wood-burning kits, books on pyrography, and copies of the *Pyrography Magazine* which existed from 1903 to 1909.

John Lewis
912 W. 8th St.
Loveland, CO 80537

We Pay

Flemish Art Co. Catalog..**25.00**
Flemish Art Co. Manual...**5.00**
Thayer & Chandler Catalog...**7.00**
Other Company Catalogs..**7.00**
Pyrography Kit...**18.00**
Unburned Plaque..**3.00**
Umbrella Holder..**25.00**
Chair..**30.00**
Table..**40.00**
Chest..**45.00**
Plaque, small..**10.00**
Plaque, medium...**15.00**
Plaque, large..**20.00**
C.D. Gibson Plaque...**30.00**
Sunbonnet Girls Plaque...**25.00**
Glove Box..**7.00**
Handkerchief Box...**7.00**
Jewelry Box..**8.00**

QUILTS

I am wanting to buy antique quilts. I am not interested in quilts with butterflies or sunbonnet designs, embroidered quilts, or any made of orange or purple fabrics. I pay top dollar, depending on the quilt. Send pictures. If a quilt is sent, I will pay postage both ways. Pictures or quilts will be returned promptly, if I'm not interested.

Evelyn Gibson
137 E. Main St.
Galesburg, IL 61401
(309) 343-2001

Handmade quilts have been very collectible for some time. Historical quilts were generally made before 1870. Many of these are red, white, and blue in color; some contain stars. I will pay up to $5,000.00 each for early historical quilts in good condition. I am also interested in buying family album quilts from before 1880.

Kittelberger Galleries
Antiques & Fine Arts
82½ E. Main St.
Webster, NY 14580
(716) 265-1230

RADIO
PREMIUMS

Between two to three thousand different premiums were made available to radio listeners by the sponsors of programs that aired from 1925 through 1955. We are interested in all premiums, with special emphasis on those from the juveniles (children's programs), juvenile-adult serials, and nighttime or weekend dramatic programs and mysteries (or, as they were called then, 'crime dramas').

We pay immediate cash for hundreds of premiums, particularly the adjustable kids' rings that incorporated some gadget, code sender, secret compartment, or glow-in-the-dark plastic. Condition is everything on premiums; we prefer premiums in mint condition. The most desirable grade is uncirculated-mint condition with the original mailing box or envelope. To sell to us, simply box up what you have and ship (UPS or USPS insured) indicating the least you will accept, or enclose your phone number and leave the price up to us. We pay the highest prices for Tarzan, The Shadow, Superman, and Dick Tracy!

Rex Miller
Rt. 1, Box 457-D
East Prairie, MO 63845
(314) 649-5048

We Pay

Capt. Midnight Skelly Maps	35.00
Buck Rogers Maps in Tubes (original only)	80.00
Dick Tracy Items in Quaker Oats Mailers or Mailing Boxes from 'Dick Tracy, Chicago, IL	1.00-75.00
Ellery Queen Pins	12.00
Rings w/Scarabs	10.00
Rings w/Dragons	10.00
Rings w/Lumps of Blue Coal	50.00
Rings w/Lightning Bolts	20.00
Rings w/Sky King	10.00
Rings w/Red Plastic Tops	10.00
Rings w/Tom Mix	10.00
Rings w/Buck Rogers	30.00
Rings w/Letter 'S'	5.00-100.00
Superman Items	4.00-400.00

Many will remember that wonderful, exciting, almost mythical time in our lives when we would send ten cents and a box top to a sponsoring company and receive an unforgettable item relating to our favorite show. The decoder badge, the ring, or the picture of our favorite hero will forever be indelible in our minds.

Captain Midnight was one of the most widely-known radio, movie, TV and comic book characters through the 1940's and 1950's. The Skelly Oil Company and Ovaltine, sponsors of Captain Midnight, showered youngsters with a wide array of premiums at little or no charge. Fond memories prompt me to collect Captain Midnight items. Please do not feel that because you may have only one item that I would not be interested or that it would be a waste of time to contact me. I am looking for any item relating to Captain Midnight and would be happy to hear from everyone.

Listed below are only some of the Captain Midnight items wanted. Prices given are approximate. Mint-condition and hard-to-find items receive higher prices. Your response will be appreciated.

DeWayne Nall
1305 Twisted Oak
Enid, OK 73703

We Pay

Flight Commander Ring	**65.00**
Sliding Secret Compartment Ring	**45.00**
Mystic Eye Detector Ring	**40.00**
Whirlwind Whistling Ring	**60.00**
Mystic Sun God Ring	**125.00**
Mexican Aztec Ring	**100.00**
Queen of Sheba Ring	**500.00**
Flight Commander Signet Ring	**90.00**
Flight Commander Pin	**200.00**
Five-Way Detect-O-Scope	**45.00**
Plane Detector	**75.00**
Spy Scope	**20.00**
Service Insignia Shoulder Patch	**50.00**
Flight Patrol Newspapers	**20.00**
Capt. Midnight Bicycle Tires	**250.00**
Airline Map of America	**75.00**
1955/56 Decoder & Membership Card	**40.00**
Service Ribbon Folder	**20.00**
Movie Stills	**10.00 +**
Lobby Cards	**20.00 +**
Manuals	**25.00 +**
Decoders	**20.00 +**
Photos	**5.00 +**
Books	**5.00 +**
Advertising	**10.00 +**
Anything Relating to Capt. Midnight	**Wanted**

I am looking for mint examples of radio premium rings, badges, decoders, etc. of the 1940's and 1950's. Items should be free of rust, tarnish, wear, and should never have been polished. Rings should not be deformed in any manner. Those that originally came with film strips or pictures should be complete and in well-preserved condition. Many premiums were not marked with the sponsoring program's name. If you are in doubt about whether an unmarked item is in fact a desired radio premium, contact me with a description or drawing. Make note of all markings and colors so that I can identify its origin. I will consider buying less-than-mint examples at reduced prices if you write me. I'm not interested in any paper items––this includes original boxes and directions that came with radio premiums. I will pay the following prices.

D. Feterman
P.O. Box 3
Newell, PA 15466

We Pay

Capt. America Sentinel of Liberty Badge	80.00
Sky King Teleblinker Ring	60.00
Sky King Electronic Television Ring	40.00
Sky King Navajo Treasure Ring	35.00
Sky King Mystery Picture Ring	70.00
Sky King Aztec Indian Ring	40.00
Sky King Magni-Glo Writing Ring	22.00
Sky King Radar Signal Ring	25.00
PF Decoder Ring	15.00
Straight Arrow Mystic Wrist Kit	40.00
Straight Arrow Face Ring	22.00
Straight Arrow Picture Ring	40.00
Superman Secret Compartment Initial Ring	125.00
Superman Crusaders Ring	30.00
Superman Pep Airplane Ring	20.00
The Shadow Crocodile Ring	45.00
The Shadow Blue Coal Ring	80.00
Roger Wilco Rescue Ring	20.00
Lone Ranger Saddle Ring	45.00
Lone Ranger Six-Gun Ring	20.00
Lone Ranger Flashlight Ring	22.00
Lone Ranger Movie Film Ring	22.00
Lone Ranger Military Ring	25.00
Gabby Hayes Cannon Ring	40.00
Buck Rogers Saturn Ring	65.00
Buck Rogers Repeller Ray Ring	50.00
Buck Rogers Flight Commander Whistle Badge	25.00
Buck Rogers Chief Explorer Badge	20.00
Capt. Video Flying Saucer Ring	40.00
Capt. Video Space Gun Ring	15.00
Capt. Video Secret Seal Ring	30.00

We Pay

Capt. Midnight Whistle Ring..**20.00**
Capt. Midnight Flight Commander Ring............................**15.00**
Capt. Midnight Initial Printing Ring................................**25.00**
Capt. Midnight Marine Corps Ring.................................**15.00**
Cisco Kid Secret Commander Ring................................**35.00**
Green Hornet Secret Compartment Seal Ring.....................**70.00**
Dick Tracy Secret Commander Ring..............................**22.00**
Dick Tracy Enameled Hat Ring....................................**22.00**
Terry & Pirates Gold Detector Ring..............................**30.00**
Rocket to Moon Ring w/Rockets....................................**25.00**
Tom Mix Sliding Whistle Ring......................................**22.00**
Tom Mix Magnet Ring...**15.00**
Tom Mix Tiger Eye Ring..**25.00**
Roy Rogers Microscope Ring.......................................**20.00**
Roy Rogers Branding Iron Ring....................................**20.00**
Major Mars Rocket Film Ring......................................**50.00**
Davy Crockett Compass Ring.......................................**15.00**
Pinocchio Ring...**15.00**
Snap, Crackle, or Pop Face Ring, each............................**20.00**
Donald Duck Living Toy Ring......................................**15.00**

During the 1930's and 1940's, every radio adventure show gave away hundreds of premiums such as rings, decoders, badges, etc. Sometimes they came in cereal boxes, but most often the sponsors asked us to send in box tops along with ten or twenty-five cents. Then we would wait with great anticipation for our latest treasure to arrive in the mail. It would be enjoyed, used until it wore out, or proudly displayed. Some of the most memorable programs were: The Lone Ranger, Green Hornet, Sky King, Jack Armstrong, The Shadow, Tom Mix, and Roy Rogers. Over the years most of these premiums were broken, lost, or thrown away. I have been spending my second childhood rebuilding my original collection and adding to it, and I've included television programs' premiums, as well. Since thousands of these trinkets were mailed all over the United States, they often turn up in old boxes, drawers, and other unexpected cubbyholes. A photo, sketch, or rubbing can help identify the piece. They may not be clearly marked. Prices listed are for examples in very fine condition.

Jan & Bruce Thalberg
23 Mountain View Dr.
West, CT 06883

We Pay

Lone Ranger Film Strip Saddle Ring...............................**35.00**
Lone Ranger Flashlight Gun (secret compartment in handle)............**30.00**

We Pay

Lone Ranger Secret Compartment Ring (4 versions: Army, Navy,
    Air Force, Marines), each..**35.00**
Sky King Aztec Indian Ring..**35.00**
Sky King Mystery Picture Ring....................................**50.00**
Sky King Radar Signal Ring..**30.00**
Sky King Electronic Television (1949)..............................**25.00**
Sky King Navajo Treasure Ring (1950).............................**30.00**
Sky King Teleblinker Ring...**35.00**
Sky King Signal Scope (1947)......................................**15.00**
Space Patrol Plastic Club Badge...................................**25.00**
Space Patrol Binoculars...**30.00**
Space Patrol Major Mars Rocket Ring..............................**35.00**
Straight Arrow Golden Nugget Cave Ring...........................**25.00**
Straight Arrow Rite-a-Lite Arrowhead..............................**30.00**
Superman Cornflakes F-87 Airplane Ring...........................**30.00**
Superman Crusaders Ring..**35.00**
Superman Secret Compartment Initial Ring.........................**65.00**
Tennessee Jed Look-Around Ring...................................**35.00**
Capt. Video Photo Ring..**25.00**
Capt. Video Flying Saucer Ring....................................**35.00**
Capt. Video Space Gun Ring.......................................**20.00**
Capt. Video Purity Bread Tab......................................**5.00**
Capt. Video Secret Seal Ring......................................**25.00**
Tom Mix Lucky Charm...**20.00**
Tom Mix Good Luck Spinner.......................................**15.00**
Tom Mix Straight Shooters Ring....................................**25.00**
Tom Mix Branding Iron..**20.00**
Tom Mix Glow-in-the-Dark Medal..................................**25.00**
Tom Mix Look-Around Ring..**20.00**
Tom Mix Signature Ring...**35.00**
Mix Magic Light Tiger Eye Ring....................................**35.00**
Terry & the Pirates Gold Detector Ring.............................**25.00**
Terry & the Pirates China Clipper Ring.............................**15.00**
Capt. Midnight Initial Printing Ring................................**25.00**
Capt. Midnight Mystic Sun God Ring................................**35.00**
Capt. Midnight Commander Ring....................................**20.00**
Capt. Midnight Whirlwind Whistle Ring..............................**25.00**
Capt. Midnight Sliding Secret Ring.................................**25.00**
The Shadow Blue Coal Glow-in-the-Dark Ring......................**100.00**
Buck Rogers Ring of Saturn Ring...................................**50.00**
Roy Rogers Saddle Ring, signed....................................**25.00**
Roy Rogers Hat Ring, signed.......................................**25.00**
Roy Rogers Microscope Ring.......................................**20.00**
Roy Rogers Iron Ring..**25.00**

RADIOS

The hobby of collecting radios has enjoyed much growth over the years, as more and more collectors learn that there are others who share their interest. More than twelve vintage radio clubs now cater to radio collectors all over the country. Radio collectors fall into three general categories. First are the wireless collectors, those who collect radio items from before the dawn of commercial broadcasting, 1905 to 1921. Second are the battery-set collectors. They collect battery-operated radios from 1921 to 1928. The last category of collectors is comprised of those who collect AC-operated radio receivers from 1928 to about the early 1950's.

Perhaps the largest problem facing individuals who wish to sell a radio is determining its value. Because of the technical nature of the hobby and the ten thousand different models manufactured from 1916 to the early 1940's, radio collecting is a subject almost impossible to cover in specific terms. Each model must be subjected to countless variables including some of these more common points: age, type, model number, rarity, physical and electrical condition, originality, manufacturer's name, and, of course, collector demand.

For these reasons, most of the prices listed below are grouped into broad classifications. Each individual radio (or radio-related item) has to be valued on its own individual merits.

Gary B. Schneider
P.O. Box 33135
Cleveland, OH 44133

References:
18 years involvement in radio-collecting hobby
member of all major vintage radio clubs
founding publisher and editor of 'Antique Radio Classified'

We Pay

Atwater Kent Models 20, 30, 32, 33, 35; 1925-1927 . . . . **25.00-60.00**
Atwater Kent Models 9, 10, 12; 1923-1925 . . . . **150.00-375.00**
Crosley Models 50, 51, 52; 1923-1925 . . . . **50.00-85.00**
Grebe Models CR-3, CR-5, CR-6, CR-8, CR-9; 1920-1923 . . . . **150.00-450.00**
Federal Models 57, 58, 60, 61; 1922-1923 . . . . **175.00-425.00**
Kennedy Models V, XV, 22, 110, 220, 281; 1921-1924 . . . . **90.00-375.00**
RCA Models III, IIIA, Aeriola Sr., RA/DA; 1922-1925 . . . . **40.00-125.00**
RCA Models 17, 18, 60; 1928-1929 . . . . **30.00-65.00**
RCA Models 20, 25, 38; 1925-1927 . . . . **50.00-125.00**
Philco Cathedral Radios Models 20, 70, 90; early 1930's **75.00-200.00**
Crystal-Set Radios, 1920's-1930's (many types) **10.00-125.00**
Battery-Set Radios, wood cabinets, 1921-1928 . . . . **20.00-300.00**
Metal Box Radios, AC-operated, 1927-1930 . . . . **20.00-50.00**
Console Radios (tall floor models), 1928-1940 . . . . **20.00-125.00**
Cathedral-Shaped Radios (beehive), 1930-1933 . . . . **40.00-175.00**
Mantel Radios (square & rectangular), wood cabinets, 1928-1940 . . . **10.00-90.00**
Plastic & Bakelite Radios, 1930-1950's **3.00-30.00**
Catalin (plastic swirled colors except brown), 1930's **40.00-300.00**
Novelty & Character Radios, 1930-1940's **40.00-300.00**
Glass-Mirrored Radios (usually blue), 1930's **125.00-475.00**
Speakers, horn shaped, for 1920's battery radios **20.00-100.00**
Speakers, paper cone shaped, 1925-1928 . . . . **20.00-80.00**
Speakers, wood & metal enclosures, 1927-1935 . . . . **10.00-40.00**
Vacuum tubes, 4-prong, 1920's **2.00-20.00**
Vacuum tubes, 5- & 6-prong, 1930's **1.00-2.00**

RAILROADIANA

Railroad collectibles can be divided into four broad categories. They are paper/printed items, lanterns/lamps, chinaware/silverware, and miscellaneous hardware. Some collectible railroad items were used strictly by employees. Other railroad items were designed for distribution or use by the general public or shipper.

The desirability and value of a railroad item is influenced by many factors. One important consideration is whether or not the railroad company name or initials appear on the item. There have been thousands of different company names throughout the history of railroading. As a general rule, the value of a collectible increases when it comes from a little-known or obscure railroad. Major railroads owned more equipment and spent more money on advertising. Consequently, collectibles from big railroads are more common, less expensive, and easier to obtain. Other important factors in evaluating railroad collectibles include age and general condition. Design, colors, and artwork on a printed item are also significant. The following price list shows average prices paid. I will pay much more for rare and unusual items. Many collectible items are not listed. Please describe what you have.

Fred N. Arone
377 Ashford Ave.
Dobbs Ferry, NY 10522
(914) 693-5858 (evenings)

We Pay

Lanterns, brass	200.00
Lanterns, bell-bottom	75.00
Lanterns, tall globe	40.00
Lanterns, short globe	20.00
Timetables, pre-1880	15.00
Timetables, 1900-1919	7.00
Timetables, 1920-1929	3.00
Timetables, 1930-1939	1.25
Timetables, 1940-1949	50¢
Cap & Hat Badges	15.00
Passes, pre-1900	5.00
Depot Post Cards	2.00
Train Brochures	4.00
Rule Books, old	8.00
Rule Books, newer	3.00
Ticket Dater Dies	15.00
Dater Machines	25.00
Brass Switch Keys	10.00
Stocks & Bonds, pre-1900	10.00

	We Pay
China Plates, large	25.00
China Plates, small	10.00
China Cup & Saucer	15.00
China Creamers	15.00
China Soup Bowls	8.00
Silver, Flatware	4.00
Silver, Creamers	15.00
Silver, Sugar Bowls	30.00
Silver, Pitchers	40.00
Posters, color, old	60.00
Posters, color, newer	20.00
Early Railroad Calendars	25.00
Builder's Plates	100.00
Wax Sealers	15.00
Equipment Catalogs	15.00
Employee Timetables	5.00

I am looking for several types of railroad collectibles. The emphasis of my collection is on fallen flag system maps and hardware items such as oilers, locks, lanterns, and metalware. However, I will consider nearly any item.

Presently I am trying to establish a collection of photographic negatives of anything relating to railroads. I need negatives of steam locomotives, early diesel locomotives, electric locomotives, and anything else pertaining to the railroads prior to 1960. I might also consider purchasing an entire collection from an estate. Of special interest would be items such as builders' plates, bells, headlights, early books and manuals relating to railroading (such as *Poor's Manual of Railroads*), and Pennsylvania Railroad calendars (complete and intact). Prices paid for these items vary greatly depending on rarity, condition, markings, and age. The following prices are only a guide.

Don Culver
3083 Balsam
Edgewood, KY 41017

	We Pay
Lantern w/Marked Globe	35.00
System Map, ca 1940's	7.00
System Map, ca 1910's	20.00
System Map on Canvas, ca 1800's	35.00
Builder's Plates	75.00
Lock w/Key	12.00
Photographic Negatives	5.00

We Pay

Pennsylvania Calendars..**40.00**
Official Guide, ca 1930's...**30.00**
Poor's Manual of Railroads.......................................**50.00**
Playing Cards..**7.50**
Cuspidors..**50.00**
Oilers...**20.00**

I pay cash for railroad dining car china, silverware, flatware, glassware, napkins, menus, and related items, as well as all telegraph instruments with railroad names, logos, or identifications on them. I especially want items one hundred years old or more.

Charles B. Goodman
636 W. Grant Ave.
Charleston, IL 61920
(217) 345-6771

RAZORS

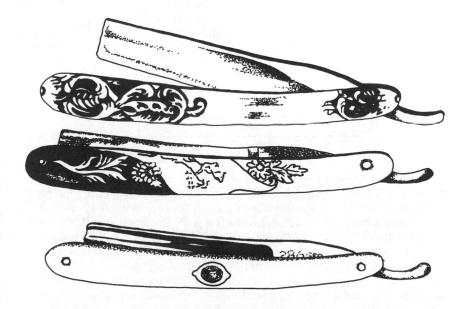

Razors are becoming popular with collectors, especially among knife traders. From the mid 1800's until the early 1900's, razor companies from England and Germany made thousands of different fancy pieces designed expressly for the American market. They embellished the handles and blades with all sorts of fancy decorations from political figures to ships, boats, and cars.

The following examples are reflective of prices now being paid for various brand names and handle materials in undamaged, excellent condition. I will buy other brands not listed as well as damaged items, if you contact me for prices.

Bill Campesi
Box 140
Merrick, NY 11566

	We Pay	Fancy, Raised Handles	We Pay
Fancy Blades	4.00-15.00	Birds	6.00-25.00
Pearl Handles	15.00-125.00	Peacocks	6.00-25.00
Cattaraugus	5.00-20.00	Elks	6.00-20.00
Winchester	12.00-75.00	Other Animals	6.00-20.00
Remington	12.00-75.00	Nudes	7.00-35.00
Case	12.00-50.00	Hunting Scenes	7.00-35.00
Keen Kutter	5.00-15.00	Flags	10.00-35.00
Silver Handles	15.00-150.00	Eagles	10.00-35.00
Picture Handles	10.00-45.00	Trains	10.00-35.00
		Ships	10.00-35.00
		Automobiles	10.00-35.00
		Babe Ruth	15.00-40.00
		Baseball Players	15.00-30.00
		Movie Stars	15.00-30.00
		7-Day Sets	15.00-90.00
		Empty 7-Day Set Boxes	5.00-12.00
		Empty Straight Razor Boxes	50¢

There was a time about ten years ago when few people collected straight razors. Even today it is not a crowded field. However, there is a demand for good razors. As with any collectible, the problem is to distinguish the desirable items from the common ones. Generally, a plain-handled razor with no embellishments is not collectible. Naturally there will be exceptions, and I have noted specific brand names that I want, even if the razor has a plain handle. Most collectors want only razors from the more desirable makers and prefer them in almost perfect condition. I am not as fussy. I will buy entire lots of razors rather than pick only one or two. I will also accept damaged razors. I answer every inquiry. The prices set forth are estimates. They can be adjusted up or down according to rarity and condition.

Denny Stapp
Rt. 3, Box 111
Georgetown, IN 47122

Fancy Celluloid Handles	We Pay
Nudes	20.00
Deer	15.00
Eagle w/Claw & Ball	30.00
Old Touring Car	50.00
Barber Pole	50.00
Stork	8.00
Cowboy & Horse	18.00
Ear of Corn	18.00
Vines & Leaves	5.00
Cupid	6.00
Mercury	6.00
Parrots	18.00
Swan	18.00
Castle	12.00
Windmill	8.00
Alligator	25.00
Bamboo	4.00

Natural Handle Materials	We Pay
Ivory, plain	5.00
Bone, jigged	20.00
Bone, smooth	4.00
Horn, stag deer	30.00
Mother-of-Pearl	40.00
Horn, raised scenes	40.00

Metal Inlaid Handles	We Pay
Words	4.00
Specific Characters	10.00
Metal Ends	4.00
Full Scenes	15.00

Man-Made, Fancy Handles	We Pay
Silver, sterling	60.00
Gold Plated	20.00
Aluminum, raised design	40.00
incised	10.00

Desirable Makers	We Pay
Winchester	25.00
Schrade	15.00
Bison	15.00
Case Bros.	14.00
W.R. Case	10.00
Hives	10.00
Holly	10.00
Crandall	15.00
Northfield	12.00
Packwood	10.00
Shepherd	10.00
Terrier	12.00
Case Mfg.	15.00
Robert Wade	18.00
W&S Butcher	18.00
Unwin & Rodgers	18.00
John Primble	10.00
New York Knife Co.	20.00
Little Valley Cutlery Assoc.	15.00

I collect straight razors and pocket knives. I buy all nice razors that are in good condition––free from defects, cracks, blade or handle damage, and excessive rust. Listed are prices I will pay for types, brands, and handle materials. Please let me know what you have. I may also be interested in damaged items.

Samuel Rogozenski
505 West 96
Kansas City, MO 64114

	We Pay		We Pay
Fancy Blades	3.00	Masonic, fancy	10.00
Famous Persons	4.00	Barlow	5.00
Political	4.00	Boker	4.00
Eagles	10.00	Case	6.00
Ships	4.00	Cattaraugus	3.00
Winchester	10.00	Colonial w/Eagle	10.00
Statue of Liberty	7.00	Cosmo w/Eagle	10.00
Military	5.00	Three Coins	3.00
Hunting Scenes	5.00	Imperial Army	8.00
Pearl Handles	20.00	Crowns	3.00
Silver Inlays	8.00	Babe Ruth	30.00
Nude Handles	10.00	Washington	10.00
Peacocks	4.00	Trains	6.00
Week Sets, boxed	12.00	Keen Kutter	6.00
Automobiles	3.00	Wade & Butcher	3.00
Elk, Deer, Stag	3.00	Flags	3.00
Corn Razors	3.50	Wostenholm	2.00
Bicycles	6.50	Common Razors	1.00
Movie Stars	2.50	Other Fancy Razors	2.50
Allan & Sons	1.50	Boxes	25¢
Masonic, plain	1.50		

RECORDS

Record collecting has rapidly become one of the major hobbies around the world. Over the last five years alone, it is estimated that the number collected in the U.S. has increased tenfold. Although there is still great interest in records of the late 1800's to the present, the greatest interest among new collectors seems to be in music of the 50's and early 60's––the roots of rock 'n roll. 45 and 33⅓ RPM recordings from this period are in demand, and those in really good condition bring top dollar.

Listed below is a small portion of the records I am seeking to buy along with the prices I will pay. Records should be in nice, playable condition: not cracked, badly worn, or scratched. I buy thousands of records by mail each year and travel to purchase large, worthwhile collections. For the convenience of sellers by mail, I offer (for $2.00, refundable when I buy) *Shellac Shack's Want List of 78 RPM Records*, a 72-page, fully-illustrated catalog listing thousands of 78 RPM records on commonly-found labels (Bluebird, Columbia, Decca, Victor, etc.), individually listed by number with specific, bona fide buying prices for each disk. It also contains information on scarce and preferred labels (78s and 45s), shipping instructions, etc. This want list is a 'live' offer to buy, backed by enough cash to handle any possible offering, and not just a vague reference.

It is not necessary, however, to buy anything from me in order to sell me records. Lists of records are welcome but should include record labels and numbers, name of artists, bands, and song titles. Return postage should accompany lists.

My book, *American Premium Record Guide*, may be useful to those seeking to learn more about popular record collecting. It identifies and lists current values for more than sixty thousand records (78s, 45s, and LPs) in the major categories of popular record collecting: dance bands, jazz, blues, hillbilly, rhythm and blues, rock 'n roll, rockabilly, etc. Ask your bookseller or write for further information.

L.R. 'Les' Docks
P.O. Box 32924
San Antonio, TX 78216

78 RPM   **We Pay**

	We Pay
Larry Abbot, Okeh Label, No. 41044	**5.00**
Irving Aaronson's Commanders, Columbia Label, No. 2946-D	**3.00**
Irving Aaronson's Commanders, Columbia Label, No. 3043-D	**3.00**
Irving Aaronson's Commanders, Vocalion Label, No. 2525	**4.00**

Records

and explains what we want, what we pay, how to ship, etc. The cost of our big catalogue is $3.00 and is refunded if we buy your records. Due to the volume of mail we receive, we do not reply unless you follow the procedures explained in our catalogue. A small sample of what we buy follows. Prices are maximum amounts paid.

Worldwide Collectors
28 Baker Dr.
Savannah, GA 31410

Artist	Title	Label	Price
Ace, Johnny	Pledging My Love	Duke	4.00
Allen, Milton	Don't Bug Me Baby	RCA	3.00
Almond, Joe	Rock Me	Trumpet	3.00
	Gonna Rock & Roll	Trumpet	10.00
Andrews, Lee		Rainbow	20.00
Anka, Paul	I Confess	RPM	10.00
	Teen Commandments	ABC	3.00
Aquatones	So Fine	Fargo	4.00
Audrey	Dear Elvis	Plus	10.00
Austin, Lovie		Victor	3.00
Autry, Gene		Champion & Clarion	5.00
Barry, Joe	I'm a Fool to Care	JIN	4.00
Beach Boys		X/Candix X	40.00
Beard, Dean	Party, Party	Atlantic	12.00
	Rakin & Scrapin	Atlantic	12.00
Beatles	Please Please Me	Vee Jay	8.00
Berry, Chuck		Chess	3.00
Berry, Mike	Tribute to Buddy	Coral	6.00
Big Bopper	Chantilly Lace	D	10.00
Blake, Tommy		Sun	8.00
Blakely, Cliff		Starday	9.00
Bob & Shari	Surfer Moon	Safari	75.00
Bond, Eddie	Flip Flop Mama	Mercury	10.00
Boone, Pat		Republic	4.00
Bop Chords		Holiday	7.00
Bowen, Jimmy	I'm Sticken w/You	Triple D	25.00
Bruce, Edwin		Sun	4.00
Burnett Trio		Coral	15.00
Burnett, Johnny		Capital & Chancellor	4.00
Burgess, Dave		Challenge	4.00
Burgess, Sonny		Sun & Phillips	4.00
Butler, Jerry	Your Precious Love	Vee Jay	4.00
Cadets	Stranded in Jungle		3.00
Capris	Moon Out Tonight	Planet	15.00
Carrol, Johnny		Decca	12.00

Records

Artist	Title	Label	Price
Carty, Ric		RCA	5.00
Cavello, Jimmy		Coral	2.00
Cellos		Apollo	2.00
Chaffin, Ernie		Sun	3.00
Chantels		End	2.00
Charles, Ray		Swingtime	4.00
Charms		Deluxe	3.00
Chicago Footwarmers		Okeh	22.00
Chordcats		Cat	6.00
Chords		Cat	3.00
Clay, Joe	Ducktail	Vik	8.00

Record collecting has become a growing phenomena over the past ten years. We've been buying and selling records for the past five years and would be interested in obtaining 33 RPM, LP, and EP singles. They must be in good condition, as we guarantee all of our used records and don't have space for marginal ones.

We also buy casette tapes—ones manufactured by a record company, not the homemade variety. Compact disks are welcome, as well. We can't take 78 RPM records or other antique sorts of recordings. 45s are only occasionally bought. Write or give us a call.

Trading Post
P.O. Box 582
221 Albany Tnpk.
Canton, CT 06019

We Pay

LP or EP..**1.00+**
Cassettes **1.00-2.50**
Compact Disks..**5.00-7.00**
    Or trade 2 used ones for 1 new one

I am interested in bluegrass and early string-band 33 LP re-recorded albums, both gospel and country. I like the banjo as the lead instrument, but not in the plectrum or riverboat style.

I pay $1.00 each for used albums if they are in serviceable condition. Names of some artists are listed below; there may be many others that I have never heard of, as well. Hopefully, someone may introduce me to new groups. Please give your telephone number and address when you respond.

Roscoe Holcomb	Wade Ward	Buell Kayee
Bascomb Lamar Lunsford	Red Parham	Hobart Smith
John Jackson	Vick Jordan	Bobby Thompson
Del McCoury	Seldom Scene	Bluegrass 45
New Grass Revival	Bluegrass Alliance	McClain Family
Bluegrass Cardinals	Mac Wiseman	Country Gazette
Roger Sprug	Flatt & Scruggs	Bill Monroe
Country Gentlemen	Stanley Bros.	Jimmy Martin
Charlie Moore	Buzz Buzby	Hylo Brown
Carl Story		

Carl Moyers
Rt. #1, Box 88C
White Pine, TN 37890

I am seeking spoken-word documentary phonograph records in 78 RPM, 45 RPM, and 33 LP dealing with historical or political events that are newsworthy. 78 RPM records must be in cardboard sleeves, and 33 RPM records must be in jackets or boxed. All records must be original recordings, not reissues. Records' subject matter may be historical, geo-political, or comedy satire and may be on an individual subject or a compilation of events; but it must be an actual phonographic recording and not a dubbed-in actor's voice. Of particular interest are 20th-century events from the New Deal to the J.F.K. assassination to Reagonomics, all related subjects, World War II, cold war, anti-communism, presidents of the United States, historical figures, events in civil rights, space, and presidential elections as well as comedy. Local news issues are welcome. I have no interest in spoken-word dramas, poetry readings, or sports events. Send a description and price quotation for each item. I will pay $3.00 to $30.00 per record depending on the subject matter, interest, and rarity. Offbeat spoken-word recordings are welcomed.

Richard A. Harrow
85-23 210 St.
Hollis Hills, NY 11427-1311
(718) 740-1088

RED WING

Red Wing stoneware jugs were made over the past one hundred years for storage of liquors, wines, molasses, and other household supplies. They were shipped all over the United States and ranged in size from a few ounces (used as salesman's samples) up to several gallons.

We will pay up to $50.00 for all jugs which are in good condition, free of chips and cracks. The jugs commanding the higher prices are usually marked on the bottom by the stoneware company's name and on the side with the dealer's advertising.

I will also consider buying marked and advertising jugs which have slight damage or small cracks. Stoneware jugs not made by Red Wing or that are not marked on the bottom will also be considered. Please send descriptions of items you have for sale, and I will be happy to contact you with a firm price.

REMINGTON CALENDARS

Long-time collector is interested in purchasing for his personal collection any pre-1935 Remington Arms Company calendars or advertising posters with hunting scenes on them—even if all of the calendar pages are missing or rats have eaten some of the item away. Feel free to call collect if you feel you have something that would be of interest to me. Thank you.

Bill Bramlett
P.O. Box 1105
Florence, SC 29503-1105
(803) 393-7390 (home)
(803) 665-3165 (work)

REVOLUTIONARY WAR

The relics associated with this era date back to the settlement of the East Coast in the early 1600's up to approximately 1830. By then the United States was expanding rapidly as a nation, and many items were starting to be mass-produced in large manufacturing centers. During the colonial era, nearly everything was handcrafted and one-of-a-kind.

I am interested in collecting almost anything associated with the Revolutionary War (colonial era). If it looks old and handcrafted, please contact me. I am always interested in corresponding with other collectors.

Larry Jarvinen
313 Condon Rd.
Manistee, MI 49660
(616) 723-5063

We Pay   **We Pay**

	We Pay
Axes	10.00-30.00
Bayonets	30.00-100.00
Belt Scabbards	20.00
Blunderbusses	400.00-1,000.00
Books	10.00-100.00
Bottles	5.00-100.00
Buckles	15.00-40.00
Bowls	20.00
Buttons	2.00-40.00
Bullet Pouches	100.00
Canteens	50.00-200.00
Cartridge Boxes	20.00-200.00
Knives	10.00-100.00
Hats	40.00
Lamps	90.00
Fascine Knives	60.00
Mortars	300.00-600.00
Muskets	200.00-1,000.00
Musket Balls	2.00
Musket Ball Molds	6.00
Pewter Plates	20.00-100.00
Pipe Tomahawks	250.00
Pistols	200.00-1,000.00
Pipes	3.00
Cannon Balls	20.00

	We Pay
Cannon Ball Gauges	100.00
Cannon Barrels	300.00-1,000.00
Cartridges	10.00-20.00
Chests	50.00
Combs	4.00
Compasses	25.00
Cooking Ware	5.00-20.00
Clocks	100.00
Coins	1.00-400.00
Gorgets	300.00
Glassware	10.00-30.00
Gunflints	1.00
Polearms	75.00-400.00
Powder Horns	10.00-150.00
Paper Money	30.00-250.00
Swords	100.00-300.00
Tobacco Containers	20.00-50.00
Tools	5.00-50.00
Silverware	2.00-15.00
Trade Axes	40.00-150.00
Trade Beads	1.00-20.00
Watches	50.00-200.00
Wood Barrels	40.00
Wood Buckets	20.00

RIFLES

I'm interested in buying antique rifles, especially target models from the 1700's muzzle loaders to the late 1920's single-shot cartridge rifles. I also collect old sights, telescope sights, loading tools, and accessories.

Premium prices are paid for nice single-shot rifles made by Winchester, Remington, Marlin-Ballard, Sharps, or rifles with the names Pope, Schoyen, Peterson, Zischang, Farrow, Zettler, Freund Schalk, or Meunier on the barrels. Prices vary considerably with condition and model. Broken, incomplete, or rough rifles are wanted for parts.

I've been buying, selling, and collecting antique rifles for over twenty-five years. I have a reputation of being fair to customers. I buy for my own collection as well as for resale. Prices listed are for nice rifles in good condition. Premium or extra nice items or pieces with a verifiable history are worth more––much more sometimes. I will travel to surrounding states for good items. Fair appraisals are made. Thank you.

Richard Binger
Rt. 1, Box 70
Morgantown, IN 46160
(317) 878-5489

We Pay

Winchester Hi Wall	200.00 +
Remington Rolling Block Sporter or Hepburn Model	250.00 +
Sharp Rifles	300.00 +

NORMAN ROCKWELL

Norman Rockwell

It is not generally known that the Goebel Manufacturing Company in Germany created a series of Norman Rockwell figurines in the 1960's. This is the same company that created and are still producing the M.I. Hummel figurines. The series that the Goebel Company created consisted of twelve to sixteen three-dimensional Rockwell studies, four or five of which were never produced for sale, as the market for such figurines was not good in the 60's. The Goebel Rockwell figurines are incised around the base with the Norman Rockwell signature, and the Goebel trademark is stamped on the underside of the base with the designation 'ROCK 201,' 'ROCK 202,' etc. ('ROCK' being used as an identifier for the Rockwell series). All 'ROCK' numbers will be in the range of 201 through 216. The Goebel Company also produced a dealer's plaque in connection with the figurines.

If you have any of these and wish to sell them, I will offer a good price. As the figurines are available on the secondary market in limited quantities, the purchase price will be negotiated on an individual basis.

Shirley & Buddy Frazier
P.O. Box 11713
Winston-Salem, NC 27117
(919) 760-0815

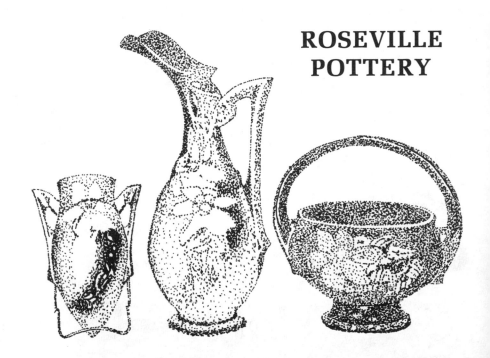

ROSEVILLE POTTERY

The Roseville Pottery Co. of Zanesville, Ohio, (not to be confused with the R.R.P. Co. of Roseville, Ohio) produced an incredible variety of art pottery and commercial wares from 1892 to 1954. Typical early lines (up to circa 1916) had painted or printed decorations with a glossy or eggshell glaze. The middle period (1910-1927) is often characterized by dripped glazes, textured surfaces, fluted bodies, molded figures, children's pieces, and Art Deco motifs. Middle-to-late items (1928-1952) generally have molded and hand-colored floral decorations. The most widely-used pattern identification and price guides are those by Sharon and Bob Huxford.

We buy all Roseville pieces that are in perfect, like-new condition, free from mold and glaze imperfections, nicks, scratches, bruises, age lines, cracks, crazing, or repairs. We buy all periods and patterns of Roseville—from the earliest to the latest. The most plentiful are the later floral lines. For most of these, we currently pay the prices shown below. On earlier, later, and rarer pieces, please contact us for specific prices.

Fenner's Antiques
Osna & Jim Fenner
2611 Ave. S
Brooklyn, NY 11229

Floral Lines   We Pay

Basket, per inch	4.00 +
Bookends, pair	40.00 +
Bud Vase, per inch	2.00 +
Cider Pitcher	45.00 +
Conch Shell, per inch	4.00 +
Console Bowl, per inch	2.50 +
Cookie w/Lid	60.00 +
Ewer, per inch	4.00 +
Flowerpot & Saucer	20.00 +
Hanging Basket	30.00 +
Jardiniere, per inch	4.00 +
Jardiniere & Pedestal	200.00 +
Lamp (complete)	50.00 +
Mug	25.00 +
Pitcher, per inch	4.00 +
Planter, per inch	3.00 +
Sand Jar	75.00 +
Tea Set, 3-piece	75.00 +
Umbrella Stand	150.00 +
Vase, per inch	4.00 +
Wall Pocket	40.00 +

The Roseville Pottery Company was established in Roseville, Ohio, in 1892 by George F. Young. Finding their facilities inadequate, the company moved to Zanesville, Ohio, in 1898, erected a new building, and entered into the art pottery market.

Animals and portraits bring higher prices than the floral designs; fine detail and good color are important, as well. Artists' signatures often increase the value of any item, especially if the artist is one who is well recognized.

The following list is reflective of prices now being paid by me. I will buy other Roseville not listed here as well as slightly damaged items, if you contact me for prices.

Barbara Rendina
27171 Lake Shore
Euclid, OH 44132

We Pay

Ash Tray, blue	10.00
Basket, #394, blue, 8″	30.00
Basket, blue, 10″	40.00
Bookends, blue, pair	30.00
Bowl, #671, blue, 4″	12.00
Bowl, #474, blue, 8″	25.00
Bowl, blue, 10″	30.00
Bud Vase, #918, blue, 7″	12.00
Candlestick, blue, 4″	10.00
Ewer, #23, blue, 10″	40.00
Ewer, #24, blue, 15″	60.00
Jardiniere, #571, blue, 8″	40.00
Tea Set, #7, blue, 3-piece	70.00
Vase, #130, blue, 6″	12.00
Wall Pocket, blue	20.00

ROUND OAK STOVES

Round Oak Stoves were the first oak-type stove. The company was founded by P.D. Bechwith in Dowagiac, Michigan, in 1871. They became famous for their Chief Doe Wah Jack Indian advertising. We buy all advertising, especially calendars, catalogs, #12-sized stoves, and Kate Lee stoves. All replies will be answered if the collector's book is mentioned. Please include SASE.

Lee Haines
P.O. Box 54
Wayne, MI 48184

ROYAL BAYREUTH

Royal Bayreuth was made in Bavaria and is usually marked with a blue shield stamp. Occasionally, the trademark is in green. I am especially interested in toothpick holders, teapots, chocolate pots or sets, bells, shoes, match holders, hatpin holders, sugar shakers, cracker jars, and humidors. I am interested in buying the following items and will pay the following prices.

Juanita Wilkins
P.O. Box 1884
Lima, OH 45802
(419) 227-2163

We Pay

Tapestry Finish Items	**30.00-500.00**
Figural Items (mouse, iris, poppy, butterfly, etc.)	**40.00-300.00**
Items Decorated w/Children	**30.00-400.00**

ROYAL DOULTON

The firm of Doulton & Co. started in 1853 by producing sewer tiles, not earning its Royal warrant until 1902. Their products became diversified and eventually included a wide range of fine china and pottery. I am interested in all examples of Doulton and Royal Doulton: figurines of ladies and animals, character jugs (erroneously referred to as Toby jugs), royal commemoratives, Rouge Flambe, and series ware. Items must be in perfect condition: no chips or missing lids. Please send a full description, including all marks and numbers on the bottom. Include an SASE for our reply. Photos will be returned.

Carol's Gallery
14455 Big Basin Way
(408) 867-7055 (Wed.-Sat. 10 am to 5 pm)

Pottery	We Pay
Teapot, half brown, applied hounds & horses, 4-cup	75.00
Teapot, half blue, incised cats, silver mounts, 2-cup	125.00
Jugs, half brown, applied figures, strap handle, 1½″	12.00
Jugs, half brown, applied figures, strap handle, 4″	20.00
Jugs, half brown, applied figures, silver mounts, 10″	75.00
Biscuit Barrel, incised deer & foxes	125.00

China	We Pay
Series Ware	
Bowl, Dickensware, 7½″	35.00
Cheese Dish, Robin Hood	50.00
Cup & Saucer, Coaching Days	22.00
Plate, Automotive, 10½″	55.00
Plate, Head Rack; Shakespeare, 10″	35.00

We Pay

Character Jugs
    Cardinal, large, 5¼″ to 7″....................................**50.00**
    Cardinal, miniature, 2¼x2½″................................**25.00**
    Cardinal, small, 3¼x4″......................................**30.00**
    Cardinal, tiny, 1¼″ or less.................................**60.00**
    Gulliver, large..**150.00**
    Gulliver, miniature...**75.00**
    Gulliver, small...**125.00**
Animals
    Chipping Sparrow by Jefferson, 7½″.......................**400.00**
    English Setter w/Pheasant.................................**125.00**
    Kitten, sitting..**15.00**
    Pig...**20.00**
    Tiger on Rock..**250.00**
Figurines
    Benmore (flag costume)...................................**200.00**
    Lily..**65.00**

ROYAL HAEGER

The prestigious Royal Haeger line was introduced in 1928 by The Haeger Pottery in Dundee, Illinois. This line is mainly comprised of figurines, console/mantel sets, vases, and lamps. The designer of this line, Royal A. Hickman, also produced pottery other than Royal Haeger. Therefore, I will buy pieces marked 'Royal Hickman-Paris' and 'Royal Hickman-California Designed,' as well as Royal Haeger pieces. (Basically, all pieces are signed and numbered on the bottom). I will pay reasonable prices for the following items: figurines, table lamps, TV lamps, vases, console/mantel sets, decanters, and miscellaneous.

Lee Garmon
Collecting Royal Haeger
1529 Whittier St.
Springfield, IL 62704

ROYAL VIENNA

I want to buy Royal Vienna porcelain in the hand-painted Rose pattern with green leaves and gold trim.

Mavis Braaten
P.O. Box 204
Trout Lake, WA 98650

We Pay

#20 Cup...**40.00**
#20 Cup & Saucer....................................**50.00**
Sugar Bowl w/Lid....................................**60.00**
Creamer **50.00**

RUMFORD BAKING POWDER UTENSILS

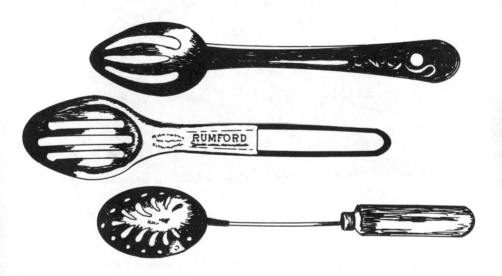

Rumford Baking Powder was introduced in 1860 as the first baking powder. It was patented in 1856 by Professor Eben Horsford, whose combination contained a blend of baking soda, cream of tartar, and cornstarch. Up to this point, these ingredients had to be added separately. In order to get people interested in buying the new product, free premiums such as kitchen tools, utensils, and cookware imprinted with the product name were given away during the late 1800's and after the turn of the century; recipe books encouraging its use were also widely distributed.

The name Rumford was taken from the Rumford Chair of Chemistry which Professor Horsford occupied at Harvard. The original Count Rumford was Benjamin Thompson, who was born in 1753 and knighted in 1784 for service to mankind while serving in the military. He was a pioneer in improving the nutritional needs of military personel who served under him. He invented the double boiler as well as the closed stove that used coal as fuel.

Pat Van Gaasbeek
631 Randolph
Topeka, KS 66606

RUSSEL WRIGHT DINNERWARE

I buy all lines of Russel Wright Dinnerware. I especially need the following in American Modern: any piece in Glacier Blue, White, Cantelope, or Bean Brown. In any color, I am looking for salad plates, divided relishes, relish rosettes, carafes, ice box jars, teapots, water pitchers, coffeepots, hostess plates, coffee-cup covers, ramekins, stack servers, mugs, covered pitchers, A.D. pots, covered butters, and children's pieces. Also, I buy any glassware.

In Iroquois, I'll buy any piece in Aqua, Brick Red, or Mustard Gold and most pieces in White, Charcoal, Oyster, or Pink. In any color, I need the redesigned gravies, family-size creamers and sugars, restyled ¼-pound butter dishes, pepper mills and single salts, restyled teapots, A.D. pots, restyled water pitchers, 10¼" oval platters, mugs, gumbos, carafes, party plates, A.D. cups and saucers, any cookware, and any glassware.

In Sterling, I buy serving pieces in any color, especially restyled pitchers, coffee bottles, ash trays, and A.D. cups and saucers.

In Highlight, I buy any piece, any color; but I especially need A.D. cups and saucers, teapots, butter dishes, gravies, mugs, and any snow glass items.

I am also interested in buying stainless flatware marked Russel Wright and Hull. I buy Russel Wright Bauer items and need any piece in Theme Formal or Theme Informal, glassware or china. I am looking for Mary Wright Country Garden dishes, as well. In addition, I am interested in finding spun aluminum items. Let me know what you have for sale. Thanks!

Dennis Boyd
211 S. Mulberry St.
Richmond, VA 23220

SALEM WITCH

Salem Witch items were made for Daniel Low of Salem, Massachusetts. There is a witch figure on each item. Some were made in sterling silver and fine china, and many souvenir-trade items were also produced. Listed below are some of the items I am looking for along with prices I am willing to pay. No reproductions please.

C.J. Russell
P.O. Box 499
Winchester, NH 03470

	We Pay		We Pay
Thimble, sterling	150.00	Salts Bottle, teal	65.00
Demi-Spoon, #2, sterling	35.00	Scissors	50.00
Soda Bottle, clear	10.00	Tea Strainer,	
Dinner Fork, sterling	85.00	double-handled, sterling	140.00
Dinner Knife, sterling	65.00		

SALESMAN SAMPLES

Salesman samples, very similar to patent models, are perfect models of large farm machinery. Most were used from the 1880's to the 1920's. Some were carried by salesmen when they traveled by train and called on their customers, but most salesman samples were found on shelves in hardware and equipment stores. Many early hardware stores sold farm equipment and machinery but did not actually stock much in the way of the full-size product. Nearly everything was ordered at the time of sale. By observing the workings of the salesman sample, the farmer was able to see exactly how the actual item would function.

Salesman samples of farm machinery can be found in the form of almost any type of equipment used on the farm. Here are a few examples: walking plows, sulky plows, hay mowers, hay rakes, bailers, cultivators, hay loaders, binders, reapers, etc. There are also windmills, silos, and pitch forks, to name but a few.

Prices on salesman samples have a very wide range; much depends on the item and the number of its working parts. Prices can range from $75.00 for a simple piece to $2,000.00 for very large examples or those that are very elaborate with many gears and chains.

Allan C. Hoover
2133 14th St.
Peru, IL 61354

SALOON MEMORABILIA

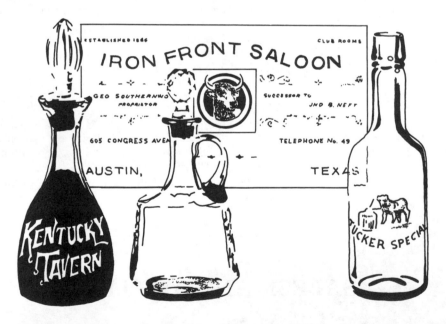

The most charming and collectible saloon memorabilia date back to the period between the Civil War and the coming of Prohibition in 1919—an era often called the 'Golden Age' of saloons. While most people think of them simply as places to drink beer or whiskey, the social life of a saloon went far beyond that. It included gambling, 'free lunch,' and all that went with them; and, in addition to spirits, cigars were sold, as well.

We are interested in pieces such as small coin-operated gambling machines, beer and liquor advertising and signs, display cases, and cash registers. Many of these and smaller items from this era are shown in our books, *An Illustrated Price Guide to the 100 Most Collectible Trade Stimulators*, Volumes 1 and 2, either of which can be purchased for $17.65 postpaid.

Richard M. Bueshel
215 Revere Dr.
Northbrook, IL 60062

We Pay

Glass Whiskey Sign	200.00
Glass Beer Sign	175.00
Cash Register	200.00
Table w/Stein Holders	150.00
Photograph of Saloon Interior	15.00
Photograph of Saloon Exterior	10.00
Card Playing 'Handout'	75.00
Etched Beer Stein	25.00
Framed Beer Advertisement	60.00
Cast Iron Coin Machine, payout	500.00
Cast Iron Coin Machine, non-payout	300.00
Wooden Coin Machine, payout	350.00
Wooden Coin Machine, non-payout	150.00
Floor Model Strength Tester	500.00
Bartop Strength/Grip Tester	150.00
Dice Game Under Glass	150.00
Mechanical Cigar Cutter	75.00
Saloon Equipment Catalog, pre-1900, per pg	1.50
Saloon Equipment Catalog, 1900-1919, per pg	1.00
Saloon Trade Magazines	2.00
National Police Gazette (magazines pre-1900), ea	3.00
National Police Gazette (magazines 1900-1919), ea	1.50

We are interested in the old tavern and bar era from the 1920's to the 1950's. We are just a couple of nostalgic collectors who will pay top dollar for those items in your basement or attic that are collecting dust.

Here is what we are looking for and the price range we will pay, if you have what we want. Help us out. Nothing is too old; whether it's working or not, we may be interested. We also trade––let's make a deal!

Bill Rosenbaum   Tom Rosenbaum
(414) 462-6072   (414) 796-0433

We Pay

Juke Boxes & Slot Machines..............................**100.00-5,000.00**
Table Radios, plastic or wood...........................**10.00-1,000.00**
Signs, neon, tin, or paper..................................**10.00-500.00**
Phone Booths, wood.......................................**up to 400.00**
Art Deco Items...**Call**
Cash Registers..**100.00-1,000.00**
Music Boxes...**up to 1,000.00**
Stand-Up Fans..**up to 500.00**

SALT AND PEPPER SHAKERS

I'm a collector and dealer wanting to buy shakers made of ceramic, porcelain, plastic, or cast iron from the 1940's through the 1980's. These must be in very good condition with no chips, cracks, or mends. Please refer to the following price list. I pay postage.

Peggy Cole
134 E-La Veta
Orange, CA 92666
(714) 997-7379

	We Pay		We Pay
Cat & Fiddle	5.00	Mickey & Minnie Mouse	8.00
Little Miss Muffet	5.00	Little Red Riding Hood	8.00
Jack & Jill	5.00	Pinocchio	8.00
Old King Cole	5.00	'Bobs' Big Boy	8.00
Humpty Dumpty	5.00	Nipper RCA	8.00
Elsie & Elmer Cow	5.00	Greyhound Bus	8.00
Cow & Moon	5.00	Colonel Sanders, plastic	8.00
Jonah & Whale	5.00	G.E. Refrigerator, milk glass	8.00
Smoky Bear	5.00	President Kennedy & Rocker	8.00
Amish People, cast iron	5.00	Campbell Soup Kids	8.00
Firestone Tires	5.00	Goebel Bellhop	8.00
Washing Machine, red plastic	5.00	Shriners, cast iron	10.00
Croquet Set, plastic	5.00	Felix the Cat	10.00
State's Famous Product	5.00	Any Black Americana	10.00
Popeye & Olive Oyl	8.00	Dogs Mustard Set, '50s	5.00
Howdy Doody	8.00	Telephone Mustard Set	5.00
Laurel & Hardy	8.00		
Orphan Annie	8.00		
Charlie McCarthy	8.00		

Plastic figural gasoline pump salt and pepper shakers that stand approximately 2½″ tall are just one example of the specialty versions of 'novelty' salt shaker collectibles. First produced in the 1940's, these miniature gas pumps are molded in the exact colors and decorated with scaled-down versions of the same decals used for most gasoline brands of the 40's, 50's, and 60's. Used as a promotional giveaway by gasoline dealers, the most commonly-found gas pump salt and pepper shaker sets naturally represent the most widely-distributed brands. As a result, brands such as as Esso, Texaco, and Phillips 66 are abundant and therefore less desirable. I'm seeking to buy gas pump salt and pepper shaker sets representing the brands of gasoline listed below. Many may still be in their original boxes; others will be unpackaged. I'll respond immediately.

Peter Capell
1838 W. Grace St.
Chicago, IL 60613

Prices range up to $15.00 a pair:

APCO	Bay	Champlin	Crown
Amlico	Boron	Chevron	Derby
Ashland	Caslo	Cities Service	Dixie

El Paso	Kan-O-Tex	Skelly	Vickers
Fleet-Wing	Marathon	SOC (Southern Oil Co.)	Zephyr
FS (Farm Service)	MFA	Tenneco	Co-Op
Getty	'M' (Midland)	Total	Keystone
Hancock	Shamrock	Union 76	Enco
Imperial	Signal		

SALVATION ARMY MEMORABILIA

The Salvation Army was founded by William Booth in London, England, in 1865. It began its work in the United States in 1878. Since that time many items that are now collectible have been made either by the Salvation Army itself or by outside organizations in their honor. Since over one hundred years have passed since the founding, there are now up to fourth-generation Salvationists who are interested in collecting bits of their heritage. The prices given below are for items in excellent condition. If you have something you are not sure about, write first, and we'll give you a bona fide quote. Some of the things we are interested in buying are noted below, but this list is by no means complete.

Major Rex McCulley
P.O. Box 9415
Colorado Springs, CO 80932

Song Sheets   **We Pay**

Salvation Lassie of Mine...**3.00**
Salvation Nell..**5.00**
Salvation Rose...**5.00**
My Doughnut Girl..**5.00**
Fires of Faith...**5.00**
They're Coming Back...**5.00**

Posters   **We Pay**
Generally of WWI Vintage

Large Size (27x38")..**20.00**
Small Size (18x24")..**10.00**
Any Other..**Write & Describe**

Magazine Covers   **We Pay**

Post, 1919 or 1920..**7.50**
Post, 1958..**1.50**

	We Pay
Leslie's, 1919	**7.50**
Pages from Harper's (or any 19th-century periodical)	
Printing only on pg	**1.00**
Engravings on pg	**2.50**
National Geographic, April 1920	**4.50**
War Crys, pre-1930	**75¢-2.00**

Pins & Buttons　　　　　　　　　　　　　　　　　　**We Pay**

	We Pay
Depending on Era (generally)	**1.00-3.00**
Older Laminated or Stamped Steel	**5.00-10.00**

SAUSAGE STUFFERS

Years ago, the sausage stuffer was a basic 'butchering-time' tool on every farm. There are many types and sizes, some of which are primitive and handmade. I am interested in buying all types. I also buy books relating to sausage making.

I pay a minimum of $15.00 and up for good, complete units. I will also buy incomplete sausage stuffers at lesser prices. When offering, please describe carefully and send a sketch or photograph.

Dale C. Schmidt
610 Howell Prairie Rd. SE
Salem, OR 97301
(503) 364-0499

SCOTTIE DOG
MEMORABILIA

In August of 1983, Donna and Jim Newton of Columbus, Indiana, published their first issue of the *Scottie Sampler*, a newsletter for collectors of Scottie dog memorabilia. As a bonus, free membership in Wee Scots, a collector's group, was offered. With subscribers all over the United States, Canada, and England, the Newtons have become aware that collecting Scottie items is a fast-growing hobby. They have also discovered that some collectors have already pursued this hobby for twenty to thirty years.

Scottie collectibles often overlap into many other areas of collectibles, making it necessary to compete with collectors who are primarily interested in other fields. As a result, it has been difficult to establish a fair level of market value. Country Scottie is interested in buying anything with a Scottie motif, but want only items that are in good or better condition. Photos are required before purchase agreements are made. For their personal collection, Donna and Jim are interested in buying such items as Cambridge glassware with a Scottie design, old greeting cards, post cards, playing cards, books, hooked rugs, and advertising items.

Country Scottie
P.O. Box 1512
Dept. 88-12
Columbus, IN 47201-1512

SCHMOO MEMORABILIA

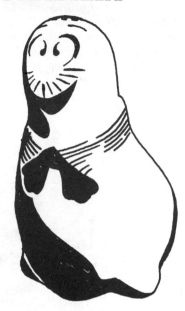

The Schmoo, designed by Al Capp in 1948, was a lovable character from the Li'l Abner comic strip. Shaped something like a gourd with feet, these little fellows were the answer to all of man's needs. They multiplied rapidly and gave milk, butter, eggs, and bread. When broiled, they became steaks; fried, they became chicken; and roasted, they became pork. Their hide was stronger than any leather or wood. So far no prices have been established, but the following items have surfaced: banks, comic books, story books, glass tumblers, figurines, room deodorizers, Lux Pendulette clocks (pink or white), ash trays, and cigarette holders. I will pay reasonable prices for Schmoo memorabilia.

Lee Garmon
1529 Whittier St.
Springfield, IL 62704

SCHOOLHOUSE COLLECTIBLES

Even though most all of us have some memento of our school days—yearbook, scrapbook, class picture, diploma, club pin, senior ring, letter sweater, etc.—as a rule, schoolhouse collectibles are not something one would deliberately set out to accumulate without good reason! Being a professional educator, I have a very exciting reason. I plan to establish a school-related museum. Someone once said that 'school is a building that has four walls . . . with tomorrow inside.' I want to preserve some of those 'tomorrows' that have made us the great country we are today.

Education is essential to a free society. We associate certain items such as bells, books, and blackboards as being tools of educators. Just as educational methodology undergoes reformation, so does the educator's equipment. New innovative methods come and go; old equipment is replaced by the new. McGuffey's Readers were essential in the 1800's, just as computers are essential today. As you gather schoolhouse-related articles, let your imagination soar. Add to the list below; let me hear from you.

Ken Norris
P.O. Box 476
Grandfalls, TX 74794

We Pay

George Washington Print	**15.00**
Abraham Lincoln Print	**15.00**
Teacher's Hand Bell	**12.00**
Inkwells, desk	**8.00**
Inkwells, molded	**5.00**
Dip Pens	**2.00**
Diplomas, Announcements	**3.50**
Yearbooks	**2.50**
Maps	**2.50**
Map Holders, oak	**20.00**
Photographs	**1.00**
Slates, single	**12.00**
Slates, double	**23.00**
Pencil Sharpeners, student	**2.50**

We Pay

Pencil Sharpeners, class	7.00
Mounted Bells	37.50
Lunch Pails	5.00
War Bond Posters	5.00
War Bond Stamp Books	5.00
Wartime Booklets for Paper, Scrap, & Metal Drives	5.00
Marbles, Jacks, Jump Ropes	5.00
Class Rings	20.00
Club Pins	2.00
FFA-FHA Articles	3.00
Athletic Equipment	5.00
Leather Football Helmets	40.00
Award Letters	3.00
Trophies	3.00
Ruler, Compass, Protractor	1.00
Pencil Boxes	6.00
Fountain Pens	4.00
Books	1.00 +
Tablets	1.00
Teaching Aids	5.00
Documents, (Local, State or Federal)	1.00
Print Stamp Sets	12.00
Eraser Dusters	7.50
Student Desk, single	20.00
Student Desk, double	50.00
Teacher Desk	100.00
Book Shelves, stackable	100.00
Potbellied Stove	200.00

SEALING WAX SEALS

Desk-type sealing wax seals come in an infinite variety of sizes, designs, and materials. The most common materials are wood, sterling, brass, bronze, and agate. Other often-used materials are china, glass, crystal, ivory, bone, and mother-of-pearl. Seals are priced from a few dollars to thousands, depending on the quality of the workmanship, materials used, beauty, and rarity. It is not possible to quote prices for seals sight unseen. Please send a description of the seal and/or a close-up photograph. Also indicate your asking price. We will contact you to discuss buying the seal and make arrangements for payment and delivery. Please note: we do not collect fob seals or Chinese chops.

Mr. & Mrs. Irwin Prince
142 Fairway Dr.
Indianapolis, IN 46260
(317) 255-1913

SEWING

Women and men have been sewing since time immemorial using tools of varying degrees of sophistication and beauty. High-quality needlework tools have been produced since about the mid- to late 17th century. Materials such as ivory, bone, exotic hardwoods, mother-of-pearl, straw, silver, gold, hardened steel, leather, and silk have all been used in the fabrication of sewing implements through the years.

I am interested in single items or entire collections. I especially look for the interesting and unusual as well as matched sets of tools, for which I pay more. Prices are determined by rarity, condition, material, and age. Because of the wide range of these factors, listing sample prices would be impossible. I am buying items such as are listed below.

Needle Cases	Crochet Ball Holders
Pincushions	Crochet Hooks
Emeries	Knitting Needle Sheaths or Guards
Thimble Holders	Stilettos & Punches
Thimbles	Tatting Shuttles
Scissors	Darning Eggs
Tape Measures	Hem Gauges
Thread Waxers	Bodkins & Ribbon Threaders
Needle & Pin Books	Fitted Sewing Boxes & Baskets
Needlework Clamps	Chatelaines
Thread Containers & Winders	Other
Lace Bobbins	

Diane Richardson
P.O. Box 993
Oak Park, IL 60303
(312) 848-3247

I want to buy pincushions made of cloth, cardboard, and various other materials. Describe and price or mail, and I'll return pre-paid if rejected.

R.L. Rice
612 E. Front St.
Bloomington, IL 61701

SHEET MUSIC

Sheet music is collected for many different reasons. Many wish to play the old familiar songs of long ago. Some collect according to the attractiveness of the cover. (Song sheets are interesting when framed and an inexpensive way to decorate.) Other collectors may seek memorabilia of a favorite movie or movie star of bygone years and concentrate on collecting covers related only to their interests. Transportation is an area of sheet music collecting that entices many collectors––trains, autos, and planes are popular subjects.

I am interested in buying sheet music in good condition——not split at the seam, torn, mutilated, folded, or with missing pages. I do not buy teaching methods, music books, or classical music. I especially want large quantities of popular music. Items may be sent by 4th Class U.S. Mail for my immediate offer. I pay according to condition, desirability, and scarcity.

Mt. Washington Antiques
3742 Kellogg
Cincinnati, OH 45226
(513) 231-6584

I am always interested in purchasing old popular sheet music, movie magazines, and downbeat magazines. Top prices are paid. I also have top-quality music for sale in all collectible categories.

Beverly A. Hamer
Box 75
East Derry, NH 03041
(603) 432-3528

SHERLOCKIANA

The stories of Sir Arthur Conan Doyle and the characters he created are enjoyed by a throng of loyal followers from around the world. With each passing year and with each new devotee, the appeal and mystique of Doyle's most-beloved figure, Sherlock Holmes, becomes stronger and more intense. Like a great work of art, each follower interprets and views Holmes and the other characters in his or her own personal way.

I collect anything and everything associated with Conan Doyle and Sherlock Holmes:

Figurines & Statuary
Dolls
Banks
Games
Books
Periodicals
Comics
Autographs
Original Works of Art
Strand Magazines
Harper's Weekly
Liberty

Collier's
Foreign Items
Personalities:
   Rathbone
   Bruce
   Gillette
   Norwood
   Paget
   F. Dorr Steele
   Brett
   Others

Robert C. Hess
559 Potter Blvd.
Brightwaters, NY 11718

SHIRLEY TEMPLE

I want to buy early Shirley Temple memorabilia. I am looking for jewelry, uncut paper dolls, sheet music, lobby cards, press books, Shirley Temple Christmas and birthday books, movie magazines with Shirley Temple as a child on the cover, clothing, pins—anything unusual. Send a description and price in your first letter. Please include a phone number and SASE. I want nothing recent and no dolls!

Frank Garcia
8963 SW 34th St.
Miami, FL 33165

We Pay

All Press Books, early Shirley Movies	50.00
Sheet Music, 'Happy Birthday Curly Top'	25.00
Paper Doll Set #2112-134, uncut, mint	50.00
Shirley Temple Jewelry, original 30's only	25.00-50.00
Scrapbooks, full of clippings of Shirley as a child only	40.00
'Little Princess' Coloring Book #1717-1936	30.00
Christmas Book #1770-1937	40.00
Birthday Book, by Dell Pub. Co. 1935	40.00
'Five Books About Me' #1730-1936, boxed	35.00
'This Is My Crayon Book' #1711-1936, mint	20.00
Movie Magazines w/Shirley on Cover, 30's, VG	12.00
Doll Trunk, intact w/all decals	50.00

We Pay

Paper Doll Set #1787-1940, uncut...................................**35.00**
Book 'Little Star' #1762-1936, VG...................................**20.00**
Book 'Little Princess' #1783-1939, VG.............................**15.00**

SILHOUETTES

Silhouettes, cut-out profile portraits or shapes (usually in black and white), were first made about 1700; some are still being made today. They were first called silhouettes about sixty years after they were introduced. These cuttings were named for an unpopular Frenchman, Etienne de Silhouette; because he was laughed out of office as Controller General of Finances, the term silhouette came to mean a man reduced to his simplest form. (The man taxed by Silhouette was indeed reduced to his simplest form.)

I buy pictures in good condition made by any of the various techniques seen today. I also consider buying silhouettes on boxes, china, glass, jewelry, lamps, etc.; and I am interested in books about silhouettes. Original frames, signed and/or dated, increase the values. Other variations of silhouettes will be considered.

Janette C. Pike
9 Brookwood Ct.
Asheville, NC 28804

We Pay

Freehand Cuttings..**12.00-100.00**
Hollow Cuttings (reverse cuts), machine-made..................**5.00-100.00**
Paintings, dense black w/no relief, on back of flat glass...........**6.00-30.00**
Paintings on back of convex glass............................**4.00-20.00**
Paintings on back of flat glass, w/various colored paints & foil
  or painted backgrounds..................................**2.00-16.00**

From the late 1700's through the late 1800's, two styles of silhouettes were popular: cut-out and backed types as well as those cut-out and applied on top of a panel. In some instances, shading and additional artwork were incorporated. Subjects range from a single profile to group scenes. Some of these pieces are signed, while others are not. Yet the artist may be identified by recognizing his unique style and technique. Sizes range from 2½" tall to 12" tall, not inclusive of the frame. As there are a variety of works available, either signed or unsigned, in various sizes, conditions, qualities, and degrees of importance, it is impossible to list prices paid with any accuracy. For price confirmation, please send a photo with any information you may have, the actual item, or call me direct. We are buying both American and English silhouettes.

Lester E. Sender
3482 Lee
Shaker Heights, OH 44120

We Pay

Profiles..**25.00-1,000.00**
Scenes **80.00-1,200.00**

SKIING ITEMS

Skiing as sport is a relatively new phenomenon with most recreational activity taking place only since the turn of this century. Until the 1930's the sport consisted primarily of jumping and cross-country. It was not until the first ski lifts were built in the mid-1930's that downhill skiing as a sport could literally 'take off.' The sport of skiing has been captured on magazine covers, post cards, equipment catalogs, skiing yearbooks, in Hollywood films, posters, and much, much more.

The following list is a range of prices I will pay for items of this type. If an item is not on the list, I may be still interested.

Gary H. Schwartz
680 Hawthorne Dr.
Tiburn, CA 94920

We Pay

Books, General; pre-1940	3.00-30.00
Books, Specific	
Caulfield, How to Ski, London	30.00
Dier, Book of Winter Sports, NY	30.00
Harris, Dartmouth Out O'Doors, Boston	30.00
Jay, Ski Down the Years, NY	15.00
Lunn, History of Skiing, London	30.00
Poulsen, Skiing, NY	20.00
Marshall & Son, Skiing, London	25.00
Syers, Book of Winter Sports, London	25.00
Winter Sports Annual, London	30.00
Catalogs w/Skiing Equipment, pre-1940	10.00-25.00
Catalogs w/Ski Clothes, pre-1940	8.00-18.00
Magazines, General (skiing covers pre-1940)	3.00-20.00
Magazines, Specific	
Life, March 8, 1937	7.00
Woman's World, February 1929	18.00
Ski, Winter 1936	20.00
Alpine Ski Club Annual 1908-1914	20.00
The Dartmouth, pre-1940	15.00
Winter Sports Review, April 1912	20.00
Photographs, General (celebrities)	3.00-20.00
Post Cards, pre-1940 U.S.	1.00-10.00
Post Cards, pre-1930 Foreign	1.00-10.00
Posters, General	25.00-250.00
Posters, Specific	
Sun Valley Serenade, 1941	125.00
Sun Valley Serenade, 1964 reissue	50.00
Sheet Music, General	25.00-250.00
Sheet Music, Specific	
Chattanooga Choo Choo (from Sun Valley Serenade)	15.00

SMURF MEMORABILIA

The Smurf cartoon character was created in Belgium in 1957 by Pierre 'Peyo' Culliford. Smurfs and Smurf products are licensed world-wide. They answer to many names in non-speaking English countries: Schtroumpf in Belgium and France, Puffi in Italy, Pitufos in Spain, Sumafu in Japan, Smolfin in Denmark and Norway, Schlumpf in West Germany, Smurfen in Holland, and Ha-dar-door-seamn' in Israel.

I buy all European Smurf merchandise. I prefer mint items in boxes. Items must bear the 'Peyo' license name. Thousands of licensed products were produced in Europe from 1957 to the present.

S. Lund
24 Cabot Rd. W
Massapequa, NY 11758

We Pay

'El Ferror' Marked Pieces	**3.00**
Belgium Postage Stamp	**2.00**
Post Cards, all languages	**2.00**
Smurf 'Fan Club Newsletter' #11	3.00
Smurf 'Fan Club Newsletter' #12	3.00
Smurf 'Fan Club Newsletter' #13	3.00
European Advertising Material	**3.00** +
Metal Cars w/Smurfs by Barago	**8.00**
Metal Cars w/Smurfs by Puffi	**10.00**
Smurf Books (no English language)	**6.00** +

We Pay

PVC Figurines w/Promotional Items (from Fanta Soda Bottle, Omo Detergent, BP
   Gas, Sport & Fitness Bodybuilder, Parodin Flue Medicine, Carl Zeiss Eyeglasses,
   Gloria Concentrated Milk)..**8.00**
Figurines, solid color (red, blue, yellow, brown, green, etc.), 2″.........**4.00**
Figurines, pewter...**6.00 +**

SNOOPY AND PEANUTS CHARACTERS

    The Snoopy and Peanuts characters collectors are coming out of the closet. They
are all over the world. The cartoon by Charles Schultz was syndicated by United
Feature Syndicate on October 2, 1950. One of the first items to be produced was
an oversized coloring book; this has been followed with toys, ceramics, music boxes,
plates, bells, dolls, clothes, banners, Hallmark paper items, books, etc. To show that
the item is 'legal,' it must carry the mark 'United Feature Syndicate.' The copyright
date is not indicative of when an item was actually produced.

    I pay very fairly; price depends on condition, rarity (rather than age), and
whether it is boxed or not. Wanted are items such as:

      See & Say, by Mattel
      Lucy & Phychiatrist Booth Music Box, by Anri, wooden

Ferris Wheel Music Box, by Anri, wooden
Piano (character's picture on top), wooden, small
Talking Story Book, by Mattel
Schroeder's Piano, by Child Guidance
Can You Catch It Charlie Brown (pinball-type game)
Cartoon Maker, by Mattel
Snap Tite Kits, by Monogram
Cookie Cutters, by Hallmark
Pop-Up Books, by Hallmark

Freddi Margolin
12 Lawrence Lane
Bay Shore, NY 11706

SNOW GLOBES

I collect any type of object referred to as a snow globe, water ball, etc. This refers to enclosed objects with water and snow inside. Any size or shape is desired. Any theme is fine––travel-related or decorative. The older they are, the better. Foreign-made snow globes are also sought. Please send a description, a photo for each if possible, and your asking price. I am also seeking any information about the history of this decorative art form.

Bruce Baron
4705 Henry Hudson Parkway, 2E
Bronx, NY 10471

SODA FOUNTAIN COLLECTIBLES

We collect the 'tools of the trade,' i.e., unusual dippers, decorated counter-top china syrup dispensers, soda glasses and ceramic root beer mugs marked with product names, syrup bottles, *Soda Fountain Magazine*, equipment and supply catalogs, hand-held advertising fans showing ice cream or soda fountain scenes, and any brand of cherry soda advertising. The one brand especially wanted is the 'True Fruit' syrups by the J. Hungerford Smith Co. of Rochester, New York. All items should be from before 1940, and condition is quite important in regard to the prices paid.

Harold & Joyce Screen
2804 Munster Rd.
Baltimore, MD 21234

We Pay

Advertising Fans, w/soda fountain or ice cream scenes	**5.00-15.00**
Soda Glasses w/Product Name, pre-1920	**20.00**
Soda Glasses w/Product Name, post-1920	**10.00**
Root Beer Mugs	**30.00-100.00**
Syrup Bottles w/Caps, flavors only	**25.00**
Syrup Bottles w/Caps, product name	**50.00**
Insulated Ice Cream Pie Containers, Eskimo Pie	**350.00**
Insulated Ice Cream Pie Containers, Kool Kub	**400.00**
Soda Fountain Magazine, 1902-1910	**15.00**
Soda Fountain Magazine, 1911-1920	**10.00**
Soda Fountain Magazine, 1921-1930	**7.00**
Soda Fountain Magazine, 1931-1935	**5.00**

Soda Fountain Collectibles

We Pay

Equipment & Supply Catalogs, pre-1900, per pg.....................35¢-50¢
Equipment & Supply Catalogs, post-1900, per pg...................15¢-35¢
Milk Shake Mixers, marble base....................................50.00
Milk Shake Mixers, light-up base..................................60.00
Mechanical Hand-Held Ice Cream Container Fillers.................100.00
Syrup Dispensers w/Original Pumps
    Jersey Creme...650.00
    Orange Julep...450.00
    Cherry Julep...500.00
    Grape Julep..550.00
    Ginger Mint Julep....................................400.00
    Afri-Kola..600.00
    Buckeye Urn..500.00
    Cherry Chic..1,300.00
    Delaware Punch.......................................350.00
J. Hungerford Smith 'True Fruit' Advertising
    Price List, w/ad cuts.................................20.00
    Paper Signs..70.00
    Cardboard Signs.....................................100.00
    Tin Signs.....................................up to 125.00
Life-like Displays of Sundaes, Sodas, Etc........................10.00
Heart-Shape Footed Ice Cream Dish................................30.00
McLaren's Ice Cream Cone Glass Jar..............................100.00

Soda fountain and ice cream memorabilia collecting has grown tremendously over the last five years. Many people start out collecting scoops and pewter molds to decorate their kitchens and expand from there.

We have an association called the 'Ice Screamers' (c/o Ed Marks, P.O. Box 5367, Lancaster, PA 17601-0387). Dues are $15.00 and include a bimonthly newsletter and an annual convention. Our organization is over five years old and has over five hundred members.

The best thing about collecting ice cream memorabilia is that it is fun, and you don't have to spend much money on any one item. The most popular items to collect are ice cream scoops, post cards, pewter molds, and ice cream trays. There are many soda fountain-related collectibles that can be acquired for a modest amount such as fans, trade cards, match covers, valentines, dixie cup lids, or booklets.

I am interested in buying the following items. All items should be in excellent condition. I am always looking for unusual soda fountain and ice cream memorabilia. I prefer a Xerox copy and price before someone sends an item.

Allan 'Mr. Ice Cream' Mellis
1115 W. Montana
Chicago, IL 60614

We Pay

Soda Fountain Magazine, pre-1925	12.00
Soda Fountain Magazine, pre-1910	25.00
Real Photo Post Card of Soda Fountains	20.00
Ice Cream Freezer Trade Card	10.00
Colorful Ice Cream Booklet, pre-1930	10.00
Paper Fan, picturing ice cream or people eating it	15.00
Pictorial Pin-Back Button of Ice Cream Companies	15.00
Ice Cream Scoop, extremely unusual	Write
Ice Cream Tray, w/image, excellent	Write
Salesman Sample of Ice Cream Equipment	75.00
Toy Ice Cream Truck	35.00
Soda Fountain Watch Fob	30.00
Ice Cream-Related Tape Measure, celluloid	20.00
Ice Cream Billhead, Letterhead, or Cover, pre-1910	15.00
Soda Fountain Related Sheet Music	15.00
Magazine Woodcut, w/ice cream scene, pre-1900	20.00
Printer's Cut, w/ice cream scene	8.00
Valentine, w/ice cream scene	5.00

Soda fountain and ice cream items are highly collectible. Burdan's Ice Cream was first manufactured in 1899 at Pottstown, Pennsylvania, and continued in production under this trade name until the mid-40's. Condition of items is most important; however, we will pay more for trays than for paper items. (Most of the trays are dated between 1913 and 1925.) We are also looking for cone-shaped dippers, sometimes referred to as dew-drop dippers!

Wm. A. Shaner, Jr.
403 N. Charlotte St.
Pottstown, PA 19464

SPORTS MEMORABILIA

Sports memorabilia as a category would include items from the sports of baseball, football, and boxing. Not only cards but books, programs, posters, uniforms, advertising items, etc. would be included. Of special interest to this collector would be pre-1920 items.

There are many baseball card collectors throughout the United States. I too collect baseball cards. I will pay premium prices for pre-1940 cards. However, I also collect a multitude of other sports items. My goal is to establish a sports museum where the various items can be displayed for public pleasure. Large posters, early photographs, early sports equipment, autographed items, etc. are what I am seeking. The following list provides a more specific indication of the types of items I buy. The prices listed will vary depending on the condition of the items.

John Buonaguidi
2830 Rockridge Dr.
Pleasant Hill, CA 94523

We Pay

Baseball Cards	1.00-5,000.00
Boxing Gloves, used by pro fighters	100.00 +
World Series Programs, pre-1920	100.00 +
19th Century Photos of Major League Players	75.00 +
19th Century Cabinet Photos	25.00 +
World Series Panorama, pre-1920	50.00 +
19th Century Non-Fiction Baseball Books	50.00 +
19th Century Non-Fiction Boxing Books	20.00 +
World Series Programs, pre-1920	100.00 +
19th Century Paintings of Players	1,000.00 +

Autographed Baseballs & Photos   **We Pay**

Cap Anson	500.00
Buck Ewing	450.00
Babe Ruth	150.00-350.00
Lou Gehrig	150.00-350.00

Boxing Tickets
We Pay

Corbett vs. Sullivan..200.00
Corbett vs. Fitzsimmons...100.00
Jeffries vs. Corbett...75.00
Johnson vs. Willard...75.00
Other 19th Century..50.00-150.00

Boxing Posters
We Pay

Johnson vs. Jeffries..250.00
Johnson vs. Willard..200.00
Corbett vs. Sullivan...400.00
Corbett vs. Fitzsimmons..350.00

Baseball Uniforms
We Pay

Babe Ruth...2,000.00
Ty Cobb...2,000.00
Other Pre-1940 Hall of Famers...............................1,000.00+

Advertising Posters
We Pay

Allen & Ginter Card Set.....................................1,000.00
Old Judge Tobacco Card Set..................................1,000.00
Testimonies by Baseball Players or Fighters, pre-1940.........500.00+

Tobacco Tins & Boxes
We Pay

Ty Cobb Pocket Tin..1,000.00+
Bambino Pocket Tin..250.00
Cigar Boxes, depicting players, early.........................50.00+

Major League baseball programs have been issued by home teams since the earliest days of the sport. The teams of the present National League date from 1876; the American League dates from 1901. A predecessor league, The National Association, dates from 1871 to 1875. Programs exist for all regular and post-season league playoff games. Post-season league playoffs pitting the champions of leagues against each other began in 1882 between the American Association and the National League. After a lapse, this practice resumed within the National League; from 1894 to 1897, it was known as the Temple Cup. Since 1903, this tradition has continued with the meeting of National and American League champions in the World Series.

The baseball All Star Game originated in 1933. This annual game pits the best players of the National League against those of the American League.

Since the 1900's, teams from the major leagues have intermittently issued yearbooks. These depict the pictures, records, and background information of all players on that year's team. I am interested in buying specific World Series, All Star, and other early programs as well as team yearbooks. A partial listing with sample prices is given below. Depending on condition, prices may be higher or lower. I am also interested in other early paper items from baseball and other sports. Contact me for specific prices I will pay for your items. Please write or call.

Bud Glick
2846 Lexington Lane
Highland Park, IL 60035
(312) 433-7484

Official World Series Programs   We Pay

1903 Boston AL	3,000.00 +
1903 Pittsburgh NL	3,000.00 +
1905 Philadelphia AL	900.00
1905 New York NL	800.00
1906 Chicago AL	900.00
1906 Chicago NL	850.00
1907 Detroit AL	850.00
1907 Chicago NL	800.00
1908 Detroit AL	850.00
1908 Chicago NL	800.00
1909 Detroit AL	750.00
1909 Pittsburgh NL	800.00
1910 Philadelphia AL	400.00
1910 Chicago NL	60.00
1911-1923	Please Write or Call

Official All Star Programs   We Pay

1933 Chicago	300.00
1934 New York	300.00
1935 Cleveland	125.00
1936 Boston	450.00
1937 Washington	100.00
1938 Cincinnati	250.00
1939 New York	150.00
1940 St. Louis	125.00
1941 Detroit	110.00
1942 New York	600.00
1943 Philadelphia	100.00

We Pay

1944 Pittsburgh **100.00**
1946 Boston **200.00**
1947-1980 . . . . **Please Write or Call**

Sports souvenirs are a sought-after link to past sporting events. Sports souvenirs consist of any sports-related items. The more coveted items are from events such as baseball, football, boxing, and auto racing. They can be related to professional teams, college teams, or sports celebrities. We are seeking souvenirs from events such as these:

Auto Racing	Boxing	Horse Racing
Baseball	Football	Olympics
Basketball	Golf	Soccer
Bowling	Hockey	Tennis

I will buy or make offers on any sports souvenir in average or above-average condition from before 1960. Any tears, ink stains, water damage, marks, or excessive wear will reduce the price I will pay. I am especially looking for pre-1900 items or items from special events such as the World Series, Super Bowl, Olympics, Indy 500, Kentucky Derby, etc.

Mark Dubiel
2336 Yemans
Hamtramck, MI 48212

We Pay		**We Pay**	
Programs **4.00**		Team Calendars **5.00**	
Team Schedules **2.00**		Giveaways . . . . **5.00 +**	
Ticket Stubs **2.00**		Yearbooks **4.00**	
Passes **2.00**		Sports Books **3.00**	
Medals & Pins **4.00**		Sports Magazines **2.00**	
Sports Buttons **2.00**		Newspaper Headlines . . . . **2.00 +**	
Autographs . . . . **5.00 +**			

I am interested in purchasing baseball memorabilia, especially from the ' York area teams, both past and present––Brooklyn Dodgers, New York Giants York Yankees, and New York Mets. World Series programs, team yearbook any other collectibles including pennants, etc. are wanted. In addition, l cards of all years are sought. Additionally, non-sport cards are wanted. I prefer to buy complete accumulations or collections.

I also have an additional interest—Beatles memorabilia (printed material or items such as lunch boxes, record players, dolls, etc.)

Steve Freedman
P.O. Box 2054-Central Station
East Orange, NJ 07019
(201) 743-2091

We Pay

Old Baseball Pennants 1.00-25.00
Yearbook, 1962 Mets 50.00
Yearbook, 1950's Yankees 25.00-50.00
Beatles Lunch Boxes 50.00

SOUVENIR SPOONS

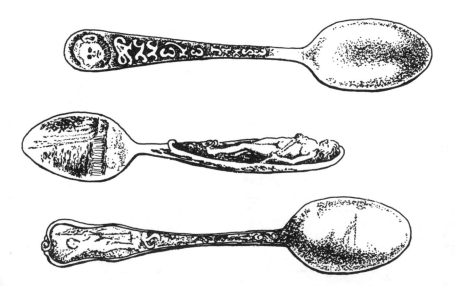

The collecting of sterling silver souvenir spoons from the 1890's to the early 's has been hampered by dealers pinning prices to the fluctuating silver market. lly, there should be no correlation, but a collector can't fight the mob. When ose to over $50.00 a troy ounce, spoons that before would sell for $5.00 to ere suddenly worth close to $50.00 if they weighed an ounce. When silver fell drastically, those dealers that had purchased spoons at weight were stuck. Not only is the silver market down, but souvenir spoon collecting is, too. However, some dealers still have spoons in their displays marked way out of sight, and there is little chance they will ever be able to sell them unless they see silver back up to that $50.00 mark or higher. In the meantime, I continue to collect in the price ranges listed below.

If you have spoons to sell, please take them to your nearest photocopying establishment; place the spoons face down on the machine and make copies of them. This is a lot faster and easier than trying to write descriptions. We will return your photocopies if we're not interested in the spoons. Price your spoons individually, by lot, or both ways. I am a big buyer.

Bill Boyd
4922 State Line
Westwood Hills, KS 66205

Teaspoon Size Only: **We Pay**

State Spoons, embossed or engraved scenes in bowl..............**10.00-20.00**
Handles, full-figured people, animals, or buildings..............**15.00-30.00**
Embossed Handles, enameled scenes in bowl, mint..............**30.00-50.00**
World's Fair Subjects, up to & including 1915...................**10.00-20.00**
Missouri Court Houses, embossed or engraved in bowl, w/state
    seal or pattern handle....................................**10.00-20.00**

I am interested in souvenir spoons. I will pay according to condition and whether or not they are sterling. I am especially interested in Dionne spoon sets.

Sandi Waddell
2791 C.R. 302
Durango, CO 81301
(303) 247-1568

STAGECOACH ITEMS

Stagecoaches date from Roman times and were the primary means of travel until the middle of the 1870's when trains made overland travel much easier. Even then, stagecoaches were used to bring passengers from the outlying areas to the railhead. Railway companies owned their own stage lines for this purpose. The late 1930's saw the last of the stage lines, as travel was taken over by car. The days of the stage driver, who was the captain, engineer, expressman, porter, and messenger of the stagecoach, have long gone; but his spirit still lives in the pictures, letters, and documents of those days. We buy most items related to stage travel: tickets, diaries, vouchers, broadside ads, waybills, abstracts of vouchers, timetables, receipts, Wells Fargo items, pictures, real picture post cards, stereoscopic views, etc. The following are prices paid for items in good condition.

AAMAC Collectibles
1316 NE 113th
Portland, OR 97220

We Pay

Picture, stage in action..**20.00**
Picture, stage station..**15.00**
Picture, stage driver...**15.00**
Stereoscopic View, stage..**9.00**
Stereoscopic View, stage station.................................**9.00**
Tickets...**8.00**
Waybills..**12.00**
Vouchers...**5.00**
Voucher Abstracts...**15.00**
Expressman..**10.00**
Timetables...**10.00**
Receipts...**10.00**
Real Picture Post Cards, stagecoaches...........................**6.00**

	We Pay
Real Picture Post Cards, stations	**6.00**
Real Picture Post Cards, drivers	**6.00**
Broadside Advertising	**20.00-50.00**
Advertising (no books or papers)	**20.00-50.00**
Strong Boxes	**45.00 +**
Wells Fargo Items	**10.00 +**

STAINED GLASS

In America, stained glass windows, beveled glass windows, doors, and side-lites were made primarily between 1880 and 1930. Stained glass artists in various studios in the United States used different techniques and types of glass than their European counterparts. Instead of painting or staining pieces of glass and firing them in a kiln, the Americans chose glass that was itself made with the color they desired. Different mineral oxides were used to produced various colors. These new variations of glass were developed by both John Laforge and Louis Comfort Tiffany.

Clear beveled glass windows were produced during the same period. Differe studios in cities across the Midwest and in the East used various designs and ty of workmanship, and certain studios are easily recognized by their style. Sta glass lamps were also produced at this time.

Numismatic Assets buys all U.S. coins in any amount or condition—singles, rolls, sets, accumulations, or entire collections. As coin retailers we can pay up to full *Red Book* or *Coin World Trends* for many coins. We consistently pay market highs—you have the satisfaction of knowing that you are receiving the highest prices you will encounter for all your coins. Handsome premiums are paid for scarce Gem coins.

We have twenty-two years of professionalism in numismatics. Perfect business references are available upon request. We are members of the American Numismatic Association. Please ship your coins with confidence by insured or registered mail for immediate, same-day, confidential cash offers. Your coins are fully insured while in our vaults. We will travel to your home, bank, or office to buy your coins if circumstances dictate. Write or call collect for details.

If for any reason you are not completely satisfied with the transaction, we will promptly return your coins to you, insured and postpaid.

Now it is up to you. Package your coins securely and take them to the post office. Keep in mind that 90% of all coin transactions are made through the mail and that it is quite safe. Your postal clerk will help you with packaging and insured-registered mail procedures to make the transaction convenient and risk-free. 'Superb service and excellent buying prices' is a hard philosophy to live up to, but we have no complaints—and neither do our customers. Listed are sample buying prices. Write for our free twenty-four page *Guide for Selling Your Coins*. We are paying top-market prices for anything gold or silver.

Numismatic Assets Co., Inc.
P.O. Box 27003
Indianapolis, IN 46227
(317) 786-7150

We Pay

Silver Dollars, very good +	**7.50**
Indian Cents, good +	**30¢ +**
Silver 10¢, 25¢, 50¢ (face value) Coins	**current market 4.5 x face value**
Large Cents	**3.50 +**

I let people spend any common, cancelled stamps of commemorative 1 x 1½″ minimum size (off paper only) at one cent each. No regular size issues are wanted. I offer all kinds of collectibles they can spend their 'paper pennies' for, if they send a long SASE for my lists.

I offer Western Americana, collector medals, post cards, and many other barter items for their common, cancelled stamps. Where others will sell for money, in effect I sell by barter, eliminating all the need for bookkeeping and tax work, as opposed to selling for cash. It works great!

Each shipment must be a minimum of 5,000 stamps. There is no maximum

I accept the dreaded Love and Christmas stamps nobody else wants! Until I came up with this project, stamp collectors had difficulty unloading Love and Christmas stamps. A shipment of 100,000 of these 'hard-to-get-rid-of' issues are worth $1,000.00. That goes for all stamps sent!

Blaine Moore
312 Jerome St.
Marshalltown, IA 50158

STANGL POTTERY

We buy and sell Stangl dinnerware––especially the following patterns:

Fruit	Country Life	Sculptured Fruit
Fruit & Flowers	First Love	White Dogwood
Country Gardens	Thistle	Golden Blossom
Blueberry	Blue Daisy	Orchard Song
Town & Country	Bittersweet	Apple Delight
Garland	Magnolia	Wild Rose
Star Flower	Golden Harvest	Chicory
Lyric	Mediterranean	

Pieces must be in perfect or near-perfect condition. Please list the patterns, number and kinds of pieces, measurements, and condition of items. We'll make you an offer if you don't have a price in mind. We also buy Stangl birds in perfect condition (and large or unusual ones in damaged condition).

We love Stangl artware vases, especially Rainbow Ware, Terra Rose in various colors, very large vases, baskets, Bronzeware, etc. We are always interested in Sportsman's Ware ash trays, mugs, plates, etc. with various birds or animals as well as Stoby mugs by Tony Sarg and Kiddieware bowls, plates, and cups.

We also want any advertising, post cards, signs, catalogs, etc. relating to Stangl or its parent company, Fulper.

Robert Perzel
Popkorn Antiques
P.O. Box 1057
Flemington, NJ 08822
(201) 782-9631

STAR WARS

The Star Wars Trilogy was a fantastic success both at the box office and in promotion and advertising campaigns. Thousands upon thousands of items have found their way to the collectibles aftermarket and have literally taken off in terms of interest and increased value. Whereas the toys and action figures still mint-in-command the highest prices, just about anything with a Star Wars, Empire Strike Back, or Return of the Jedi logo is of some interest to an avid collector.

Currently we are especially interested in toys, games, figures, etc. that are of mint-in-the-box, undamaged condition; but we are interested in all items. Below is a sample listing of items readily available (if a person wants to look for them) and the prices we pay. Please note that prices reflect mint-in-the-box condition. Open and/or used items command a somewhat lower cash value (usually about 50% less).

Wayne Tobias
1738 SE Place
Portland, OR 97216

Star Wars Action Figures   **We Pay**
  Dated 1977-78, 2¼″ to 4¼″

R2D2 . . . . 3.50
C3PO 3.50
Jawa 3.50
Storm Trooper 2.00

Large Action Figures   **We Pay**

Boba Fett, cape & back pack, w/rifle, 13½″ 50.00
Han Solo, belt & medallion, w/hand blaster, 12½″ 50.00
IG-88, bandoleer & rifle, 12½″ 60.00

STATUARY

I am interested in Art Deco, Art Nouveau, and Victorian statuary of Galle and Mucha design. Pieces may be bronze and ivory, bronze and marble, spelter, porcelain, etc., with or without lighting, 1920 to 1930—no reproductions. All or any pieces considered.

Mrs. Wm. H. Lidey
2109 Sunland Ave.
Las Vegas, NV 89106
(702) 383-4009

STEINS

I want to buy miniature and advertising beer steins. I want antique miniature beer steins, especially Mettlach sample miniatures. I pay $100.00 for these. I am also interested in buying glass beer steins with inlaid porcelain lids advertising beer brands or breweries. I will pay $50.00 for these.

Donald A. Shaurette
#21 1240 Bryant Ave.
St. Paul, MN 55075

STERLING SILVER AND SILVERPLATE

Sterling and silverplated flatware are our main interest. We buy all sterling items made in the United States and other countries. We buy all silverplate made in the United States. We prefer to buy complete sets but will buy single pieces of better patterns as well as serving pieces. We prefer to buy mint, non-monogramed pieces of both sterling and silverplate, but we will make quotes on monogramed pieces.

Prices listed below are for mint, non-monogramed pieces. There must be no wear on the silverplated flatware. Let us know what you have, as we buy all patterns, all of the time. Thanks to all!

Windmill Antiques
600 W. Burt
Lincoln, NE 68521

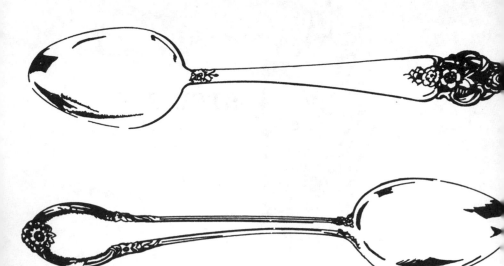

Silverplate   We Pay

Brides Bouquet, Gorham...**1.00**
Diana, Gorham...**1.00**
Vanity Fair, Gorham...**1.00**
Grape, Our Very Best..**1.00**
Moselle, American...**1.50**
Bride, Holms & Edwards..**1.00**
Danish Princess, Holms & Edwards..................................**1.00**
Arcadian, 1847 Rogers...**1.50**
Siren, 1847 Rogers..**1.50**
Columbia, 1847 Rogers...**1.50**
Bershire, 1847 Rogers...**1.50**
Vintage, 1847 Rogers..**1.50**
Charter Oak, 1847 Rogers..**1.50**
Old Colony, 1847 Rogers...**1.50**
Berwick, Rogers...**1.50**
Arbutus, Rogers...**1.50**
Orange Blossom, Rogers..**1.50**
Holly, Wards..**1.50**
La Vigne, 1881 Rogers...**1.50**
Hanover, Rogers...**1.50**
Carnation, Keystone...**1.50**

Sterling   We Pay

Place Fork..**10.00**
Salad Fork..**8.00**

We Pay

Place Knife..3.00
Lunch Knife...3.00
Teaspoon...4.00
Butter Knife..4.00
Cream Soup Spoon..6.00
Large Tablespoon..12.00
Sugar Spoon..5.00
Jelly Spoon...5.00
Iced Tea Spoon...6.00
Large Meat Fork...13.00
Lunch Fork...8.00
Pickle Fork...5.00
Cream Ladle..7.00
Gravy Ladle...12.00
Cake Server..6.00
Pie Server..8.00
Tomato Server...15.00
Demi Spoon...3.00
Oval Soup Spoon..9.00

Sterling hallmarked items by major American companies have been manufactured since the mid-19th century. Over the years, millions of American families have purchased sets from among the fifteen hundred patterns issued since that time.

W.F.N. currently makes an aftermarket for new and used sterling items. Being in business since 1974, W.F.N. will guarantee to purchase all items offered at some mutually-agreeable market price. As an example, in late 1986 with the silver market based at $5.75, W.F.N. guaranteed a minimum value of $4.85 for all scrap items and regularly paid prices of $5.00 to $15.00 per ounce for usable, non-monogramed sets of sterling flatware and non-monogramed and clean, undamaged American sterling holloware.

A booklet describing W.F.N.'s major services is available for the asking. Quotes for flatware are given upon request. Please remember that gross troy weight is 10% less than bathroom-scale weight for the same number of ounces weighed (i.e., 16 ounces on a bathroom scale equals 14.5 troy ounces). In addition, please do not weigh hollow-handle knives, butter spreaders, or serving pieces: they figure from ¼ to 1 ounce each depending upon size and pattern.

W.F.N. Enterprises, Inc.
2300 Henderson Mill Rd., NE Suite 318
Atlanta, GA 30345
(404) 938-0745

Atlantic Silver is a major national sterling silver matching service. We buy sterling silver flatware at premium prices. All inquiries are expeditiously and courteously answered. You may call collect.

Attention: Paul Aimis
Atlantic Silver
401 State Rd. 584 East
Suite 1106
Oldsmar, FL 33557
(813) 854-1555

American silverware manufacturers made many unusual place and serving pieces at the turn of the century. Individual strawberry forks, individual asparagus tongs, pastry forks, ice cream forks—a complete place setting in some patterns could be as many as twenty-five different place pieces! We are collecting old, ornate flower patterns such as Whiting's 'Lily' and 'Violet'; Durgin's 'Chrysanthemum,' 'Iris,' 'Dauphin,' 'Tulip', and 'Jonquil'; Tiffany's 'Chrysanthemum' and 'Japanese'; Scheibler's 'American Beauty'; Reed & Barton's 'Les Six Fleur' and 'Intaglio'; Watson's 'Wild Rose,' 'Lily,' and 'Orchid'; Alvin's 'Bridal Rose,' 'Orange Blossom,' and 'Raphael.' I will buy other items not listed here and damaged items, as well, if you contact me for prices. Monogrammed items are also purchased. Send a Xerox of your unusual items; we will identify and offer to purchase. If it is fancy, unusual, and flowered—we buy! We pay according to condition and wear.

Overtons
200 Ave. Santa Margarita
San Clemente, CA 92672
(714) 498-5530

We Pay

Strawberry Forks, 3-tine	12.00-20.00
Asparagus Tongs	20.00-40.00
Pastry Forks	20.00-40.00
Salad Forks	20.00-45.00
Ice Cream Forks	20.00-30.00
Fish Forks	25.00-45.00
Fish Knives, a/s	35.00-55.00
Breakfast Knives, a/s	35.00-55.00
Unusual Serving Pieces	35.00-200.00

I want to buy silver tea caddy ladles. These tiny silver 'spoons' are very lightweight as a rule, and the average measurement is a mere three inches. The bowl is large and often as wide as the spoon is long. Usually, the bowl is in the shape of a leaf, shell, or hand; but that is not always the case, as some were very plain and others very ornate. These were used to measure tea from the caddy during the time when tea was an expensive commodity.

We buy tea caddy ladles and spoons and any other unusual silver items, preferably small. Condition and style as well as the maker are very important. Items such as these bring a wide range of prices on today's market, but we will pay your price when feasible. Do not hesitate to write, but please include SASE for reply.

Betty Bird
107 Ida St.
Mount Shasta, CA 96067

STICKERS

I collect all holiday 'lick and stick' package stickers made through the 1950's. These are not to be confused with seals put out by various charitable organizations. The oldest stickers are quite small and were usually sold boxed in quantities; each box sold for two to five cents each. Generally, later stickers were marketed in glasine envelopes, window envelopes, booklets, and die-cut sheets. They were produced by a large number of manufacturers including Raphael Tuck, Dennison, Whitney, Stanley, Gibson, and Tipco. Others may only be marked 'USA,' 'Germany,' 'Saxony,' etc.

I am especially interested in those stickers which read 'Santa Claus Post,' 'Christmas Post,' and 'X mas Post.' These first appeared about 1905 and continued to be made through 1925. They are frequently found on old post cards and letters mailed during the Christmas season.

E.L. Sikinger
695 Greencrest St. NE
Salem, OR 97301

We Pay

'Santa Claus Post,' 'Christmas Post,' or 'X mas Post'
    per sticker . . . . **50¢**
    on post card . . . . **60¢**
Raphael Tuck, Germany, or Saxony, boxed . . . . **50¢**
Stanley, Dennison, Whitney, Gibson, etc., boxed . . . . **35¢-50¢**
Booklets, Glasine Envelopes, Window Envelopes, Full-Package
    Die-Cut Sheets, Etc. . . . . **25¢-35¢**
Old Trade Catalogs (illustrating stickers) **3.00-4.00**

STOCK CERTIFICATES
AND BONDS

Scripophily (collecting stock certificates and bonds) is the newest and most fascinating hobby in the collectible world. As early as 1670, stock certificates were being issued. The development of the West, the Era of the Gold Rush, and the Era of the Iron Horse are examples of important periods in our nation's history that are often represented in scripophily. The fine engravings appearing on stocks and bonds were designed by the same world-renowned banknote companies who are also known for their excellent stamp and currency engravings. Because of their attractiveness, certificates and bonds are being prominently displayed in homes, offices, banks, hotels, libraries, etc. by decorators as well as collectors.

Since rarity, condition, and many other factors determine the worth of a certificate, we prefer to recieve photocopies so that we many submit the highest bid possible. The following prices are broad guidelines.

Phyllis L. Barrella
Buttonwood Galleries
P.O. Box 1006
Throggs Neck Station
New York, NY 10465

	We Pay	Signed Certificates	We Pay
Railroad, pre-1930	**5.00 +**	Thomas A. Edison	**150.00 +**
Railroad, pre-1900	**10.00 +**	John D. Rockefeller	**400.00 +**
Mining, pre-1930	**5.00 +**		
Mining, pre-1900	**10.00 +**		
General, pre-1930	**5.00 +**		

Since the mid-1970's, stock certificates are more collectible than ever before––there are an estimated ten thousand collectors in the U.S. today. Many factors determine the collector value: age of the certificate, industry represented, autograph value, how ornate it is, condition, demand, and whether it has been issued or not. There are many collecting fields represented such as mining, railroad, aircraft, automobiles, territorials, banking, and manufacturing.

Stock certificates have great appeal because of their unique illustrations, mining scenes, street scenes with horses and buggies or horse-drawn streetcars, train tunnels, old locomotives, state buildings and seals, famous personalities and Presidents, and old smoke-belching factories. Many are well worth framing as conversation pieces and date back to the mid-1800's.

Other documents that are of interest to collectors are discharge papers, land grants, sheriff's writs, leases, military orders, waybills, checks, invoices, and those relating to specific subjects such as mining, railroads, slavery, politics, legal deeds, mortgages, etc. Some date back to Colonial, Civil War, Revolutionary, and early Western eras. The following list is reflective of prices paid according to material and condition.

Georgia Fox
Foxes' Den Antiques
P.O. Box 846
Sutter Creek, CA 95685
(209) 267-0774

Stock Certificates   **We Pay**

	We Pay
Chicago, Burlington, & Northern Railway, 1888	12.00
Deluxe Mining & Milling Co., Colorado, 1897	10.00
Silver Mining Co., Buena Vista, Colorado, blank	6.00
Smuggler Gold Mining & Milling Co., 1889	8.00
Park, Davis Drug Co., 1927 or any date	3.00
New Orleans, Great Northern R.R., LA, wine print, vignette, 1913	8.00
Richfield Copper, Arizona Territory, brown print, 1910	8.00
Spokane, Valley, & Northern Railway, Washington, 1917	10.00
Johnnie-Wonder Gold Mine, Arizona Territory, issued/uncancelled, 1907	8.0
United Verde Consolidated Copper, Arizona, issued/uncancelled, 1916	7.6

We Pay

Wastach Oil & Refining, Utah, scene w/train, issued/uncancelled, 1919. . . . **8.00**
Any Gold Mining Co. in California Motherlode. **7.00**
Any Silver Mining Co. in California or Colorado. **5.00**

Documents   We Pay

Auctioneer's Receipt, slave for sale, 1863. . . . . **15.00**
Slave Bill, sale of girl, handwritten. **15.00**
Check, Mt. Jackson Quicksilver Mining Co., wages, 1876. . . . . **6.00**
Comstock Lode, written, 1888. . . . . **10.00**
Land Grant, 40 acres to Cherokee Nation, red seal, 1906. . . . . **15.00**
Civil War, re: moving of troops, handwritten. **4.00**
Any Documents Dealing w/Comstock Lode. **5.00**
Any Documents Dealing w/California Motherlode, 1850's. **7.00**

STONEWARE

We are looking for stoneware manufactured in the state of Iowa. A number
of potteries existed in Iowa from the 1870's to the 1900's. Although a large amount
of stoneware was made there, because of age and hard use, few examples are found
day.

Many pieces are Albany-glazed (dark brown) with incised stamps which identify the potter and the town. Other pieces are salt-glazed—some with cobalt designs either stenciled or slip trailed. Crocks, jars, jugs, churns, and bowls are the most commonly-found objects.

We are looking for any Iowa stoneware, but especially items from the following towns: Sioux City, Red Oak, Eldora, Auburn, Sergeant Bluff, and Mason City. We are not interested in Albany-glazed stoneware from Fort Dodge. Although condition of the stoneware is important in determining value, because of rarity, even damaged pieces are of value. We pay $100.00 and up for undamaged, marked pieces of Iowa stoneware.

Andy Brenner
814 9th St.
Sheldon, IA 51201

SUMMER RESORT SOUVENIRS

Between the 1880's and the 1930's, summer resorts were favorite vacation spots. Usually located on the seashore, along the Great Lakes, or in scenic mountain areas, resorts featured large hotels, swimming, theatrical performances, concerts, fine dining rooms, and (often) famous boardwalks. Although not really amusement parks, many included roller coasters, carousels, and a variety of other rides. While we are interested in all resorts, we are particularly seeking souvenir items from Atlantic City, Coney Island, and Cedar Point (Sandusky, Ohio). If in good condition, we will pay the following prices for souvenir items.

D.W. Francis
Box 16
Wadsworth, OH 44281

	We Pay		We Pay
Post Cards	1.00-2.00	Dolls	10.00+
Post Card Folders	2.00-4.00	Paperweights	5.00+
Souvenir Booklets	5.00	Glass Hatchets	5.00
Original Photographs	5.00	Glass Canoes	5.00
Souvenir Spoons	5.00+	Leather Items	2.00-4.00
Plates, one color	5.00+	Seashell Items	3.00-5.00
Plates, multi-color	7.00+	Hats	3.00-5.00
Cup & Saucer Sets	7.00+	Metal Sand Pails	5.00-10.00
Ruby-Flashed Glass	5.00+	Tickets	50¢
Custard Glass	15.00+	Convention Badges	2.00-5.00
Jewelry	3.00+	Convention Ribbons	2.00-5.00
Felt Pennants	2.00-4.00	Brochures	2.00-5.00

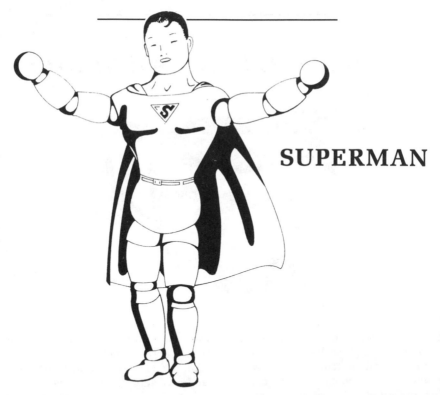

SUPERMAN

Superman was first introduced in 1938, and since that time thousands of items bearing his likeness have been produced. One of the most popular fictional characters ever created, he has had a long and faithful following by both fans and collectors. I have been collecting Superman memorabilia since 1962 and have what considered to be the largest collection of its kind in existence. Although I have usands of items, there are still many others I'm looking for.

I collect all Superman items I don't already have that are in good condition, complete, and manufactured between the years 1938 through 1960. All items should be accurately described, noting defects and giving the manufacturer, dimensions, copyright, etc. The list below represents average prices I will pay. I will also buy other interesting or unusual Superman items not listed. Prices paid vary, depending on condition, rarity, and desirability of the item.

Danny Fuchs
209-18th Ave.
Bayside, NY 11360

	We Pay		We Pay
Games	15.00	Puppets	8.00
Figures	5.00	Greeting Cards	3.25
Dolls	18.00	Watches	20.00
Coloring Books	10.00	Puzzles	12.00
Buttons	10.00	Playsuits	9.00
Rings	15.00	Photos	1.50
Banks	12.00	Gum Cards	3.00
Paint Sets	12.00	Lunch Boxes	10.00

TELEGRAPH INSTRUMENTS

Thanks for your interest. Please feel free to call or write if in doubt about my wants. A photo or rough sketch is greatly appreciated. Condition is not of primary concern, but missing parts may affect offering price. Formal appraisals are not ordinarily offered but may be negotiated subject to an agreement and fee.

A minimum of $35.00 will be paid for any complete keys, sounders, or relays with the following markings. These are among the major telegraph manufacturers from the period of 1860 to 1890.

Avery, Thomas C.
Bradley, Dr. L.
Buell, M.A.
Caton Instr. Shop
Chester, C.T. & J.N.
Chester & Partrick
Chubbuck, A.S.
Clark, James J.
Cleveland, W.B.
Davis, William E.
DuBois, Charles H.

Electrical Construction Co.
Greeley, E.S.
Hall, Thomas
Hughs, David
Jones, C.E. & Bro.
Knox & Shain
Lannert, J.A.
Longstreet, J.H.
Lyman, A.B.
Moses, I.H.
New Haven Clock Co.

Palmer & Hall	Redding, Jerome
Partrick & Bunnell	Tillotson, L.G.
Partrick & Carter	Watts
PRR-Altoona Shops	Williams, Charles
Phelps, G.M./W.P.	Western Elec. Mfg.
Pope, F.L.	Any Other Pre-1890 Maker

A minimum of $50.00 will be paid for peg boards, early messenger or alarm call boxes (other than type 6-B), early porcelain or wood telegraph signs, C.C. White 3-arm resonator stands, and box relays.

A minimum of $100.00 will be paid for early registers (pen or stylus, but not fire alarm) and pocket relays or linemen's sets.

A minimum of $500.00 will be paid for early stock tickers. Early telegraph textbooks, broadsides, and telegrams (pre-1900) are also wanted.

The following intruments are rather common and are not sought unless priced under $10.00: key 2-A; sounders 1-A/B, 15-B, 17-A; and relays 3-A/C and 4-A/B/C/D. These are usually made by J.H. Bunnell & Co., Western Electric, Foote, Pierson & Co., and Manhattan Electric Supply Co. (MESCO). Equipment made by Signal or Menominee is not wanted, nor are war-surplus keys J-37 or J-38.

Practice or 'learner's' sets consisting of a key and sounder with gold-striped, black, cast-iron bases mounted on a wood board about 5″ x 8″ are of interest only if under $20.00. Any set marked with a maker's name from the pre-1890 list of manufactures already given is especially sought. I will pay a minimum of $50.00 for any of these.

Roger W. Reinke
5301 Neville Court
Alexandria, VA 22310
(703) 971-4095

I am paying cash for telegraph books; instruments such as keys, sounders, relays, resonators; and everything that had to do with telegraphy––postal telegraphy, Western Union items, etc., old stock tickers, etc.

Charles B. Goodman
636 W. Grant Ave.
Charleston, IL 61920
(217) 345-6771

TELEPHONES

Old telephones, phone parts, and telephone company memorabilia are increasingly becoming sought-after collectibles. The wooden wall telephones and candlestick models from of the turn of the century share in popularity with the more common cradle telephones of the 1930's and 1940's. There were many different manufacturers of telephones with each company making its own variation. It would be an impossible task to list everything I am specifically interested in buying due to the various designs, shapes, and sizes produced by each of the telephone manufacturers. Condition, scarcity, desirability, and manufacturer are all factors in determining a price.

I also buy other telephones and related items not listed as well as incomplete telephones. The prices given below are only a general indication of what I am paying. For more specific prices, I would need detailed information and a sketch or photo.

Thomas Guenin
310 N. Hambden St.
Chardon, OH 44024

We Pay		We Pay	
Pins	3.00	Transmitter Cups	3.00
Pens	1.50	Switch Hooks	2.00
Mechanical Pencils	1.50	202, w/Dial	20.00
Mouthpieces	2.50	202, No Dial	15.00
Receivers	8.00	Metal Nameplates	2.00
Transmitters	5.00	Bells	1.00

	We Pay		**We Pay**
Transmitter Arms	15.00	Tools	5.00
Receiver Cords	2.00	Dial, 3″	2.50
Magneto Cranks	1.25	F1 Handsets	2.00
Telephone Signs	25.00	E1 Handsets	3.50
Glass Mouthpieces	25.00	Blake Transmitters	350.00
Pay Phones	50.00	Colored 302's	25.00
Blotters	1.00		

We Pay

Receiver w/Top Binding Post, 5½″	35.00
Receiver w/Top Binding Post, 7½″	75.00
Wall-Phone Cabinet, wood, empty	28.00
Wall-Phone Shelf, wood	5.00
Candlestick Telephone	35.00 +
Wall Telephone, wood	100.00 +
Candlestick Phone, shaped	175.00 +

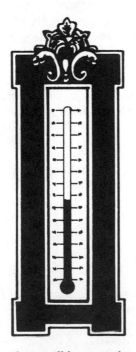

THERMOMETERS

    Like their well-known advertising cousins, decorative thermometers have been around for at least one hundred years. They have been made in free-hanging, wall-mounted, or desk/mantel versions and have been manufactured from nearly every conceivable material—mahogany, sterling, brass, and plastic being the favorites.

Decoratives have tested the artistry and technical skills of many of Europe's and America's finest craftsmen. Most household or light commercial varieties are simple tube-on-backing types. Fewer yet are the exquisitely ornate sterling silver Tiffanies or gold-plated Bradley & Hubbards.

Decorative thermometers exemplify the best qualities associated with the unique skills of an artisan and the scientific precision of a technician. Insofar as sheer beauty, decorative thermometers are not without peer in the field of scientific instrumentation. Many devices, in fact, are prized no less for their design features as their ability to accurately record temperature.

Because so few ornate Victorian mantel models have survived the perils of time, those remaining specimens that can be found intact are usually one-of-a-kind and are valuable by that standard alone. Decoratives were fabricated out of every conceivable material from walrus tusk to sterling silver.

The golden age of decoratives ended in the early 1940's, as modern manufacturing methods and the extensive use of plastic materials robbed them of their distinctiveness. Most American, early 20th-century thermometers were produced by Taylor (Tycos). Their models of today, while primarily utilitarian, still remain the most plentiful. Decoratives with mercury tubes, figural designs, or customized features fetch correspondingly higher prices.

We buy all pre-1940, non-advertising, and non-commercial decorative thermometers—the older, the better. Mercury-in-the-tube varieties are preferred. Thermometer company catalogs are also purchased. I will buy other types of thermometers not listed here if you provide me with a description. Damaged thermometers bring considerably lower prices due to the cost of specially manufactured replacement tubes.

Harris Catalog Library
6130 Rampart Dr.
Suite 209
Carmichael, CA 95608
(916) 487-6964

We Pay

Adam Kilt, Desk; brass portico/scalloped roof, F&R scales/mercury, 4½"..**25.00**
Alexandre, Folding; F&R scales/mercury, 1850's.......................**35.00**
Anonymous, Desk; walrus tusk, inlaid scales/mercury, 9".............**30.00**
Bargess Reversible Box, brass scales/mercury, oak case, 5½"...........**25.00**
Bertrand Mumser, Desk; cast/cathedral, months rotate, mercury, 12"...**800.00**
Bradley & Hubbard, Desk; ornate w/brass lion, brass scales/mercury, 9"..**45.00**
Bradley & Hubbard, scroll back, steel/cardboard, Mensh, mercury, 8"...**160.00**
Brannan, brass case, F&C stainless scales/mercury, 1932..............**28.00**
Brown Penzance, Desk; brown marble, ivory scales/mercury, 6".........**51.00**
C Wilder Co., bear & billboard figural brass, mercury, 6½"............**35.00**
CE Large, Hanging; Cottage Barometer, 2-tube, 1918..................**20.00**
CE Large, Kitchen; The Modern Thermometer, tin, permacolor.......**110. 00**
Chester, Desk; stainless scales/mercury, sterling bezel, 2x6"...........**70.00**
Clark, Desk; ivory pedestal, crown, mercury, 1904, 7"................**35.00**

We Pay

Cloister, inkwell, stainless back & vase w/side angels, 1901 . . . .**490.00**
Creswel, Travel; ivory case/mirror, removable scales/mercury, 2½" **1,200.00**
Desk-Type, carved walrus tusk, 2-tier disk base, 1860, 9" **85.00**
E Berman Co., Desk; brass/filigree, scrollwork atop, mercury, 8" **40.00**
Fahrenheit, Indoor; oak w/brass scales, permacolor, 1889, 7" **28.00**
Freeborn, Desk; bronze w/lead decoration, brass scales/mercury, 8" **30.00**
G Barnes, oak fold-out box, plastic scales/mercury, 2½" **61.00**
G Cooper, Desk; bell shape w/cupola, sterling, dial, 2x3" **40.00**
Gloucester Scientific, stainless case, glass front, permacolor, 42" **790.00**
Golub, Hanging; mahogany/brass bulb cap, large scales/red spirit, 9x2" . .**42.00**
H Lauramark, Hanging; gold stipple on boxwood, 0-120, mercury **40.00**
Harcatlib Ltd, Desk; brass pedestal on griffin, mercury, 9" **20.00**
Helmut, Desk; scrolled edge, stainless & plastic, easel pedestal, 6" **16.00**
Hiergelsell Bros., Indoor; cabinet w/oak back, blue liquid, #159 . . . .**2.00**
Hohmann Maurer Co., steel F&C scales & back, mercury, 12" **19.00**
Jed Sirrah, Hanging; silver, umbrella, mercury, 8" **45.00**
Jedseth Ltd, Desk; mercury figure w/base filigree, mercury, 7" **50.00**
LC Tower, Weather Prognosticator, cherry w/brass scales, mercury **18.00**
Mensch, Mantel; castle, round mercury tube, 10" **60.00**
Moeller Instrument Co., metal w/brass scales, permacolor, 12" **17.00**
Mova Products, Desk; round, glass encased, dial scales, pat. 1923 . . . .**38.00**
Orchard, iron case, brass face, glass intact, 14" **28.00**
Phila Therm Co., Hygrometer; brass scales, rotating bezel, 1928 . . . .**30.00**

We Pay

Any Outdoor, Non-Advertising, Pre-1940 Thermometer **10.00-50.00**
Any Indoor, Hanging, Non-Advertising, Pre-1940 Thermometer **15.00-60.00**
Any Desk or Mantel Pre-1940 Thermometer, any material **20.00-200.00**
Any Pre-1940 Thermostat **10.00-50.00**

THREE STOOGES COLLECTIBLES

The 'Three Stooges' started as Ted Healy's sidekicks in the 1920's. They performed in vaudeville, on Broadway, and in feature and short films at M.G.M. from 1933 through 1934 before splitting up with Ted Healy and going out on their own at Columbia. They made 190 short films at Columbia, working continuously until 1058. For the first time in 1959, their films were aired on television. This created a new generation of fans. They began making feature films geared to younger audiences and started releasing promotional items such as toys, comic books, rings,

bubble gum cards, puppets, and records. I am interested in all items. Prices listed
are based on items in good condition.

Peter Moment
537 Bright St.
San Francisco, Ca 94132

We Pay

Book, Stroke of Luck	**75.00**
Lobby Card	
w/Curly, 1930's	**85.00+**
w/Curly, 1940's	**75.00+**
w/Shemp	**65.00+**
One Sheets	
w/Curly, 1930's	**315.00+**
w/Curly, 1940's	**285.00+**
w/Shemp	**100.00+**
w/Joe Besser	**55.00**
Autographs, Letters, or Cancelled Checks	**100.00+**
Pillsbury Moving Picture Machine, 1937	**200.00**
16mm Exel Films	**25.00**
8mm Home Movie Versions	**10.00+**
Hand Puppets, 1930's, per set	**500.00**
Hand Puppets, 1960's, each	**40.00**
Gum Cards, 1959, each	**2.25**
1959, set	**265.00**
1959, wrapper	**25.00**

We Pay

1959, pack..**40.00**
1959, full box..**700.00**
1959, box..**45.00**
Gum Cards, 1965, each.......................................**1.00**
    1965, set...**85.00**
    1965, wrapper..**4.00**
    1965, pack...**8.00**
    1965, full box...**175.00**
    1965, box..**20.00**
Toys, Games, Puzzles, Hats, or Candy Boxes.....................**20.00 +**
Record, Happy Birthday.......................................**4.00**
Record, Any 45 RPM...**8.00**
Record Album...**12.00**
Record, Snow White & 3 Stooges..............................**20.00**
Comic Books
    Jubilee #1 & #2, each......................................**100.00**
    St. John #1 through #7, each............................**20.00-80.00**
    March of Comics..**10.00**
    Dell, Gold Key, or Little Stooges.......................**5.00-10.00**
Flicker Rings, set...**10.00**
Photos, Columbia Originals..................................**10.00 +**
Scripts...**250.00 +**
Moe Ventriloquist Dummy......................................**35.00**
Theater Programs, Vaudeville Items, Personal Appearance Handouts,
    Playbills 'A Night in Venice,' 'A Night in Spain,' 'Passing Show of
    1932,' 'George White's Scandals of 1939,' or Items w/Ted Healy.....**45.00 +**
Stooge Feature Films
    One Sheet, 1960's...**15.00**
    Lobby Cards, 1960's, set...................................**35.00**
    Lobby Cards, 1960's, each...................................**4.00**
    Inserts, ½-Sheets..**15.00**
    Pressbooks..**8.00**

TIRE ASH TRAYS

The second decade of this century saw a great increase in the sale of automobiles as they became affordable to the masses. Perhaps the most important (and troublesome) replacement part of the auto was the tire. The many tire companies in business at the time turned to advertising to secure their share of the market. One form of this advertising was the tire ash tray. A few tire ash trays with glass or metal tires were popular in the teens. The familiar rubber tire ash tray appeared in the early 1920's and is still being produced today. The ash tray tires are nearly perfect, minature replicas of actual tires. Passenger car, truck, tractor, heavy equipment, aircraft, and motorcycle tires have all been issued in ash tray form. They can be found worldwide, as most industrialized nations have produced them.

I'm interested in buying most types of tire ash trays. Prices I pay for some are shown below. Capital letters indicate lettering on tire. Contact me for a price quote on any not listed.

Jeff McVey
P.O. Box 201
Moffett Field, CA 94035

We Pay

Allstate, any w/colored tire	15.00
Allstate Fleet Tested Rayon	15.00
Armstrong 6.00-16	15.00
Atlas Bucron	15.00
Avtoexport (USSR)	25.00
Bridgestone Super Speed Radial (Japan)	15.00
Brunswick Balloon	13.00
Dayton Thorobred, w/whitewall tire	15.00
Diamond Balloon	13.00
Diamond Deep Cleat HB	13.00
Dominion Royal Heavy Duty (Canada)	15.00
Dominion Royal Centipede Grip (Canada)	15.00
Dunlap 25 Jahre Reifen-Kiotz (W. Germany)	20.00
Dunlap Fieldmaster	15.00
Falls Evergreen Tube (inner tube ash tray)	30.00
Firestone, w/4″ diameter red tire	20.00
Firestone 32 x 4½ RMC	35.00
Firestone 36 x 10	25.00
Firestone 40 x 12	25.00
Firestone, w/World's Fair glass	17.00
Firestone 6.00-18 (Canada)	15.00
Fisk, any	15.00
General 40 x 12	15.00
Goodrich 6.50-20 (Canada)	20.00
Goodrich, w/World's Fair glass	20.00
Goodyear 36 x 10	35.00
Hood Arrow, w/'Bee, Inc.' sticker	15.00
India, w/electric lighter	30.00
Michelin, w/rubber tire	50.00
Miller Deep Cleat HB	15.00
Mobil, any	20.00
Mohawk, w/'wheel' glass	15.00
Overman, any w/devil figure	50.00
Pennsylvania, w/white tire	20.00

We Pay

Pennsylvania Vacuum Cup	30.00
Republic, any	25.00
Saxon	15.00
Swinehard, any	25.00
Tyer Rubber Co., any	25.00
United States, w/spoked wheel	50.00
US Royal Fleet Carrier	25.00
US Royal Heavy Duty Six	15.00

TOBACCIANA

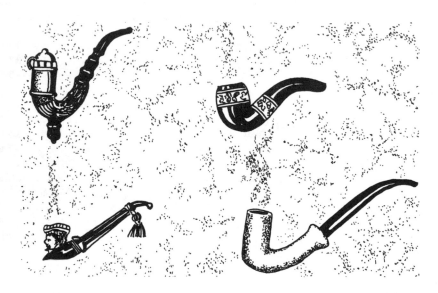

Antique smoking pipes are defined as those used in smoking dry tobacco only. However, other categories of smoking implements such as opium pipes, chibouks, nargilehs, hookahs, and other versions of the water pipe can be included, as well. These pipes are not defined so much by their age as they are by their materials: meerschaum, boxwood, walnut, cherry, porcelain, metal, ivory, amber, silver, and even gold. Their shapes, sizes, and intricate carvings are not found in today's expressions of similar materials. Older meerschaum pipes, choroot holders, cigar and cigarillo holders customarily were carved in full (high) or bas (low) relief, were accompanied by amber/amberoid stems, and included a fitted case (etui) lined with satin, plush, or chamois. Their size had no specific range; but their ornamentation, accouterment, and imagination are not found in pipes made anywhere in the world today. Ancillary collectibles include old catalogs, ephemera, lithographs of pipes and pipe smokers, literature on the history and culture of smoking artifacts, tampers, and associated utensils. Prices reflect the generic type of artifact when offered in excellent condition and can vary depending on material, theme, size, and execution. Photographs, line drawings, and descriptions are most useful in assessing the current value of an item in this category for sale.

Benjamin Rapaport
5101 Willowmeade Dr.
Fairfax, VA 22030

We Pay

Meerschaum Pipes, relief carving	100.00-1,000.00 +
Meerschaum Cheroot Holders	50.00-250.00 +
Opium Pipes	250.00-2,000.00
Porcelain Pipes	50.00-500.00
Meissen, Chinoiserie, Wedgwood	100.00-750.00
Assorted Metals	50.00-250.00
Cloisonne, Champleve	300.00-1,000.00
Other (requires more descriptive information)	Varies

Tobacco products are popular collectibles whether they are sacks, packs, tins, cigar bands, boxes, or even old cigarette packs. Also collected are any cabinets, cases, shipping boxes, or display items. By the turn of the century, there were hundreds of different brand names. Because of the Depression and World War II, many tobacco companies went broke and were bought out by those remaining. I am buying the following pre-1950 items—empty or full.

Terrell W. Allen
1705 2nd Ave.
Manchester, TN 37355

We Pay		We Pay	
Sack Tobacco	5.00 +	Cardboard Boxes	10.00 +
Cigarettes	5.00 +	Shipping Boxes	10.00 +
Tins	5.00 +	Display Items	50.00 +
Cabinets	100.00 +	Chewing Tobacco	5.00 +

Beginning as a marketing device in the late 1800's, cigarette cards have enjoyed a long and colorful history. Efforts to attract smokers to a particular brand gave rise to keen competition among tobacco companies and resulted in outstanding artwork and a wide diversity of subject matter. There are thousands of themes, titles, and interests to be found on cards, including art, architecture, literature, scouting, animals, flags, fish, birds, butterflies, aviation, flowers, railroads, motor cars, stage, screen and radio personalities, history, geography, occupations, explorers, general knowledge, etc. A unique feature of most British cigarette cards is the fact that the majority of card backs contain carefully researched descriptions and information, providing a valuable legacy of the life and times of the English-speaking peoples.

All types of cards are wanted, especially pre-WWII. British and German cards sets, singles, albums, American tobacco and cigarette cards (especially sports) are sought. I am also looking for unusual items such as uncut sheets, original artwork, etc.

Robert C. Hess
559 Potter Blvd.
Brightwaters, NY 11718

TOASTERS

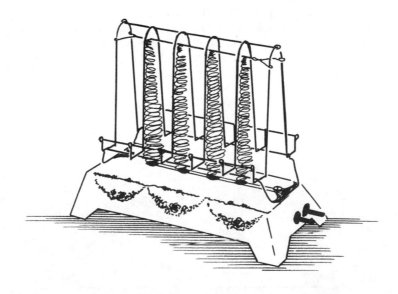

Electric toasters have been collectible for some time now, and they gain in popularity every year. They are still affordable with prices ranging from $20.00 to $150.00 depending on the toaster. The earliest toaster was horizontal in shape; it was made by American Electric Heater Co. in 1908. In 1909 the first upright toasters appeared on the market. The list below contains prices I am paying now; I also buy toasters not mentioned on the list. Take into consideration that prices below are for examples in good or near-mint condition, free from chips or breaks, and not pitted or corroded. However, I do buy damaged ones for parts.

J. Allen Barker
P.O. Box 592
Hawley, PA 18428

We Pay

American Beauty	25.00
American Electric	35.00
Bersted #78	30.00
Bigelow Electric	25.00
Birtman 1 Slice	45.00
Cadillac Electric	35.00
Copeman Electric Stove	25.00
Cutler Hammer	30.00
Dalton Electric Heater	45.00
D.A. Rogers Self Timing	75.00
D.C. Hughes & Co.	35.00
Double Action Junior	30.00
Edicrat Junior	20.00
Electric Specialties 'Okeco'	30.00
El Toasto	35.00
Estate	45.00
Excelsior	65.00
General Electric D-12	65.00-125.00
Gold Seal	30.00
Hold Heat	40.00
Hot Point #129T31	75.00
Liberty Gage	25.00
Manning Bowman #1209, #1221, #1226	45.00
Mecky & Co. (Philadelphia)	100.00
Mesco	60.00
Millar #100	40.00
Monarch	25.00
Pan Electric	100.00
Paragon	35.00
Pelouze	65.00
Phelps Mfg. 'Cozy Toaster'	65.00
Porcelier	100.00
Radiant Helion	50.00

We Pay

Rimco	40.00
Rochester Stamping (Percher)	35.00
Rogers Electric Laboratories	35.00
Saluta	100.00
Security 190, 220, 230	20.00
Simplex T-211, T-215	50.00
Steel Craft	25.00
Tamco Reversible	30.00
Thermax E1942	70.00
Trimble	35.00
Truitt	35.00
Universal #9410	65.00
Victory	45.00
Visible	60.00
Vita Electric	20.00
White Cross	25.00
Wicks	50.00
White Beauty	35.00

Electric toasters date from about 1908. It all began with a patent granted to Albert March on February 6, 1906, for an electrical resistance element which made the electric toaster possible. Out of the period between 1908 and the mid-1930's came many different toaster manufacturers, all competing for a piece of the market. They produced a seemingly endless variety of toasters with charm and style. After that they grew bulbous, automatic, monotonous, and commonplace.

I am interested in buying and trading electric toasters from this period, especially porcelain toasters and ones that are very unusual. I am not interested in rusted or corroded examples.

The fair retail price of an antique toaster varies greatly and like anything else depends on condition, desirability, and rarity. The following is a general price range for toasters I am looking for. If in doubt about the value of a toaster, please contact me for specific prices.

Joe Lukach
7111 Deframe Ct.
Arvada, CO 80004

We Pay

Turnover Toasters, open grillwork	12.00 +
Turnover Toasters, solid sides	8.00 +
Unusual Shapes or Unusual Mechanisms	15.00 +
Porcelain Toasters	30.00 +

TOKENS

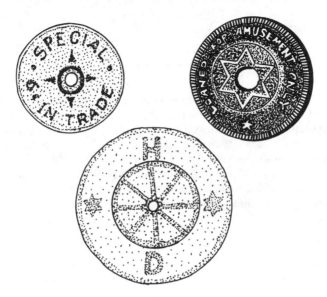

What a fantastic way to enjoy and learn about our past! Tokens have become the 'fun' side of numismatics with many a coin collector having switched to searching for that ever elusive 'Good For' token. There are tokens 'good for one shave or one drink,' tokens from your home state, tokens with your last name as a merchant—there are hundreds of ways to collect them.

Tokens are usually made of metal but may also be paper, fiber, wood, or even in the form of the advertising 'Good For' mirrors. By 1900 tokens had become a very common type of coinage by which merchants not only advertised but created good will and repeat business, as well.

We buy all types of tokens except sales tax, common transportation, OPA tokens, etc. We prefer tokens listing a town and state on them, but we buy those without, as well. If it says 'Good For (something),' chances are we are interested! Quantities are invited, although hordes of the same token won't be so valuable to me as that rare, unique piece—so send for my offer! I will pay up to $500.00 for certain tokens; give me a chance to make you an offer you can't refuse.

Jim Hinton
920 Millbrook #11
Jefferson City, MO 65101

We Pay

Common 'Good For'...50¢-5.00
'Good For' Mirror...10.00-150.00 +
Hotel to Depot..15.00 +
Saloon ....3.00-30.00 +
Missouri ....1.00 +

We Pay

C.C.C. . . . . **5.00 +**
Animal Pictorials . . . . **10.00 +**

All tokens, medals, exonumia wanted for outright purchase or consignment. We are seriously interested in purchasing all types of tokens, medals, counterstamps, buttons, badges, pocket advertising mirrors, World's Fair items, Masonic items (all types: tokens, medals, fobs, other early relics, etc.), political items, banners, china, and all related material. No collection is too large or too small.

We will travel to purchase. Please write or call collect. Consignments also are wanted for our quality public auctions and mail bid sales of tokens and medals (write for further consignment information). Sample catalogs are available for $3.00 (includes prices realized). For the best price, ship your material (insured or registered) with price desired, or I will make an offer.

Ask for your free copy of my detailed *Buying Guide* giving prices paid for many types of tokens and medals. We pay highly competitive prices. We purchase everything––common, scarce, or rare! Large quantities of the same item are wanted.

Rich Hartzog
P.O. Box 4143XW
Rockford, IL 61110-0643

I am a collector of tokens and transportation items as well as items relating to these areas of interest. I would appreciate any help you might give. I seek transportation items such as bus and streetcar tokens; tokens reading 'One ride, One fare'; hotel to depot; one toll; ferry tokens; bridge tokens; old tokens that read good for something: 5¢ in trade, one shave, bath, milk, bread, etc. Also wanted are Civil War tokens; hard-times tokens; store cards; pictures (actual photos of transit systems, bus lines, streetcar lines, street scenes showing same); passes; paper tickets; transfers; etc. Any old books on any of these subjects are sought. Also wanted are old medals from fairs, expos, any foreign medals, old coins or paper money, and books or catalogs on these categories.

I have been a collector of these items for many years and will pay top dollar for any material I can use. Please describe for offer or ship insured. If material is sent, I will make an offer. If my offer is not acceptable, I will return the material intact and pay postage both ways. I hope we get together.

Lee Schumacher
10609 Eastern
Kansas City, MO 64134

I want to buy tokens and all engraved awards or medals. I seek military, political, merchant advertising, early American, foreign, and historical tokens. I want to buy examples relating to the military, historical, agricultural, and industrial as well as awards or medals relating to mechanics, associations, expositions, and life-saving.

Stanley L. Steinberg
P.O. Box 512
Malden, MA 02148

TOOLS

I am wanting to buy old letter and number stamps for stamping metal in 1″, ⅛″, ³⁄₃₂″, and ¹⁄₁₆″ characters only. Good prices paid for nice stamping sets.

Richard Binger
Rt. 1, Box 70
Morgantown, IN 46160
(317) 878-5489

TOYS

Toys

The toys made during 1960 to 1969 were some of the most imaginative, distinctive, and outrageous ever to be unleashed upon the young. It was a decade that saw the birth of cartoon characters like the Flintstones, Jetsons, and Bullwinkle. Boys began playing with dolls like Captain Action and GI Joe. There were crazy fads such as the rediscovery of movie monsters which led to such popular TV shows as 'The Munsters' and 'The Addams Family.' And the creation of the spy craze James Bond initiated over twenty years ago is still evident today. Aurora Plastics revolutionized the model kit industry with their introduction of monster and superhero-figure model kits. Creativity was at its peak in every area of the toy market.

I buy all TV, cartoon, monster, superhero, and other interesting **toys from the 60's.** Many toys do not have to be mint or even complete. I buy loose plastic figures from playsets, loose uniforms from GI Joe and Captain Action dolls, assembled figure kits, and empty toy boxes! I also buy cereal, candy, and gum boxes.

Toy Scouts
15354 Seville Rd.
Seville, OH 44273
(216) 769-2523

We Pay

Capt. Action Doll, boxed	50.00
Capt. Action or Green Hornet Costume	50.00
Action Boy Doll, boxed	50.00
Action Boy or Superman Costume	50.00
Lost in Space Model Kits, boxed	50.00
Lost in Space Puzzles or Games	20.00
Lost in Space Playset by Mattel	100.00
Marx Gunsmoke Playset	100.00
Marx Alaska Missile Base Playset	50.00
Marx Untouchables Playset	100.00
Marx Ben Hur Playset	100.00
Outer Limits Puzzles or Games	20.00
Outer Limits Gum Card Box	35.00
Monster-Operated Frankenstein	100.00
Addams Family Puppets, Games, or Dolls	20.00
Munsters Puppets, Games, or Dolls	20.00
Munsters Hat, Pajamas, or Costumes	20.00
Munster Model Kit, boxed	100.00
Jetsons Puzzles, Games, or Lunch Box	15.00
Bullwinkle Games, Lunch Box, Etc.	15.00
Green Hornet Games, Paint Sets	15.00
Batman Switch & Go Playset by Mattel	50.00
Batman Shoes, Pajamas, or Sheets	15.00
Matt Mason Dolls & Equipment	15.00
Time Tunnel Games or Puzzles	20.00
Voyage to Bottom of the Sea Playsets	35.00
007 Road Race Set	75.00

We Pay

007 Attache Case	40.00
U.N.C.L.E. Dolls or Games	20.00
U.N.C.L.E. Guns or Model Kits	25.00
Justice League of America Playset	100.00
Supergirl or Batgirl Dolls by Ideal	50.00
Wonder Woman (Mera Doll) by Ideal	50.00
Twinkles or Jets Cereal Boxes	10.00
Land of the Giants Game, Colorforms	20.00
Land of the Giants Model Kits	40.00
GI Joe Dolls, boxed	40.00
Marx Big Loo, Great Carloo Robots	50.00
Superman Gumball Flasher Rings	5.00

Toys made prior to 1960 are becoming one of the top items in the current collectibles market. While cast iron toys, once considered the only collectible toy, have gradually dropped in value over the last several years, tin lithographed toys made in Europe and the USA have risen at a remarkable rate. Japanese toys made in the 1950's are now climbing as fast as toys made before WWII. As in most areas of the collectibles market, the condition of the toy means everything; and an original box for a rare toy can be worth as much as the toy itself. I buy many types of collectible toys; if you write to me, I will send you a free three-page illustrated want list of the types I am looking for. As an example of the prices I pay, I will offer the following amounts for these unboxed toys in excellent condition.

Larry Bruch
P.O. Box 121
Mountaintop, PA 18707
(717) 678-7395 (after 5 pm EST)

We Pay

Hubley 'Say It w/Flowers,' cast iron, 3-wheel motorcycle, 10¾"	3,000.00
German Tin Litho Clockwork Battleships, 24" or longer	2,000.00 +
Buddy L Tugboat	3,000.00
Toonerville Aunt Eppie Hogg Truck	2,500.00
Ives Walking Santa Claus	1,500.00
Battery-Operated Robby Space Patrol	2,000.00
Tommy Toy Jack & Jill, lead figure	350.00

Old toys are our specialty. We're buying **battery robots from the 1950's and 1960's**, Japanese tin toy cars, Matchbox, Corgi, Dinky, Tootsie Toy, Solido Military, Buddy L, Marx, and Fisher-Price toys as well as plastic model kits by Revell, Monogram, AMT, MPC, Johan, and Aurora. Plastic, promotional toy automobiles by Chevrolet, Ford, Plymouth, Studebaker, and others are also wanted. We buy **toys produced from 1900 to 1970**. Exceptionally high prices are paid for toys in like-new condition, but toys in any condition are desired! No item is too small or too large. We're buying single items or entire collections. Contact us if you have quality toys, boats, trains, cars, trucks, etc. for sale.

Ronald Moss
The Attic Fanatic
9017 Reseda Blvd.
Northridge, CA 91324
(818) 886-3959

We Pay

Batmobile by Corgi	50.00
Robby the Robot	300.00
Buddy L Steel Trucks	200.00-1,000.00
Marx Charlie McCarthy Car	300.00
Buck Rogers Space Ship	300.00
Lincoln Futura Car, tin	400.00
Atom Racing Car	400.00
Lil Abner Dogpatch Band	300.00
Howdy Doody Band	350.00
Marx Merrymakers Band	400.00
Amos & Andy Fresh Air Taxi	400.00
Metal Battleships, 2″	500.00

Wanted: **toy automobiles from 1900 to 1950**. Of particular interest are the larger, pressed-steel types: Buddy L, Keystone, American National, Turner, Son-ny, Structo, Kingsbury, Sturditoy, Steelcraft, and Kelmet. I am also interested in **pedal cars and live steam toys** of all types.

Dickie McCoy
The Toy Boy
1119 Michigan Ave.
St. Joseph, MI 49085

We are looking for **sand toys**, though they are really not very old or collectible. A sand toy is a small box-like toy containing a clown or trapeze artist. The clown dances or spins on the trapeze when the box is inverted. We are looking for any sand-operated toy that is self-contained. Also sought are **toy scales**. These may be any small tin scales and are similar old penny toys. I am not looking for the pencil sharpener-type scale replica.

Donald Gorlick
P.O. Box 24541
Seattle, WA 98124

We will pay high, wholesale prices for older **tin, wood, cast iron, and composition toys**, especially those related to Easter, Halloween, and Christmas. Please let us hear from you.

Childhood Memories
P.O. Box 96
Ashford, CT 06278
(203) 429-8876

Toys and pedal cars are wanted by collector. Highest prices are paid. Send photos with first letter. Remember: any price, any condition, anywhere!

Jack L. Callaway
P.O. Box 6906
Lincoln, NE 68506

As a long-time collector of old **tin toys**, I will purchase single items or collections at extravagant prices––providing they are complete, original, and manufactured by F. Martin, G. Bing, E. Lehman, Guntherman, Ives, F. Strauss, or other particularly well-respected toy makers. A picture and description will help. All inquires will be answered. I also want dolls, Rolly toys, musical instruments (other than pianos), uniforms, circus animals, tents, and many more items made by **A.O. Schoenhut** of Philadelphia from 1876 to 1939. The following prices will be paid for original items in good or better condition. All inquires will be answered. Write or call.

Harry McKeon
18 Rose Lane
Flourtown, PA 19031
(215) 233-4904

Toys

Tin Toys	We Pay	Schoenhut Toys	We Pay
F. Martin	100.00 +	Dolls	175.00-950.00
G. Bing	100.00 +	Rollys	50.00-250.00
E. Lehman	100.00 +	Circus Animals	50.00-350.00
Guntherman	100.00 +	Bond & Circus Wagons	100.00 +
Ives	100.00 +	Tents	250.00-900.00
F. Strauss	100.00 +	Teddy Roosevelt African Trip	Let's Talk

I'm looking for **any type of antique toys**--comic character, windup, friction, pedal cars, advertising clocks that light up, slot machines, Tootsie toy cars with white rubber tires, old neon signs, GI Joe stuff, and Courtenay model soldiers (as well as lead toy soldiers). Cash is always waiting for all of the above. Call or write!

Gary Darrow
309 E. 61 St.
New York City, NY 10021
(212) 838-0730

Wanted: old toys by the following toy makers and in the following categories --Soljertoys, Unknown, Molded Products Inc., Beton, Plastic, Ausley, Miller, Lincoln Log, Tootsie Toy, Arcade, American Soldier Co., Ideal, McLoughlin Bros., Marx, Warren, Comet, Britains, Playwood Plastics, premiums, comics, character, movies, radio, TV characters, Disney, guns, aircraft, ships, Fisher-Price, miscellaneous, and bibliography. Please price and give complete description in first letter.

William Lester
P.O. Box 303
Rosedale, VA 24280
(703) 889-0542

Character toys have been around as long as the characters that inspired them have existed. The list of characters whose likenesses were reproduced in toys over the years could fill volumes. It is because of past creative and successful merchandising that character collectors of today are offered a wide array of colorful, highly unique, and inventive toys based on the best of all comic characters.

I will buy all toys in excellent condition with no missing parts. If windup or battery-operated, the toys should be in working condition. Those listed below are not the only toys of interest to me; I will also buy others.

Richard T. Rautwein
437 Dawson St.
Sault Ste. Marie, MI 49783

We Pay

Barney Google Windup	400.00
Powerful Katrinka Windup	225.00
Andy Gump Arcade Car	350.00
Charlie Chaplin Windup, tin & cast iron	300.00
Felix the Cat on Scooter Windup	160.00
Mickey Mouse Emerson Radio	350.00
Mickey Mouse Steiff, pull toy	325.00
Popeye the Champ Windup	310.00
Katzenjammer Kids, pull toy, cast iron	390.00
Andy Gump Arcade Car	290.00
Maggie & Jiggs Windup	320.00
Uncle Wiggly Car, tin	530.00
Buttercup & Spare Ribs Windup, tin	425.00
Blondie's Jalopy	350.00
Santa Claus Hand Car	325.00
Popeye Dippy Dumper	200.00
Bluto Dippy Dumper	115.00
Superman Tank Windup	125.00

We are collecting the **tin robots** made by Japan in the 50's and early 60's. We only buy robots in excellent condition with no dents, cracks, or rust. We are also buying tin **character toys** made by Marx and Linemar and wood character toys made by Ideal or Schoenhut (such as Mickey Mouse, Pluto, Donald Duck, Felix, Flintstones, Jetsons, Popeye, etc.).

John & Jenny Tarrant
67 May Valley
Fenton, MO 63026

We Pay

Robots, tin	45.00 +
Character Figures, wood	25.00-75.00
Character Toys, tin, w/scratches	25.00-85.00
Character Toys, tin, missing ears or tail	25.00-60.00

Toys

Character Toys, tin, near-mint condition...................25.00-200.00
Character Toys, tin, mint in box.........................75.00-300.00

We are buying **Fisher-Price pull toys**. Herman Fisher and Irving Price organized their company on October 1, 1930, in East Aurora, New York. Margaret Evans Price, wife of the founder, was the company's first artist and designer. As Fisher-Price began operations, numbers as well as a name were assigned to each toy. When a toy has been out of production for awhile, its number is re-assigned to a new toy. The majority of toys were made of colorful, paper lithographs applied over wood. During the 1950's, plastic came into use; by the 1960's, it was the main material.

The logo can be used as a guide in dating the toys. A black and white rectangular logo appears on all toys made prior to 1962. After that, toys were marked with a red F and a blue P on a yellow background.

I am interested in pull toys only. They should be in good shape with none of the lithograph missing. I will also buy others not listed.

Frank Fazzini
227 Castner Ave.
Donora, PA 15033

We Pay

11 Ducky Cart	15.00
132 Dr. Doodle	15.00
151 Happy Hippo	10.00
156 Circus Wagon	20.00
166 Bucky Burro	15.00
175 Gold Star Stagecoach	20.00
312 Running Bunny Cart	6.00
333 Butch the Pup	6.00
462 Barky	6.00
480 Leo the Drummer	15.00
540 Granny Duck	20.00
634 Tiny Teddy	10.00
678 Kriss Kricket	10.00
703 Bunny Engine	10.00
712 Teddy Tooter	10.00
735 Juggling Jumbo	15.00
745 Eldie's Dairy Truck	20.00
755 Jumbo Rollo	10.00
777 Squeaky the Clown	15.00

Incomplete or damaged toys can be restored, or parts can be used to restore other toys. We will buy the following toys, parts, or original toy boxes. Write, describe finish, size, and parts missing. Price or ask for a quote. I buy one item or a box full.

Robert J. Cufr
3319 County Road L
Swanton, OH 43558

Tin Windup   We Pay

Broken Springs	5.00-100.00
Parts Missing	5.00-75.00
Figures for Jigger & Band Toys	5.00-50.00
Bases for Jigger Toys	10.00-50.00

Cast Iron Toys   We Pay

Wheels & Figures	1.00-25.00
Hitches (horses) or Rear	10.00-50.00
Complete, Broken, or Missing Parts	10.00-250.00

Battery-Operated Toys   We Pay
Complete, Excellent Condition; Not Working, No Rust

Robots, tin	20.00-250.00
Robots, part tin	5.00-50.00
Character (Popeye, etc.)	25.00-150.00
Monsters or Gorillas	15.00-150.00
Animals, People, or Autos	5.00-50.00
Any Above, w/rust in battery box or parts missing	2.00-35.00
Original Boxes	5.00-75.00
Farm Tractors, wheels missing or broken	3.00-100.00

I need **parts and wheels for toy electric trains made before 1945** by Lionel, American Flyer, Marx, etc. I also will buy damaged cars and engines. Write, describing what you have and the price wanted.

Don Luke
1310 Bryson
Independence, MO 64052

Toy soldiers of the type generally known as dime-store soldiers were made by American manufacturers from the 1920's through the 1950's. Most soldiers are three inches high and are made of hollow-cast lead; however, they were also made of iron, natural rubber, and––during the war––wood, flour, or other composition materials. In addition, there were a large number of paper soldiers and related items (planes, tanks, etc.) made during the war when metal was unavailable. Prices of soldiers vary widely by type, design, and condition.

Allen W. Smith
102 N. Cherry St.
Falls Church, VA 22046

	We Pay		We Pay
Barclay	2.00-20.00	Playwood	1.00-10.00
Monoil	2.00-20.00	Molded Products	1.00-10.00
Grey Iron	2.00-15.00	Jones	5.00-25.00
Auburn	2.00-15.00	Built-Rite Fort	25.00-50.00
Alnu	2.00-20.00	Various Paper	1.00-25.00
Tommy Toy	2.00-20.00		

I want to buy **toy tractors and other farm-related toys** in any condition. Please ship; after I inspect them, I will quote you a price. If you're not satisfied with the price I quote, I will return them immediately. Listed below are approximate prices that I am paying for these toys. I pay substantially more if the toys are in original boxes and in mint condition. These are just a few of the many toys I want.

Paul Ashby
602 Circle Dr.
Enid, OK 73703
(405) 237-8442

We Pay

Case 930 Tractor, by Ertl, 1960	75.00
Case 1030 Tractor, by Ertl, 1960	55.00
Case 1070 Tractor, by Ertl, 1960	65.00
Case International 1256 Tractor, by Ertl, 1968	50.00
Allis Chalmers 190 Tractor, by Ertl, 1960	40.00

I want to buy iron or die-cast aluminum **toy tractors and farm machinery** in sizes ⅟₁₆, ⅟₆₄, and ⅟₄₃.

Chester Ashby
2232 E. Maple
Enid, OK 73701-4613

I am interested in direct purchase or consignment for my auctions of S, O, 1, 2, and Standard gauge toy **trains** by such manufacturers as Ives, Lionel, American Flyer, Fundamentions, Dorfan, Marx, and others, as well as clockwork toys, character toys, trucks, boats, and airplanes circa 1900 through 1965.

Prices listed are examples of what would be offered for top-quality, original-boxed specimens. Prices vary due to condition, manufacturer, and individual model number. I am interested in one piece or complete sets.

Richard Giedroyc
P.O. Box 4145
2103 N. Broadway
Sidney, OH 45365
(513) 498-1872 (after 6 pm)

We Pay

Ives 3250 Series Engine	up to 150.00
Ives Clockwork Engine	up to 75.00
Ives Rolling Stock, O Gauge	up to 25.00
Ives Accessories	up to 100.00
Ives Standard Gauge Engines	up to 400.00
Lionel GG1 Series	up to 400.00
Lionel Diesels, post-war	up to 400.00
Lionel 238-265 Series Locomotives	up to 400.00
Lionel Pink Train Set	up to 2,000.00
Lionel 60 Trolley	up to 110.00
Lionel Rolling Stock, plastic	up to 60.00
Lionel Rolling Stock, 2800 Series	up to 100.00
Joy Line Train Set	up to 120.00
Dorfan Train Set	up to 160.00
Ives Rolling Stock, Standard Gauge	up to 140.00
American Flyer 300 Series Engine	up to 60.00
American Flyer Pacific Engine	up to 300.00
American Flyer S Gauge Diesel	up to 1,000.00
American Flyer O Gauge Engine	up to 300.00
American Flyer Standard Gauge Engine	up to 800.00
Fundamentions Trains	Call

We Pay

Marx Train Sets	**up to 100.00**
Clockwork Toys, tin	**Call**
Clockwork Toys, other	**up to 80.00**
Battery-Operated Robots	**up to 200.00**
Erector Sets	**up to 200.00**
Arcade Automobiles	**up to 400.00**
Lionel Boats	**up to 600.00**
All Early American Manufactured Toys	**Call**

Joshua Lionel Cowen was a pioneer in the electric train industry. He made a high-quality product and was an innovative marketer. Collectible Lionel trains are broken down into several categories: early standard gauge, classic standard gauge, pre-war O gauge, and post-war O gauge. These categories span the period from 1900 to 1969.

Listed below are **Lionel trains** I buy with prices reflecting what I will pay for items in excellent condition. To facilitate selling trains, the following grading system should be used:

Excellent: minute scratches or nicks, no dents, and no rust. The train has been carefully used and protected when stored.

Very good: few scratches, no dents or rust—exceptionally clean.

Good: scratches, dirty, small dents, and no rust.

Fair: scratches, chipped, dented, rusted, or warped.

Warren Burdine
830 Geneva Dr.
Prescott, AZ 86301

We Pay		**We Pay**	
#8 Electric 0-4-0	**90.00**	#1835, w/tender	**400.00-500.00**
#10 Electric 0-4-0	**120.00**	#2035, w/tender	**30.00**
#248 Electric 0-4-0	**75.00**	#2020, w/tender	**70.00**
#249 w/tender	**100.00**	#2065, w/tender	**100.00**
#252 Electric 0-4-0	**90.00**	#2343 A.A.	**130.00**
#332, #337, or #338	**50.00**	Cars, post-war	**3.00-50.00**
#629 or #630	**10.00-15.00**	Engines, post-war	**5.00-500.00**
#800, Freight Series	**10.00-15.00**	Accessories, post-war	**5.00-200.00**
#1666, w/tender	**40.00**		

Trains and train parts wanted: all types of Lionel, American Flyer, Ives, and foreign trains. We buy those in any condition if honestly and accurately described for rust, dents, missing parts, etc., as I need parts for repairs. Collector grade is also desired, and we pay good prices for premium grades. No HO or N gauges are wanted. I do not want track or small transformers unless they come with a train set. **Train accessories** of any kind are wanted in any condition. Foreign trains such as Bing, Bassett Lowke, Marklin, Karl Bub, etc. are also wanted.

We need locomotives, freight cars, and passenger cars of all makes, except HO and N gauge. Please describe and price in first letter. I pay before you ship, and I pay UPS fees, also.

Allison M. Cox
18025 8th Ave. NW
Seattle, WA 98177

I am looking to buy **Lionel, Marx, and American Flyer trains**, especially American Flyer 0 gauge, 027 gauge, and standard gauge. I am willing to pay $20.00 to $350.00 for engines in any condition from the pre-war era. All tenders from the pre-war era are purchased for $5.00 to 100.00. I am also willing to pay $5.00 to $110.00 for train cars of that time. Any **pre-war train items** such as transformers, street lamps, tunnels, track, switches, and cranes––in any condition––will bring $1.00 to $100.00.

Randy Deerdoff
10222 Lafferty Oaks
Houston, TX 77013

Lionel (pre- or post-war)   We Pay

Cars, any condition...5.00-70.00
Engines or Tenders, any condition...........................7.00-500.00
Transformers, any condition...................................5.00-50.00
Track, O Gauge or 027 Gauge, any condition...................10¢-1.10
Lamppost, Tunnels, Houses, Etc.; any condition...............1.00-100.00

American Flyer (pre- or post-war)   We Pay

Cars, any condition..15.00-110.00
Engines or Tenders, any condition.........................20.00-350.00
Transformers, any condition...................................2.00-35.00
Track, all sizes, any condition...............................1.00-1.10
Lamppost, Tunnels, Houses, any condition....................1.00-100.00

Marx (pre- or post-war)   **We Pay**

Cars, any condition...50¢-25.00
Engines & Tenders, any condition...........................7.00-100.00
Transformers, any condition................................2.00-50.00
Track, all sizes, any condition................................50¢-75¢
Lamppost, Tunnels, Houses, any condition.....................1.00-30.00

Electric toy trains of any size, any year . . . we buy **toy trains produced from 1900 through 1980**—Lionel, American Flyer, Marx, LGB Trains, Buddy L, and Tootsie Toy. We are paying up to $5,000.00 for clean, original Lionel trains in original boxes. Wanted are passenger cars, freight cars, bridges, stations, track, and switches. No collection too large or too small; we need them all. So either call, write, or snap a picture of it, and send it along. Also wanted are toy train catalogs of any brand. If you have a toy train needing a new engineer—contact us at once.

Ronald Moss
The Attic Fanatic
9017 Reseda Blvd.
Northridge, CA 91324
(818) 886-3959

I want to by older **toy trains and toys**. I am looking for Lionel, American Flyer, and other brands—any condition or amount. Cash paid. I also want to buy older toys—cars, trucks, etc. Please write or call.

Private Collector
P.O. Box 1533
Northbrook, IL 60065-1533
(312) 299-0268

TRADE CATALOGS

As America's industrial revolution took hold and as new crafts, skills, industries, and businesses expanded, the trade catalog was born. These catalogs describe a wide variety of products and their uses. They were used by the growing army of engineers, businesses, and merchants in their work, showing them what to look for, why they needed this or that product or machine, and why the item in the catalog was better than the one made by the competition.

We are primarily interested in trade catalogs printed before 1900. In select areas such as saloon equipment, slot machines, coin-operated arcade machines and ceiling fans, we are interested in those produced up to the 1950's. We also buy wholesale and mail-order catalogs for a number of select consumer products such as toy banks, games, and gambling equipment. You may also have other trade catalogs not listed here in which we might be interested. If you think you do, please contact us, and we will let you know if we decide to purchase them. We have written a book that is a primer for trade catalogs and other paper items; it is called *A Guide to the Collecting of Slot Machines, Paper, Catalogues, and Advertising*. It can be purchased for $17.65 postpaid.

Richard M. Bueschel
215 Revere Dr.
North Brook, IL 60062

	We Pay
Electrical Equipment, pre-1900	10.00
Electrical Equipment, 1900-1920	7.50
Ceiling Fans, pre-1900	15.00
Ceiling Fans, 1900-1950	10.00
Saloon Equipment, pre-1900, per pg	1.50
Saloon Equipment, 1900-1919, per pg	1.00
Slot Machines, pre-1900, per pg	1.00

We Pay

Slot Machines, 1900 & later, per pg	1.00
Penny Arcade Machines, per pg	1.00
Amusement Park Rides, per pg	75¢
Mills Novelty Co., pre-1905	100.00
Mills Novelty Co., 1906-1951	25.00
Industry Novelty Co.	35.00
B.A. Stevens-Toledo	25.00
R. Rothschilds Sons, pre-1905	75.00
Peck & Snyder Sporting Goods	35.00
D.N. Schall & Co.	75.00
Watling Mfg. Co., pre-1905	75.00
Watling Mfg. Co., 1906-1951	25.00
Kernan Mfg. Co.	35.00
Gambling Equipment, pre-1900, per pg	1.50
Gambling Equipment, 1900-1917, per pg	1.00
N. Shure & Co.	15.00
Richard K. Fox, pre-1910	25.00
Bott Bros. Co., Columbus, Ohio	75.00
Albert Pick & Co., pre-1912	100.00
Soda Fountain, per pg	1.00
Tin Ceilings	10.00
Store Counters & Fixtures, pre-1917	10.00
Ogden & Co., pre-1905	50.00
H.C. Evans & Co.	10.00
Exhibit Supply Co.	10.00
Samuel Nafew & Co.	25.00
Albert Pick & Co., 1912-1935	10.00

For over five years I have been researching the glass companies of the Western Pennsylvania area—in particular, those of Beaver Valley. Currently, I am trying to compile a complete and accurate history of the Phoenix Glass Company of Monaca, Pennsylvania, where my grandfather was employed as a glassblower for many years. My book on this subject will cover the period from 1880 to 1980.

I'm interested in buying original glass company catalogues and advertising brochures, especially those of the Phoenix Glass Company at Monaca, the Consolidated Lamp & Glass Company at Coraopolis, the CoOperative Flint Glass Company at Beaver Falls, the Fry Glass Company at Rochester, the Dithridge Glass Company at New Brighton, the Whitla Glass Company at Beaver Falls, the Beaver Falls Glass Company at Beaver Falls, the American Glass Specialty Company at Monaca, and the Rochester Tumbler Company at Rochester. I also buy related items such as magazine ads showing glassware, company letterheads, workers' badges, and post cards of glass companies and of Monaca, Pennsylvania. Please price and describe each item fully. I answer all letters.

Kathy Kelly
1621 Princess Ave.
Pittsburgh, PA 15216
(412) 561-3379

TRAPS

Collector is buying old, unusual traps from mouse to bear sizes. These include all types of traps--mouse, mole, gopher, rat, fly, minnow, roach, bird, handmade, or inventor's models. These can be made of tin, glass, wire, plastic, steel, or cardboard. Old or new steel traps with teeth are of particular interest. Call or write describing what you have. I will answer all letters. Thank you.

Boyd Nedry
728 Buth Dr.
Comstock Park, MI 49321
(616) 784-1513

	We Pay		We Pay
Mouse	50¢-75.00	Mole	1.00-50.00
Rat	50¢-65.00	Fly	4.00-65.00

	We Pay		We Pay
Gopher	**50¢-20.00**	Steel Traps,	
Roach	**2.00-40.00**	hand-forged	**10.00-200.00**
Minnow	**2.00-75.00**	Bear	**50.00-600.00**
Bird	**4.00-40.00**		

Traps have recently become more popular as shown by a greatly increased number of collectors and new publications on the subject of trap collecting. There are literally thousands of traps of many types (rat, gopher, mole, animal, fly, fish, minnow, etc.) around today, many of which are still in use. Several have no names, numbers, or identification on them; but a collector usually knows what they are and when and who made them. However, this may not be said of very primitive homemade versions.

To determine the value of a trap, there are two main factors to consider: whether or not the trap is complete (this consideration has top priority) and how hard it is to find (rarity comes in a close second). Because there are so many traps made by many different manufacturers with hundreds of models and variations, pricing for the novice dealer is difficult at best.

The current trap pricing trend is from $1.00 up to $3,000.00 with many plateaus in between. Traps with factory-made, cast iron teeth start at $20.00. Cast iron traps of any kind start around $30.00 to $90.00 and go up rapidly.

Terry Burger
2323 Lincoln
Beatrice, NE 68310
(402) 228-2797

TROLLS

They're fat-bellied and fuzzy-haired. They're companions and good luck charms. They are troll dolls, and they are collectible. The most notable are the ones that were designed by Thomas Dam in Denmark around 1964. The troll dolls were as much in demand in the 60's as the Cabbage Patch dolls are in the 80's.

They come in all sizes—from from less than an inch to more than eighteen inches. There are animal trolls, celebrity trolls, astronaut trolls, monster trolls, and a whole assemblage of troll accessories.

I am looking for any trolls and troll items in any condition. I also buy items that are not listed, as there are so many different things in circulation. Contact me first for my offer. Remember, that one poor-condition troll you have could be the one I want.

Debbie Brown
541 South St. Clair St.
Painesville, OH 44077

We Pay		We Pay	
Trolls	1.00-50.00	Outfits	to 5.00
Troll Houses	3.00-15.00	Animals	1.00-40.00
Handlebar Covers	2.00-10.00	Halloween Outfits	3.00+
Charms	to 3.00	Coloring Books	1.00-5.00

TURTLES

Turtles are becoming very collectible, especially those with advertising on their backs or bellies. In the 1800's and early 1900's, turtles were made as spittoons, tape measures, ash trays, pin holders, jewelry of various designs, and for use as paperweights.

I buy all small to medium size old turtles in good condition and turtle spittoons complete with containers. The following list indicates the average prices I will pay.

Prices will vary according to condition. I will also buy other turtles not listed here. When contacting me, a photo would be very helpful in determining value.

Lloyd Hedman
5033 Spencer
Omaha, NE 68104

We Pay

Spittoon, tin & cast iron	**60.00-90.00**
Tape Measure, metal	**5.00**
Tape Measure, sterling	**15.00**
Ash Tray, cast iron	**5.00**
Ash Tray, brass or china	**7.00**
Pin Tray, metal	**3.00**
Paperweight, cast iron	**4.00**
Paperweight, brass or china	**7.00**
Paperweight, solid w/advertising, cast iron	**6.00**
Jewelry	**2.00-8.00**

TYPEWRITERS

The first production-line typewriters were manufactured by Remington in 1874. These clumsy behemoths had many features adapted from the company's sewing machines, including foot-treadle carriage returns. Sales were very slow since these machines worked poorly, printed only capitals which struck underneath the platen (out of sight), and––worse yet––the contraptions sold for $125.00. Beginning in the early 1880's, scores of machines weighing five pounds or less that typed just as well began to compete at prices ranging from $10.00 to $20.00. Most of the little machines used pointers or indicators to select letters that were printed on a paper index and typed from molded, rubber strips rather than by using typebars. These small typewriters are today referred to as indicators or index machines, while the big machines patterned after the Remington are called blind writers. I buy unusual early machines which appear to be in good condition with little rust at the prices listed below. I will also negotiate to purchase broken specimens of rarer typewriters and machines not listed.

Mike Brooks
7335 Skyline
Oakland, CA 94611

We Pay		**We Pay**	
American, square index	100.00	Dollar	100.00
American Visible	200.00	Eagle	100.00
Automatic	500.00	Edison	1000.00
Baltimore	100.00	Edland	500.00
Bennington	500.00	English	100.00
Blickensderfer Electric	1000.00	Eureka	150.00
Boston, index	500.00	Farmer	500.00
Brooks	600.00	Fitch	1000.00
Burns	700.00	Ford	500.00
Cahill	1200.00	Gardner	500.00
Carpenter	500.00	Hall, index	200.00
Cash	500.00	Hamilton	200.00
Century, index	300.00	Hartford	100.00
Champion, index	300.00	Horton	1,500.00
Cleveland	100.00	Index Visible	300.00
Coffman, index	500.00	International	300.00
Conde	100.00	Jackson	500.00
Conover	125.00	Jewett	100.00
Crandall New Model	700.00	Keystone	125.00
Crary	600.00	Lambert	200.00
Crown, index	500.00	Lasar	500.00
Darling	100.00	Liliput, index	100.00
Daugherty	100.00	Martin	150.00
Daw & Tait	500.00	Maskelyne	500.00
Dennis Duplex	200.00	McCool	300.00
		McLoughlin	300.00
		Mercury	200.00

Typewriters

We Pay		We Pay	
Merritt	150.00	Pocket	200.00
National, curved front	150.00	Rem-Sho	125.00
Niagra	500.00	Sholes & Glidden	500.00
Norths	400.00	Sun, index	300.00
Odell	100.00	Travis	300.00
Pearl or Peoples	150.00	Victor, index	200.00

Collectible typewriters are generally those which pre-date 1920 and have mechanisms which differ from the conventional format. Look for machines which do not have four rows of keys, front-striking type bars, and a ribbon for inking. This would include machines with odd shapes, single-element printing mechanisms, odd keyboards—and even those with no keyboards.

Condition is very important to typewriter collectors, and the prices shown are for machines in truly excellent, fully-functional condition. The list which follows is incomplete, as hundreds of different typewriters were made before 1920. If you have a question, don't hesitate to contact me.

Darryl Rehr
3615 Watseka Ave. #101
Los Angeles, CA 90034
(213) 559-2368

We Pay		We Pay	
American	100.00	Franklin	75.00
Automatic	500.00	Garbell	75.00
Blickensderfer Electric	1,500.00	Hammond #1	150.00
Brooks	500.00	Jackson	500.00
Chicago	100.00	Index Visible	500.00
Coffman	500.00	International	500.00
Columbia	300.00	Keystone	200.00
Crandall	300.00	Lambert	200.00
Commercial Visible	300.00	Merritt	100.00
Crown	300.00	Morris	300.00
Daugherty	150.00	McCool	500.00
Duplex	150.00	National, curved	350.00
Edison Mimeograph	1,000.00	Niagra	1,200.00
Emerson	100.00	Pittsburgh, #1-11	100.00
Fay-Sho, bronze	200.00	Postal	125.00
Ford	500.00	Pullman	125.00
Fitch	1,500.00	Rapid	500.00
		Rem-Sho, bronze	200.00

	We Pay		We Pay
Sholes Visible	500.00	Victor	300.00
Sholes & Glidden	5,000.00	Williams	200.00
Sterling	200.00	World	250.00

U.S. MARINE CORPS

U.S. Marine Corps memorabilia is wanted by collector. I want to buy items such as recruiting posters, books, photos, sheet music, belt buckles, cigarette lighters, steins and mugs, toy soldiers, trucks, planes, documents and autographs, artwork, post cards, trench art, bronzes, novelties, and John Phillip Sousa items.

Dick Weisler
53 07 213th St.
Bayside, NY 11364
(718) 428-9829 (home)
(718) 626-7110 (office)

U.S. MILITARY CAMPAIGN MEDALS

U.S. Military Campaign Medals

Campaign medals are given in recognition for service in a theatre or during a period of military action. U.S. military medals from the older campaigns prior to World War II are the ultimate collectibles. They range from the Civil War to service in China just before the outbreak of World War II. These medals began to be struck in 1905 and are still being minted periodically to this time. The dates on the medals refer to the time of the involvement and not to the time of mintage.

The earlier strikes had serial numbers on the lower edge of the medal. These numbered issues are the most collectible and are the ones I seek. Some medals (with Commodore Perry and Admiral Sampson) will not be numbered but may have the name of the recipient on the edge. Due to many variables, these medals would be best evaluated on an individual basis.

The campaigns and branches of service listed below are for numbered medals only. Prices are basic and other details could enhance the value of some. Other U.S. and unnumbered campaign medals will be considered. Please write first.

'Cap'n Nemo'
Cecil E. Lawhon
Rt. 1, Box 176F
Edwards, MO 65326

Campaign	We Pay
Civil War, Army	100.00
Civil War, USN	175.00
Civil War, USMC	300.00
Indian Wars	200.00
West Indies, USN	200.00
West Indies, USMC	250.00
Spanish Campaign, Army	40.00
Spanish Campaign, USN	75.00
Spanish Campaign, USMC	150.00
Spanish War Service	20.00
Philippine Campaign,	
Army	35.00
USN	75.00
USMC	150.00
Insurrection	40.00
Cuban Occupation,	
Army	45.00
Puerto Rico Occupation,	
Army	85.00

China Relief 1900-01

Army	175.00
USN	200.00
USMC	300.00

We Pay

Pershing Medal WWI,
    No Number..15.00
Cuban Pacification,
    Army...50.00
    USN...100.00
    USMC..150.00
Nicaraguan, 1912,
    USN...200.00
    USMC..350.00
Mexican Service,
    Army...50.00
    USN..70.00
    USMC..125.00
    Border Service.....................................20.00
Haitian Campaign,
    USN, 1915...100.00
    USN, 1919-20.......................................75.00
    USMC, 1919-20.....................................125.00
Dominican Campaign,
    USN...100.00
    USMC..150.00
2nd Nicaraguan,
    USN, 1926..70.00
    USMC, 1926...90.00
Yangtze Service,
    USN..70.00
    USMC..100.00
Expeditions, USMC.....................................50.00
China Service, USN....................................90.00
China Service, USMC..................................125.00

U.S. PRESIDENTIAL CAMPAIGN RIBBONS

From 1840 until the appearance of celluloid political buttons in 1896, the manufacture and distribution of silk campaign ribbons played a major role in publicizing the candidates and the issues of the day.

I am looking for nice-quality campaign (not memorial) ribbons that picture the presidential candidate alone or with his running mate (jugate). The buy prices listed below are for the more common varieties from each campaign. I will pay more for more scarce varieties. Ribbons should have no major stains, separations, or other damage.

Larry Leedom
7217 Via Rio Nido
Downey, CA 90241

Year	Presidential Candidate	Single Portrait	Jugate
1840	M. Van Buren	500.00	1,500.00
	W.H. Harrison	100.00	300.00
1844	J. Polk	300.00	600.00
	H. Clay	100.00	400.00
1848	Z. Taylor	500.00	1,500.00
	L. Cass	1,500.00	3,000.00
1852	F. Pierce	500.00	1,500.00
	W. Scott	800.00	2,000.00
1856	J. Buchanan	200.00	400.00
	J. Fremont	75.00	300.00
	M. Fillmore	100.00	300.00
1860	A. Lincoln	400.00	800.00
	S. Douglas	400.00	800.00
	J. Breckinridge	300.00	600.00
	J. Bell	300.00	600.00

Year	Presidential Candidate	Single Portrait	Jugate
1864	A. Lincoln	400.00	800.00
	G. McClellan	500.00	1,000.00
1868	U.S. Grant	100.00	300.00
	H. Seymour	200.00	300.00
1872	U.S. Grant	100.00	500.00
	H. Greeley	1,500.00	3,000.00
1876	R.B. Hayes	50.00	50.00
	S. Tilden	50.00	50.00
1880	J. Garfield	50.00	75.00
	W.S. Hancock	100.00	150.00

VIEW-MASTER REELS AND PACKETS

View-Master, the invention of William Gruber, was first introduced to the public at the 1939-40 New York World's Fair. To this day, thousands of reels and packets on subjects as diverse as life itself have been produced. The product has been owned by four different companies, the original Sawyer's View-Master and G.A.F. in the middle 60's, by View-Master International in 1981, and now by the Ideal Toy

Company. Unfortunately, Ideal has no intention of making View-Master anything more than a toy item used to view only cartoons. Therefore, the early non-cartoon single reels and three-packet sets are now desirable items. Sawyer's items are becoming especially collectible since they are of the best quality and are credited for making this hobby a fascinating 3-D experience.

The company produced two cameras for the general public which enabled them to take their own 'personal' reels in 3-D; then they designed a projector so that people could show their pictures in full-color 3-D on a silver screen.

I am a collector and dealer and can pay well for good items in nice condition. Condition is important, but please let me know what you have, regardless.

Walter Sigg
P.O. Box 208
Swartswood, NJ 07877

We Pay

Sawyer's Single Reels, early	25¢-5.00
Movie Preview Reels	25.00
TV & Movie Star Reels	2.50-7.50
TV & Movie Star Packets (Sawyer's & G.A.F.)	1.00-25.00
#401 Girl Scout Reel	20.00
Mushroom Set w/Book	100.00
Scenic Packets (Sawyer's & G.A.F.)	1.00-25.00
Commercial Reels	5.00-50.00
'DR' Reels, early	5.00-30.00

WATCHES

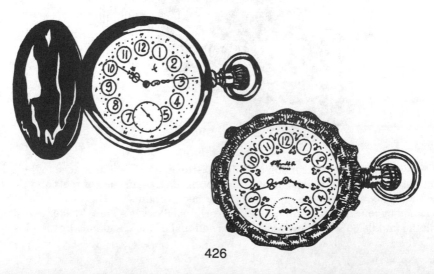

Pocket watches are unique collectibles. Since the beginning of civilization when man scooped up a handful of sand and created the hourglass, portable timepieces have held a fascination that demanded the attention of the wealthy and the poor alike. Man has constantly sought to improve his time-measuring instruments, sometimes even by making them of the finest metals and jewels. The pocket watch in particular became an item of ornamentation often highly valued among families for generation after generation.

There are many factors that make a pocket watch desirable and contribute its value, and there are no two pocket watches alike. This makes setting a price very difficult. Furthermore, values are constantly changing, due in part to the fluctuating silver market.

I buy only prime-condition watches. If you are interested in selling your watch, describe it, its condition, and the price you desire in your first letter. Listed are minimum prices I pay for watches of various manufacturers. I am also interested in many not listed, and some without manufacturers' names. Watches in fancy or solid gold cases will bring much more. Those that strike or have moving figures can bring in excess of $4,000.00. If you have any prime-condition watch, contact me.

Irving Lipsky
P.O. Box 2094
Vista, CA 92083

	We Pay		We Pay
Waltham	50.00	Fredonia	400.00
Columbia	50.00	Illinois	65.00
Elgin	50.00	Ball	75.00
Hampden	50.00	Rockford	70.00
Aurora	70.00	Hamilton	75.00
Howard	100.00	Southbend	70.00

Over seventy-five million wind-up wrist watches were made in the last one hundred years. Where are they? Most are in a drawer or a box. Because of the high cost of repair, most people turn to quartz-type watches.

We buy all wrist watches listed below. The face must be in good condition. We buy wrist watches that do not work and those with minor problems such as missing stems. We also buy all 24- and 25-jewel watches. If you're not sure, contact me for prices. Beware of reproductions. The days of the pyramids are over; you can't take them with you! If the watch has a working band, add $1.00.

James Lindon
11002 N. 64th Lane
Glendale, AZ 85304

	We Pay		We Pay
Audemars Piquet	20.00	Leroy	20.00
Auburndale		Lonville	30.00
porcelain dial	30.00	Lucerne	10.00
Broquet	20.00	Movado	10.00
Bulova	4.00	Marconi	20.00
Benrus	4.00	Mozart	80.00
Breitling, 18K	20.00	Nashua	100.00
Bowman, E.F.	50.00	Omega	20.00
Breguet	20.00	Ojay	40.00
Cressarow	10.00	Paillet	10.00
Cyma	5.00	Paul Ditisheim	30.00
Cartier	50.00	Piaget	50.00
Elgin	4.00	Reed, J.P.	30.00
Flint, E.H.	20.00	Rolex	50.00
Fasoldt, Charles; USA	100.00	Tavannes	20.00
Freeport	40.00	Tiffany Porcelain	40.00
Glycine	20.00	Touchon/Wolf	20.00
Gruen	4.00	Vacheron & Constantin	40.00
Hamilton	4.00	Waltham Chevalier	4.00
Henry, Capt.	50.00	West End, 18K	10.00
Lange & Sons	20.00	24-Jewel	1.00
Longines	4.00	25-Jewel	4.00
Lucien Picard	50.00		

Maundy International is one of America's leading mail-order dealers in fine, vintage wrist watches and rare pocket watches of all shapes and sizes. We have been buying and selling watches on a regular basis now for many years. Watches need not be running. We purchase the common railroad watch to the rare museum specimen, the better-name vintage wrist watches to those not so well known, repeaters, enamels, keywinds––all kinds of watches. If you have a watch for sale, give us a call toll free at 1-800-235-2866/(800) 23J BUNN or drop us a line telling us as much as possible about your watch. We also buy collections, estates, and accumulations. We offer prompt, confidential, and knowledgeable service to customers and collectors. If you have a watch for sale or if you know of a collection for sale (we pay handsome finder's fees!), write or call!

Maundy International Watches
Miles Sandler, Horologist
P.O. Box 128WB
Overland Park, KS 66212
(800) 235-2866

I am interested in buying any comic, character, promotional, or advertising watch from the 1930's through the 1980's, working or not working. However, it is important that the dial of the watch is bright and free of any imperfections. It is also important that both the original hands are still in place and that the watch case is in good condition. Should the watch be in its original box or have its original band, please indicate the condition of these. Some of the watches I am particularly interested in are those that carry names such as Ingersoll, Ingraham, New Haven, or U.S. Time, or promotional watches with Mr. Peanut, Ritz Crackers, Kool-Aid, etc. Please be sure to state how much you want for the watch or watches.

Maggie Kenyon
One Christopher St., Suite 14-G
New York, NY 10014

WATCH FOBS

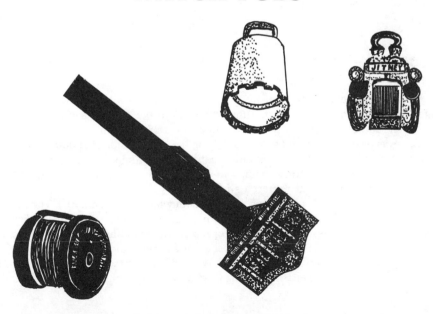

The advertising watch fob was designed with a bail to accommodate a strap which was then attached to the watch. The watch itself was kept in a special pocket, and men found it easier to remove with a gentle tug on the fob than by sticking grown-up fingers into such a small opening. Many reproductions have been made over the years; but the old, authentic fobs are very desirable collectibles. In general, the old farm-equipment fobs are the most valuable.

Many varieties were made of each brand, and some are rarer than others. Case fobs are worth from $5.00 to $200.00 depending on the variation. Send fobs on approval, if you'd like; or send Xerox copies for my offer. I'm interested in buying all fobs––not just those that are listed.

Dave Beck
P.O. Box 435
Mediapolis, IA 52637

We Pay

John Deere, black porcelain	**150.00**
John Deere, red, white, & blue porcelain	**100.00**
John Deere, mother-of-pearl	**60.00**
Dan Patch, porcelain	**100.00**
Automotive	**30.00-75.00**
Holt Tractor	**50.00-150.00**
Saddle	**45.00**
Dead Shot	**75.00**
DuPont	**75.00**
Hunter, Trader, or Trapper	**100.00**
Stationary Engine	**75.00**
Thresher	**75.00**

Watch fobs are collectibles usually associated with watches. They are appendages to the watch and are worn either attached to the watch itself or as a part of a watch chain. Fobs come in all shapes and materials; some have gemstones. Watch keys were used to wind watches before they were pendant wound and were sometimes also used as fobs. Another collectible associated with watch fobs is the watch chain, which hung from a man's vest, often with a fob attached to it. Ladies used fobs occasionally, but prefered slide chains.

I am interested in fobs, keys, and chains (mainly ladies' slide chains). The many forms, materials used, weight of pieces, and their individual uniqueness make pricing impossible without a description. Some representative minimums are listed below. These prices are bare minimums with most going for much more. Send full description or picture (if possible) with price desired. If you wish, you may send item––quote price. You'll either have the item returned or a check in the next mail.

Irving Lipsky
P.O. Box 2094
Vista, CA 92083

We Pay		**We Pay**	
Plain Fobs	**20.00**	Plain Watch Keys	**20.00**
Fancy Fobs	**50.00**	Fancy Watch Keys	**50.00**

	We Pay		We Pay
Short Slide Chain	**75.00**	Men's Watch Chains	**40.00**
Long Slide Chain	**100.00**		

Watch fobs are becoming popular collectibles. I collect watch fobs advertising old road or farm machinery or related items. I also collect fobs advertising fur, traps, powder, and gun companies. I'll pay $25.00 and up depending on age and condition.

John W. Cline
609 N. East St.
Carlisle, PA 17013

WATT
POTTERY

We have been collectors of Watt pottery for many years now. We have been unable to find information such as catalogs or listings in price guides, so we do not know the going prices. Perhaps someone out there is also interested in Watt; if so, we would like to hear from them. We are looking for plates, cups and saucers, canister sets, and glasses.

David R. Hagen
Star Rt., Box 116
Sarona, WI 54870
(715) 469-3306

WELLER POTTERY

I want to buy a pair of Weller Wild Rose candle holders. These are six inches tall. I will pay $60.00.

Mavis Braaten
P.O. Box 204
Trout Lake, WA 98650

WESSON OIL MAYONNAISE JARS

I want the Wesson oil jar with the metal plunger inside and the recipe written on the outside––perfect condition only, no cracks or chips. I will pay $10.00 each.

Margaret McDermott
153 Charles
Shreveport, LA 71105

WESTERN AMERICANA

Western relics from the frontier up to the time of the early rodeos hold a fascination for many. Collectors tend to focus on a period from about 1860 to the late 1890's. This was a time of rapid change in the west. The gold rush of 1848 brought in thousands of people from all over the world. This influx of people led to the Indians being placed on reservations and property being divided by barbed-wire fences, thus bringing the end of an era.

Craftsmen that came to the west developed styles in the manufacture of their goods that was unique in all the world. Below is a partial list of items I want to buy. I will pay the prices listed for relics in good condition. I will pay more for anything rare or unique.

Charlie Smith
1006 NE 4th Ave.
Milton-Freewater, OR 97862
(503) 938-6298

	We Pay
Silver Inlaid Spurs	200.00
Silver Inlaid Bits	100.00
Studded Batwing Chaps	125.00
Wooly Chaps	150.00
Shotgun Chaps	90.00
Holsters w/Money Belts	85.00
Studded Cuffs	45.00

We Pay

Braided Horsehair Bridles	250.00
Braided Horsehair	35.00-75.00
Large Brim Cowboy Hats	100.00
Early Western Law Badges	60.00
Saddle Watch Fobs	40.00
Sterling Belt Buckles	30.00
Roundup Silk Scarves	20.00
Western Photos	Varies
Rodeo Post Cards	2.00
Western History Books	Varies
Will James Books (Scribner editions)	10.00
Saddle Catalogs, pre-1938	25.00
Ivory Poker Chips	10.00
Pendleton & Oregon City Indian Blankets	60.00
Indian Artifacts	Varies
Back Bar Bottles	25.00
Bottles, label under glass, colored enamel	100.00
Counter Top Cigar Cutters & Lighters	85.00
Professional Gambling Equipment	Varies
Miniature Western Items	Varies
Express Signs	100.00
Express Seals	50.00
Other Express Items Needed	Call or Write

I want to buy Hutchinson sodas and whiskeys from western mining towns; mining antiques including carbide lanterns, sunshine lamps, candle holders, assay equipment; and photographs. Especially wanted are antiques from Black Hawk, Breckenridge, Buena Vista, Central City, Cripple Creek, Georgetown, Idaho Springs, Leadville, Ouray, Silverton, Telluride, and Victor, Colorado. Also wanted from all states are embossed round milk quarts, druggists, Hutchinson sodas, amber whiskeys, and bitters.

Ed Krol
Star Rt. 2, Box 15A
Derning, NM 88030
(505) 546-4368

Towns, cities, states, counties, and territories of 'West of the Mississippi' America began publishing brochures and booklets promoting their particular area, aimed to entice Easterners to 'Go West' (and bring your money). They expounded the marvels of their towns, the climate, the potential for growth, and gave other reasons why settlers should go there. They often gave descriptions of lands for sale, the marvelous developments of the past few years, railroads, agriculture, mining, etc. Most were published with paper covers. State the exact title and information on the title page, including date and location of publication. State condition carefully, noting any soiling or tearing. Check to see if pages are missing, as we do not buy defective copies.

View books were popular from the 1870's through 1900. Some were published as paper-covered booklets, others as hard-covered, 'accordion-type,' fold-out views. Very good condition would be clean, complete, and no torn pages. State the title, number of pages, date and place of publication along with the price wanted. Condition, age, location, and type of material are the important factors in determing prices paid. We buy single items or entire collections. We have been 'buyers of old Western promotionals and view books since 1965.' Prices below are for view books and booklets in very good condition.

Treasure Hunt
P.O. Box 3862-WB
New Haven, CT 06525

Promotional Booklets 1850-1910	We Pay	View Books Pre-1900	We Pay
California	5.00-15.00 +	California	5.00-15.00 +
Texas	10.00-25.00 +	Texas	8.00-18.00 +
New Mexico	8.00-25.00 +	New Mexico	6.00-15.00 +
Arizona	8.00-20.00 +	Arizona	5.00-12.00 +
Montana	12.00-30.00 +	Montana	10.00-22.00 +
Dakotas	15.00-40.00 +	Dakotas	10.00-25.00 +
Kansas	10.00-20.00 +	Kansas	6.00-15.00 +
Colorado	7.00-25.00 +	Colorado	7.00-15.00 +
Washington	7.00-15.00 +	Washington	5.00-12.00 +
Nevada	12.00-30.00 +	Nevada	6.00-10.00 +
Idaho	10.00-20.00 +	Idaho	8.00-20.00 +
Wyoming	12.00-20.00 +	Wyoming	8.00-20.00 +

Many types of Western Americana are collected; but for us nothing is more representative of the Old West than the whiskey bottles of the early mining, logging, and cattle towns. Western whiskey bottles have a wide price range. Three elements make a bottle more desirable and expensive: (1) crudeness, characterized by a drippy or glob applied top and a whittled or mottled appearance to the surface of the glass; (2) an image in the embossing (usually a bird or an animal but may also be things such as teacups, people, barrels, etc); and (3) as with everything, rarity.

Condition is of great importance. All bottles must be free of cracks and chips.

Bottles that have been dug up are often stained, and this greatly reduces value. The presence of original labels enhances value.

We buy embossed pumpkinseed, coffin, and regular whiskey bottles from all the western states. We pay $10.00 to $25.00 for most clear pumpkinseed and coffin flasks. Most crude amber flasks are purchased for $30.00 to $100.00 each. For quart-sized bottles, consult the following list. There are hundreds of different bottles, so please contact us concerning anything not listed.

Old Bottle Museum
P.O. Box 1570
Cedar Ridge, CA 95924

We Pay

N. Ahrens	200.00
Ahrens, Bullwinkle	75.00
Barry & Patten, 116 & 118	500.00
G.O. Blake, Pond, Reynolds	125.00
Buffalo Old Bourbon, amber	175.00
Buffalo Old Bourbon, clear	75.00
California Club	1,000.00
Clinch	15.00
Copper Distilled	75.00
Hotaling of P.S.	300.00
Milto J. Hardy	400.00
Denaveaux	150.00
Eagle Glen	35.00
The Elite	200.00
Golden Eagle	75.00
N. Grange	200.00
Kane, O'Leary	225.00
Durham	200.00
Phoenix	40.00
J.C. Nixon	300.00
Old Signet	1,000.00
Wm. Provis	75.00
Renz's Blackberry Brandy	200.00
Rothenberg (rooster)	200.00
C.W. Stuarts	100.00
John Wold	100.00

A great number of photographers began photographing the American West from the 1850's through the turn of the century in the form of mammoth photos (very large), CDV photos (approximately 2″ x 3″), cabinet cards (5″ x 8″), and stereoviews (twin photos mounted on a single card to be viewed in a stereoscope).

We have been active buyers of western photos taken prior to 1900 for over twenty years. We buy pre-1900 photos of Texas, Colorado, Utah, California, Nevada, Idaho, Montana, the Dakotas, and all states and territories west of the Mississippi.

Among the many categories of photos we need are those of towns, cities, frontier, settlers, mining, Indians, soldiers, street scenes, famous people, trains, stagecoaches, cowboys, buffalo hunting, emigrants, etc. by western photographers such as Watkins, Houseworth, Savage, Carter, Jackson, Muybridge, Tabor, and hundreds of others! We buy single photographs or entire collections. We also need letters and documents by these photographers or about them. Describe the photo, state the photographer, and give all information printed on the photo. Carefully state its condition and note any tears, soiling, or scars. A photocopy would be helpful. Please state your asking price. Curved stereoviews are generally later than 1900 and are not wanted. Condition is very important; for examples in very good condition, we pay as listed below.

We have other related areas of interests. We would like booklets and pamphlets published in 'West of the Mississippi' America prior to the 1880's—especially those printed in the territories; collections of letters and documents relating to Western American travel, mining, military, Indians, cowboys, buffalo hunting, or relating to the early settlement of many western towns, the gold rush, or the silver rush; pre-1900 Western American ephemera of any kind; pre-1900 letters and documents relating to Alaska or the Klondike; letters and documents relating to American exploring expeditions through 1900; early aviation photos, documents, ephemera, and letters; letters, photos, and documents relating to Adolph Sutro; and the letters, photos, ephemera, and pre-1920 documents relating to any Chinatown west of the Mississippi; and Hawaii or Sandwich Islands pre-1900 photographs, letters, documents, pamphlets, etc. 'Buyers of old Western photographs since 1965.'

Treasure Hunt
P.O. Box 3862-WB
New Haven, CT 06525

Subject	Mammoth	CDV	Cabinets	Stereos
Western towns/cities	150.00	10.00 +	10.00 +	8.00 +
Mining in the west	150.00	10.00 +	10.00 +	10.00 +
Indians	175.00	15.00 +	15.00 +	12.00 +
Military	125.00	15.00 +	15.00 +	12.00 +
Stagecoaches	165.00	18.00 +	15.00 +	13.00 +
Trains	125.00	14.00 +	16.00 +	10.00 +
Photos by Wm. Jackson	100.00 +	20.00 +	10.00 +	8.00 +
Photos by Houseworth	125.00 +	18.00 +	12.00 +	8.00 +
Photos by Watkins	135.00 +	16.00 +	12.00 +	8.00 +

Western stars originated over the radio, on television, and through comic books. Some of the more famous western stars are Tom Mix, the Lone Ranger, Gene Autry, Roy Rogers, and Hopalong Cassidy. They were enjoyed by the young, old, rich, and poor. Items were acquired either through the mail as premiums from advertising companies such as Ralston Cereal, Ovaltine, Wheaties, etc. or purchased at stores. Names of western stars associated with premiums are listed below.

I will always pay the prices listed for items in above-average condition. Any tears, ink stains, water damage, or excessive wear will reduce the price I will pay. I am especially looking for items in their original boxes, and I will pay large bonuses to acquire them.

Lone Ranger	Tom Mix	Annie Oakley
Cisco Kid	Buffalo Bill	Sky King
Gene Autry	Davy Crockett	'Wild' Bill Hickock
Roy Rogers	Dale Evans	John Wayne
Hopalong Cassidy	Daniel Boone	Gabby Hayes

Mark Dubiel
2336 Yemans
Hamtramck, MI 48212

We Pay

Rings & Whistles	3.00	Belt Buckles	6.00
Comic Books	3.00	Flashlights	10.00
Compasses	5.00	Coloring Books	5.00
Badges & Buttons	3.00	Wrist Watches	10.00
Manuals & Magazines	4.00	Drinking Mugs	5.00
Lunch Boxes	10.00	Drinking Glasses	5.00
Toy Guns & Games	10.00	Dolls	20.00+
Pocket Knives	6.00	Decoders	5.00

WHITE HOUSE MEMORABILIA

The hobby of collecting authentic White House memorabilia has been growing for the past several years. Items collected include dishes, plates, and dinnerware used in the White House; White House silverware; jewelry used or given by any President or First Lady; pieces of the building itself during a remodeling or renovation; or personal possessions of any President or First Lady. Prices for White House memorabilia vary greatly depending on scarcity and condition. I am always interested in buying White House artifacts. Let me hear what you have.!

Paul Hartunian
47 Portland Place
Montclair, NJ 07042

WIZARD OF OZ

In 1939 Metro-Goldwyn-Mayer Studios produced the now-classic motion picture *The Wizard of Oz*. Although the film was neither the critical nor commercial success its makers had hoped for during its initial release, *The Wizard of Oz* was one of the most highly-promoted and exploited movies of its time. This meant that the public was saturated with all kinds of related merchandise and ephemera which included dolls, toys, figurines, valentines, face masks, stationery, clothing, sheet music, coat hangers, and soap characters (just to name a few!). In addition, there was also an extremely elaborate publicity campaign for *The Wizard of Oz* that consisted of numerous movie posters and other theater material as well as massive magazine and newspaper coverage across the United States and abroad.

Although it's hard to say exactly how much of *The Wizard of Oz* memorabilia has appeared in the last five decades, my goal is to obtain as much of it as I can find. Please contact me if you have the following items or any other memorabilia relating to this wonderful movie.

1939 Judy Garland as Dorothy, Doll by Ideal
1939 Ray Bolger as the Scarecrow, Rag Doll by Ideal
1939 Leo Feist Souvenir Album Songbook
Minicam Magazine, Aug 1939, Ray Bolger, Scarecrow Cover
Movie Life Magazine, Aug 1939, Judy Garland, Dorothy Cover
Kerk Guild's Soapy Characters from the Land of Oz Figurines
1939 Wizard of Oz Rayon Hankerchief
Any of the Set of 5 Wizard of Oz Pin-Back Buttons from 1939
1939 Wizard of Oz Game by Whitman Publishing Company of Racine, WI
Original Souvenir Program from the Film Premiere Entitled 'The Wizard of Oz Comes to Life'
Any of the 1939 or 1949 Oz Valentines
Original 1939 Movie Posters and Lobby Cards
1949 Reissue Pressbook
1949 Reissue Window Card Poster
1955 Reissue Insert Poster (14x36")
1955 Reissue Window Card Poster
1955 Reissue Cardboard Standees of 4 Main Characters
1939 Loew's Wizard of Oz Drinking Glasses, especially Lion, Bad Witch, Wizard, & Scarecrow
1939 Wizard of Oz Children's Writing paper, 10 sheets/envelopes, Whitman Publishing Co.
1939 Oz children's Wooden Coat Hangers
1939 British Wizard of Oz Card Game
1939 British Sheet Music for Film's Song
1939 British Folio Booklet for Film
1939 British Movie Edition Hardcover Book of The Wizard of Oz
1975 4" Mego Munchkin Dolls in Original Boxes

Jay Scarfone
985 Parma Center Rd.
Hilton, NY 14468

WOODEN NICKELS

Since 1932 when first introduced at Tenio, Washington, wood has been used as money, souvenirs for various celebrations, and as advertising for many different businesses. My interest lies in wood actually used as money (depression script, generally flat pieces), all woods issued by governmental units to celebrate various anniversaries and local events, and in specific advertising done by restaurant chains. Please write describing the wooden money you have and the price you expect to receive for it.

Norman R. Boughton
1356 Buffalo Rd.
Rochester, NY 14624

Flats (Unbroken)	We Pay
Tenino, WA 25¢	25.00
Tenino, WA 50¢	35.00
Tenino, WA $1	50.00
Tax Tokens-Tenino, WA	1.00
Other Flats	50¢-10.00

Rounds	We Pay
Celebrations	25¢-10.00
McDonald's	25¢
Dairy Queen	50¢
Dunkin Donuts	25¢
Sambo's	35¢

WOODENWARE

Wanted: any small wooden item (pre-1930 only) with original blue paint or blue stain on the outside. I will consider boxes, bowls, firkins, chests, cupboards, stools––anything wooden with at least 50% of the original blue paint. Since there is such a wide variety of items, I can't quote prices. Also wanted are wooden checkerboards in orginal blue, red, mustard, or dark green paint, pre-1920's only. I am paying $75.00 and up for these. In every category, I need a full description and price. photo is most helpful.

I am also interested in buying twig art log cabins and buildings, barns, fen small pieces of furniture, etc. These are made of permanently nailed-together (not Lincoln Logs) and were popular up through the 1930's. Any of the above will be considered. The smallest log cabins were bird houses; the largest on made with glass windows and swinging doors. Prices paid depend upon s and condition but would start at $25.00. As to condition, the twigs or

be natural, darkened twigs with some bark. Here also please send a full description and price. A photo is appreciated.

Linda Grunewald
P.O. Box 311-X
Utica, MI 48087
(313) 739-4053

WORLD WAR II

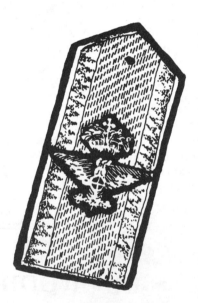

I am seeking collectibles and memorabilia of the WWII allied forces only. Commemoratives are wanted from mass-produced items to folk art relative to patriotic home front aid, the war effort toward victory, and anti-fascist propaganda. I am particularly interested in the unusual and scarce, but I accept descriptive price quotations on all items except weaponry and uniforms. Materials are wanted from the actual period of the war (1939-1945), the Jewish holocaust period of those same years, and the occupation of Germany and Japan through 1950. Items past 1950 are not wanted except specific WWII anniversary commemorations of the Axis Surrender liberation of occupied countries. I especially seek home front material of USA England; soldier benevolent aid; women and children during wartime living; y and political leaders of America, Britain, Russia; aid to occupied coun-rtoons or other art; and books on liberation, chaplaincy, or bullet art. These y be made from pottery, china, metal, glass, or wood, and range from Toby dolls to games and plaques. I will pay $2.00 to $200.00 and up, depending on interest in a piece––anything from a pin-back button to a post card or a painting. Price depends on scarcity and uniqueness.

Richard A. Harrow
85-23 210 St.
Hollis Hills, NY 11427-1311
(718) 740-1088

It has been almost fifty years since the beginning of World War II. Perhaps the most important operations and highest casualties were with the bombing crews and fighter pilots of the war. Casualties among these men were higher than those among front-line troops. Because of this, the element of luck and lucky mascots became a very popular and personalized part of the war. Every plane had a picture on it of a mascot such as a comic character or a pin-up style girl, and each plane seemed to carry a name such as Misseducer, Sterile Errol, Pistol Packin' Mamma, Old Scarface, etc. This was called nose art, as it often covered the nose section of the plane. Many men would have their favorite nose art painted onto round squadron patches which they would sew onto their leather flying jacket or heavy leather and sheepskin bomber coats. They would also paint large figures onto the backs of their coats. These are now becoming desirable and are wonderful pieces of Americana. These coats were either of simple leather with knit waistbands and cuffs or were of the heavier variety––dark brown outside and sheepskin inside. Every military coat can be identified as such because it will have a black cloth contract-maker's tag in it. An example might read: Model M-445a, Contract #236745, DWG ##%, Bu-Aero Leather Company, etc.

Other aviation collectibles from World War II are goggles, metal breast wings, squadron and unit books, all patches and pins, parachutes, oxygen masks, equipment, uniforms, photos, and medals. If you have any of these, contact me.

Timothy Gordon
2700 Eaton St.
Missoula, MT 59801
(406) 251-3617

We Pay

Painted Coat or Jacket, any	250.00 +
Coat w/Squadron Patch, any	175.00 +
Goggles, marked AN-6530	40.00
Loose Leather or Cloth Squadron Patches	20.00 +
Metal Fliers Wings	15.00
Squadron Wing Group Books	25.00 +
Silk Escape Maps	15.00
Leather or Silk Jacket Flags (Chinese or American flag)	35.00

WORLD'S FAIRS

World's Fairs and Expositions began in this country with the Crystal Palace Exposition in New York in 1853, and collectors have shown increased interest in souvenirs and memorabilia from these events in recent years. A few of the more notable expositions and world's fair held in this country are:

1876 Centennial Exposition (Philadelphia)
1893 Chicago World's Fair (Columbian Exposition)
1898 Trans-Mississippi Exposition (Omaha)
1901 Pan-American Exposition (Buffalo)
1904 St. Louis World's Fair (Louisiana Purchase Exposition)
1933/34 Chicago World's Fair (Century of Progress Exposition)
1939/40 New York World's Fair

I buy souvenirs and memorabilia from these and most other world's fairs and expositions. I prefer that the owner state prices for items they wish to sell but will make offers on desirable material if an adequate description is furnished. The desirability and value of these souvenir items vary greatly, but the following are representative prices that I will pay for items in fine, undamaged condition from the 1904 St. Louis World's Fair. Comparable items from other fairs might be worth more or less.

D.D. Woollard, Jr.
11614 Old St. Charles Rd.
Bridgeton, MO 63044
(314) 739-4662

We Pay

Pocket Watches	100.00 +
Clocks	50.00-150.00
Stock Certificates	50.00 +
Award Metals	20.00-50.00
Pin-Back Buttons	5.00-20.00
Hold-to-Light Post Cards	10.00 +
Pocket Knives	15.00-25.00
Straight Razors	20.00-35.00
Souvenir Spoons, sterling	
full size	15.00-25.00
demitasse	10.00-15.00
w/enameled bowls	35.00-75.00
Thimbles, sterling	25.00 +
Thimbles, gold	75.00 +
China Souvenirs, w/buildings or scenes of fair	
Plates	15.00 +
Bowls	15.00 +
Vases	15.00 +
Pitchers	15.00 +
Cups	10.00 +
Cups & Saucers	15.00 +
Banks	20.00 +
Employee Badges	15.00 +
Officials' Badges	25.00 +
Other Badges, Ribbons	10.00-35.00
Steins	25.00-100.00
Tickets, Passes, Etc.	2.00 +
Pocket Mirrors	15.00-35.00
Watch Fobs	10.00-25.00
Fans	15.00-35.00
Invitations	5.00-25.00
Books, large, hard-bound	15.00-50.00
Booklets, Pamphlets, Etc.	1.00-10.00

There has been huge amounts of material issued with various World's Fair logos or emblems. I am interested in pre-1935 material other than post cards and books. Top prices are paid for odd and unusual items--the larger, more ornate, and expensive, the better! Examples given below are for some of the more scarce items. We purchase everything!

Richard Hartzog
P.O. Box 4143XW
Rockford, IL 61110

We Pay

1893 Columbian Expo	**All Wanted**
1893 Columbian Expo Official Medal, in case	**55.00 +**
1893 Badge or Ribbon	**10.00-35.00 +**
1901 Pan-American Badge or Ribbon	**3.00-20.00 +**
1904 St. Louis Expo	**All Wanted**
1904 St. Louis Expo Unusual Token or Badge	**20.00-35.00 +**
1909 Alaska-Yukon Expo	**All Wanted**
1909 Alaska-Yukon Expo Unusual Token or Badge	**15.00-35.00 +**
Century of Progress	**All Wanted, Especially Unique Items**
Century of Progress Unusual Token or Medal	**8.00-15.00 +**
Century of Progress Unusual Badge or Ribbon	**10.00-25.00 +**

Souvenirs of all World's Fairs since 1851 are sought by collectors of World's Fairs memorabilia. Items from fairs of earlier days were often made of fancy types of china and glassware. Large medals, books, post cards, tapestries, demitasse spoons, silverware, etc. were sold, as well. In more recent years, many of the same items were sold but tended more often to be made of plastic, pewter, or paper.

The Society is always looking for items to add to its Official World's Fair Library and Museum Collection. We especially need books, reports, correspondence, posters, medals, tokens, stamps, post cards, and similar items. Some sample prices are listed below.

World's Fair Collectors Society, Inc.
P.O. Box 20806
Sarasota, FL 34238-3806

We Pay

Modern Spoons	**2.00-6.00**
Older Demitasse Spoons, silverplate	**8.00**

We Pay

Older Demitasse Spoons, silver....................................**15.00**
Large Bronze Medallions...**10.00**
Modern Posters...**5.00**
Post Cards, post-World War II....................................**40¢**
Post Cards, pre-World War II...................................**50¢-4.00**
Wooden Nickels...**50¢**
Elongated Cents..**50¢-8.00**
Official Guide Books..**3.00-9.00**
Pennants..**2.00-8.00**

ZELL DUTCH SCENE EARTHENWARE

Zell Dutch Scene tableware is becoming quite hard to find, especially in my state. Produced in Zell-Harmersbach, Germany, at the Georg Schmider pottery during the period of 1900 through 1907, the pieces are on a white to ivory background decorated with colorful figures of a Dutch boy and Dutch girl with their dog or geese, a Dutch man with his pipe, or a Dutch woman with her chickens. There are many different motifs on pieces ranging from small to large plates and bowls, cups and saucers, creamers and sugar bowls, pitchers, vases, water jugs, children's dishes, and so on.

The designs on the Zell pieces were individually applied and handpainted, so the decorations may differ slightly. Pieces marked with a pottery mark and 'Baden' were produced for local trade; those marked with a pottery mark and 'Germany' were made for export to the United States.

I also buy items made in Austria that are decorated with a Dutch scene so similar that they can hardly be distinguished from the Zell line. These were made by an unknown pottery company.

I will pay a fair price depending on the piece and its condition. Items in my collection have been purchased for $3.00 to $45.00.

Audrey Domenick
7735 E. Jefferson Place
Denver, CO 80237
(303) 779-5221

OTHER INTERESTED BUYERS OF MISCELLANEOUS ITEMS

In this section of the book we have listed some 250 buyers of miscellaneous items and related material. When corresponding with these collectors, be sure to enclose a self-addressed stamped envelope if you want a reply. Do not send lists of items for appraisal. If you wish to sell your material, quote the price that you want or send a list and ask if there are any articles on the list that they might be interested in and the price they would be willing to pay. If you want the list back, be sure to send a SASE large enough for the listing to be returned.

ADVERTISING
(signs)
Norm & Judy Sherbert
3805 S. Valley Dr.
Evergreen, CO 80439

(Philip Morris 'Johnny')
Jim Fredrick
918 W. Co. Rd. C-2
Roseville, MN 55113

AMERICAN ILLUSTRATORS & PRINTS
The Rocking Chair Emporium
123 N. Glassell
Orange, CA 92666

APOLLO XI MEMORABILIA
(First Moon Landing)
Bernard Passion
3517½ Kinney St.
Los Angeles, CA 90065

ART DECO
(figurals)
K. Hartman
7459 Shawnee Rd.
North Tonawanda, NY 14120

(figurals)
Vivian Riegelman
P.O. Box 384
Waxhaw, NC 28173

ART GLASS
Lenore Monleon
33 Fifth Ave.
New York, NY 10003

ART NOUVEAU
(porcelain)
Vivian Riegelman
P.O. Box 384
Waxhaw, NC 28173

(figurals)
K. Hartman
7459 Shawnee Rd.
North Tonawanda, NY 14120

ART POTTERY
Jeanne Delarm-Neri
Art for Life
122 Center St.
Stamford, CT 06906

(Longway)
The Antique Gallery
8523 Germantown Ave.
Philadelphia, PA 19118

AUTOGRAPHS
(operatic)
Jose W. Perez
2427 SW 21 St.
Miami, FL 33145

AUTOMOBILIA
James E. Fredrick
918 W. Co. Rd. C-2
Roseville, MN 55113

(advertising & literature)
Bruce Raymond
30715 9 Mile Rd.
Farmington Hills, MI 48024

(Brush paper ephemera)
R.L. Rice
612 E. Front St.
Bloomington, IL 61701

BAKELITE
(jewelry & radios)
Cookie's Collectibles
15 Arthur Rd.
Bridgewater, NJ 08807

BALLOON TIRE BICYCLES & ACCESSORIES
Ray Zeak
1105 Broadway
Altoona, NJ 16601

BANKS
(cast iron)
Esther B. Lundblade
57 Calhoun Rd.
Pueblo, CO 81001

(Washington or Lincoln)
Ed's Islander
Books & Bookends
1136 Loma, No. 7
Coronado, CA 92118

(glass bottle)
Jim & Bonnie Hare
311 Fairview St.
Carlisle, PA 17013

BARBER EQUIPMENT
Roland Granger
Times Past Antiques
R.D. #2, Box 97
Wellsville, NY 14875

BASEBALL CARDS
John Cook
Rt. 1, Box 176
Remer, MN 56672

Dick Soffey
17 Seaview St.
Chatham, MA 02633

BEER CANS
(and keys)
J.W. Cates
3241 Eastwood Rd.
Sacramento, CA 95821

BICYCLES & LITERATURE
Antique Cycle Supply
Cedar Springs, MI 49319

BILLIARDS
Leonard Fondini
P.O. Box 304
37 Springvale Ave.
Chelsea, MA 02150

Mark Stellinga
1168 Briar Dr.
Iowa City, IA 52240

Dillworth Billiards
300 E. Tremont Ave.
Charlotte, NC 28203

BLACK MEMORABILIA
Judy Posner
R.D. Box 273
Effort, PA 18330

San & Jan Spencer
3671 E. Highland
Highland, CA 92346

BLACKSMITH WHIMSIES
Linda Franklin
2716 Northfield
Charlottesville, VA 22901

BLUE RIDGE POTTERY
Santiam Sales Co.
P.O. Box 471
Mill City, OR 97360

BLUEBIRD CHINA
Betty Gilmore
292 Brevoort Rd.
Columbus, OH 43214

BOOKENDS
(Washington or Lincoln)
Ed's Islander
Books & Bookends
1136 Loma, No. 7
Coronado, CA 92118

BOOKS
Carl Sciortino, Militaria
Box 6424
Scottsdale, AZ 85261

Connecticut Yankee Bookshop
95 Main St.
East Hampton, CT 06424

(out of print needlework)
Galerie de Boicourt
250 Martin St.
Birmingham, MI 48011

(Civil War or Kentucky)
Donald Mull
1706 Girard Dr.
Louisville, KY 40222

(first editions)
Jack Hewitt
St. Johns, AZ 85936

(horticulture, lighting, toys & science)
Lee Troutt
Westdell Dr.
St. Louis, MO 63136

(Puerto Rico, Tampa & Key West, FL)
Frank Garcia
8963 SW 34th St.
Miami, FL 33165

Mark Wilkinson
Box 73
Mansfield, OH 44903

Owen's Antiques
Rt. 5, Box 240
Vashon Island, WA 98070

Joy McDowell
39872 Duran Ct.
Fremont, CA 94538

Dinah Henderson
Fifth & Main
Greenwood, MO 64034

E.S. Radcliffe
3732 Colonial Lane SE
Port Orchard, WA 98366

BOTTLES
Peyton L. Youmans
2109 Norwood Ave.
Savannah, GA 31406

BOY SCOUT
(patches)
Greg Souchik
Star Route, Box 53
Lewis Run, PA 16738

BUDDHA
(stone heads)
M. Margvlies
Box 7376
Washington, D.C. 20044

BURMA SHAVE ITEMS
Steve Soelbert
29126 Laro Dr.
Agoura Hills, CA 91301

BUTTER MOLDS
Mrs. Wilson Taylor
154 Files Creek Rd.
Beverly, WV 26253

CAMPAIGN COLLECTIBLES
William Lester
P.O. Box 303
Rosedale, VA 24280

CARTOON COLLECTIBLES
Mark Dubiel
2336 Yemans
Hamtramck, MI 48212

CARVED WAXES

Blair Museum of Lithophanes & Carved
Waxes
P.O. Box 4557
2032 Robinwood Ave.
Toledo, OH 43620

CHILDREN'S DISHES

Kaydee Cooper
39 Park Ave.
Harahan, LA 70123

(enamel)
Jeri Lucht
1481 W. 240th St.
Farmington, MN 55024

('Laurel' pattern)
Harriet Joyce
16144 Woodhaven Ct.
Granger, IN 46530

CHILDREN'S THINGS

Debz & Val's Doll Hospital
P.O. Box 281
Bethany, OK 73008

CHINA

(Noritake 'Polka')
(Aynsley 'Queen's Garden')
Mrs. L.W. Hultgren
2033 13th St.
Moline, IL 61265

(Japanese by Jonroth Studios)
Mrs. V.R. Lewis
Rt. 1, Box 102
Stafford, KS 67578

(Krautheim, Selb-Bavaria)
Mrs. James F. Smith
R.R. 2, Box 89
Elmore, MN 56027

(U.S. Army Medical Dept.)
Pat Van Gaabeek
631 Randolph
Topeka, KS 66606

CHINESE MINIATURES

James E. Williams, Jr.
335 Monticello St.
Eden, NC 27288

CHOCOLATE MOLDS

(2-piece, any kind)
Shirley Baumann
2109 Floyd Ave.
Iowa Falls, IA 50126

CHRISTMAS

(silver ornaments)
Overtons
Avenida Santa Margarita
San Clemente, CA 92672

CHURNS

(1-qt., marked Daisy)
L.D. Hanner
Box 16
Kansas, IL 61933

CIGARETTE HOLDERS

Pat Tschudy
3816 Wooded Creek Dr.
Dallas, TX 75244

CIVIL WAR

Alex Peck
Antique Scientifica
P.O. Box 710
Charleston, IL 61920

CLOCKS

Daniel's Den Antiques
P.O. Box 405
Aransas Pass, TX 78336

(antique French, for parts)
Don Luke
1310 Bryson
Independence, MO 64052

CLOTHING

(vintage)
Alberta Chambless
1004 Pratt Hwy.
Birmingham, AL 35214

COAL CARVINGS

Linda Franklin
2716 Northfield
Charlottesville, VA 22901

COCA-COLA
Gael deCourtivron
4811 Remington Dr.
Sarasota, FL 33580

Debbie Brown
541 S. St. Clair St.
Painesville, OH 44077

COIN-OPERATED MACHINES
William F. Rosenbaum
8057 W. Herbert St.
Milwaukee, WI 53218

Joseph S. Jancuska
619 Miller St.
Luzerne, PA 18709

COLLECTOR PLATES
Mrs. Wilson Taylor
154 Files Creek Rd.
Beverly, WV 26253

COLORED GLASSWARE
(all periods)
Heritage Antiques
516 S. Holland
Bellville, TX 77418

Daniel's Den Antiques
P.O. Box 405
Aransas Pass, TX 78336

COMIC BOOKS
Howard Weinberg
1725 York Ave. 18H
New York, NY 10128

COOKIE JARS
Debbie Brown
541 S. St. Clair St.
Painesville, OH 44077

DECOYS
John Cook
Rt. 1, Box 176
Remer, MN 56672

DENTAL
Kem DuVal, D.D.S.
P.O. Box 1668, Suite 88
Oceanside, CA 92054

DEPRESSION GLASS
Carolyn Metcalf
R#1, Box 484
Aurora, KY 42048

Janet M. Davis
4433 Third Ave. North
Great Falls, MT 59401

DESK SETS
Jeanne Delarm-Neri
Art for Life
122 Center St.
Stamford, CT 06906

DICK TRACY COLLECTIBLES
Larry Doucet
2351 Sultana Dr.
Yorktown Heights, NY 10598

DISNEY TOYS
Steve Soelbert
29126 Laro Dr.
Agoura Hills, CA 91301

DISNEYANA
Judy Posner
R.D. Box 273
Effort, PA 18330

DIVING HELMETS
Larry Pitman
5424 Bryan Station Rd.
Paris, KY 40361

DOLLS
Debz & Val's Doll Hospital
P.O. Box 281
Bethany, OK 73008

(composition)
Debbie Brown
541 S. St. Clair St.
Painesville, OH 44077

Doll Chest
3413 Amalfi Cove
Austin, TX 78759

Joy McDowell
39872 Duran Ct.
Fremont, CA 94538

(also dollhouses)
Carol Ann Kachur
3096 E. Detroit Rd.
Niles, MI 49120

(all bisque)
S. Weintraub
2924 Helena
Houston, TX 77006

DOORSTOPS
Terry Burger
2323 Lincoln
Beatrice, NE 68310

(dog)
Mrs. Wm. H. Lidey
2109 Sunland
Las Vegas, NV 89106

ELVIS
Eddie Hammer
773 Roosevelt Ave.
Carteret, NJ 07008

Janet M. Davis
4433 Third Ave. North
Great Falls, MT 59401

ESTATE AUCTIONS
Bear & Associates
718 Broadview Dr.
Green Bay, WI 54301

Estate Services
N.W. 316 Harrison
Pullman, WA 99163

Greater Chicago Enterprises, Inc.
37419 N. Hwy. 45
Lake Villa, IL 60046

EXPOSITIONS
D.D. Woollard, Jr.
11614 Old St. Charles Rd.
Bridgeton, MO 63044

FANS
Howard Weinberg
1725 York Ave. 18H
New York, NY 10128

FARM MACHINERY
Larry Pitman
5424 Bryan Station Rd.
Paris, KY 40361

FISHING
(wooden plugs)
Machairologist
Gerald A. Shaw
1928 Causton Buff Rd.
Savannah, GA 31404

FLASHLIGHTS & CATALOGS
Bill Utley
7616 Brookmill Rd.
Downey, CA 90241

FLOW BLUE
Carolyn Metcalf
Rt. 1, Box 484
Aurora, KY 42048

Barbara Amster
15 Bellevue Ave.
Bass River, MA 02664

FOUNTAIN PENS
Dick Soffey
17 Seaview St.
Chatham, MA 02633

FRUIT KNIFE HOLDERS
Esther B. Lundblade
57 Calhoun Rd.
Pueblo, CO 81001

GOLD TIMEPIECES
Carter & Sons
P.O. Box 209
Galena Park, TX 77547

GREEN-HANDLED KITCHEN UTENSILS
Rey Y. Pierce
643 W. 11
Casper, WY 82601

HARDWARE
(door & window)
Dan Kelley
SRB Box 397
Franklin, LA 70538

HAT PINS & HOLDERS
The Rocking Chair Emporium
123 N. Glassell
Orange, CA 92666

HULL POTTERY
Dennis & Joyce Billiet
#3 Maplewood Dr.
Geneseo, IL 61254

HUMMELS
Rue Dee Marker
220 W. Fry Blvd.
Sierra Vista, AZ 85635

Eva Flynn
Box 4111
Thousand Oaks, CA 91359

Andreas Tarcsai
Hummel specialist Von Austria
Gallmayergasse 17
A-8020 Graz
Austria

ICE SKATING
(skates, lanterns, programs)
Keith Pendell
1230 N. Cypress
La Habra, CA 90631

IRONSTONE
Barbara Amster
15 Bellevue Ave.
Bass River, MA 02664

Mrs. Wm. H. Lidey
2109 Sunland
Las Vegas, NV 89106

JAPANESE SWORDS
Greg Souchik
Star Route, Box 53
Lewis Run, PA 16738

JEWELRY
(marcasite)
Pat Cavoli
P.O. Box 103
Homecrest Station
Brooklyn, NY 11229

Timepiece Antiques
P.O. Box 26416
Baltimore, MD 21207

Doll Chest
3413 Amalfi Cove
Austin, TX 78759

Follies
Nob Hill Antique Center
3310 Central S.E.
Albuquerque, NM 87106

Christie Romero
P.O. Box 1904
Hawaiian Gardens, CA 90716

Andrea P. Richter
405 E. Coolspring Ave.
Michigan City, IN 46360

Pat Tschudy
3816 Wooded Creek Dr.
Dallas, TX 75244

(costume or estate)
Old Magic Antiques
117 SW Evangeline Thruway
Lafayette, LA 70501

(signed)
Beatrix Brockerman
730 W. Gaines St.
Tallahassee, FL 32304

(signed, costume, antique)
Bird-in-the-Cage Antiques
201 King St.
Alexandria, VA 22314

Joy McDowell
39872 Duran St.
Fremont, CA 94538

JUDAICA
M. Margvlies
Box 7376
Washington, D.C. 20044

LAMPS, FIXTURES & CATALOGS
Robert Kwalwasser
168 Camp Fatima Rd.
Renfrew, PA 16053

(prior to 1930's)
Merlin Merline
P.O. Box 16265
Milwaukee, WI 53216

(reverse-painted)
Mrs. Wm. H. Lidey
2109 Sunland
Las Vegas, NV 89106

(reverse-painted)
Paul Aimis
13721 Attley Place
Tampa, FL 33624

MAGAZINES
Alberic Gerard
P.O. Box 97
Lafayette, OR 97127

Joy McDowell
39872 Duran Ct.
Fremont, CA 94538

MAJOLICA
Mrs. Wm. H. Lidey
2109 Sunland
Las Vegas, NV 89106

MARX MAIN STREET ROOMS
Harriet Joyce
16144 Woodhaven Ct.
Granger, IN 46530

MEDALS
(Washington or Lincoln)
Ed's Islander
Books & Bookends
1136 Loma, No. 7
Coronado, CA 92118

MEISSEN PORCELAIN
The Antique Gallery
8523 Germantown Ave.
Philadelphia, PA 19118

MILITARY & NAUTICAL
Larry Pitman
5424 Bryan Station Rd.
Paris, KY 60361

MINI BOAT MOTORS
Craig Lillemoe
1815 Nicollet Ave. S.
Minneapolis, MN 55403

MINI STONEWARE JUGS
Craig Lillemoe
1815 Nicollet Ave. S.
Minneapolis, MN 55403

MINING LAMPS & ACCESSORIES
Ray Zeak
1105 Broadway
Altoona, PA 16601

MODEL CAR KITS
Bruce Raymond
30715 9 Mile Rd.
Farmington Hills, MI 48024

MOTORCYCLES
Antique Cycle Supply
Cedar Springs, MI 49319

(paper memorabilia)
R.L. Rice
612 E. Front St.
Bloomington, IL 61701

MOUSETRAPS
Mike Brooks
7335 Skyline
Oakland, CA 94611

MOVIES & MOVIE STARS
Jay Scarfone
985 Parma Center Rd.
Hilton, NY 14468

Bob Havey
Box 3
W. Sullivan, ME 04689

MUSIC
Ervin Erickson
1211 N. 18th St.
Bismarck, ND 58501

MUSIC BOXES
David Broker
820 S. Main
Hutchinson, KS 67501

NAUTICAL & OCEAN LINER
New Steamship Consultants
P.O. 9696
El Cajon, CA 92022

NEWSPAPERS
Alberic Gerard
P.O. Box 97
Lafayette, OR 97127

OCEAN LINER ITEMS
E.S. Radcliffe
3732 Colonial Lane SE
Port Orchard, WA 98366

PALMER COX BROWNIES
Norm & Judy Sherbert
3805 S. Valley Dr.
Evergreen, CO 80439

PAP BOATS
(invalid feeders)
Ken Odiorne
Rt. 2, Box 22
Bertram, TX 78605

PAPER DOLLS
Loraine Burdick
5 Court Place
Puyallup, WA 98372

PAPERWEIGHTS
(advertising)
Don E. Burnett
P.O. Box 178
East Greenwich, RI 02818

Mrs. E.L. Kramer
3725 Huaco Lane
Waco, TX 76710

PATENT MEDICINE MEMORABILIA
Steve Ketcham
P.O. Box 24114
Edina, MN 55424

PEDAL CARS
Barbara Amster
15 Bellevue Ave.
Bass River, MA 02664

PENCIL SHARPENERS
Robert Kwalwasser
168 Camp Fatima Rd.
Renfrew, PA 16053

PERFUME BOTTLES
Daniel's Den Antiques
P.O. Box 405
Aransas Pass, TX 78336

Leona Barnes
P.O. Box 1364
Sandy, OR 97055

PEWTER
(18th & 19th century)
Louis Picek
Main Street Antiques & Art
Box 340, 110 W. Main
West Branch, IA 52358

PHONOGRAPHS
David Broker
820 S. Main
Hutchinson, KS 67501

PHOTOGRAPHICA
Alberic Gerard
P.O. Box 97
Lafayette, OR 97127

PHRENOLOGY
Donald Gorlick
P.O. Box 2451
Seattle, WA 98124

POCKET WATCH STANDS
Steve Katz
2923 E. Thompson St.
Philadelphia, PA 19134

POLITICAL
(also Uncle Sam items)
Central City Antiques & Collectibles
527 14th St. West
Huntington, WA 25704

(parade torches)
Robert Kwalwasser
168 Camp Fatima Rd.
Renfrew, PA 16053

POST OFFICE LOCK BOX DOORS

Oscar Hubbert
P.O. Box 1415
Fletcher, NC 28723

POST CARDS

(lighthouses only)
Betty Auman
3928 Ferndale Ave.
San Bernardino, CA 92404

(pre-1945, Cape May, NJ)
Virginia Walsh
920 Benton Ave.
Cape May, NJ 08204

(pre-1920, Puerto Rico)
Frank Garcia
8963 SW 34th St.
Miami, FL 33165

Dick Soffey
17 Seaview St.
Chatham, MA 02633

PRIMITIVES

Louis Picek
Main Street Antiques & Art
Box 340, 110 West Main
West Branch, IA 52358

PRINTS

(original Icart)
Mrs. Wm. H. Lidey
2109 Sunland
Las Vegas, NV 89106

PURSES

Barbara Rossi
712 27th Ave.
San Mateo, CA 94403

QUILTS

The Margaret Cavigga Quilt Collection
8648 Melrose Ave.
Los Angeles, CA 90069

Follies
Nob Hill Antique Center
3310 Central SE
Albuquerque, NM 87106

Santiam Sales Co.
P.O. Box 471
Mill City, OR 97360

Owen's Antiques
Rt. 5, Box 240
Vashon Island, WA 98070

RADIO & CEREAL PREMIUMS

Bob Havey
Box 3
West Sullivan, ME 04689

RADIOS

William F. Rosenbaum
8057 W. Herbert St.
Milwaukee, WI 53218

RAGGEDY ANN & ANDY

(early)
Bunny Walker
Box 502
Bucyrus, OH 44820

RAILROADIANA

Howard K. Page
The Old Depot
651 W. Hwy. 12
Dassel, MN 55325

RAZORS

John Holak
611 Mosher Lane
Houston, TX 77037

Sigmund Wohl
24 N. Greeley Ave.
Chappaqua, NY 10514

RECORDS

Carl E. Moyers
Rt. #1, Box 88C
White Pine, TN 37890

(opera, 78 RPM Victor)
Jose W. Perez
2472 SW 21 St.
Miami, FL 33145

ROBJ

Randall B. Monson
P.O. Box 1503
Arlington, VA 22210

ROSEVILLE
(Futura & Falling)
Randall B. Monsen
P.O. Box 1503
Arlington, VA 22210

(tea pots & sets)
Normans Enterprises
542 Gettysburg Rd.
San Antonio, TX 78228

SALT & PEPPER SETS
Helene Guarnaccia
52 Coach Lane
Fairfield, CT 06430

SAMPLERS
The Margaret Cavigga Quilt Collection
8648 Melrose Ave.
Los Angeles, CA 90069

SEWING MACHINES
Mike Brooks
7335 Skyline
Oakland, CA 94611

SHEET MUSIC
L.D. McNeill
117 S. Taylor Ave.
Oak Park, IL 60304

SHIRLEY TEMPLE
Loraine Burdick
5 Court Place
Puyallup, WA 98372

SHOOTING GALLERY TARGETS
R.S. Tucker
P.O. Box 262
Argyle, TX 76226

SILVER
(marked Mecum or Mecom)
The Museum
4111 Farhills Dr.
Champaign, IL 61821

SNOW DOMES
Helene Guarnaccia
52 Coach Lane
Fairfield, CT 06430

SOFT DRINK ITEMS
Mr. & Mrs. Marion Lathan
Rt. 1, Box 430
Chester, SC 29706

SOUVENIR SPOONS
(sterling, Cuban)
Frank Garcia
8963 SW 34th St.
Miami, FL 33165

SPANISH AMERICAN WAR
Richard M. Bueschel
215 Revere Dr.
Northbrook, IL 60062

SPORTING GOODS
Gary L. Medeiros
1319 Sayre St.
San Leandro, CA 94579

Machairologist
Gerald A. Shaw
1928 Causton Bluff Rd.
Savannah, GA 31404

Ron Adelson
13447 N. 59th Place
Scottsdale, AZ 85254

STAFFORDSHIRE FIGURES
Heritage Antiques
516 S. Holland
Bellville, TX 77418

STANHOPES
Donald Gorlick
P.O. Box 24541
Seattle, WA 98124

STEIFF TOYS
(specialty, early bears)
Bunny Walker
Box 502
Bueyrus, OH 44820

Cynthia Brintnall
11924 W. Forest Hill Blvd.
Suite 1
West Palm Beach, FL 33414

(also catalogs)
Susan Cleff
1712 Redwood
Hanover Park, IL 60103

STERLING
(silverware)
Overtons
200 Avenida Santa Margarita
San Clemente, CA 92672

(and/or metals)
Christie Romero
P.O. Box 1904
Hawaiian Gardens, CA 90716

TEDDY BEARS
Debz & Val's Doll Hospital
P.O. Box 281
Bethany, OK 73008

Carol Ann Kachur
3096 E. Detroit Rd.
Niles, MI 49120

Joy McDowell
39872 Duran Ct.
Fremont, CA 94538

TELEPHONES
Dennis F. Kukhofel
20863 Lancaster Rd.
Harper Woods, MI 48225

TENNESSEE MEMORABILIA
Carl E. Moyers
Rt. 1, Box 88C
White Pine, TN 37890

TEXTILES
(multi-cultural)
Galerie de Boicourt
250 Martin St.
Birmingham, MI 48011

TIFFANY
Kem DuVal, D.D.S.
P.O. Box 1668, Suite 33
Oceanside, CA 92054

TIRE ASH TRAYS
Normans Enterprises
542 Gettysburg Rd.
San Antonio, TX 78228

TOYS
(Hot Wheels, Matchbox)
Eldon Sutton
13345 N. Linden Rd.
Rt. 2
Clio, MI 48420

Debz & Val's Doll Hospital
P.O. Box 281
Bethany, OK 73008

TRADE MAGAZINES
(prior to 1924)
Richard M. Bueschel
215 Revere Dr.
Northbrook, IL 60062

TRAMP ART
Louis Picek
Main Street Antiques & Art
Box 340, 110 W. Main
West Branch, IA 52358

TRANSPORTATION
(Greyhound or Trailways Bus)
Eugene Farha
P.O. Box 633
Cedar Grove, WV 25039

TRAPS
(rat, mouse, & fly)
Robert Kwalwasser
168 Camp Fatima Rd.
Renfrew, PA 16053

TRAVELING INKWELLS
Robert Kwalwasser
168 Camp Fatima Rd.
Renfrew, PA 16053

TYPEWRITERS
(pre-1900)
Mark Stellinga
1168 Briar Dr.
Iowa City, IA 52240

U.S. NAVY
F.M. Hoak III
P.O. Box 668
New Canaan, CT 06840

VALENTINES
Jeri Lucht
1481 W. 240th St.
Farmington, MN 55024

VICTORIAN PARLOR GARDENS 'WARDIAN CASES'
Steve Katz
2923 E. Thompson St.
Philadelphia, PA 19134

VICTORIAN PICTURE NAILS
Kaydee Cooper
39 Park Ave.
Harahan, LA 70123

WAR POSTERS
Mark Wilkinson
Box 73
Mansfield, OH 44903

WATCH FOBS
Allan C. Hoover
4015 Progress Blvd.
Peru, IL 61354

WAVECREST
Betty Bird
107 Ida St.
Mount Shasta, CA 96067

WELLER
(Hudson, Woodcraft, Knifewood)
Ann McDonald
Box 3721
Arlington, VA 22207

WHISKEY MEMORABILIA
Steve Ketcham
P.O. Box 24114
Edina, MN 55424

WINCHESTER
Ralph Lipeles
Ridgedale Rd.
Monroe, CT 06468

WINDMILL WEIGHTS
R.S. Tucker
P.O. Box 262
Argyle, TX 76226

WORLD'S FAIRS
(especially 1939)
Pat Cavoli
P.O. Box 103
Homecrest Station
Brooklyn, NY 11229

Index

Schroeder's Antiques Price Guide

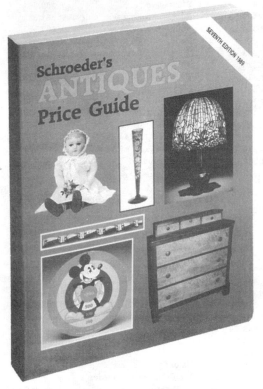

Schroeder's Antiques Price Guide has climbed its way to the top in a field already supplied with several well-established publications! The word is out, *Schroeder's Price Guide* is the best buy at any price. Over 500 categories are covered, with more than 50,000 listings. From ABC Plates to Zsolnay, if it merits the interest of today's collector, you'll find it in Schroeder's. Each subject is represented with histories and background information. In addition, hundreds of sharp original photos are used each year to illustrate not only the rare and the unusual, but the everyday "fun-type" collectibles as well. All new copy and all new illustrations make Schroeder's THE price guide on antiques and collectibles. We have not and will not simply change prices in each new edition.

The writing and researching team is backed by a staff of more than seventy of Collector Books' finest authors, as well as a board of advisors made up of well-known antique authorities and the country's top dealers, all specialists in their fields. Prices are gathered over the entire year previous to publication, then each category is thoroughly checked. Only the best of the lot remains for publication. You'll find the new edition of *Schroeder's Antiques Price Guide* the one to buy for factual information and quality.

No dealer, collector or investor can afford not to own this book. It is available from your favorite bookseller or antiques dealer at the low price of $12.95. If you are unable to find this price guide in your area, it's available from Collector Books, P.O. Box 3009, Paducah, KY 42001 at $12.95 plus $2.00 for postage and handling.

8½ x 11, 608 Pages $12.95